NORTHEAST LIGHTS

LIGHTHOUSES AND LIGHTSHIPS

Rhode Island
to
Cape May, New Jersey

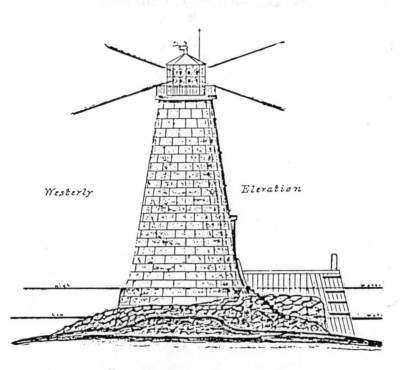

Westerly   *Elevation*

Execution Rocks Lighthouse, 1850

Also by the author

Scuba Northeast, Volume 1

Scuba Northeast, Volume 2

NORTHEAST LIGHTS

LIGHTHOUSES AND LIGHTSHIPS

Rhode Island

to

Cape May, New Jersey

Robert G. Bachand

Sea Sports Publications
Box 647, Belden Station
Norwalk, CT 06852

Library of Congress Cataloging in Publication Data

Bachand, Robert G.
  Northeast Lights: lighthouses and lightships, Rhode
Island to Cape May, New Jersey / Robert G. Bachand
  Biliography: p.
  Includes index.
  ISBN 0-9616399-3-8
  1. Lighthouses -- New England. 2. Lighthouses --
Middle Atlantic States. 3. New England -- History,
Local. 4. Middle Atlantic States -- History, Local.
  I. Title
VK 1024. N38B33   1989
387 . 1 '55 -- dc20   89-60652
                                           CIP

Printed in the United States of America

To Kathy

ACKNOWLEDGEMENTS

In producing a manuscript of this magnitude, there were many people who shared their valuable knowledge and time with me. I would, however, especially like to thank the staff of the Coast Guard Academy Library, George Briscoe and Bill Sherman of National Archives, Dr. Robert Scheina, Coast Guard Historian, Wayne C. Wheeler of the U. S. Lighthouse Society, Ken Black of the Shore Village Museum, Charlotte Johnson of the Rose Island Lighthouse Foundation, Doina Dubitsky of the Stony Point Lighthouse, the staff of the Maritime Center at Kingston, the staff of the Newport Historical Society, Richard Black of the Cedar Island Lighthouse, and my wife Kathy who helped me wade through the enormous stacks of documents at National Archives.

CONTENTS

CONTENTS

Foreword

I was delighted to learn that I had the honor of writing the foreword for this impressive work on lighthouses of the northeast. Even when I first read the rough manuscript, I knew a comprehensive and valuable work on lighthouses in the area from Rhode Island to New Jersey was about to unfold. It was humbling to be a part of this extensive manuscript.

So very many books on the romantic subject of lighthouses and lightships have been produced over the years that they tend to blend together, many repeating the same misinformation in a spectrum of styles running the gamut from 'dry as dust' to 'dripping adjectives', often with the ubiquitous ghost lurking in the lantern room. Most are based on newspaper morgues and erroneous writings of others.

At last a refreshing, major work on the subject has been produced by author Bachand. Early on it was obvious to me that he had labored long and hard to get "just the facts ma'am." Yet these facts are well organized and presented in a flowing manner. The prelude to each light station (containing such basic information as cost, construction dates, major alterations, characteristic changes, etc.) nicely set forth basic, pertinent information. From this accurate and interesting beginning the author tip toes through each lighthouse in the region he has selected paying attention to important aspects of its life, be it construction, a shipwreck, pathos or tragedy. And always, "just the facts ma'am."

I am doubly honored to foreword this fine book in the year 1989, the Bicentennial of our Lighthouse Service. The work, dedicated to detail and love that went into this work is a suitable tribute to those long gone keepers of the flame and a punctuation mark to the end of that era, the era of manned Lighthouse Americanus.

Wayne C. Wheeler
President, U. S. Lighthouse Society
San Francisco, CA April 1989

Preface

T here is something special about a lighthouse. It is a welcome sight to a sailor lost in a fog, an aesthetic signpost, a romantic vision of the sea, and a look into our maritime past.

Northeast Lights examines 133 light stations (lighthouses and lightships) from Rhode Island to Cape May, NJ, parts of an area once known as the Third and Fourth Light House Districts. The Third District extended from Gooseberry Point, MA, to Squam Inlet, NJ, and included Narragansett Bay, New York Bay, Providence and Hudson rivers, Lake Champlain and Lake Memphemagog. The Fourth District extended from Squam Inlet, NJ, to Metomkin Inlet, VA.

Some of the lighthouses within the area discussed in this book are still operational, and, some which have been extinguished, are owned by individuals, organizations or local governments. Others were torn down or were destroyed, and a few, never having developed a concerned constituency, slowly decayed into obscurity. Still standing or lost forever, each has its own unique history.

The story of these beacons is not only of the structures themselves, but it is also of the keepers, their dedication, heroism, misfortunes, misdeeds and madness. Following a geographic pattern from Rhode

Island to Cape May, each of the 133 light stations is explored.

Research and writing of *Northeast Lights* took nearly four years. Sources included all available lighthouse and lightship logs (1800-1943) held at National Archives, Suitland, MD, a wide variety of documents held at National Archives, Washington, DC, and the Library of Congress. Other sources included state archives, local historical societies and libraries, the *New York Times* (1851-1988), local newspapers and first person accounts. Students of light-houses for this region will find that apart from the National Archives, the libraries at the Coast Guard Academy, Mystic Seaport, and New York City hold the greatest amount of research materials.

Robert (Bob) G. Bachand
Norwalk, CT
April 1989

1 EVOLUTION OF THE NATION'S LIGHTHOUSE SYSTEM

T he lights are much better in all parts of Europe," wrote Capt. W. B. Cropper, "than they are in the United States." In his letter of June 28, 1851, to the Secretary of the Lighthouse Board, the veteran mariner of twenty-three years and master of the ship *Isaac Webb* found only one of the nation's lights that was the equal to those of Europe's, the Highlands of Navesink (NJ).

"The light-vessels in the United States which I have seen," he continued, "are all inferior to those in Great Britain, and are badly lighted and badly attended." He went on to describe the English system of marking channels. The buoys that were on the starboard side (right) as one entered a harbor were painted red, and those on the port side (left) were black; buoys marking a turn in the channel were painted with stripes. "They are also marked and numbered, and have the name of the channel to which they belong. The buoys on different sides of channels are of different shapes and form."

The captain's views were shared by many others. In July of 1851, Lt. David D. Porter of the United States mail-steamer *Georgia* reported that "our light-houses as at present arranged are so wretched, that any seafaring man must desire a change." The naval officer echoed Capt. Cropper's observation regarding the twin lights of Navesink. "The Navesink fixed and revolving lights I consider the only perfect lights on our coast, not only as regards regularity of lighting, but in the brilliancy of the light." Going on, he related that from the wheelhouse of his vessel, thirty-two feet above sea level, he could see the revolving light from a maximum distance of twenty-five miles in ordinary weather, and from about thirty miles on a clear winter's day.

By 1852, the United States had 325 lighthouses and lightships, numerous buoys, monuments, and other navigational aids, but there was no uniform system for these aids. Lighthouses, lightships, and buoys often looked so much alike that it was difficult to distinguish one from another. Lights shown from some of the beacons were so dim or so poorly managed that they were of little use except under the best atmospheric conditions. Approaches to New York and other major harbors and bays (Delaware and Chesapeake bays) were insufficiently marked; certain navigational obstructions, especially at the southern tip of Florida, were left totally unmarked.

There were ten lighthouses at the time that the colonies broke away from England in 1776: Little Brewster Island, Boston Harbor, MA, 1716; Brant Point Light, MA, 1746; Beavertail Light, RI, 1749; New London Harbor, CT, 1760; Sandy Hook, NJ, 1764; Cape Henlopen Light, DE, 1765; Charleston Light, SC, 1767; Plymouth Light, MA, 1768; Portsmouth Light, NH, 1771; and Cape Ann Lights, MA, 1771. Three-quarters of a century later, aids to navigation had grown tremendously in numbers, but the system had yet to mature into an efficiently run organization.

Birth of a Lighthouse System

The history of the nation's lighthouses began in colonial Massachusetts when a group of Boston merchants, led by John George, petitioned for permission to establish a lighted tower at the entrance of Boston Harbor. Little Brewster Island was selected for the beacon and on September 14, 1716, a light was shown for the first time from what is thought to have been a stone tower. Largely through the efforts of Keeper John Haynes, a fog signal was established at the lighthouse in 1719; the "signal-cannon" was fired in answer to ships approaching the harbor in the fog.

A lighthouse system was especially important to the young nation's commerce, and on August 7, 1789, the first session of Congress enacted a law that allowed acceptance of title and joint jurisdiction over all then-existing lighthouses and other aids to navigation. The ninth law passed by Congress also provided for their maintenance and repair, and for the salaries of keepers and others directly involved in lighthouse connected matters.

Care and superintendence of the Light House Establishment was placed under the Treasury Department, and as Secretary of the Treasury, Alexander Hamilton became its first superintendent. During its early years of operation, however, many contracts and orders were reviewed and signed by George Washington himself.

In May of 1792, the Office of Commissioner of Revenue was established, transferring the superintendence of lights to that office; ten years later, it reverted to the Secretary of Treasury. In 1813, the pendulum swung back to the Commissioner of Revenue, and finally on July 1, 1820, the superintendence of lights was placed under the Fifth Auditor of the Treasury Department; Stephen Pleasonton was appointed to the post.

The Light House Establishment, 1820 – 1852

When Pleasonton moved into the position in 1820, the number of lighthouses in the United States stood at fifty-five. Congress appropriated funds for lights and their repairs and detremined the location of new lights, their kind (lighthouse versus lightship, day-beacon, etc.) and the strength of their beacons; Pleasonton executed the orders of Congress, and he was given certain discretionary powers.

The collector of customs nearest to the lighthouse was usually also made its local superintendent. He helped select the site of a proposed lighthouse, and armed with its plans, he hired a consultant to oversee its construction. The local superintendent was

Fifth Auditor and Superintendent of Lights Stephen Pleasonton.
Courtesy United States Lighthouse Society

expected to make yearly inspection tours of all facilities in his district, and report back on their condition to the fifth auditor's office.

Stephen Pleasonton initiated a system that entailed obtaining bids from contractors who were to furnish all of the supplies needed for the Light House Establishment. The contractors' obligations also included keeping the stations' illuminating apparatuses in good repair, inspecting and reporting on any other repairs needed at the stations, and reporting on the keepers' maintenance of their lights. The keepers reported on the quality of the supplies and on the general condition of their stations.

Problems began to surface as the Light House Establishment grew in size. The publishers of the *American Coastal Pilot* wrote a letter to the Secretary of the Treasury on November 30, 1837, citing complaints related to them by ships' captains. Listing the problems as they saw them, the publishers concluded, "The establishment has increased beyond the ability of any single individual at Washington to superintend it in more important details, and the efficiency of the whole has become greatly lessened." Though they lauded Pleasonton's efforts, they felt that he had depended too much on the contractors, who, as they said, would always present themselves and their services in the best possible light.

Congress had recognized by 1837 that it had been too liberal with its appropriations for new light stations. On March 3, 1837, legislation was passed to institute a Board of Navy Commissioners. Its duty was to examine whether or not proposed aids were necessary, and, if so, what were the best sites for their construction. Twenty-two naval officers were assigned to the project. When they had concluded their investigations, they reported that thirty-one of the proposed light stations, some of which were already funded, were unnecessary; all of the proposed lighthouses were canceled.

In July of 1838, the president divided the Atlantic coast into six districts and the Great Lakes into two. Each district was assigned a naval officer who had a revenue cutter or a hired vessel at his disposal. The officers were to inspect all of the navigational aids in their district, submit a report on their condition, and make recommendations for any future needs.

The area extending from Rhode Island to New York, including the Hudson River, was designated as the Third District. During the summer of 1838, Lt. George M. Bache inspected the district's thirty-three lighthouses, and its lightships at Bartlett Reef and Middle Ground (Stratford Shoals) and proposed sites for additional light stations. On November 22, 1838, he submitted his report.

All of the officers' reports were in many ways less than complimentary. There was evidence of poor management: lamps were found "in bad order," arrangement of the lighting apparatuses was sometimes faulty, the silver was often worn off from the lamps' reflectors, and some towers and/or keepers' dwellings were found to have been poorly constructed. Most damaging, however, was the revelation that too many lights had been established and that some of them had been erected in the wrong place. Lt. Bache's report included recommendations for improving the Light House Establishment, some of which were later instituted.

On February 18, 1842, the House of Representatives directed the Committee of Commerce to look into the expenditures of the Light House Establishment since 1816. In a wide-ranging report, the committee concluded that the administration of the system had been adequate. One of its most important recommendations was for the appointment of full-time inspectors, who would make frequent site visits to all of the aids to navigation. Congress failed to act on the report.

A civil engineer, I. W. P. Lewis, was appointed in 1843 to survey many of the coastal lighthouses. He examined about one-third of the nation's lighthouses, and his report that followed was critical of the system; it was not well received by Pleasonton, and Congress adjourned before taking any action.

In 1845, Secretary of the Treasury Robert J. Walker dispatched two naval officers to Europe to examine improvements made in its lights, construction of its lighthouses and its system's organization. Their reports were submitted to Congress, but again no action was taken.

Lighthouse Equipment

From the start, the nation's lighthouse system was slow to adopt European improvements. Parabolic reflectors began to be used in English lights around 1761, but it was not until about 1812 that they were introduced in this country. Using bowl-like reflectors with highly polished surfaces, the light sources were set at a predetermined distance from the center of the reflector. The light was thereby intensified and focused into a beam. In order to make the tower's light visible over a wide arc however, multiple lamps had to be used, each with its own reflector. In 1838, Point Judith Light, on the coast of Rhode Island, used ten lamps and reflectors; Little Gull Island Light, at the eastern entrance of Long Island Sound, had fifteen lamps and fifteen reflectors.

In 1780, Aime Argand of Geneva, Switzerland, found that an oil lamp using cylindrical wicks that were confined in a glass chimney produced a more brilliant flame. The Argand lamps were introduced in the United States in 1812, along with the parabolic reflectors.

Incandescent oil vapor lamps were first used in France in 1898. The burner that used kerosene vapor with an incandescent mantle proved to vastly increase candlepower while using less fuel. In 1904, a unit was installed at North Hook Light (Sandy Hook, NJ), and three years later the lamps began to gain wide use at other United States light stations.

In 1823, French citizen Augustin Jean Fresnel designed a lens system that eventually revolutionized the world's lighthouse systems. Through a group of lenses that collected and focused the light into a horizontal beam, the light's intensity was greatly magnified. In the United States, Highlands of Navesink, which marked the approach to New York Harbor, was the first lighthouse to be equipped with the Fresnel lens. When installed in 1841, the light station was immediately proclaimed as the country's most powerful light.

Coal and tallow candles were used in early European lighthouses as a source of light, but oil lamps were probably the first illuminants to be used in the United States lighthouse system. Because of the country's large whaling fleet, sperm oil was the nation's standard illuminant for many years, but when its price rose to $2.43 per gallon in 1863, lard oil gradually replaced it. Lard oil held its position as the principal illuminant until 1877, when kerosene began to be introduced. In 1917, it was estimated that 600,000 gallons of kerosene per year were used in the nation's light stations, over half of which was said to be used for lighthouse illumination.

In 1884, electric lights were used from Hell Gate's tower in an attempt to "light up" the dangerous passage. Two years later, the Statue of Liberty, then regarded as an aid to navigation, also used it, and Sandy Hook Light, situated at the entrance of New York Harbor, was electrified in 1889. Bridgeport Harbor Light, discontinued in 1953, is thought to have been the country's last lighthouse to regularly use an oil-lamp system.

Light House Board, 1852 — 1910

On March 3, 1851, Congress finally acted on the reports that it had been receiving since the mid-1830s. It authorized the Secretary of the Treasury to begin introducing Fresnel lenses in the nation's lighthouses. It also instructed him to appoint a board composed of two naval officers, two army engineers, and "two civilians of high scientific attainments." Signed by President Fillmore on August 31, 1852, the group known as the Light House Board took over the responsibilities that had rested with Fifth Auditor Stephen Pleasonton for thirty-two years. In the end, Pleasonton was recognized for his accomplishments in helping the lighthouse system grow. His skills as a "money manager," however, were blamed for the "lack of zeal exhibited for his adoption of modern improvements."

The Light House Board immediately began classifying the nation's lights in orders, modeled on the French system. The order of lights ran from first-order to sixth; first-order lights, the most powerful, were coastal beacons, and sixth-order lights were generally relegated to the role of marking minor harbors or river channels. In 1855, Rondout Creek, a Hudson River light, was refitted with a sixth-order lens, as was Cedar Island, a harbor light. Robbins Reef Light, located in the lower part of New York Harbor, received a fourth-order lens, and in 1858, the coastal lights at Fire Island and Shinnecock Bay were fitted with first-order lenses.

The board designated a light's characteristic as fixed, flashing, or revolving, and red or white. A designation could also be listed as a combination of those characteristics. It was also decided to phase out the Argand-lamp/parabolic reflector system in favor of the French-design illuminating apparatuses. Finally, the lighthouse system was made more professional by using the talents of scientists with knowledge of illumination, engineers, well-qualified contractors, people who knew the needs of commerce, and good managers.

In 1872, officials from England's lighthouse system traveled to the United States to inspect the country's fog signals and lighthouses. The signals were regarded as generally better than those in Europe, but our nation's lights still lagged behind those in Europe.

At the invitation of the British, Maj. George H. Elliot, a member of the Light House Board, made a reciprocal inspection tour in 1873 of the English and French lights. In a 288-page document, the Army officer described how some of the European lights had the capacity to vary the strength of their lights to fit the atmospheric conditions. United States first-order lights produced only 210-candlepower; English and French first-order lights could vary from 342 to 722-candlepower. Europeans had also switched from animal fat to the more efficient kerosene, and some were already using gas or electricity as the source of their illuminants.

Lighthouse Bureau, 1910—1939

The Light House Board continued to manage the lighthouse system until June 17, 1910, when an act of Congress created the Bureau of Lighthouses. The system, which had become known as the Lighthouse Service, consisted of 1,397 lights, 54 lightships and 225 light buoys. George R. Putnam was appointed Commissioner of the Lighthouse Service.

During the next twenty-nine years, there was considerable progress in aids to navigation, but possibly one of the most important and useful was the development of the radio direction signal.

On May 1, 1921, the Lighthouse Service established three radio fog signal stations in the area of New York Harbor. The transmitters were installed at Sea Girt Light, NJ, Ambrose Lightship and Fire Island Lightship. Radio signals of a certain characteristic were broadcasted during heavy weather or fog, allowing navigators using a radio compass to obtain definite bearings. The equipment was gradually improved, and by 1935, all of the lightships and many of the more important lighthouses were equipped with radiobeacons. These signals continued to play an important part as navigational aids into the late 1980's, but the development of a LOng RAnge Navigation (Loran A) during the Second World War, began to lessen the importance of radiobeacons. In the late 1950s, the Department of Defense further developed Loran, which then became known as Loran C. Its accuracy, within certain limits, could fix a mariner's position within less than 100 feet, but, as a vessel traveled farther from shore, it tended to become less and less accurate. A satellite navigational system was thus developed for offshore waters, and it continues to be refined.

United States Coast Guard, 1939 —

On July 7, 1939, the Lighthouse Bureau was dissolved and the Coast Guard took over all aids to navigation. Some of the Lighthouse Service personnel were absorbed directly into the Coast Guard, while others remained as civilian keepers. The Coast Guard's last female keeper, Fannie M. Salter, retired in January of 1948. She had been appointed keeper of Turkey Point Light in Chesapeake Bay following her husband-keeper's death in 1926. The service's last male civilian keeper, Frank Schubert, was expected to remain on at the Coney Island Light even after its scheduled automation in 1989.

Floating Beacons

As the master of an English coastal vessel, Robert Hamblin had noted the shortcomings of lighthouses in their ability to mark the changing positions of sandbars. Joining forces with David Avery, the two men established what was perhaps the world's first lightship in 1732. The small vessel, equipped with a light, was anchored at the eastern end of Nore Sands, in the Thames estuary.

The two entrepreneurs immediately set out to make their fortunes by levying tolls on all passing ships. The corporation of Trinity

House, which had jurisdiction over all English lighthouses, was quick to note the pair's financial and navigational success and their plans to expand their fleet of lightships. Protesting that private individuals had no right to tax marine commerce, the corporation tried to have the Nore lightship discontinued. Matters were finally settled when Hamblin and Avery agreed to turn over ownership of their vessel to Trinity House, with the provision that tolls could be levied by the two entrepreneurs or their heirs for a period of sixty-one years, on payment of a yearly sum of 100 pounds to Trinity House.

United States Lightships, 1819–1983

The use of lightships in the United States began in 1819, when Congress appropriated funds to build two vessels, the first stationed at Willoughby's Spit, VA, and the other, at Wolf Trap Shoal, VA. The seventy-foot, wood-hull Willoughby's Spit lightship was built by James Pool of Hampton, VA. Anchored at the northernmost tip of the shoal, the small vessel, it was realized, could not long withstand its exposed position. It was thus moved to a more sheltered site off Craney Island, near Norfolk, VA. In 1822, Congress approved the construction of New York Harbor's first lightship, which was stationed off Sandy Hook, NJ. It became operational in the late spring of 1823.

The early history of American lightships was sometimes also marred by inefficiency and incompetence. The Light House Report of 1852 noted that, during inspection, both the captain and mate were absent from one lightship and the other was found with the entire crew ashore; the ship had been left in charge of a twelve or thirteen-year-old black boy. Other lightships were found in such a poor state of maintenance that their illuminating apparatuses were no brighter than an ordinary household lamp. "Nothing could be much worse than the floating-lights of the United States," concluded the report. "The want of care and attention in wetting the decks and keeping them clean, scrubbing the vessels outside, and keeping them properly painted and well ventilated, will account for the rapid decay of them, especially in warm climates."

The first lightships were generally held in position by a single anchor. Vessels often drifted off their stations, and, when taken into port for repairs, the sites were sometimes left unmarked, since there were no relief vessels available to replace them.

During the Civil War, the Confederate forces sank or captured a number of lightships, including the vessels at Rattlesnake Shoal, SC, Frying Pan Shoal, NC, Harbor Island, NC, Bowlers Rock, VA, and Upper Cedar Point, MD. By April of 1861, most of the lighthouses had been extinguished, and the remaining lightships had been with-drawn from the Chesapeake to the Rio Grande. The exception seems to have been a few that remained operational in the area of the Florida Keys. Other lighthouses and lightships south of the Chesapeake were relit during the course of the war to help the Union forces, and a few more became operational as conditions permitted.

In the First World War, Nantucket Shoals Lightship was responsible for the recovery of crewmen from at least six torpedoed merchant vessels. The Diamond Shoals Lightship *LV* (light vessel) *71* however, was itself attacked and sunk by a German submarine on August 6, 1918; all of the vessel's crewmen made it to safety.

The Second World War saw many of the lightships withdrawn from their stations and used as examination vessels. A notable exception, however, was Ambrose Lightship, which remained on station during the entire war. A lightship was lost during those years, but it was not from enemy action. On September 19, 1944, a hurricane struck the east coast. Five of the crewmen from the Vineyard Sound Lightship *LV 73* were on leave and were due back on the following morning; their absence saved their lives. As the storm approached, the anchored vessel began to be battered by high winds and waves. In seas that were estimated to have reached a height of one hundred feet, the vessel succumbed and took with it the entire shipboard crew of twelve.

Other lightships were lost because of storms or collisions while moored at their stations. These included Relief *LV 24* which was lost at Five Fathom Bank in a September 1889 hurricane, and Buffalo Lightship *LV 82*, which sank during a 1913 Great Lakes storm. On April 24, 1919, Relief *LV 51* was rammed and sunk at Cornfield Point. Nantucket Lightship *LV 117* capsized in 1934, when White Star liner *Olympic* collided with it in a heavy fog, and Ambrose Relief *WAL 505* went to the bottom on June 24, 1960, after being struck by the steamer *Green Bay*. It was not, however, the danger of losing these vessels that ended their use in the United States. Rather, it was the high cost of maintaining them which led ultimately to replacing all of them.

In 1909, the United States reached its maximum of fifty-six light-ship stations, and, when the Coast Guard took over the Lighthouse Service in 1939, the number had dwindled down to thirty. The country's last lightship, Nantucket Shoals, was extinguished in 1983 and replaced with a large navigational buoy.

BIBLIOGRAPHY

Adams, W.H. Davenport. *Lighthouses and Lightships.* London: T. Nelson. 1870.

Commissioner of Lighthouses Annual Report. 1921.

Compilation of Public Documents and Extracts from Reports and Papers Relating to Lighthouses, Light-vessels and Illuminating Apparatus. 1789-1871. Washington, D.C.: Government Printing Office. 1871.

Chronology of Aids to Navigation and the Old Lighthouse Service. 1716-1939. United States Coast Guard CG-458, 1974.

Flint, Willard. *Lightship Data.* Held by the U.S. Coast Guard Academy Library.

Johnson, Arnold Burgess. *Modern Lighthouse Service. Washington, DC:* U.S. Government Printing Office. 1889.

Lighthouse Service Bulletin. September 1, 1927. 3:205-209.

Lighthouse Site Files. RG 26, 66 Boston light station, MA DC:NA

Loran C User Handbook. Department of Transportation, United States Coast Guard. COMDTINST M16562.3 May, 1980.

Modern Lighthouse Practice. Birmingham: Chance Brothers and Co. 1910.

New York Herald Tribune. September 20, 1924.

New York Times. August 31, 1874.

New York Times. October 25, 1874.

New York Times. May 16, 1934.

New York Times. November 20, 1935.

New York Times. June 30, 1939.

New York Times. June 21, 1942.

Putnam, George R. *Lighthouses and Lightships of the United States.* New York: Houghton Mifflin. 1917.

Report of the Light House Board. Washington, DC. A. Boyd Hamil ton, 1852.

Report of the Light-House Board. 1867-1909.

Stebbins' Illustrated Coast Pilot: Atlantic and Gulf Coast. Boston: N. L. Stebbins. 1896.

Weiss, George. *Lighthouse Service.* Baltimore: John Hopkins. 1926.

2   *Rhode Island Lights*

SAKONNET POINT LIGHT

Appropriation:	August 7, 1882	$20,000
Established:	1884	
First lighted:	November 1, 1884	
First keeper:	Clarence Otis Gray, appointed October 6, 1884	

Illuminating apparatus (IA): fourth-order Fresnel lens

IA	*	(1891) fourth-order lens, fixed white (FW) for 30 sec. 3 red flashes (Fl R) at intervals of 10 seconds.
IA:		(1939), fourth-order Fresnel lens, FW alt. Fl red, white light 2,900 cp, red light 3,200 cp.
Illuminant:		(1939), incandescent oil vapor.
Fog signal:		(1939), air-diaphram horn.

Height of tower above sea level: (1891) 70 feet

*** Date in brackets ( ), signifies information
obtained from the Light List of that year.**

Struggling against an unbroken series of steep swells, the small boat reached the waves' crests only to slip back to the depths of their troughs. It must have seemed an eternity before the assistant keeper had reached his new post at Sakonnet Point, situated almost 800 yards offshore on Little Cormorant Rock. The January cold, seeping through the iron tower's brick-lined walls, greeted Lucius E. Chadwick as he began inspecting his new surroundings. There were two small rooms on the first deck and two on the second. He climbed the tower's wooden steps to the lantern, looked out over the frigid waters, and, with few words, asked to be returned to the mainland. With his two feet planted firmly back on solid ground, Chadwick resigned the appointment that he had received just two days earlier.

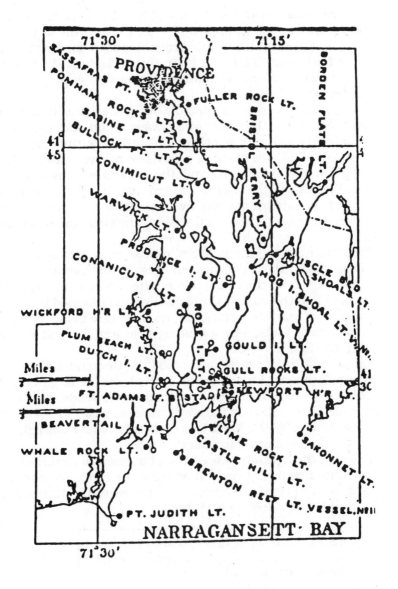

Rhode Island Lights, Narragansett Bay, 1895

Established, 1884

Construction of the Sakonnet Point Light began in 1883, but, as the season progressed to late autumn, waves began to break almost continuously over the exposed site. Luckily, the tower's iron pier had already been filled with concrete, and it was capped for the winter. Work resumed in the spring, and by late October the structure was completed. Fitted with a fourth-order Fresnel lens, the station displayed a fixed white light with intermittent flashes. The weights for the beacon's clockwork mechanism were suspended through a pipe in the center of the tower.

Life at the lighthouse was difficult. Heavy seas often limited access to and from shore, the tower was always damp, and the structure was not equipped with a privy until 1920. During the storm of August 26, 1924, the stations's boats were swept away, the boat landing severely damaged, and the tower's windows shattered. Keeper William Durfee later recounted that the spray easily cleared the top of the lantern seventy-five feet above sea level, and waves broke on the main galley's roof, shaking the structure to its foundation.

The 1938 hurricane demolished over seventy cottages at Sakonnet Point, with the loss of thirteen lives. In one incident, four men sought refuge from the rising tide on the roof of a two-story home. The wind lifted the roof off the structure and dropped the four into a cove not far from the lighthouse. As they were being swept out to sea, they came along side a quahog boat and were able to climb aboard; the four survived.

Somehow, the lighthouse withstood the tremendous force of the hurricane's waves, but, when it had passed, a large crack was discovered in the tower's base. Repairs were made, and in 1954 Hurricane Carol again damaged the masonry base. Faced with an estimated cost of $100,000 to tear down and rebuild the lighthouse, the Coast Guard elected to abandon it.

In 1961, the lighthouse was sold at auction to Carl Haffenreffer who maintained it for twenty-four years. In 1985, Haffenreffer donated it to the Friends of Sakonnet Light with the stipulation that money would be raised to preserve it.

The Sakonnet Point Light is best seen from the water. It can, however, be observed from a distance at Sakonnet Point, Little Compton, RI.
   * *NOAA Chart #13221*

---

*   *Nautical charts published by National Ocean Service, NOAA, Rockville, MD, 1988. Chart numbers are occasionally changed as the charts are updated.*

Sakonnet Point Lighthouse, 1988

BRISTOL FERRY LIGHT

Appropriation:	*March 3, 1837*	*$5,000*
Appropriation:	*August 3, 1854*	*$1,500*
Established:	*1855*	
First lighted:	*October 4, 1855*	
First keeper:	*George G. Pearse, appointed December 30, 1854*	
Illuminating apparatus (IA): (1863) sixth-order Fresnel lens, fixed white light (FW).		
Refitted:	*August, 1902, fifth-order Fresnel lens, FW.*	
IA:	*(1907) fifth-order Fresnel lens, FW.*	
Fog signal:	*none*	
Height of light above sea level: (1907) 35 feet		

"Those of us who have to pass through this strait on dark and stormy nights, or else are brought to a stand in the attempt to grope our way through, realize that, as it is now, we are subjected frequently to a responsibility more weighty than to be placed on any one." In his petition to the Light House Board of

November 22, 1853, William Brown, master of the steamer *Bay State*, argued for the establishment of a lighthouse at Bristol Ferry to mark the narrow passage connecting Narragansett and Mount Hope bays.

The strait connecting the two bays had about six hundred yards of navigable water, but its approach from Narragansett Bay was equally difficult. A shoal, which ran from Hog Island, reached nearly one thousand yards out into the waterway, and, less than a quarter mile east, another shoal reached out from the opposite shore; both sites were later marked with lighthouses.

The passage at Bristol Ferry had been marked in 1846 by a privately maintained wood-frame beacon, but it was dim and unreliable. Captain Brown's emotional plea was joined by a chorus of other ships' captains, and on August 3, 1854, Congress appropriated funds for the establishment of a light station at the site.

The Light House Board lost no time preparing the way for its construction. In October of that same year, the necessary land was purchased from George Pearse at a cost of $100, and, within a short time, work had begun.

George Pearse was appointed keeper of the station's temporary beacon, and he held the position until shortly after the lighthouse first showed its sixth-order, fixed white light on October 4, 1855. In December of 1855, Henry Dimon was appointed keeper of the Bristol Ferry Light.

Standing only fifty-three feet N. 1/4 W. from the former, privately maintained beacon, the station's twenty-eight-foot brick tower rose from the front of the brick-walled keeper's dwelling. The front door of the dwelling opened to a narrow hall that had stairs leading to the second floor. To the right was a small room, six feet by six feet, that was directly below the tower. On the left was a sitting room that connected to the dining room; beyond that room was a wood-frame kitchen, which extended out from the main building. The second floor had two to three bedrooms.

Keeper Henry Dimon was not to enjoy his stay at Bristol Ferry for long; he died on August 7, 1856. His widow, Elizabeth, took over, but the station's only female keeper did not hold the position for long either; she passed away six months later.

The station's sixth-order lens was replaced in August of 1902 with a more powerful fifth-order Fresnel lens. In 1916, a routine inspection of the tower revealed that the original wooden lantern and deck were in such poor condition that they were not worth repairing. An iron lantern and deck that had been removed from the discontinued Rondout Light on the Hudson River, was shipped to Bristol Ferry. The tower was then raised by six feet to accommodate its new iron structure.

Bristol Ferry Lighthouse, 1884. National Archives, 26-LG-11-23

Bristol Ferry Lighthouse, 1988

On December 14, 1917, Keeper Baldwin wrote in the lighthouse log, "NE to SSE gale. Heavy seas and high tide flooded station throughout the ground floor, 2-3 inches in depth, washed bulkheads and walks away." The light station stood in a depression that tended to collect water; the dwelling was flooded nearly every year.

On visiting the site a week after the most recent flooding, Inspector Luther of the Lighthouse Service recommended creating better drainage for the area and raising the height of the dwelling's floors by twelve inches. There was barely enough time to clean up; a month after the December storm, the station was again flooded. "Station surrounded by water from rain flowing into the pond, causing a back up and surround the station. Cistern filled with water which made it unfit for use." Funds were expended to create better drainage around the lighthouse, but it was not possible to determine if the floors were ever raised.

In 1927, the Bristol Ferry Light was discontinued and a thirty-foot skeleton tower, equipped with an acetylene light, took its place. With the construction of the Mount Hope Bridge and the lighting of its piers, the steel tower was no longer needed. It was discontinued and removed in the spring of 1930.

The lighthouse itself, with its lantern removed, was put up for auction in November of 1928. It was purchased by Anna Santulli of Bristol, RI, in April of 1929; the purchase price was $2,050.

> *The Bristol Ferry Light stands on the northwest side of the Mount Hope Bridge, near its steel and stone pilings. The structure is a private dwelling.*
> *NOAA chart #13221*

MUSSELBED (Muscle, Mussel Bed) SHOALS LIGHT

Appropriation:	*March 3, 1873*	*$3,000*
Appropriation:	*March 3, 1877*	*$6,000*
Established:	*1873*	
First lighted:	*August 1, 1873*	
First keeper:	*Dennis Shea, appointed August 5, 1873*	
Illuminating apparatus (IA): (1873) sixth-order 270o Fresnel lens,		
	fixed red light (FR).	
Rebuilt:	*1877*	
IA:	*(1907) sixth-order Fresnel lens, FR*	
IA:	*(1939) fourth-order Fresnel lens, FR, incandescent oil vapor, 870 cp.*	
Fog signal:	*1873, fog bell, one blow every 20 seconds.*	
Height of light above sea level: 1873, 31 feet. 1877, 35 feet		
Discontinued:	*1939*	

The channel leading from Narragansett Bay to Mount Hope Bay was an obstacle course of dangerous rock reefs. A steamboat company had, for some years, maintained a light at Hog Island Reef, and, on the opposite side of the channel, Musselbed Shoals was marked by a stone tower. In the late 1860s, Congress was petitioned to establish a lighthouse at Hog Island Reef, but, when it failed to appropriate the necessary funds, the less costly Musselbed Shoals Light was erected.

The first structure at Musselbed was a wooden keeper's dwelling, with a hexagonal tower rising from the center of the front of the building. Equipped with a sixth-order Fresnel lens and fog bell, it became operational on August 1, 1873.

In 1879, the lighthouse was found to be beyond repair, and it was rebuilt, but the new building was hardly an improvement; it had but one room, which was twelve feet square. The station's fixed red light was displayed from the gable, and the fog bell was located on the roof.

"I wish to inform you," wrote Keeper Otis Barstow on February 9, 1920, "that heavy ice has carried away part of the foundation from under this station leaving the light in a threatening condition." Ice jams had often formed in the narrow channel off Musselbed Shoals. During the winter 1874-1875, much to the dismay of Keeper William Dunnell, the entire station was moved four feet as ice piled up against the stone pier. Despite the serious damage, the station continued to operate for two more years before repairs were made. The pier was then torn down and rebuilt of granite, and the old dwelling was moved back on the new pier.

Following the damage caused by the ice in 1920, Superintendent of Lighthouses Yates inspected the station. Describing the unsightly structure as "a mere shanty," he recommended that both the foundation and dwelling be rebuilt.

The walls and ceilings of the new four-room dwelling leaked almost continuously from the time the structure was erected. The exterior of the tower and dwelling was waterproofed in the late 1920s, yet the window and door casings and the floors near exterior walls, were always wet. In July of 1938, the keeper wrote the Superintendent of Lights that a five-foot by ten-foot section of the living room ceiling had fallen; life at the lighthouse had become unbearable. In the following month, even before damage was inflicted on it by the September hurricane, the decision had been made to discontinue the station. In 1939, the lighthouse was torn down, and a skeleton tower with a fixed red acetylene light was erected in its place.

Standing on the southwest side of the Mount Hope Bridge, the skeleton tower at Musselbed Shoals continues to direct vessels through the narrow channel, showing its flashing white light every six seconds.

Hog Island Shoal Lighthouse, 1987

HOG ISLAND SHOAL LIGHT

Hog Island Shoal Lightship
Established lightship: 1886
Became operational: August 12, 1886
Lightship: LV 12,   sail-schooner rigged
Built: Philadelphia, 72 ft long, 20.6" beam

Hog Island Shoal Lighthouse
Appropriation, lighthouse: March 3, 1899 $35,000
Lighthouse built: October, 1901
First keeper (lighthouse):   Ernest W. Borgstrom
Illuminating apparatus: 1901, fifth-order Fresnel lens.
Refitted: September 15, 1903, fourth-order Fresnel lens,
                             fixed white light, dark sector.
Illuminant: November 25, 1912, changed from oil to
                             incandescent oil vapor.
Fog signal: April 5, 1902, siren.
Height of light above sea level: (1907) 54 feet (lighthouse)

In the United States, the use of light-boats or beacon-boats seems to have predated lightships by at least thirty-one years; two of the earliest beacon-boats were located at Cross Ledge, DE, and Brandywine, DE. Usually equipped with a single mast and lantern, the small boats were often privately maintained. From approximately 1866, the Old Colony Steamship Company operated such a boat, which was anchored at the southern end of Hog Island. Warning mariners of the area's dangerous shoals, the vessel's light was so dim that it was generally inadequate; in inclement weather, it was of no use at all.

With the establishment of Latimer Reef Light at the east end of Fishers Island Sound, the Eel Grass Shoal Lightship, *LV 12*, was permanently withdrawn. The vessel was then towed to Hog Island Shoal, and, under the command of Keeper Augustus Hall, it became operational on August 12, 1886. The "schooner rigged" vessel showed a fixed light and was equipped with a fog bell. Its lead-color hull had "Hog Island Shoal" painted in large black letters on its port and starboard sides.

Keeper Hall, a native of Massachusetts, died six months after being appointed keeper of the lightship. His assistant, August Wholstrom, assumed the post and remained there until his death four years later.

In 1889, after having developed a serious leak in its wood hull, the aging *LV 12* was taken off station for repairs. The seventy-one-foot vessel had been built at Philadelphia in 1846 and first saw duty as a relief vessel. It was then assigned to York Spit, VA (1863-1864), Wolf Trap Shoal, VA (1864-1870), and Cornfield Point, CT (1872-1882), and it was stationed twice at Eel Grass Shoal, CT (1871-1872, 1882-1884) before being transferred to Hog Island. By 1891, it had become obvious that *LV 12* was beyond repair, and over the next few years various proposals were made for a new lightship. When it was determined that the cost of building such a vessel was about twice that of erecting a lighthouse for the site, Congress appropriated funds for the latter.

Work on the conical tower began in the early summer of 1901, and during its construction, *LV 12* remained on station. On July 12 of that year, the tender *Cactus* pulled up alongside the Hog Island Shoal Lightship to deliver supplies and provisions. Lt. Spencer Wood boarded the vessel and asked for Keeper William Wallin. When the keeper arrived on deck, he was obviously drunk. "I accused him of it," wrote Lt. Wood, "and he said he had only been drinking tea; after a few further questions I ordered him to go below." The naval officer then went to find the mate, who had gone for provisions. "When I returned the assistant keeper was on board, and I placed the assistant in charge with orders not to allow the keeper on board again." Following an investigation, the keeper was dismissed from the service.

The regulations concerning intoxication had always been very specific, and an infraction of the rule generally always led to immediate dismissal. Even minor incidents, however, could sometimes lead to removal from office. Setting the tone for strict enforcement of the rules, President Thomas Jefferson wrote in December of 1806, "I think the keepers of light houses should be dismissed for small degrees of remissness, because of the calamities which even these produce."

Constructed to a height of fifty-four feet above sea level, the Hog Shoal Light was completed in October of 1901; a foghorn was installed and the lantern was fitted with a fifth-order Fresnel lens. When the lightship was withdrawn to the New London Lighthouse Depot, a recommendation was made to turn it over to the Navy for use in target practice. Apparently the Navy was not interested in the aging hulk; on February 9, 1903, *LV 12* was sold at auction.

The automated Hog Island Shoal Light has continued to show its white light for six seconds followed by a dark period of equal duration. Its foghorn gives two blasts every thirty seconds.

Hog Shoal Light can be approached on the water, from its south side. It is visible in the distance from the Mount Hope Bridge. NOAA chart #13221

NAYATT (NAYAT) POINT LIGHT
CONIMICUT LIGHT

Nayatt Point Lighthouse
Appropriation:	May 23, 1828	$3,500
Appropriation:	August 18, 1856	$6,500
Appropriation:	April 7, 1866	$6,500
Established:	1828	

Illuminating apparatus (IA): (1842) 6 lamps, 9" reflectors, fixed white light (FW).
IA:	(1850) 6 lamps, 14" reflectors, FW.
First keeper:	Daniel Wightman
Rebuilt:	1856
IA:	(1863) fourth-order Fresnel lens, FW.
Discontinued:	1868

Height of light above sea level: (1838) 38 feet, (1863) 31 feet.

Conimicut Lighthouse
Apporpriation:	March 2, 1867	$15,000
Appropriation:	March 3, 1877	$5,000
Established:	1868	
First lighted:	November 1, 1868	
IA:	(1873) fourth-order Fresnel lens, FW	
Rebuilt:	1882-1883	
IA:	(1939) fourth-order Fresnel lens, FW, red sector. Incandescent oil vapor. White light, 2,900-candlepower (cp), red light, 870 cp.	
Fog signal:	(1873) bell struck by machine, every 12 seconds.	

Height of light above sea level: (1883) 60 feet

"A s there is no option left us by law but to accept the lowest offer," wrote Stephen Pleasonton of the Treasury Department, "you are authorized to accept and enter into contract with them [William Halloway and Westgate Watson] accordingly." The law forcing the acceptance of the lowest bid with seemingly little regard to a contractor's qualifications was to haunt the Light House Establishment on more than one occasion (see Execution Rocks Light). Almost from the time that it was built in 1828, the stone keeper's dwelling at Nayatt Point was in a constant state of disrepair. The tower's winding wooden stairs were narrow and difficult to negotiate; the height of the lantern was, at best, for persons of very slight build and short stature.

The light from the twenty-three-foot brick tower was generated by six lamps and reflectors. It served to mark the narrow passage between Nayatt Point and the shoal off Conimicut Point.

A winter gale in 1855 undermined the tower and produced cracks from top to bottom, and the sea wall that protected the lighthouse reservation was also nearly destroyed. After a survey of the damage, it was determined that the old tower was not worth repairing, and, in the following year, a twenty-five-foot square tower was erected next to the dwelling.

In the mid-1860s, the Light House Board erected a round granite tower to mark the sand shoal off Conimicut Point. Originally intended as a day-mark, the tower was lighted at the urging of ship owners and captains. Following its completion, the Nayatt Point Light was discontinued, and its fourth-order Fresnel lens was transferred to the new facility.

T he lighting of the Conimicut Point Beacon on November 1, 1868, was a great improvement for vessels navigating the Providence River, but it was hardly a blessing for Keeper Davis Perry and his assistant. No provision had been made at the granite tower for keeper's quarters, forcing the attendants to travel back and forth by small rowboat. The one-mile trek was all too often made while fighting dangerous seas or avoiding ship traffic in the narrow channel.

A five-room dwelling was built on Conimicut's landing pier during 1873-1874, but the keepers were to enjoy its use for only a short time. In March of 1875, Keeper Horace Arnold and his son barely escaped with their lives as a large field of ice bore down on the station and demolished the dwelling; all of the keeper's furniture and possessions were lost. With its destruction, the keeper returned to the dwelling at Nayatt Point; later that year, the quarters were enlarged, and an assistant was hired.

Staffed by two keepers, the tower was occupied at all times by one attendant while the other remained on shore. Duty at the tower was not always pleasant, especially when it rained. The structure leaked badly and there was only a small stove that provided inadequate warmth during the colder months.

In 1882, the stone tower was torn down and a cast-iron, cylindrical lighthouse was erected in its place; it was the duplicate of those at Stamford Harbor, Latimer Reef, Whale Rock, and Tarrytown. The Nayatt Point Light and its grounds were then placed in charge of a caretaker; he remained there until the station was sold at auction in 1890.

Most keepers welcomed the interruption provided by visitors, but Conimicut's keeper may have had second thoughts. Local fishermen were in the habit of making their way out to the lighthouse to fish off its riprap foundation. By 1935, things were getting out of hand, with as many as forty to sixty people crowding on the rocks at once. The keeper tried to restrict the numbers on several occasions but he had no success with the generally rowdy individuals. With the help of the Coast Guard, however, the station was posted and the keeper returned to the splendid isolation of his rock-surrounded light-

Nayatt Point Lighthouse, 1987

Conimicut Lighthouse, 1987

house.

Conimicut Light was manned until the early 1960s when it was automated. It continues to operate, flashing its white light every 2.5 seconds and sounding its fog bell every 15 seconds.

> *Nayatt Point Light, a private residence, is located on Nayatt Point Road in Barrington, RI. On the water, it can be approached only aboard a "shallow draft" vessel.*
>
> *Conimicut Light is clearly visible from Nayatt Point. It can be reached only by boat.*   *NOAA chart #13221*

BULLOCK(s) POINT LIGHT

Appropriation:	*June 20, 1860 (day beacon)*	*$3,000*
Appropriation:	*June 20, 1872*	*$1,000*
Appropriation:	*June 23, 1874*	*$15,000*
Established:	*1872*	
First lighted:	*October 1, 1872*	
First keeper:	*Joseph Bower, appointed November 7, 1872*	
Illuminating apparatus (IA):	*(1872) sixth-order Fresnel lens, fixed red light (FR).*	
IA:	*1876, sixth-order Fresnel lens, FR.*	
IA:	*(1924) FR, 20 cp. (1939), 375 mm lens, 140 cp, flash 1 second.*	
Rebuilt:	*1876*	
Fog signal:	*(1924) fog bell, 2 strokes every 15 seconds.*	
Height of light above sea level: (1873) 26 feet		
Height of light above sea level: (1883) 50 feet		
Discontinued:	*1938*	

For about twenty-two years, a day-mark had warned mariners of Bullock Point's dangerous shoals on the east side of the Providence River. In November of 1872, a portable beacon, which rested on a granite pier, was established in its place; Joseph Bowes, the keeper of Sabin Point Light, was given the responsibility of maintaining the fixed red light.

The portable beacon had been in operation for only a few months before it became apparent that a keeper's dwelling was needed. In 1874, funds were appropriated for the expansion of the pier and for construction of a dwelling; it was a little over two years before the project was completed. The new lighthouse was a two-story Victorian structure, which had chimneys at both ends of its gable roof. The tower rose from the center of the roof and it was surmounted by a black lantern with a black railing. The station's privy hung over edge of the deck on the front and left-hand side of the lighthouse.

In 1907, the American Association of Masters, Mates, and Pilots petitioned the Light House Service for the establishment of a fog signal at Bullock Point. The well-respected organization argued that

Bullock Point Lighthouse, February 1918. National Archives, 26-LG-11-24

a signal was "of great importance for the safe navigation of all classes of vessels." Within four days, the request was granted, and, a short time later, a 1000-pound blow fog bell was installed.

The Great Hurricane of 1938 struck a devastating blow to the sixty-one-year-old lighthouse. The granite pier on which it was erected was undermined, leaving the entire structure in a precarious position. The keeper escaped unharmed, but the dwelling was heavily damaged and the square tower, which rose from its center, was described as "unsafe." All of the furnishings, supplies, and the station's boat were washed away.

At Palmer Island Light, MA, about thirty miles to the east, only the station's tower remained standing in the wake of the storm. The keeper's dwelling and all of the other buildings were leveled and swept away. The keeper's wife took refuge at the tower, but, when she saw her husband caught up in heavy surf, she went to his aid; the attempt cost the woman her life. Somehow Keeper Arthur Small managed to get back to shore, and carrying the enormous emotional burden of the loss of his wife, he managed to continue maintaining the light until the storm had passed.

The light station at Bullock Point was discontinued following the 1938 hurricane.

SABIN'S (Sabine) POINT LIGHT

Appropriation:	March 3, 1871	$42,000
Established:	1872	
First lighted:	November 4, 1872	
First keeper:	Joseph Bower, (Bowes?) appointed November 7, 1872	

Illuminating apparatus (IA): (1873) sixth-order Fresnel lens, fixed white light.
IA: (1907) sixth-order Fresnel lens, fixed red light (FR).
IA: (1939) fourth-order Fresnel lens, FR, incandescent oil vapor, 870 cp.
Fog signal: (1899) fog bell. (1907) bell struck by machine every 9 seconds.
Height of light above sea level: (1873) 48 feet. (1891) 54 feet. (1939) 49 feet.

Sabin's Point Lighthouse was located about a quarter of a mile offshore in eight feet of water. Standing on the east side of the Providence River, it marked a sharp turn in the river's channel. A vessel venturing outside the channel, on either side, could expect to find itself immediately aground in soft mud or sand.

A square pier, fabricated of irregular blocks of granite and riprap, formed the dwelling's foundation. The station's octagonal tower, which rose from the front of the structure, reached a height of forty-eight feet above sea level.

Rainwater was collected from the roof and filtered through charcoal as it flowed into the cistern; the 4,215-gallon capacity cistern was located in the cellar. The first story had an oil room, kitchen, dining room, and sitting room. The second floor consisted of bedrooms and a watch room; a wooden ladder led to the lantern.

Equipped with a sixth-order Fresnel lens, Sabin's Point exhibited its fixed white light for the first time on November 4, 1872. From their vantage point on the river channel, the keepers could easily see the lights at Pomham, Conimicut, and Fuller Rock.

John Weeden, the station's second keeper, recorded several instances of rendering aid to the occupants of small boats. On April 16, 1877, he wrote in the station's log of an accident near the lighthouse. "Schooner collided with steamer *Panther*. Schooner grounded 300 yards from lighthouse." He went out to the schooner and helped its occupants to safety. Keeper Charles E. Whitford, who succeeded Weeden, also had his share of rescues.

Keeper Whitford was probably the station's most colorful personage. He had served five years as assistant keeper at Orient Point before being transferred to the station on October 27, 1916. His career at sea, however, had begun even earlier when, at the age of twelve, he enlisted in the Navy as an "apprentice boy." During the Spanish-American War, he saw action in the Philippines, and later,

Sabin's (Sabine) Point Lighthouse, undated. National Archives, 26-LG-14-54

aboard the gunboat *Vicksburg*, he witnessed the sinking of two Russian ships by the Japanese Navy.

At Sabin's Point, Keeper Whitford settled down to the routine of keeping the light, and, together with his wife, Annie, they raised three daughters. Two of the girls, Myrtle and Eleanor, were married at the station. Years later, the then seventy-two-year-old Myrtle recalled having to be taken ashore by her father every time she had a date, "and I always got wet." In addition, a child was born at Sabin's Point, the keeper's granddaughter, Beverly Ann Beach. For the most part, however, Sabin's Point seems to have been a great place to sit back and watch the world go by. In a 1943 interview, Keeper Whitford recalled how vessel traffic had changed over the years; luxurious passenger steamers had given way to oil tankers.

The 1938 hurricane found Keeper Whitford ashore with Annie left in charge of the light. "The station was damaged quite a lot on September 21st 1938, by hurrycane and tidal wave. There was five foot of water in the kitchen, all of the old journals & all other records were lost," he later entered in the log. The keeper continued, "Furniture on lower floor was lost and most of the governments property on lower floor and cellar lost." The 160-pound fog bell and its 10,000-blow striking machine, which had been installed in 1900, were carried away by the sea along with most of the equipment kept

Northeast Lights

outside the lighthouse. At the height of the storm, the keeper later recounted that his wife "had been washed off the runway of the lighthouse three times." Annie who had been trying to secure equipment, nearly had lost her life in the attempt. In the aftermath of the great storm, Whitford put in a claim of $1,725.98 for loss of personal effects.

The keeper stayed on at the lighthouse until his retirement on April 1, 1943. He was then relieved by Coast Guardsman J. B. Watkins.

In July of 1968, the Rhode Island State Division of Harbors and Rivers ordered the ninety-six-year-old structure burned and removed, to make way for the widening and deepening of the river channel.

POMHAM (Pumham) ROCKS LIGHT

Appropriation:	(Fuller Rk, Sassafras, and Pomham) July 15, 1870 $20,000
Appropriation:	March 3, 1873 $1,200
Established:	1871
First lighted:	December 1, 1871
First keeper:	C.H. Salisbury, appointed December 8, 1871
Illuminating apparatus (IA):	(1873) sixth-order Fresnel lens, fixed red light (FR).
IA:	(1939) fourth-order Fresnel lens, FR. Incandescent oil vapor, 870 cp.
Fog signal:	(1902) fog bell.
Fog signal:	(1924) bell, 2 strokes every 20 seconds.
Height of light above sea level:	(1873) 69 feet
Discontinued:	1974

A fog siren had been operating at Pomham for about a year, but the new signal installed in 1900 was greeted by a local newspaper as "THE GREATEST NUISANCE IN THE HISTORY OF THE STATE." "Did you hear the siren this morning?" asked the conductor of a Providence street car. "Great Scott!! I didn't hear anything else. I haven't heard anything else since 3 o'clock this morning" was one man's answer. Unfortunately, almost everyone for miles around had also been subjected to its unrelenting wail. The signal had "a sound to make the flesh creep, indescribably lonesome and cheerless, creepy and dreary." Another man was quoted as having said, "It beats the dutch how that Light House Board, sitting in Washington, and considered the fattest snap [with the most influence] in the navy, can tell what is best for the mariners and residents of Narragansett Bay, better than they can tell themselves."

Even many of the ships' captains and pilots were in favor of

Pomham Rocks Lighthouse, 1989

removing the experimental signal, since they felt that its uninter-rupted blast made it difficult to locate the lighthouse in the fog. Though suggestions were made to substitute a fog bell, one already existed a short distance away at Sabine Point. The use of one bell near another, it was argued, might confuse mariners. The charac-teristic of the siren was thus changed to a three-second signal, with twelve-second silent intervals. Three years later, the siren was removed and a fog bell installed.

Established, 1871

In December of 1871, C. H. Salisbury was appointed keeper of the eight-room wood-frame lighthouse. Located on the east side of the Providence River, the station's tower rose from the front of the dwelling. The lantern was accessible from the second floor watchroom via a wooden stepladder.

In 1872, Mary Salisbury applied for an appointment as assistant keeper, but she was turned down. Following the death of her husband in 1893, the widow was appointed acting keeper, a post she held for only a few months.

Pomham had few of the amenities that were normal for home-owners living along the shoreline, less than a mile away. The station had no telephone, electricity, or running water. Light was provided by oil lamps, and water was obtained from rainwater collected in a brick and concrete cistern.

A trip back and forth from shore to the light station always necessitated the use of a small boat. When Keeper Adolph Aronson's wife had appendicitis, she was too ill to be moved. The doctor and his staff went out to Pomham and performed the emergency surgery right at the lighthouse. During the winter, when the river was frozen solid, access to Pomham Rocks was easy. There were many times, however, when the ice was too thin, and the keeper had to cut his way slowly through the ice to make way for the station's boat.

Leisure time at the lighthouse for the Aronsons included reading and playing the family piano. The keeper transported the instrument to the station aboard a schooner. Lines were tied to the piano, and it was hung above the deck by lines, strung between the two masts. With the vessel pulled tightly up against the island's rocks, the crew shifted weight to one side and tipped the boat sufficiently to lower the precious cargo gently to the ground.

Pomham Rocks' light was extinguished in 1974 and replaced by a skeleton tower. In 1980, the structure was sold to the Mobil Oil Company, and it continues to be maintained by them.

> The lighthouse can be seen from the parking lot of the Stone Gate Apartments on Pawtucket Avenue, (Route 103), in East Providence.
> NOAA Chart #13221

FULLER ROCK/SASSAFRAS POINT LIGHTS

Fuller Rock and Sassafras Point Lights

Appropriation:	July 15, 1870	$20,000
Established:	1872	
Illuminating apparatus:	(1873) sixth-order lens, portable beacons.)	
Characteristic (Fuller Rock):	1873, fixed white. 1912, flashing red, every 3 sec.	
Characteristic (Sassafras Point):	1873, fixed red.	
Height of light above sea level:	(1873) 25 feet (Fuller Rock)	
Height of light above sea level:	(1873) 25 feet (Sassafras Point)	
Sassafras Rock discontinued:	July 23, 1912, shoal dredged away.	
Fuller Rock discontinued:	1923	

Keeping the lights at Sassafras Point and Fuller Rock was by no means an easy task. The portable beacons stood about a mile apart on either side of the Providence River. Reaching them meant fighting current, wind, and waves and dodging steamers in heavy fog as they traveled up and down the river channel.

Sassafras Point, which was located on the west side of the river, showed a fixed red light. Fuller Rock, situated near the channel's edge and on the east side of the river, showed a fixed white light; both were established in 1872. Hexagonal in shape, the wood-frame towers were erected on granite piers.

A year after the lights became operational, the Light House Board went to Congress asking for funds to build quarters at Fuller Rock. "The purchase of a site and the erection of a dwelling for the keeper are recommended, as very great difficulty is experienced in securing a suitable person to attend the lights at the compensation fixed for such beacons." Congress appropriated $5,000, but landowners, fearing that the construction would depreciate the value of their property, refused to sell a parcel; the dwelling was never built.

Lorenzo Clark, the stations' first keeper, held the post for only five months; his successor lasted five and a half months. During the first twelve years of operation, the stations had eight keepers who either transferred, resigned, or died. John (Jack) Mullen, appointed keeper on April 20, 1886, was, however, one of a more hardy breed; he remained at the post for over a quarter century.

On a cold December day, Capt. Jack Mullen, dressed in an overcoat, heavy sweater, and rubber outer garments, rowed across the river in his yawl to Sassafras Point. The wind was brisk, and the cold spray covered his face. Having tended to the beacon, he turned

Acetylene tank following its explosion at Fuller Rock, February, 1923.
National Archives, 26-LG-12-3A

his boat around and raised its small sail. Just off Kettle Point, a strong gust caught the sail and flipped the boat over; Capt. Mullen fell headlong into the icy waters. Luckily, a local resident, Ed Grogan, spotted the struggling keeper and went to his aid. "Surely you were thinking of the Lord when you were in the water," said a religious-minded lady to the captain. "Not all of the time," admitted the keeper. "I was also thinking how in blazes I was going to get ashore!"

In 1911, work was begun on widening of the river channel, and in the following year, Sassafras Point Light was dismantled. Having only one light left to maintain, Keeper Mullen found his position reduced to that of a laborer and his pay cut to less than one-half.

On February 5, 1923, crewmen from the lighthouse tender *Panzy* were servicing Fuller Rock Light. During the installation of new acetylene tanks for the automated beacon, one of the tanks exploded. The force of the blast hurled the men through the air, burning and injuring five of them, and in the process, the tower was totally destroyed. Within hours a temporary beacon had been set up, and sometime later a structural steel tower was erected.

Fuller Rock Light was discontinued in 1923 and replaced by a pyramidal skeleton tower.

WARWICK (Neck, Point) LIGHT

Appropriation:	*March 3, 1825*	*$1,000*
Appropriation:	*March 14, 1826*	*$2,000*
Established:	*1826*	
First keeper:	*Edmund Burke (declined)*	
First keeper:	*Elisha Case*	
Illuminating apparatus (IA): (1838) 8 lamps, 9" reflectors, fixed white light (FW).		
Refitted:	*1856, fourth-order Fresnel lens, FW.*	
Rebuilt:	*1889*	
IA:	*(1891) fourth-order Fresnel lens, FW.*	
Rebuilt:	*1932*	
IA:	*(1939) fourth-order Fresnel lens, fixed green light, electric, 5,100 cp.*	
Fog signal:	*(1882) fog bell.*	
Fog signal:	*(1907) compressed air siren, blast 3 seconds, interval 3 seconds.*	
Fog signal:	*(1939) horn.*	
Height of tower, base to lantern: (1842) 30 feet		
Height of light above sea level: (1891) 54 feet. (1939) 51 feet		

D aniel Waite arrived at Warwick Light in July of 1831 to find that the man he was replacing, Elisha Case, refused to turn over the station to him. The former keeper wanted first to be assured that he would be allowed to continue to grow and harvest a crop that he had planted on the lighthouse grounds. He also asked to be compensated for a barn that he had erected on the public land.

Warwick Neck Lighthouse, undated. Courtesy U. S. Coast Guard

Shelters for keepers' horses and other farm animals were generally not provided at most early light stations. If keepers chose to build such structures on lighthouse property, the government took the position that the builders also had to take the responsibility of removing them; the United States would never pay for "buildings erected without their previous knowledge and consent." Elisha Case was allowed to keep and harvest his crop, but he received no payment for his barn.

Established, 1826

Completed in 1826, Warwick's light tower was an odd-shaped structure that might have been more comfortable as a windmill than as a lighthouse. Built of stone, the outer walls of the structures were covered with a lime-gravel mix about ten years after their construction, and later they were sheathed with wood shingles. The keeper's dwelling, which was connected to the tower, had "but two rooms, each about eleven feet square, and very wet and damp owing to the imperfect manner in which they were built." At Keeper Waite's request in 1832, a one-story, three-room frame house was built to join the back of the original structure. Six years later, the dwelling was reported to be leaking badly at the junction between the frame addition and the original dwelling. Improvements were made, and the dwelling was used for another half-century. In 1888, the frame addition was moved and converted into a barn, and the keeper's dwelling was rebuilt.

Standing near the water's edge at Warwick Neck, the lighthouse afforded its keepers a commanding view of Narragansett Bay. The beacon served to mark the narrow passage between the point on which it stood and the northern tip of Patience Island. It also aided those traveling on either side of Prudence Island. When the light was established in 1826, mariners sailing toward Providence were instructed after proceeding to the Dutch Island Light, to "steer N. 1/2 E. 14 miles, for the light on Warwick Neck, leaving it on the larboard (left) hand one-quarter of a mile, where you anchor in 3 fathoms of water." Mariners were warned that the channel from that point was marked with only wood stakes and that they should not proceed any farther without a pilot. Though a light was established at Nayat Point two years later, it was forty to fifty years before the well-traveled Providence River channel was better marked.

Erosion was always a problem at Warwick. During an 1869 gale, a large portion of the bank in front of the station was washed away. The property fence had to be moved back on at least two occasions to prevent it from toppling over the edge. In 1932, the continual loss of sand began to endanger the light station, forcing the Lighthouse Service to erect a new beacon. The old lighthouse was left standing during construction, and in June of that year, the thirty-one-foot-tall steel tower was completed. Just six years later, the 1938 hurricane caused so much erosion that the new tower found itself within inches of the bank's edge. Massive jacks lifted the thirty-five-ton tower onto logs and moved it fifty feet inland, where it was raised up on an eight-foot-high concrete pedestal. During the entire move, the tower never stopped showing its light.

The light shown from Warwick' tower was originally generated by eight lamps and reflectors, which were arranged on a circular table. In the mid-1850s, the lantern was refitted with a fourth-order Fresnel lens, and, with construction of the new tower in 1932, the beacon was electrified. A fog signal was added to the station at the turn of the century. Automated in the 1980s, the conical tower continued to exhibit its flashing green light.

Warwick Neck Light can be reached by following Route 117 from Interstate 95, to Warwick Neck Avenue. The white conical tower stands a short distance past Rock Point Beach, at the end of Warwick Neck Avenue.
NOAA chart #13221

PRUDENCE ISLAND (Sandy Point) LIGHT

Appropriation: September 28, 1850 $3,500
Established: 1852
Refitted: 1855, fifth-order Fresnel lens, fixed white light (FW).
Characteristic: (1924) FW, alternating with flashing red (Fl R), 5 seconds.
Illuminating apparatus: (1939) fourth-order Fresnel lens, FW, Fl Green, every 5 seconds.
      Electric. White light 5,000 cp, green light 33,000 cp
Fog signal: (1891) bell struck by machine every 15 seconds.
Height of light above sea level: (1863) 30 feet. (1939) 28 feet

As the winds picked up and the swells grew in the channel between Prudence Island and the shores of Portsmouth, seventy-one-year-old Martin (Martie) Thompson became convinced that the keeper's dwelling was the safest place to be. Having served as the station's keeper for about twenty years, "he'd seen a lot of weather on Prudence Island. If he said the building would stand it, it would stand it."

Martie Thompson found a married couple, the Lynches, as guests at the lighthouse, along with Keeper George T. Gustavus, his wife, and his son. Together, they chose to ride out the hurricane at the dwelling. As the storm waters rose, all of the occupants, with reportedly the exception of Keeper Gustavus, elected to move to the floor above; his decision may have saved his life.

A storm-generated "tidal wave" swept up Narragansett Bay, swallowing everything in its path. In an instant, it reduced the keeper's dwelling to rubble, leaving only the stone tower standing. George Taber, an eighteen-year-old island resident, managed to help pull Keeper Gustavus to safety, but horrified onlookers watched as his wife and son were swept away, clinging to parts of the dwelling. No one ever saw the other occupants; the hurricane of 1938 had taken five lives at the lighthouse.

Established, 1852

The station's twenty-five-foot octagonal tower was built on Goat Island in 1823, but, fourteen years later, it was found no longer to be of use at the site. It was moved in 1851 to Sandy Point on the east side of Prudence Island. The lighthouse became operational on the following year, and three years later, the lantern was refitted with a fifth-order Fresnel lens that displayed a fixed white light. A stone stairway led to the upper landing, and from there an iron ladder reached the lantern. In the mid-1880s, a fog signal was added to the

Prudence Island Lighthouse, undated. National Archives, 26-LG-14-26

Prudence Island (Sandy Point) Lighthouse, 1987

station.

The keeper's dwelling was located about 190 feet west of the tower. It had six rooms and a kitchen which was attached to the west side of the structure. An elevated walkway connected the tower and residence.

The one-acre lighthouse reservation stood entirely on beach sand. Over the years, the keepers were allowed to maintain a garden and a variety of farm animals on neighboring land owned by the family of Lewis Herreshoff. A rift developed between the parties after the Herreshoff's cattle wandered into Thompson's garden and ate all of his vegetables. In throwing stones to frighten them away, the keeper badly injured one of the animals and it later died. Herreshoff expressed the desire to allow the keeper to continue having his garden, but he asked to have it surrounded by a fence. Thompson, however, who had a wife and four children, was apparently too poor and did not have the necessary resources to build one himself. The plot was eventually purchased by the government for $540, and apparently a fence was later erected.

Electric lights had been recommended for the Prudence Island Station in 1937, but the installation had been deferred pending results of the Rose Island Light's electrification. On the very night of the 1938 hurricane, Milton Chase, general manager of the Homestead Utilities Company, installed an electric light in the damaged tower. In the spring of the following year, it was decided not to rebuild the keeper's dwelling and to automate the station, using power drawn from the local generating station. A standby generator was installed, and the weight-revolving lens was replaced with a fixed fourth-order lens that exhibited an occulting green light.

In the late 1980s, the station continued to show its green light and sound its fog signal.

The Prudence Island Light can be reached via the Island Transport Ferry from Portsmouth, RI, or the Prudence Island Ferry from Bristol, RI. NOAA chart #13223, 13221

CONANICUT ISLAND LIGHT

Appropriation:	*July 7, 1884*	*$18,000*
Established:	*1886*	
First lighted:	*April 1, 1886*	
First keeper:	*Horace W. Arnold, appointed March 23, 1886*	

Illuminating apparatus (IA): (1891), fifth-order Fresnel lens, fixed white light.
IA: *(1907) fifth-order lens, fixed red light (FR).*
Fog signal: *(1891) fog bell struck by machine, double blow, every 30 seconds.*
Fog signal: *January 13, 1903, compressed-air siren, blast 3 sec, silent 17 sec.*
Height of light above sea level: (1891) 47 feet
Discontinued: *1933, replaced by skeleton tower.*
Lightshouse sold at auction: Mahlon G. Dunn, August 27, 1934, $2,875.
IA: *(1939) skeleton tower 375 mm lens, FR, electric, 2,800 cp.*

T he lighthouse at Conanicut, located on the northernmost point of the island, consisted of a six-room dwelling with a square tower rising from its northeast corner. Congress appropriated $18,000 for its establishment in July of 1884, but difficulties in obtaining a title from the site's owner, the Conanicut Park Land Company, delayed its construction. Work began in mid-1885, and by the end of the working season, the structure was nearly completed. Over the winter, a temporary beacon lamp was apparently shown from the point, but it proved to be of no help to the steamer *Eolus.* Bound from Wickford to Newport in a raging snowstorm, the steamer's captain miscalculated his position and his vessel went aground on a shoal just west of the lighthouse. No one was injured in the incident; the passengers were taken to shore in small boats and housed at local farmhouses. Work resumed on the lighthouse in late winter, and when it was completed, the tower was equipped with a fifth-order Fresnel lens. The station's fixed white light was shown for the first time on April 1, 1886.

Conanicut's first keeper, Horace W. Arnold, must have found life just a little dull at his new post, in comparison to that at Conimicut Light where he had spent thirteen years. When pack ice threatened to topple his former station in 1875, according to one account, the keeper launched himself (official records indicate that his son was also with him at the time, -see Conimicut Light) on an "ice floe on which he placed a mattress." Describing Arnold, who was seen sitting on a mattress in the middle of the ice floe, Capt. Sutton of the tug *Reliance* recalled that the keeper was "sitting like a man on a magic carpet." He was taken aboard the tug with his mattress. Arnold served some twenty years at Conanicut.

Not much is actually known about the light station. By 1932, it was

Conanicut Island Lighthouse, 1989. (Lantern removed from the tower)
determined that the amount of ship traffic no longer justified the cost of the attended light, and preparations were made to discontinue it. Over the next few years, the trend toward the use of automated lights accelerated throughout the service, and by the end of the Second World War, only thirteen of Rhode Island's lights remained manned; four were kept by civilians, the others were watched by Coast Guardsmen. In 1988, Rhode Island's last manned lighthouse was Block Island's Southeast Light, and in the entire United States, only twelve lighthouses remained under the care of keepers.

Conanicut Light was replaced by a fifty-foot steel tower, erected some fifty-five feet east of the old lighthouse. Operated electrically, the automatic beacon began showing its fixed red light in 1933. In the following year, the lighthouse and its half-acre of land were sold at auction to Mahlon G. Dunn, but the small section on which the new tower stood was retained by the Lighthouse Service. In the early 1980s, the skeleton tower itself was discontinued by the Coast Guard.

The gingerbread trimmed, Victorian style lighthouse is a private residence. It is located at 64 North Bay View Drive, Conanicut Point, Jamestown, RI.   *NOAA chart #13223*

POPLAR POINT LIGHT
WICKFORD (Old Gay Rock) HARBOR LIGHT

Poplar Point Lighthouse
Appropriation: March 3, 1831 $3,000
Purchased from: Thomas Albro
Contractor: Charles Allen, 1831
Illuminating apparatus provided by: Winslow Lewis, 1831
Established: 1831
First keeper: Samuel Thomas, Jr.
Illuminating apparatus: (1838) 8 lamps, 14.5" reflectors
Refitted: 1855, fifth-order lens, fixed white light.
Refitted: 1871, fifth-order Fresnel lens, fixed white light.
Height of light above sea level: (1838) 48 feet
Discontinued: 1882
Land sold at auction to: October 15, 1894 Albert R. Sherman

Wickford Harbor Lighthouse
Appropriation: June 15, 1880 $45,000
Established: 1882
First lighted: November 1, 1882
First keeper: Henry F. Sherman
Illuminating apparatus: fifth-order Fresnel lens, fixed white light.
Fog signal: (1891), fog bell struck by machine, every 20 seconds.
Height of light above sea level: (1891) 52 feet
Discontinued: 1930
Skeleton tower, IA: (1939), 375 mm lens, 390 cp, flashing white.

Poplar Point Light was probably never meant to direct vessels through Narragansett Bay's West Passage. It stood well within the recesses of a shallow bay, about two miles from mid-channel. Few mariners attempted to enter Wickford Harbor at night, preferring instead the easy access of the well-protected anchorage between Dutch and Conanicut Islands. Even within the harbors it served, Wickford and North Kingston, in 1838 only six schooners and fourteen small sloops made them their home ports.

The station's one-story stone dwelling with its octagonal tower was erected in 1831; it showed a fixed white light produced by eight lamps and reflectors. The structure's wooden tower had been left unfinished, with its studs exposed; entry was through a small bedroom that had no windows. In the winter, the tower became a virtual wind tunnel that fed biting cold air and snow into the uninhabitable room.

In the early 1870s, a dormer window was installed in the access bedroom, and a partition was created to separate it from the tower. The inside walls of the tower were finished, and a new lantern and

Poplar Point Lighthouse, 1987

an iron deck were set into place. Just ten years later, it was decided to abandon Poplar Point and erect a new lighthouse on Old Gay Rock, 200 yards offshore and northeast of the old station.

The land for the Poplar Point Light Station had originally been purchased from Thomas Albro for $300. After the light was discontinued, the parcel and its buildings were sold at auction to Albert R. Sherman of Pawtuxet, RI. Over the years it was resold several more times and used mainly as a summer home; it later became a year-round residence.

Known as the Wickford Harbor Light, the new lighthouse was built on an iron pier. Its wooden dwelling had eight rooms and a 2,500-gallon cistern built within the foundation. The outhouse hung over the outside deck; it is doubtful that anyone lingered there for long in the winter!

The tower, which was attached to the dwelling, rose to the height of fifty-two feet above sea level; it was equipped with a fifth-order Fresnel lens that showed a fixed white light. The station also had a Stevens fog bell.

The lighthouse inspector was impressed with the condition of Wickford Harbor Light during his 1905 tour of the station: "It was in most excellent order," wrote the inspector. "The Board commends you on this." The glowing report did not, however, save Keeper

Edward Andrews from nearly being dismissed two years later over an infraction of the rules.

A resident of Wickford complained that Keeper Andrews was in the habit of permitting "certain persons," not in the employ of the Light House Board, to remain at the station. A naval inspector went out to the lighthouse and reported that the keeper indeed allowed two or more people to stay there for extended periods of time; these people were reportedly of "bad reputation."

Further investigation revealed that one of the people was Aaron Sprague, the keeper's brother-in-law, and another was Elam Littlefield, Block Island North Light's keeper and a family friend. Keepers were allowed to have only immediate family members residing at their light station, and the board alone could grant exceptions to the rule.

Andrews freely admitted that he had not obtained the necessary permission to have these people remain at the lighthouse. In replying to the charges, the keeper wrote, "Aaron Sprague my wive's brother is to this station at the present time to row the children to school mornings & get them at nights." The keeper, who had been ill, asked if he could have his brother-in-law remain, at least until he had time to recover fully. The board replied that Andrews could have someone stay at the lighthouse during his illness, but that person could not be any of those who had been named in the complaint, including Aaron Sprague.

Wickford Harbor Light continued to be manned until 1930. It was then discontinued and replaced by a square tower with a white tank house at its base.

> *Located at 1 Poplar Avenue, in Wickford, RI, the old Poplar Point Light has been greatly expanded. The structure can easily be approached by water.*
>
> *All that remains of Wickford Harbor Light are parts of its metal pier, in the middle of which stands an automatic beacon. NOAA chart #13223*

PLUM BEACH LIGHT

Appropriation:	March 2, 1895	$20,000
Appropriation:	June 11, 1896	$40,000
Appropriation:	July 1, 1898	$9,000
Established:	1897 -completed 1899	
First lighted:	February 22, 1897 -temporary red lantern light.	
First keeper:	Joseph L. Eaton (temporary light)	

Illuminating apparatus (IA): (1899) temporary lens apparatus; not described.
IA: (1907), fourth-order Fresnel lens, flashing white light every 5 sec.
Fog signal: 1897, 1,028-pound fog bell struck by machine,
double blow every 30 seconds.
Height of light above sea level: (1907) 54 feet

"We thank God that all was not lost at Plum Beach, RI, in the blizzard Saturday night," wrote contractor H. Toomey. His construction schooner had lost anchorage and was swept down Narragansett Bay's West Passage. At the last moment, the vessel's anchor fouled itself on a cable off Beavertail, saving the schooner and its crew from being smashed on nearby rock reefs or carried out to the open sea. Pleading to be allowed to stop work for ninety days, the contractor, in his letter of December 3, 1898 went on, "Plum beach, Narragansett Bay is the stormiest place we ever worked. It is either raining or blowing half of the time." The Light House Board was slow to answer the contractor's request, and exasperated with its delay, Toomey suspended operations on January 17, 1899. Work was resumed later that spring.

The Plum Beach Light was being erected in response to complaints by ships' captains. Steamers attempting to avoid Dutch Island in dense fog often came dangerously close to going aground on the opposite side of the narrow waterway; the steamer *Pequot* had already done so a few years earlier. A site was selected and surveyed in 1895, and on February 1, 1897, a temporary red lantern and fog bell were established at the work site. The cylindrical tower was completed in mid-1899, but the funds remaining for the project proved insufficient to equip it with a lens. A temporary apparatus was thus obtained from the Lighthouse Depot. After more money was allocated, the station was equipped with a fourth-order Fresnel lens, showing a flashing light every five seconds.

During construction, Joseph L. Eaton was placed in charge of the temporary lantern light, and on July 1, 1899, Judsen Gallen was made head keeper of the new tower. When Assistant Keeper Arthur White resigned from the light station in 1901, finding a replacement

Plum Beach Lighthouse, 1987

proved to be difficult. In April of that year, the position was offered
to at least two persons, but they declined, stating that the station
was too remote. The station's luck with assistants was not much
better when Andrew Smith was hired. He was dismissed from the
service for not changing the lamp at the appointed time and for allowing the clockwork to run down and the lens to stop revolving.

The winter of 1918 proved to be difficult on the iron lighthouse. A
one-inch crack developed around the entire circumference of the
tower at about two feet above low tide; an additional three or four
vertical cracks extended below the waterline. Bids for repair of the
structure proved to be too high, and little was done for the next four
years. Repairs were made in 1922, along with placement of 9000
tons of riprap to protect the foundation. In 1938, the September hurricane reopened the old cracks, created others, and caused extensive damage to the gallery and landing dock. Somehow, though, the
structure withstood the unrelenting pounding by the mountains of
water that totally destroyed its neighbor, Whale Rock Light, five and
a half miles to the south.

With the completion of the Jamestown Bridge in 1941, the cylindrical tower became obsolete. It was turned over to the state of Rhode
Island in the mid-1950s, and, within a short time, vandals had
broken all of the tower's windows. The lighthouse then became a

rookery for pigeons.

In September of 1970, the Rhode Island Department of Resources offered the forlorn structure for rent to the highest bidder. In the announcement, it was mentioned, however, that the lighthouse lacked a "few" amenities: electricity, heat, fresh water, and sewage disposal. A local radio station expressed some interest, but nothing more happened. In 1988, the Plum Beach Light avian refuge was still in dire need of repair.

> *Plum Beach Light stands just a few*
> *hundred feet north of the Jamestown*
> *Bridge. It is best seen from the water.*
> *NOAA chart #13221*

DUTCH ISLAND LIGHT

Appropriation:	*March 3, 1825*	*$3,000*
Appropriation:	*March 14, 1826*	*$2,000*
Established:	*1826*	
First keeper:	*William Dennis*	

Illuminating apparatus (IA): (1842), 8 lamps, 9" reflectors, fixed white light (FW).

IA:	*(1850), 8 lamps, 14" reflectors, FW*
Rebuilt:	*1857*
Refitted:	*1857, fourth-order Fresnel lens, FW*
IA:	*(1924), occulting red light, 10 seconds, 150 cp*
IA:	*(1939), fourth-order Fresnel lens, incandescent oil vapor, 870 cp, occulting red, 10 seconds.*
Fog signal:	*(1891) fog bell struck by machine every 15 seconds*

Height of light above sea level: (1838) 56 feet. (1891) 56 feet

"**M**y father," wrote Robert Dennis, keeper of the Dutch Island Light, "was master of a vessel and was in Europe at the time of the Tea excitement in Boston Harbor. Having heard of the affair, he returned home and fought during the war of the Revolution in behalf of his country. He has been keeper of this light 15 years, and is now 95 years of age, being very infirm." Robert Dennis, who had assumed the post in April of 1843, was making an impassioned plea to the Light House Board for postponement of his removal from office. He wanted to have his father, William Dennis, live out his remaining time at the lighthouse.

The young Dennis had not resided at the lighthouse from the time

Dutch Island Lighthhouse, 1988

he had taken it over, and he had been warned that his appointment obliged him to do so. Records seem to indicate that he stayed on until November of 1844, when William Babcock received the appointment. Two years later, Dennis returned to the post and was there until 1853.

The lighthouse at Dutch Island was established in 1826. Erected at the south end of the island, it served to guide vessels plying the west passage of Narragansett Bay and those entering Dutch Island Harbor.

The tower and the dwelling, which were connected, were constructed of slate and other stones found on the island. From its thirty-foot tower, the station showed a fixed white light generated by eight lamps and reflectors. The keeper's dwelling, a four-room structure, was described in 1838 as poorly kept. Within a few more years, it had assumed the unenviable reputation of being the "worst constructed of any in the state." The stairs to the tower were of "rough cut stone, dark, cramped and slippery in the winter," and the lantern was described as "wretched." In modern parlance, the tower was a disaster!

Funds for reconstruction of the tower and for providing it with a new illuminating apparatus were made available in 1856, and over the next two years about $4,000 was spent in making improvements.

Fire threatened the station in 1923. The keeper's mother-in-law, who had piled up remnants of the previous year's crops behind the lighthouse, decided to burn the materials. There was no wind at the time she started the fire, but within a short time the wind picked up and scattered sparks to a nearby field. The keeper was away from the station on business, but his wife reacted quickly and summoned help from Fort Greebe.

At the time, there were only a few men stationed at the fort, but all of them turned out. The fire changed direction and spread toward the fort igniting a one-story storage building, and then shifted back toward the lighthouse. With still another shift in the wind, the exhausted group finally was able to check the fire's advance; the only casualty of the blaze was the storehouse. An investigation concluded that the fire was accidental, and there was no action taken.

In the late 1950s, the Dutch Island Light Reservation was transferred to Rhode Island, but the light continued to burn automatically. When the Coast Guard announced in 1972 its intention to discontinue the light, local boaters protested vigorously. Their efforts paid off, but seven years later vandals succeeded in extinguishing the light; it has not burned since.

> *Just the square tower is left standing at the south end of Dutch Island. The light can be reached only by boat. NOAA chart #13221*

GOULD ISLAND LIGHT

Appropriation: March 3, 1887 $10,000
Established: 1889
First lighted: June 10, 1889
First keeper: Edmund Taylor, appointed June 6, 1889
Illuminating apparatus (IA): (1891) fifth-order Fresnel lens,
                     flashing white (Fl W) every 10 seconds.
IA: (1939) fourth-order Fresnel lens, Fl W
                     every 10 seconds, incandescent oil vapor, 11,000 cp.
Fog signal: 1889, fog bell struck by machine every 15 seconds.
Height of light above sea level: (1891) 52 feet.   (1839) 50 feet.

June 8, 1889: "Store keeper of the Light House Depot arrived this morning and delivered the outfit of supplies for the light, and instructed me on my duties." Two days later, Keeper Edmund Taylor wrote in the log, "Lit the light for the first time at 7:25 pm. Fog, wind SW, fresh breeze."

Prior to being appointed to the post, Taylor had, for a time, tended the Fall River Line's beacon, which stood 250 feet northeast of the newly constructed lighthouse. During its operation, the privately maintained navigational aid was regarded as undependable and inadequate by the Light House Board. In 1887, it was argued before Congress that "the great steamers of the Old Colony Steamboat Company, which pass Gould Island, carrying thousands of passengers and millions of dollars' worth of freight, should not be jeopardized by the failure of a private light." The board estimated that $18,000 was needed to establish a light and fog signal for the site; Congress appropriated $10,000.

Gould Island's conical brick tower was described as located about thirty feet north of the keeper's dwelling. The house's first story was red brick, and the second story and roof were naturally-colored shingles. The station's tower, which was thirty feet high, was equipped with a fifth-order Fresnel lens, showing a flashing white light every ten seconds; its fog bell was struck by machine every fifteen seconds.

In 1901, Capt. John Bebber, master of the steamer *City of Tauton*, reported that trees obscured the light while travelling north from Rose Island to almost halfway to Gould Island. The answer seemed simple enough; trees were cut down. The heavily wooded center of the island, however, made it impossible to remove enough trees, and the obstruction continued to plague mariners. In 1931, the National Organization of Masters, Mates, and Pilots petitioned the Lighthouse Service to correct the problem. In the following year, a skeleton tower which was lit by acetylene, was erected on the south end of the island.

The Gould Island Light was discontinued in 1947, and it was replaced with by a white steel tower. The automated tower continued to operate until October 24, 1988, when its base crumbled and it toppled over.

Gull Island Rocks Lighthouse, post-1928. Courtesy U. S. Coast Guard

GULL ROCKS LIGHT

Appropriation:	August 4, 1886
Established:	1887
First keeper:	Frederick W. Puriton, appointed August 26, 1887

Illuminating apparatus (IA): (1891) tubular lanterns,
east light fixed red (FR), west light fixed white (FW).

IA:	(1907) lens lanterns, east FW, west FR
IA:	(1924) lens lanterns, east FW, 160 cp, west FR 50 cp
Fog signal:	(1891) fog bell struck by machine every 5 seconds.

Height of light above sea level: (1891) 44 feet. (1939) 45 feet.

Discontinued:	1928, replaced by skeleton tower.

IA skeleton tower: (1939) 375 mm lens, flashing green every 3 seconds,
acetylene, 120 cp.

January 1, 1931: "New Years Day. All dressed up and no place to go, James Gallen, keeper."

The A-frame lighthouse on Gull Rocks, was located just north of what is now the bridge from Newport to Jamestown. It might have seemed more at ease, however, nestled away at a ski resort than clinging desperately to its small, low-lying rock-reef. Each night like clockwork, the keeper hoisted its tubular lanterns to platforms at each end of the A-frame's peak. The east light was fixed red and the west light was fixed white. Seen at a maximum distance of about twelve-and-one-half miles, they marked the north entrance to Newport Harbor.

Established, 1887

Gull Rocks, which was said to be difficult to spot even under the best of conditions, prompted the establishment of a privately maintained beacon sometime prior to 1885. In that year, the Light House Board recommended that a "proper light and fog signal" be erected and maintained by the government; the cost of its construction was approximately $10,000.

The station's first keeper, Frederick W. Purinton, arrived at Gull Rocks on September 15, 1887. Along with the usual entries in the lighthouse log concerning weather and chores, the keeper often made mention of being able to clearly discern Beavertail's fog signal, a distance of nearly five miles over water.

During an inspection tour of the light station in 1898, Keeper Purinton was cited for "not being in uniform," but all of his subsequent inspections were said to be in "good order." That evaluation was not true, however, for at least two other keepers at the station.

J. O. Bouley was appointed to the post in July of 1912. His log was generally sloppy, and, in his last month at the lighthouse, he made a total of only four entries. The log seemingly reflected the general state at Gull Island; "station left in very dirty condition by retiring keeper," wrote Inspector Luther of the Third District. When Keeper George Denton, Jr. took over in 1927, he wrote in the log, "station found in bad shape by me." He apparently was not impressed with his predecessor either.

It was impossible to maintain a garden on the rock-reef station but its residents usually managed to keep chickens. The hens sometimes roosted among the rocks and below the high tide line. As the tidal waters rose, some of the chicken eggs occasionally washed away and reportedly landed on the shores of Newport, leaving the town's residents with the mystery of how they had come to land there.

Because of the great amount of damage sustained by other Rhode Island lights, the precariously positioned Gull Island Light might have been expected to have been destroyed in the 1938 hurricane. The eighteen-foot storm tide washed away the station's front and back steps and its boat, salt water contaminated its cistern, and the keeper's chickens were introduced to a swimming lesson from which they never recovered. The light itself, however, emerged relatively unscathed.

Gull Island's two lights were replaced in 1928 by a skeleton tower that was erected on the east side of the dwelling. Equipped with a new fog signal, the tower displayed a flashing green acetylene light.

With the change, Keeper George Denton was also made responsible for the Newport Harbor Light; it had previously been maintained, for about six years, by Navy personnel.

Gull Island Light continued to be manned until the mid-1950s, when the tower was automated; soon after, the keeper's dwelling was torn down. With construction of the Newport Bridge in 1969, the beacon was no longer necessary, and, on January 8, 1970, a helicopter from the Coast Guard Station at Salem, MA, lifted the 600-pound light off its base. It was then flown to the Coast Guard Depot at Bristol, RI.

NOAA chart #13221

ROSE ISLAND LIGHT

Appropriation: *July 20, 1868*   *$7,500*
Established: *1870*
First lighted: *January 20, 1870*
First keeper: *John Bailey Cozzens, appointed November 25, 1869*
Illuminating apparatus (IA): (1873) sixth-order Fresnel lens, fixed red light (FR).
IA: *(1939) fourth-order Fresnel lens, FR, electric, 2,700-candlepower.*
Fog signal: *1885, fog bell struck by machine.*
Fog signal: *November 12, 1912, first-class reed horn, blast 2 sec., silent 2 sec.*
Fog signal: *(1939) second-class reed horn, 2 second blast, 13 second silent.*
                     Emergency fog bell, sounded by hand
Height of light above sea level: (1891) 50 feet

R ose Island Light was built on the southwest corner of the island, within the ruins of a circular bastion that had been part of Old Fort Hamilton. Administered by the War Department, the island was considered a point of defense for the East Passage of Narragansett Bay.

For a long time, there were no specific boundaries between the lighthouse property and the military grounds. The keepers maintained a garden and a variety of farm animals, some of which wandered onto the military compound — as the officers often complained. Keeper Charles Curtis stabled his cow behind the lighthouse, in a long building that also served as a storage area for explosives. Fortunately, the keeper's cow did not kick over the oil lamp as did Mrs. Murphy's cow in the Chicago fire!

In 1889, a portion of the island was used as a rifle range, and as a practice area for rapid-fire and machine guns. During the First World War, Rose Island served as a storage depot for torpedoes. Under those circumstances, it would seem that one of the prerequisites for being a keeper at the Rose Island Light must have been nerves of steel!

Rose Island Lighthouse, 1987   – prior to restoration.

Built in 1869, the Rose Island Light's tower rose from the front of a one-story keeper's dwelling. Its lantern, which was equipped with a sixth-order lens, exhibited a fixed red light; the beacon served mariners traveling the East Passage of Narragansett Bay and those entering Newport Harbor.

John Bailey Cozzens[1] the station's first keeper, was appointed to the post on November 25, 1869, two months before it became operational. The keeper remained at Rose Island for three years and he was replaced by George C. Williams, a veteran of the Civil War who was reportedly wounded twice while serving in the Fourth Rhode Island Regiment.

Rose Island, in easy reach of Newport's commerce, did not impart the sense of isolation that accompanied many other island stations. The weather in 1876 however, made life there less than desirable.

On February 2, 1876, a storm moved over the Newport area changing from rain to snow as it grew in intensity. Wind gusts that reached near-hurricane force shook the keeper's dwelling and vibrated the tower violently. Two weeks later, a northeaster dragged the station's boat and its 600-pound mooring up on the beach, heavily damaging the small vessel. Keeper George Williams had

1. Difficult-to-read pay records indicate the the station's first keeper's name was either spelled Cozzens or Cozzans.

attempted to save the boat, but the tide was out and there was insufficient water to move it to safety. At the height of the storm, the wind swayed the tower about "1 1/2 inches each way so that it broke the plaster inside of the house and the glass chimney in the lantern."

On April 4, another northeaster brought heavy rains and gale-force winds. The roof leaked to such an extent that it was almost "as wet inside as out." At one stage of the storm, an unusually strong gust carried away the dwelling's chimney. The weather seemed to calm down during the next few months, but in November a storm flooded the station, ruining the keeper's entire winter supply of vegetables. December did not improve. Commenting on that month's weather, Keeper Williams entered in the lighthouse log, "stormiest December on record, much damage to property and according to report, much loss of life at sea." The keeper made no specific note of "bringing in the new year," but he was no doubt happy to "ring out the old."

Rose Island was the scene of a number of maritime accidents. In 1889, the ferry *Conanicut* ran up on Spindle Rock in a heavy fog, a short distance from the lighthouse. Though Keeper Charles Curtis had been sounding the station's fog bell, none of the crew or the passengers had heard its toll.

Capt. Elijah Davis met his match on Rose Island, just five years later. Nicknamed the Fog Eater for his fearless navigation in zero-visibility, the master of the steamer *Plymouth* brought his vessel to an abrupt halt on the south shore of the island. The steamer's 700 passengers were safely removed, but the vessel remained stuck there for several more weeks.

Rose Island Light was abandoned by the Coast Guard in 1971, and was turned over to the University of Rhode Island for use as a research station. After a short time, the university found its maintenance too expensive, and the facility was boarded up. In October of 1985, the General Services Administration (GSA) transferred the property to the city of Newport, and the Rose Island Lighthouse Foundation, a private, non-profit group, has raised funds to restore the handsome structure.

Rose Island Light stands just south of the Newport Bridge. It is easily seen by motorists crossing the bridge in an easterly direction.
Boaters approaching the lighthouse should avoid the shallows on the south side of the island.
NOAA chart #13221

NEWPORT HARBOR (Goat Island) LIGHT

Appropriation:	March 3, 1823	$2,500
Appropriation:	May 18, 1842	$13,000
Appropriation:	July 2, 1864 (keeper's dwelling)	$6,000
Established:	1823	
First lighted:	January 1, 1824 *	
First keeper:	Samuel Watson *	

Light characteristic: (1827) fixed white
Illuminating apparatus (IA): (1838) 8 lamps, 9" parabolic reflectors, fixed white light (FW).
Rebuilt tower: 1842
(IA): (1842) 8 lamps, 9" reflectors, FW
Refitted: 1857, fourth-order 270o Fresnel lens, FW
IA: (1907) fourth-order Fresnel lens, FW 15 seconds, eclipse 5 seconds.
Characteristic: (1924) fixed green light (FG), 6,000 cp.
IA: (1939) fifth-order Fresnel lens, FG, electric.
Fog signal: 1873, fog bell struck by machine every 15 seconds
Height of light above sea level: (1873) 33 feet

    * **Information obtained from secondary sources**.

Keeper Pardon Stevens was away from his post during an 1851 inspection of the Newport Harbor Light, a situation that often led to negative comments by inspecting officers. A little over a decade earlier, a tour of the Beavertail Light had not been to the inspector's liking. "On my late excursion," he wrote, "the Captain and myself landed with some difficulty at New Port Light[1] [Beavertail], and was much mortified to find that the Keeper was absent with the key in his pocket." The keeper was informed that there was no possible excuse for his not being there, and "none will hereafter be admitted." In Keeper Stevens case however, the report was good despite his absence. "Everything managed better than in any light visited before." The inspector's remarks were in sharp contrast to those of Lt. Edward R. Carpenter, who had visited the station in 1838. "I found this light, late in the afternoon, in the filthiest condition of any light in the district. The reflectors had the appearance of not been cleaned for a length of time; the glass in the lantern was darkened with smoke, and oil left upon the table and lamps showed the slovenly manner in which preparations for the night had been made."

Established, 1823

From the early 1700s, Newport had gradually developed into an important center of maritime commerce, but it was not until 1823

1. Until the early 1850s, Beavertail Light, located at the south end of Conanicut Island, was referred to as the New Port or Newport Light; The Newport Lighthouse, located at the north end of Goat Island, was, at that time, referred to as the Goat Island Light.

Newport (Goat Island) Lighthouse, 1989   *Photo by Rob P. Bachand*

that a lighthouse was established to mark the entrance to its harbor. Erected at the northernmost tip of Goat Island, the beacon did not sufficiently mark the shallow reef that extended out from it. At night, vessels rounding the point occasionally ran aground on the shoal.

The tower's lantern was only five feet high and four feet wide, giving the keeper little room to maneuver when adjusting its equipment. In 1838, the station was listed as having eight lamps and reflectors that were arranged around a circular table, so as to be seen from every direction. The reflectors were held in place by small hooks on their lamps. The lantern itself was said to be very damp, and ventilation was poor. The resulting condensation on the lantern glass often froze during the colder months.

In 1842, a breakwater was constructed over the top of the reef, and its outer end was marked by a new twenty-nine-foot tower. The original tower was then discontinued and later moved to Prudence Island. For the next twenty-two years, the keepers remained quartered at the original six-room dwelling, but in 1864 a new structure was erected connecting it directly to the tower. Four years later, the old structure was demolished, and its cellar was filled.

The new tower was initially equipped with fifteen lamps and reflectors, and in 1857, it was refitted with a fourth-order Fresnel lens. A fog bell, struck by machinery every fifteen seconds, was added in

1873.

In the late 1800s, steamboat companies maintained a beacon at the south end of the island. Known as the Goat Island Shoal Dolphin, the private beacon consisted of piles driven into the sea bottom, which were held together by wires; a light was kept on top of the structure. Around 1891, the Old Colony Steamboat Company replaced the oil lamps with an electric light, and in 1905 the government took over the beacon.

The Light House Service continued to use an electrical light from the five-pile beacon, and an electrically operated gong was installed. The fog signal however, immediately came under criticism by maritime interests. It was sounded at five and ten-second intervals, followed by a forty-second silent period and ships' captains felt that the latter interval was too long for the narrow channel. The signal was changed, and in 1912 a skeleton tower replaced the old pile structure.

The Newport Harbor Light was made electric in 1922, and the keeper's dwelling was later torn down. In the late 1980s, the white stone tower continued to direct mariners into the busy harbor, showing a flashing green light.

> *Newport Harbor Light is located at the north end of Goat Island. It is accessible via the Goat Island Sheraton Hotel property.*
> *NOAA chart #13221*

LIME ROCK LIGHT - IDA LEWIS ROCK LIGHT

Appropriation: *March 3, 1853*   *$1,000*
Appropriation (dwelling): August 18, 1858   *$1,500*
Established: *1854*
First keeper: *Hosea Lewis, appointed November 15, 1853*
Illuminating apparatus (IA): 1854, sixth-order Fresnel lens, fixed white light (FW).
IA: *(1873) sixth-order Fresnel lens, FW*
IA: *(1883) sixth-order Fresnel lens, FR*
Fog signal: *none*
Height of light above sea level: (1863) 30 feet
Renamed: *1925*
Discontinued: *1927, replaced by a skeleton tower*
IA skeleton tower: (1939) 200 mm lens, Fl W, 3 seconds, acetylene, 70-candlepower.

On March 24, 1925, Commissioner of Lighthouses G. R. Putnam recommended that the name of Lime Rock Light Station, RI, be changed to Ida Lewis Rock Light Station. Going against a long-held Light House Service rule of naming a light station after the natural feature on which it was located, the change

Ida Lewis. National Archives, 26-LG-69-60

was a fitting tribute to America's best known lighthouse keeper.

Lime Rock's first keeper, Hosea Lewis, was appointed to the post on November 15, 1853. For the first two years of the station's operation, Keeper Lewis commuted by boat to Lime Rock, about 220 yards offshore. There was a small shanty next to the tower that allowed the keeper to remain at the station in heavy weather, but it was obvious that the station would be better served if the keeper lived on the site. In 1856, a dwelling was built to connect to the square granite tower.

Keeper Lewis suffered a disabling stroke in 1857. Since his wife was fully occupied taking care of the ailing keeper and an invalid daughter, the lighthouse duties fell on the shoulders of the couple's "black eyed, dark haired" teenage daughter, Ida. The sixteen-year-old proved to be exceptionally well suited for the task. She faithfully kept the light, and, during her long residence at Lime Rock, she was credited with the rescue of at least eighteen people from the waters

Lime Rock Lighthouse, circa 1926. National Archives, 26-LG-12-55

surrounding the lighthouse.

The accounts of Ida's feats vary from one source to another, but there is no doubt that she was a true heroine. As is often told, her first rescue occurred in the fall of 1858, when four boys who had been sailing near Lime Rock capsized their small vessel. Ida launched her rowboat and expertly plucked each of the lads from the water by pulling them individually over the boat's stern.

There were many other rescues during the next eleven years, but, after the 1869 rescue of two soldiers from their overturned skiff, Ida attained overnight fame. From that time, many of the rich and famous sought out the modest keeper. Ida was awarded a silver medal from the Life Saving Benevolent Association in 1869 and was later the first woman to receive the Congressional Medal of Honor.

Hosea Lewis died in November of 1872, and though Ida had kept the light for all those years, her mother, as was the custom, was appointed to the post. On January 21, 1879 Ida Lewis Wilson was officially appointed keeper of Lime Rock.

Ida had taken the name of Wilson in her marriage to Capt. William Wilson of Black Rock, CT, but the union did not go well. Two years after the wedding, the couple separated and the captain was never heard from again.

In October of 1911, Ida was found lying on the floor of her bedroom by her brother, Rudolph. A physician was summoned from Newport, but a couple of days later the seventy-two-year-old lighthouse heroine passed away. Rudolph, who had assisted his sister for a number of years, remained at Lime Rock until the new keeper, Edward Jansen, arrived.

Keeper Jansen, a native of Bristol, RI, had served at Sandy Hook

Light prior to being assigned to Lime Rock. He and his wife barely had time to settle in at the lighthouse when a little girl was born to them. Headlined by the *New York Times* as the "First Baby of Lime Rock," she was christened Ida Lewis Jansen; that year, there was a special Christmas tree at Lime Rock.

Jansen proved also to be a vigilant keeper. In 1918, he saved the lives of two men whose boat had been swamped during a storm. The keeper remained at the lighthouse until it was deactivated on July 18, 1927; a month later he was transferred to Borden Flats Light.

The Ida Lewis Rock Light was replaced with a thirty-foot skeleton tower, which was erected just to its northeast. Using a 200-millimeter lantern, the new structure's acetylene light was visible for one second, followed by a one-second dark period.

In the summer of 1928, the 110-foot long, 80-foot wide Ida Lewis Rock and its buildings were sold at auction. Purchased for $7,200, the buildings and grounds were made into the Ida Lewis Yacht Club. Four years later, Dr. Horace Beck, one of the club's members, located the sixth-order light that had once produced the station's fixed red light. It was brought back to the club and displayed there for a time; it is now part of an Ida Lewis exhibit at the Newport Historical Society.

> *The Ida Lewis Yacht Club is located off Wellington Avenue, in Newport. Ida's boat can be seen at the Museum of Yachting, Fort Adams State Park, and a large collection of the keeper's memorabilia is on display at the Newport Historical Society, 82 Tours St., Newport, RI.*   *NOAA chart #13221*

CASTLE HILL LIGHT

Appropriation:	March 3, 1875	$10,000
Appropriation:	August 4, 1886	$10,000
Appropriation:	March 30, 1888	$5,000
Appropriation:	March 2, 1889	$5,000
Established:	1890	
First lighted:	May 1, 1890	
First keeper:	Frank W. Parmele, appointed March 27, 1890	
Illuminating apparatus (IA):	(1891) fifth-order Fresnel lens, flashing red (Fl R) every 10 sec	
Refitted:	1899, fifth-order Fresnel lens (5-order).	
IA:	(1907) 5-order, Fl R, every 30 seconds.	
IA:	(1939) 5-order, FL R, flash 9 seconds, eclipse 21 sec, oil lamp, 270 cp.	
Fog signal:	1890, fog bell machine operated, triple blow every 10 seconds.	
Height of light above sea level:	(1891) 42 feet.	

F rank W. Parmele, a native of Connecticut, had been keeper of the Saybrook Breakwater Light for four years before being transferred to Castle Hill Light on March 27, 1890, as the station's first keeper. In moving to his new post, his wages dropped

Castle Hill Lighthouse, 1986

from $540 to $520 per year, but the convenience of a land-based station no doubt more than made up for the loss in pay.

A lighthouse and fog signal had been considered for Castle Hill as early as 1869, and, in March of 1875, Congress appropriated $10,000 for its construction. Alexander Agassiz, a well-known American oceanographer/zoologist, owned the property on which the station was to be erected. In that very year, he had built an elaborate summer residence on his land, and he opposed the station's construction on the basis that it might devalue the property. As purchase of the necessary parcel of land could not be negotiated, condemnation of the site was considered under Rhode Island law, but it was found to be impractical; the value of the land was more than had been appropriated for the light station.

Since the proposed lighthouse site was considered ideal for directing mariners through Narragansett Bay's East Passage, the Light House Board persisted in its attempts to secure it. In 1886, Congress reappropriated the $10,000, and in the following year, Professor Agassiz deeded the property to the government for $1, but there was a "fly in the ointment"; he had transferred the property without granting a right-of-way to it. The site, which was on a steep rock face, was, for all practical purposes, inaccessible by water. William Wilbor of Newport, RI, won the contract to erect the lighthouse, but he had made his bid contingent upon being permitted to use "the most accessible route in the vicinity of the proposed site."

In a letter to the engineer of the Third Light House District, the professor refused to change his mind and grant a right-of-way across a corner of his land. "It is impossible for me to make any further concessions in the matter of the light house. What with one thing and another I stand an excellent show of having my place ruined and nobody to foot the bill. I must protect myself of all hazards. I have signed a deed to the U. S. on the only terms which I will agree to and if the Government cannot carry out its part of the programme I shall take the necessary steps to re-enter the land."

On May 20, 1888, Agassiz relented. He deeded the .198 acres of land to the United States "without condition and without expenses to the Government."

Construction of the twenty-five-foot granite tower began in 1889 and, on May 1 of the following year, the station showed its flashing red light for the first time. The keeper's dwelling was erected a short distance away at Castle Hill Cove; it had six rooms and an attached summer kitchen.

The station's triple-blow fog bell must have irritated the professor, since, on November 30, 1891, the signal was discontinued at his request. Five years later, the 1,286-pound fog bell was reinstalled, and shortly thereafter it was replaced with a more efficient 2,000-pound bell. The controversy did not stop there. "The Light House Board had not treated me fairly in the matter of the Bell at Castle Hill and had not kept their agreement with me," wrote Agassiz. The matter was finally put to rest in 1898 when a fog bell screen was set in place to deflect the sound.

In 1899, the color of the upper half of the tower was repainted from gray to white and its original fifth-order lens was changed for a newer model of the same order. Still showing a red light and sounding a fog signal in the late 1980s, the automated station was expected to continue to operate for the foreseeable future.

Visitors to the Inn at Castle Hill in Newport, RI, will find it easy to understand why Alexander Agassiz did not want to chance changing the idyllic setting of his summer home. During his leisure time, he could look out over his promontory and see much of the East Passage. Nearby, the Harvard professor often collected marine specimens for study in a laboratory that he had built behind the main building.

The Castle Hill Light is accessible from the bottom (south end) of the parking lot at the Inn at Castle Hill, and from the barely perceptible remains of an access road that runs from Castle Hill Cove.
NOAA chart #13221

BRENTON REEF LIGHTSHIP

Established: 1853
First keeper: *David C. Champlin (?)* *
Lightship LV 14 (Ledyard),   1853-1856.   *Built 1852, $15,000*
Lightship LV 11,   1856-1897.   *Built 1853, $13,462*
Lightship LV 39,   1897-1935.   *Built 1875, $42,200*
Lightship 102/WAL 525,   1935-1962.   *Built 1916, $110,065*
    * ***(?) unable to confirm against pay records.***

T
he men on the bridge of the steamer *Newport* strained to hear the sound of the lightship's fog bell, but nothing could be heard through the dense fog. Bound for Newport on December 3, 1873, the ship was right on course, but when it reached the lightship's station, only buoys were found at their anchors. Capt. A. Simmons ordered the *Newport's* engines stopped, and from the distance came the faint ring of a fog bell. Proceeding slowly toward the sound, the steamer located Brenton Reef Lightship, *LV 11*, just off Beavertail Point. The wayward vessel was taken under tow and brought to safe anchorage at Newport Harbor.

It was not the first time that *LV 11* had parted its moorings. In February of 1855, while stationed at New South Shoal, the vessel was blown ashore at Montauk Point. It was salvaged, repaired and then assigned to Brenton Reef in 1856; it remained there until 1897.

The two-masted *LV 11* was the second of four lightships assigned to Brenton Reef. The station's first, the *Ledyard (LV 14)*, was built at Newport in 1852 at a cost of approximately $13,000. The ninety-one-foot long lightship had a single lantern with eight lamps; it was also equipped with a hand-operated fog bell and horn.

In January of 1854, the schooner *Mozelle* reportedly struck Brenton Reef within sight of the lightship. Throughout the night, heavy snow and seas battered the grounded vessel, and water washed freely over its decks. In the morning, the schooner began to break up forcing the crewmen to seek safety by clinging to its rigging. On shore, more than two miles away, Seth Bateman spotted the shipwrecked sailors and sent for help, but, by the time the rescue boat had arrived, all of the crewmen had perished.

Why had Capt. John Heath of *LV 11* failed to launch the station's boat for the stranded schooner? Had he not seen the *Mozelle* or did he simply choose to ignore its plight? Did he feel that the seas were too choppy to risk going to the crewmen's aid? Capt. Heath declared that he had a clear conscience, but the reasons for his inaction remained unanswered. Samuel Dunn was temporarily named as his

Brenton Reef Lightship, LV 39, 1897-1935. National Archives, 26-LS-39-1

replacement, and on December 19, 1854, Joseph Pitman was appointed captain. Nine years after the incident, John Heath was named keeper of the Goat Island Light; he remained there until his death in 1868, whereupon his wife took over and kept the light for an additional five years.

Charles V. Steijen joined the crew of the Lightship *LV 11* in 1890 as a deckhand. Over the next six years, Steijen worked as ship's cook and was later promoted to mate. When Capt. Edward Fogerty retired in 1912, Steijen became the ship's master.

The Swedish-born captain had begun his sailing career at the age of fourteen. Over the next decade, he wandered the world aboard Swedish and British vessels and finally settled in New York where he was employed as a harbor pilot. In 1888, the captain joined the Light House Service and, after serving four years at Brenton Reef, he returned briefly to his native Sweden to find himself a bride. He continued on at the lightship station until June of 1927, when he retired and was replaced by another seafaring man, Theodore Anderson.

On November 4, 1897, Lightship *LV 39* relieved *LV 11*. The white oak *LV 39* had been built at Pelham, NY, in 1875. It was 119 feet, 6-inches long and was sail-schooner rigged. The vessel had two masts, two lanterns, a twelve-inch steam whistle, and a hand-operated fog

Lightship LV 102/WAL 525, prior to serving as the Brenton Reef Lightship. Stationed at Southwest Pass, LA, 1917-1919, and South Pass, LA, 1919-1933, Brenton Reef, 1935-1962. National Archives, 26-G-126-21130.

Brenton Reef Tower, 1987

bell.

The *LV 39* began its career in 1875 at Vineyard Sound. It spent about one year there, a year at Five Fathom Bank, and twenty years as relief. From 1897 until March of 1935, it was posted at Brenton Reef. On its final day, a tug took *LV 39* in tow and brought it to Chelsea, MA, where Capt. Theodore Anderson and his crew transferred to Brenton Reef's last lightships, LV 102/WAL 525. After its retirement, *LV 39* was used as a floating restaurant at Glouster, MA, and it later served as a clubhouse for the Coast Guard Auxiliary, in Boston. While being towed to a shipyard in 1975, *LV 39* sank off Beverly, MA; it was never salvaged.

LV 102/WAL 525 was self-propelled and capable of 8 knots; it was 101 feet, 10 inches long and constructed of steel. The lightship had a single large-diameter tubular lantern, which was equipped with an electric lamp in 1932. *WAL 525* was equipped with a radiobeacon in 1931 and in 1945 it was fitted with radar.

During the Second World War, many of the nation's lightships were discontinued, but though enemy submarines often approached the Rhode Island coast, *WAL 525* remained on station, unarmed.

On September 28, 1962, a steel tower, which had been erected at Brenton Reef, replaced the lightship. In a farewell gesture, Capt. E. Godlewski sailed Lightship *WAL 525* up the East Passage of Narragansett Bay, circled Conanicut Island, and returned through the West Passage. Each time it passed a light station, the vessel's foghorn was sounded in a final salute. *WAL 525* served for less than a year at Cross Rip, MA, and was decommissioned in October of 1963. Two years later, the vessel was sold and it was used as a crab-processing plant at Seattle, WA.

When Hurricane Gloria swept the coast of Rhode Island on September 30, 1985, it destroyed the light's rotating apparatus. The Coast Guard replaced the light with an emergency beacon, but after discovering that a great deal of asbestos had been incorporated in the square platform tower's structure, minimal maintenance was ordered; the temporary light remained. In 1988, the Coast Guard began considering the discontinuance of the Brenton Reef Light.

Standing in seventy-eight feet of water, the square black tower is marked "Brenton" on its sides. Though visible on a clear day from Brenton Point, in Newport, it can be approached only by water. NOAA chart #13221

BEAVERTAIL (Newport, New Port) LIGHT

Authorized: *1738 Colony of Rhode Island*
Established: *1749*
Appropriation: *August 3, 1854*   *$14,500*
Rebuilt: *1754*
Illuminating apparatus (IA): (1838) 15 lamps, 9" reflectors, fixed white light (FW).
IA: *(1842) 15 lamps, 15" reflectors, FW.*
Rebuilt: *1856*
IA: *(1856) third-order Fresnel lens, FW.*
IA: *(1907) fourth-order Fresnel lens, group of 8 white*
                          flashes(G FL W),interval between groups 15 seconds
IA: *(1939) fourth-order Fresnel lens, G Fl W 15 seconds, 2 flashes.*
                          Electric, 240,000-candlepower.
Height of light above sea level: (1842) 98 feet.   (1863) 96 feet

Beavertail Lighthouse fog signals
March, 1829: hand-rung fog bell
1851: horse-powered fog horn
1857: 5-inch steam whistle
1868: Ericsson hot-air engine, Daboll horn
1870: replaced worn-out fog trumpet
1872: first-class fog signal, Daboll trumpet
1881: two, ten-inch steam whistles
1888: Crosby automatic fog signal controller
1899: 13-horsepower oil engines for fog signal
1901: conical siren
Late 1930's: electric motors to drive air compressors

R hode Island's first settlers were primarily engaged in agriculture, but within a short time the young colony with its 450 miles of coastline, began to develop a maritime economy. By 1708, markets had been established from Boston to South Carolina and to the West Indies. At the time, it is estimated that of Newport's population of 2,203, "one in four men (white males) may have looked to the sea for their livelihood." Early on, exports included maize, tobacco, lumber, livestock and rum. It was the latter, however, that became the basis of a profitable but sinister triangular trade in rum, slaves and molasses. Loaded with "spirits," Rhode Island's vessels sailed to the African coast where their cargo was traded for slaves. In the second leg of the triangle, the ships transported their human cargo, in numbers of up to 150 individuals, to the West Indies. There they were exchanged for molasses, sugar, and specie. The vessel then returned to the colony and the molasses was processed into rum. In a five-year period, between 1736 to 1739, fifty-four vessels participated in the triangular trade, delivering over six thousand blacks to Caribbean markets; Rhode Island's slave commerce operated for about a one hundred years.

Beavertail Lighthouse, 1988

The rising importance of shipping prompted the colony's General Assembly, in 1738, to propose the establishment of a lighthouse at Beavertail Point. War however, between England and Spain, postponed its construction for another ten years.

There is evidence that the widely recognized first lighthouse at Beavertail may not have been the first beacon on the site. A chimney was built on, or next to, the watch house at Beavertail in 1712 (or 1705). Ordered by Jamestown's Town Council, it is believed by some that the chimney was in fact a platform of stone upon which a beacon fire was maintained. If it was so, then Beavertail may have been the first navigational light in North America.

Construction of the Beavertail Light was begun in 1748, and it became operational on the following year. Built of wood, the sixty-nine-foot tower was twenty-four feet in diameter at its base, and tapered to thirteen feet at the bottom of its gallery. Considered to have been the third lighthouse erected in what is now the United States, it stood for only four years before it was totally destroyed by fire. The station's second tower, constructed of brick and stone, was made sixty-four feet high. Access to its lantern room was by means of a wooden spiral staircase.

During the early part of the Revolutionary War, the British controlled Newport Harbor. In October of 1779, mounting pressure from

the American and French forces compelled the British to evacuate,
and in doing so, their troops were thought to have taken much of the
Beavertail's equipment before setting the tower ablaze. Though
badly damaged by the fire, it was restored, and then continued to
operate until 1854.

Standing near the water's edge, the light station at Beavertail often
caught the full brunt of onshore storms. In the early 1800s, Keeper
Philip Caswell and his family were driven from their home as gale-
driven waves struck and threatened to topple the entire structure.
Repairs were made to the small two-room dwelling but in the
onslaught of the 1815 hurricane, it was finally destroyed. Having
feared the worst, the keeper moved his wife to a neighbor's farm-
house and returned later, to ride out the storm in what was left of
the structure. Though the masonry tower fared much better, all
twenty panes of glass in its lantern were broken.

A five-room dwelling was built on the following year, and though
an improvement in size, its construction was generally poor. An inspection by Lt. George M. Bache in 1838, found portions of the
masonry being supported solely by the cellar's window frames.

The station's fixed light was generated by fifteen lamps with reflectors, arranged on two copper tables. The upper table held seven
lamps, the lower had eight. Unlike the negative comments made by
Lt. Bache concerning many other light stations of the time, his report
seemed to indicate that Beavertail's beacon was being properly cared
for.

Robert H. Weeden was appointed keeper of Beavertail Light in April,
1844, and when he died four years later, his wife, Damaris, became
the station's first and only female keeper. Aided with the lighthouse
chores by her son, the widow remained at the post for nine more
years. During that time, Congress appropriated funds for a new
granite tower, brick keeper's dwelling and fog signal. The station's
illuminating apparatus which was changed to a third-order Fresnel
lens, was lit for the first time in 1857.

In its early history, Beavertail was known as the Newport (New Port)
Light. The station became an important field testing site for various
types of fog signals. Its first signal, a fog bell rung by hand, was
established in March of 1829. In 1851, Celadon Daboll, a New
London, CT, inventor, installed his fog horn. Consisting of a vibrat-
ing metal reed inside of a long trumpet, the signal was sounded by
a horse-operated air compressor, which was mounted on top of a
cylindrical air storage tank. The unusual looking device was replaced six years later by an entirely new type of signal, the steam
whistle. It was followed by a number of other improved signals, with
Beavertail usually one of the first light stations to field-test the new
devices.

The keepers at Beavertail were not always at peace with their neighbors. In 1907, Joseph Wharton who had property adjoining the lighthouse, disputed the station's right-of-way and he blocked the roadway leading to the lighthouse with large boulders. The obstructions were finally removed, but it was several years before the right-of-way was resolved.

Living near Fort Adams also proved to be a disadvantage to the keepers. Artillery men had often practiced firing dummy shells into the water, but in December of 1908, the gunfire sent the keepers running for cover. One 5-inch shell narrowly missed the tower, one landed in the yard behind the dwelling, and another crashed into the foundation. The War Department repaired the damage and assured the Light House Board that it would not happen again.

The hurricane of September 21, 1938, brought tragedy to the family of Keeper Carl Chellis. On the way home from school, the storm toppled his daughter's school bus; she and the bus driver perished. The wind and waves also swept away the station's fog signal building, revealing the foundation of Beavertail's first lighthouse.

In the early 1970s, Beavertail Light's fog signal was controlled by a "watch-stander," from the Coast Guard Station at Castle Hill, and its light was lit by means of a light-sensor. In 1988, the fog-signal was automated and the light was shown on a continual basis.

> *Beavertail Light is located at the south end of Conanicut Island (Jamestown). It can be reached after crossing the Jamestown or Newport Bridge, and going south to the end of Beaver Tail Road. A museum is housed in the former keeper's dwelling.*
> *NOAA chart #13221*

WHALE ROCK LIGHT

Appropriation: March 3, 1881
Established: 1882
First lighted: October 1, 1882
First keeper: Nathaniel Dodge, appointed September 2, 1882
Illuminating apparatus: (1883) fourth-order Fresnel lens, fixed red light.
Fog signal: (1883) fog bell struck by machine, double blow every 20 seconds.
Height of light above sea level: (1883) 73 feet

B reaking the surface waters like the back of a great whale, the rock reef was a danger to all who navigated the west channel of Narragansett Bay. On a cold January evening, about fifteen years before the establishment of Whale Rock Light, the schooner *Pearl* struck the rock and tore a large hole in its hull. The vessel went

Whale Rock Lighthouse, undated. National Archives, 26-LG-17-48

Remains of Whale Rock Lighthouse, 1988

to the bottom in a depth of fifty to sixty feet, with its masts still above the surface. Five perished with the ship; Capt. Benjamin Hudson was able to make his way to the surface, and climb the main mast where he remained until rescued on the following day.

A lighthouse and fog signal was proposed for Whale Rock in 1871, but funds for its establishment were not appropriated for another decade. When work began on the site in 1881, a hollowed-out ring was cut into the natural rock, to which was secured the first section of the cast-iron pier; it was then filled with concrete. The upper portion of the conical pier served as basement for the lighthouse. In it was placed the cistern, coal storage bins, and general storage. The kitchen of the four-story high conical tower was on the pier level, and there was one bedroom for the keepers on each of the next three decks. The three lower decks had windows; the fourth had port holes typical of a ship.

The isolated station which was first lit on October 1, 1882, was hardly an enviable assignment. Nathaniel Dodge, the first keeper remained four years, but for the next 27 years, there was a turnover of fifteen head keepers.

Nelson Sprague was less than enthusiastic with his assignment at Whale Rock. He was appointed keeper on July 6, 1900, and over the next 9 months, he was absent from his post for a total of 146 days. In a letter to the Light House Inspector, Assistant Keeper Silas Staton wrote, "I think it is time there was something done about the Keeper. He is away nearly half of his time." The assistant went on by describing how there had been a great deal of fog and because the head keeper was so often absent from the station, he "had to be up most of the time."

The allegations proved to be true, and Sprague was dismissed from the service. The assistant was then appointed head keeper, but he remained at Whale Rock for just three more months.

Weather often prevented personnel from going ashore, and once there, it was sometimes impossible to return. Exposed from the south and east to the full force of the sea, in was not unusual to have waves breaking against the tower's port holes, four-stories above sea level. In August of 1924, Keeper Alfred Auger recounted his experience during a gale. "Solid water going over the roof of the main galley and spray over the top of the lantern." During the storm, about half of the galley's roof was torn away, and cast iron gutters and sections of railings were carried away by the sea. Yet, the worst was still to come!

The winds were light and the sea relatively calm on the morning of September 21, 1938, as Keeper Daniel Sullivan set out for shore to purchase supplies. By late morning, however, the winds had picked up and the seas had become increasingly menacing. The change prompted the keeper to decide that it had become too dangerous to return to Whale Rock and he remained ashore; his action saved his life.

Left in charge of the station, Assistant Keeper Walter Eberle, the father of six children, had been with the Lighthouse Service for only one year. As the hurricane approached, the lighthouse was battered by gradually larger waves that shook the entire structure and weakened it for a final blow. Sometime during the height of the storm, a wall of water, described as a tidal wave, struck and tore the tower away from its base, taking with it the assistant keeper.

After the hurricane had passed, the tower's basement and the concrete deck were found to be intact. The kitchen floor and the cast-iron basement stairs were still in place, but everything above deck level was either gone or totally wrecked. The cast-iron plates that remained were so badly distorted, that it was difficult to determine how they had once fitted together.

The assistant keeper's body was never recovered, nor was any portion of the structure above the second deck ever located.

In 1939 the remaining structure was removed, and a cylindrical steel tower was erected in its place. Fueled by acetylene, the automatic beacon showed a green light.

Only the concrete which was once surrounded by the cast-iron base, remains of Whale Rock Light. In 1988, the site was marked by a lighted gong buoy which flashed green every four seconds.
NOAA chart #13223

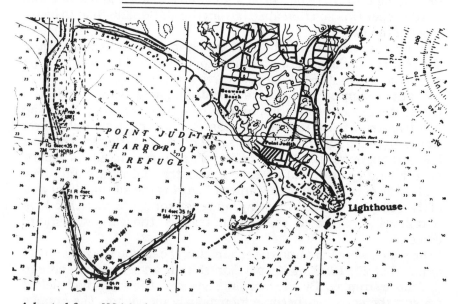

Adapted from NOAA chart #13219, Point Judith Harbor of Refuge, 1987

POINT JUDITH LIGHT

Appropriation:	February 10, 1808	$5,000
Appropriation:	February 26, 1810	$200
Appropriation:	April 27, 1816	$7,500
Established:	1810	

Lighthouse contractor: (1809) Daniel S. Way
Illuminating apparatus (IA): (1838) 10 lamps, 8.5" reflectors, revolving white light (Rv W)
IA: (1842) 10 lamps, 9" reflectors, Rv W.
Rebuilt: 1817
Rebuilt: 1857
Refitted: 1857 fourth-order 360o Fresnel lens, Rv W.
IA: (1891) fourth-order Fresnel lens (4-order),
        flashing white (Fl W) every 10 seconds.
Illuminant: 1907, changed from oil to incandescent oil vapor.
        Power increase from 6,000-candlepower (cp) to 75,048 cp.
IA: (1907) 4-order, FL W every 15 seconds.
IA: (1939) 4-order, fixed white light, electric, 15,000 cp.
IA: (1987) 4-order, occulting white every 15 seconds, 1000 watt lamp.
Fog signal: (1867) Daboll trumpet, Wilcox hot-air engine
Fog signal: May 1, 1873, first-class steam siren, blast 6 sec.
Radiobeacon established: November 11, 1931
Height of light above sea level: (1838) 74 feet.   (1891) 67 feet

I t was a natural site for a lighthouse. Extending out for over a mile from Rhode Island's coast, Point Judith was once regarded as the junction at which the waters of Narragansett Bay and Long Island Sound met. Even before establishment of a beacon, vessels sailing toward the Rhode Island shore watched for the prominent landmark that was described as shaped in the form of a "nags head."

Navigating around the point was fraught with hazards. Impenetrable fog and heavy seas contributed all too frequently to mishaps on Squid Ledge, one and a half miles west of the lighthouse, or on the point itself. Construction of a light at Point Judith in 1810 no doubt helped prevent many maritime losses, but the toll continued. In 1855 alone, sixteen vessels were reportedly stranded or wrecked within sight of the light.

The station's first tower, which was octagonal in shape and of wood construction, stood on a two-foot-high stone pedestal. Its lamps were suspended by iron chains, and an eclipser obscured the light for twenty seconds, every two and a half minutes. On September 23, 1815, a hurricane swept over coastal Rhode Island; its winds proved to be devastating to the five-year-old station. "The lighthouse at Point Judith," wrote Superintendent William Ellery, "was thrown down and utterly destroyed, and in the fall injured a corner of the roof, and the Southeast part of the dwelling House."

A new thirty-five-foot-tall tower, erected the following year, was "built of rough stone, faced with free-stone laid in courses, and coated with cement." The station's lighting apparatus was described in 1838 as having ten lamps and reflectors. Divided into two equal clusters, the lamps sat on two copper rotating tables, producing a revolving light. The tables turned by means of a 228-pound weight that was attached to a rope, and wound around a horizontal barrel. The simple "power" mechanism proved to be fairly trouble-free, and as far as the keeper knew, it had failed once. The keeper, however, had no watch or any other means of accurately measuring the time of revolutions; they were found to be consistently slow in an 1838 inspection of the station.

As was the case at many other regional light stations, dampness in the tower sometimes caused ice to form on the lantern glass. At times the ice became so thick that the keeper had to wait for a warming trend to allow him to remove it without fear of breaking the glass in the process.

The station's original dwelling had only one bedroom, which was located in the attic. To keep warm in the winter, the keeper and his family are said to have slept in the kitchen. However, conditions had improved considerably by 1838 when Lt. Bache inspected the dwelling. By that time, the structure had apparently been expanded to seven rooms and he described it as only "requiring some painting and a new kitchen floor." In 1857, the dwelling was rebuilt to connect to the tower. The station's illuminating apparatus was then replaced with a fourth-order lens.

Petitions were received in 1871, asking to change the station's fog signal from a horn to a whistle. Point Judith was at the hub of an important route for vessels traveling between many of New England's ports and New York; ships' captains complained that the foghorn was often "drowned out" by the pounding surf. Besides being more effective, it was argued, the whistle would also help to distinguish Point Judith's signal from Beavertail's siren. Two years later, the station was fitted with the new signal, yet vessels continued to become stranded on the point.

It was a foggy evening in April of 1908 as Assistant Keeper Willis Green walked along the beach and heard the sound of a schooner's distress signal. Quickening his pace toward its source, he sighted the misty outline of the schooner *Clara E. Comee* aground at Sand Hill Cove.

Bound for Boston, the schooner had been sailing the Rhode Island coast in an increasingly dense fog. As the vessel neared Point Judith, Capt. Barster decided to seek the safety of Point Judith's Harbor of

Point Judith Lighthouse, 1987

Refuge, where he planned to remain until morning. Making his approach, the captain spotted several schooners lying at anchor just inside the breakwall. In trying to give them a wide berth, he ventured too close to shore and went aground.

After discovering the stranded schooner, Assistant Keeper Green notified the Life Saving Station, and all of the crewmen were removed to safety. Two years after the incident, the assistant was named head keeper at Point Judith, and in 1911 he was transferred to the Bridgeport Harbor Light.

The Point Judith Harbor of Refuge, formed by the construction of three breakwaters, was erected to provide safe anchorage to the large number of vessels plying the waters off Point Judith. Soon after their completion, the breakwaters were marked by unmanned acetylene lights. Records in 1907 indicate that 22,680 vessels traveled past Point Judith Light in daylight hours, and it was estimated that twice that number passed at night. When compared to vessels entering the port of New York in that same year, ship traffic off Point Judith was four times greater. Reflecting concern for the safety of these mariners, Bill H.R. 11270 was introduced in Congress on January 10, 1906, for establishment of a lightship station off Point Judith. The proposal for the additional navigational aid was dropped two years later, when it was opposed by the Light House Board. The board assured Congress that Point Judith Light, which stood close to deep water, was a very efficient light and that the station was equipped with a powerful fog signal. It was recommended, however, that a combination acetylene and whistling buoy be stationed at that same site in lieu of the lightship.

The 1938 hurricane destroyed 250 feet of the station's seawall and eroded one point of the beach 30 feet inland. The old tower, however, withstood the full brunt of the storm. In that same year, the original Life Saving Station, built around 1872, was burned to the ground; it was rebuilt the following year. The keeper's dwelling was torn down in 1954.

In the late 1980s, Point Judith Light was operated at a throw of a switch from the site's Coast Guard Station. In addition to their minimal duties in connection with the lighthouse, the twenty-three guardsmen serve in search and recovery operations, law enforcement, and national defense.

Point Judith Light may be reached by taking Route 1 to Wakefield and then following Route 108 south, to Point Judith. NOAA chart #13205

BLOCK ISLAND NORTH LIGHT
(Sandy Point Light)

Appropriation:	March 2, 1829	$5,500
Appropriation:	March 3, 1837	$5,000
Appropriation:	August 18, 1856	$9,000
Appropriation:	July 28, 1866	$15,000
Established:	1829	
First keeper:	William A. Weeden	
Rebuilt:	1837	
Illuminating apparatus (IA):	(1838) two towers, 7 lamps, 15" reflectors (each), fixed white light (FW).	
IA:	(1842) two towers, 18 lamps, 15" reflectors, FW	
Rebuilt:	1857	
IA:	1857, fourth-order Fresnel (4-order), FW	
Rebuilt:	1867	
IA:	(1873) 4-order, FW	
Illuminant:	1907, changed from 1-wick oil to incandescent oil vapor. Power increase from 475-candlepower (cp) to 4,308 cp.	
Height of light above sea level:	(1842) 58 feet. (1863) 65 feet. (1891) 61 feet.	
Discontinued:	1973	

E lam Littlefield was the second of what proved to be a rapid succession of keepers at Whale Rock Light. Life at that station, surrounded by its often turbulent waters, left little opportunity for contact with the outside world. When the keeper

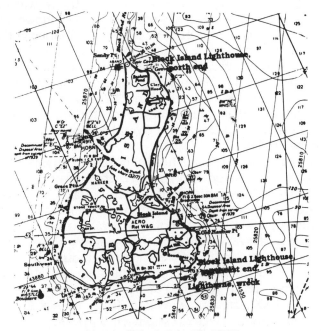

Chart of Block Island, 1987

learned of his transfer to the Block Island North Light, he no doubt
felt that he would finally be able to lead a more normal life, with a
chance of developing closer relationships with some of his neighbors.

Keeper Littlefield reported for duty at Block Island on April 21,
1891. The windswept lighthouse at the northern end of the island
was isolated, but fishermen frequented the point, visitors called at
the lighthouse, and the keeper became a familiar face among the
island's year-round residents.

In 1912, the island's postmaster, Eugene Rose, built a small fishing
shanty on lighthouse property. Keeper Littlefield informed him that
he could not keep the structure on government land, a small war
broke out between the two. In a letter to the Light House Service, the
postmaster wrote, "I can give you ample proof that this man is
physically unfit for any government position, I can also furnish proof
that there has been Government oil sold, from a Government
Reservation." When asked for proof, he had none. The "shanty feud"
went on for five years. To help settle the matter, the service granted
Rose a "revocable license," giving him permission to maintain a
fishing shack on government property; the license carried an annual
rental fee of $10. The postmaster never paid the license fee, and the
keeper probably longed, at times, for the peace and quiet of Whale

Rock.

Established, 1829

The lighthouse at Block Island's north end was erected on twenty acres ceded to the United States on May 14, 1829, by the State of Rhode Island and Providence Plantations. Established in that same year, the station consisted of two towers that rose to a height of fifty-eight feet above sea level. Twenty-five feet apart, they were attached to opposite ends of the keeper's dwelling. To a sailor approaching the island, the lights looked like a single beacon until less than three miles away; the shoal at the northern end of Block Island extended out nearly two miles.

Though the lights were established in response to the large number of shipwrecks off the island's north end, there was an actual increase in mishaps the year the lights became operational. From about 1800 to 1945, there were well over 350 reported wrecks in the vicinity of Block Island. In 1831, the schooner *Warrior*, which had been at anchor off the northwest point, was driven aground in a heavy gale. An estimated twenty-one lives were lost, including thirteen of the ship's crew. Other mishaps included the schooner *Almira* -1841, schooner *Harriet*-1851, schooner *John A. Matherson*-1895, schooner *Montana* -1907, steamer *Grecian* -1932, tanker *Lightburne* - 1939, and the *U-853*, a German submarine sunk in action on May 5, 1945. Had it not been for the island's beacons, however, there no doubt would have been many more losses.

The original lighthouse stood at the extremity of the island's northwest point, exposed to the constant battering of wind and sea. Beach erosion began to undermine the entire stone structure, and, despite construction of a protective wall, the station had to be abandoned. A proposal was made in 1836 to change the station to a single tower, but Superintendent of Lights Stephen Pleasonton disagreed. "Now it appears to me," wrote Pleasonton, "that as this Light house has for several years past exhibited two Lights, to which vessel have been accustomed, it would be extremely dangerous to change the form, and exhibit but one Light." Going on, he stated, "It will be necessary to keep the old Light in operation while the new one is building, and consequently none of the old materials can be used in the new Light house, with the exception of the Lamps."

Rebuilt in 1837, the new station was situated farther from the sea. Constructed of granite laid in cement, it also had two towers that were attached at either end of the keeper's dwelling. From their position fifty feet above sea level, they showed fixed white lights generated by seven lamps having fifteen-inch reflectors.

Mariners were again warned of the deceptive lights. "The two lights cannot be made separate when to the Northward, unless in a position to make Point Judith light N E, when they appear like lights

Block Island North Lighthouse, post-1867. National Archives, 26-LG-11-14

of a steamboat." Vessels approaching the island from a southerly or westerly direction, were instructed, "they appear as one light until you are within 2 and 3 miles of them."

In 1857, loss of sand again threatened the lighthouse, and it was rebuilt at a cost of about $9,000. A single tower was constructed that rose to sixty-five feet above sea level, and it was equipped with a fourth-order Fresnel lens. The wind and sea, however, continued to wash away sand from the base of the new tower and dwelling, forcing Congress in 1866, to appropriate an additional $15,000, for what was the fourth and last lighthouse erected at Block Island's north end.

Similar in appearance to many other lighthouses built at about the same time (Morgan Point -1867, Great Captains -1868, Plum Island -1869, Norwalk Island -1869, Old Field Point -1869), the new structure was constructed of stone, with a tower rising from the front of the keeper's dwelling. Hiram D. Ball, who had been keeper for six years at the old light, exhibited the station's fourth-order light for the first time on September 15, 1867. Keeper Ball remained posted there for thirty years.

With construction of the north end's fourth light, the old facility was torn down, and its materials were used to control erosions. Despite other measures that included stakes driven into the ground and interlaced with brush, the sand continued drifting, and the light station was once more at risk. Finally, in 1873, grading and paving arrested much of the problem.

 The lighthouse was automated in 1955, and it operated until 1973, when it was abandoned and replaced by an offshore beacon. In 1984, the United States Fish and Wildlife Service turned over the lighthouse and two acres to the town of Block Island.

> *The old lighthouse stands at Sandy Point at the northwest end of the island. Though it is boarded up, vandals have managed to enter it on a regular basis.*
> *NOAA chart #13217*

BLOCK ISLAND SOUTHEAST LIGHT

Appropriation: *June 10, 1872*   *$75,000*
Purchased land from: George Sheffield, Jr., July 14, 1873
Established: *1875*
First lighted: *February 1, 1875*
First keeper: *Henry W. Clarke, appointed November 4, 1873*
Illuminating apparatus (IA): 1875, first-order Fresnel 270o (1-order),
                      fixed white light (FW).
IA: *(1907) 1-order FW, incandescent oil vapor.*
Characteristic changed: April 16, 1929, flashing green, every 3.7 seconds.
Fog signal: *January 1, 1874 first-class steam siren, 6 sec. blast, 20 sec. interval.*
Fog signal: *(1907) first-class automatic compressed-air siren,*
                      4 sec. blast, 30 sec. interval.
Height of light above sea level: (1891) 204 feet

F loating on a bed of mercury, the massive first-order light turns slowly, casting its flash of green light every 3.7 seconds. Until April 16, 1929, Block Island's octagonal tower had shown a fixed light. The immobile glare, however, was sometimes mistaken for the mast light of another vessel, prompting the American Association of Masters, Mates, and Pilots to petition for a change in the light's characteristic.

 Congress in 1871 appropriated $75,000 for the construction of a lighthouse and steam fog signal at Block Island's southeast corner. After some delays, land was purchased from George Sheffield, Jr. for the sum of $1,350, and construction began.

 As the fog signal neared completion, Henry W. Clark(e) of Kingston, RI, was appointed keeper, and on January 1, 1874, the signal became operational. It was another thirteen months, however, before the lighthouse itself was finished and a light was installed.

Block Island Southeast Lighthouse, undated.
National Archives, 26-LG-11-5

Standing on a promontory, the tower rose from the keeper's dwelling to 204 feet above sea level. The station's lens, large enough for several grown men to stand in, was expressly built for the lighthouse at a cost of $10,000. Resembling a grandfather clock, the light's mechanism turned by means of a 100-pound weight that was hung in the tower's stairwell.

On the morning of September 21, 1938, Keeper Earl Carr noted in the station's log that the winds had picked up, changing from a fresh breeze to strong gusts; by mid-afternoon, the winds had reached hurricane force. In its position high on a bluff, the lighthouse received the full brunt of the storm. Windows in the tower were blown out, shingles on the dwelling tore off, the radio beacon tower toppled over, the oil house was destroyed, and power and communications were lost. For the next few days, the lens had to be turned by hand. In comparison to so many other Rhode Island lights, however, the station's damage proved to be relatively minor.

Repairs were made to the light station during the remaining autumn, and eventually Keeper Earl Carr settled into a winter routine. On February 10, 1939, a heavy fog enveloped Block Island's waters. At about 7:00 pm, the keeper, from inside the lighthouse, thought he'd heard a vessel's fog whistle. Going out to investigate, he could not see anything, but from the strength of the sound, it was apparent that the ship was quite near shore. A half hour later, the vessel ceased sounding its signal.

The 416-foot Texaco tanker *Lightburne* had also heard a fog signal —that of the lighthouse. The vessel's chief officer, Page Augustin, later reported that they had been running a course on the lighthouse's radiobeacon, "but we estimated that we were 3 or 4 miles off shore." Loaded with 72,000 barrels of gasoline and kerosene, the tanker ran aground on rocks just below the lighthouse bluff, and it immediately began taking on water. A large floating pool of gasoline that had spilled from the ship, was ignited when an emergency buoy flare was washed overboard. For nearly an hour, the flames performed a deadly dance on the water's surface, no more than fifty yards away from the ship. Luckily, a favorable wind kept the blaze at a safe distance, and the lives of the crewmen were spared.

The *Lightburne* was later blown up by the Coast Guard to eliminate it as a hazard to navigation, but much of the wreck remains on the bottom; it has become a favorite dive site for scuba enthusiasts.

In 1984, the U.S. Coast Guard considered demolishing Block Island's famous landmark in favor of an automated steel tower. Erosion was threatening the structure. Estimates varied, but it was said that it could topple over the edge of the sandy precipice in ten to twenty years. The Block Island Historical Society had the engineering firm of LeMessurier and Associates examine the possibility of moving the structure inland from the edge of the bluff. The report came back assuring that it could be done at a cost of $1.7 million. The society hoped to raise the necessary funds from private, state, and federal sources before nature took away the National treasure.

In 1988, Block Island Southeast Light was the last Rhode Island lighthouse to remain manned.

> *The handsome Southeast Light stands at the top of Mohegan Bluffs on the southeast side of Block Island. It can be easily seen from the water.*
> *NOAA chart #13217*

WATCH HILL LIGHT

Appropriation:	*January 22, 1806*	*$6,000*
Appropriation:	*February 10, 1808*	*$1,000*
Appropriation:	*August 3, 1854*	*$8,300*
Established:	*1807*	
First keeper:	*Jonathan Noah, appointed February 10, 1808*	
Illuminating apparatus (IA): (1838) 10 lamps, parabolic reflectors,		
	revolving white light (Rv W).	
IA:	*(1842) 8 lamps, 9" reflectors, Rv W.*	
Rebuilt:	*1856-1857.*	
Refitted:	*1857, fourth-order Fresnel lens, fixed white light (FW).*	
Characteristic:	*(1924) FW alternating with group of 2 flashes red (R) 15 seconds.*	
	W 1,700 cp, R 4,300 cp.	
IA:	*(1987) FA-251 lens, Alt occulting Fl R every 15 sec*	
Fog signal:	*(1924) second-class reed horn, blast 5 seconds, silent 25 seconds.*	
Height of light above sea level: (1838) 73 feet. (1891) 62 feet.		

On June 28, 1918, the freighter *Onondaga,* bound for Jacksonville, FL, ran up on Watch Hill Reef in a heavy fog. Loaded with a general cargo, the ship went to the bottom in fifty feet of water. Two months later, the fishing steamer *George Hudson* struck a nearby reef and sank. These vessels were hardly the first to be claimed by Watch Hill's dangerous rock reefs, nor, no doubt, will they be the last.

The colony of Rhode Island apparently had erected some type of beacon at Watch Hill during the mid-1700s, but it was destroyed in a 1781 gale. A number of ships' captains petitioned the government for its replacement, while others felt, instead, that navigation would be better served by erecting a light on Little Gull Island.

In February of 1793, the Senate ordered a inquiry to determine the necessity of a light at Watch Hill. Directed to various maritime interests, questions included the size and range of light that would answer the intended purpose, the type of shoals that existed in the area, the area tides and currents, the distance to the nearest five families, the nature of the local soil, and the type of vessels likely to depend upon the light.

The consensus was that a first-class light was not necessary since it would not be serving arriving transatlantic ships. It was felt, however, that establishment of a small light would be of great help to coastal vessels. The soil in the vicinity was deemed fertile, and it was determined that five families resided within half of a mile from the proposed site. The latter information was apparently a gauge of labor costs; they would have been expected to be higher if outsiders

Watch Hill Lighthouse, undated. National Archives, 26-LG-17-36

Watch Hill Lighthouse, 1980

had to be brought in to help maintain the station. On January 22, 1806, an act of Congress signed by President Thomas Jefferson appropriated $6,000 for the construction of a lighthouse at Watch Hill.

When the new beacon was completed in mid-February of 1808, Secretary of the Treasury Albert Gallatin ordered it immediately lighted. In his letter to William Ellery (superintendent of lights for Rhode Island), the secretary also asked to have Jonathan Noah of Westerly, RI, notified of his appointment as keeper; his annual salary had been set at $200.

The station's tower, which rose to a height of thirty-five feet, was entirely wood frame; "the outside was weatherboarded and painted." Located just a short distance away, the keeper's dwelling was a five-room wood structure.

In 1838, the lantern was described as having ten lamps with parabolic reflectors, arranged around two movable iron frames. The light was made to rotate by means of a large weight tied to a rope, which was wound around a barrel. As the weight dropped, it moved the clockwork mechanism, which in turn rotated the iron frames. Unfortunately, the machinery often malfunctioned and stopped, creating concern that the light might be mistaken for Stonington's stationary light, located just two and a half miles to the northwest.

By 1855, the station's dwelling was deemed not worth repairing, and the tower was in danger of being destroyed. Funds were appropriated, and, in the following year, construction of a brick dwelling and attached stone tower were begun. The two-story house had a sitting room, dining room, kitchen, three bedrooms, lamp maintenance room, and an oil storage cellar. The ten-foot square, forty-five-foot-high tower, displayed a fixed white light generated through a fourth-order Fresnel lens.

Keeper Jonathan Nash remained at Watch Hill until about 1833, when he was succeeded by Enoch Vose. In April of 1879, Sally Ann Crandall became the first of two females that kept the light at Watch Hill; she took over the position following her husband's death. The widow remained until October 11, 1888, and she was succeeded by Fanny K. Sckuyler. The station's last keeper, Coast Guardsman Charles Merritt, was stationed there for about two years before the light was automated on August 31, 1986.

As one follows Scenic Route 1A from Westerly, RI, the Watch Hill Light stands only a short distance from Watch Hill's business district. The grounds and station are maintained by the Watch Hill Improvement Society.
NOAA chart #13214, 13205

3   **Fishers Island Lights**

STONINGTON HARBOR LIGHT —
STONINGTON BREAKWATER LIGHT (CT)

Stonington Lighthouse
Appropriation:	May 7, 1822	$3,500
Established:	1824	
Contractor:	Benjamin Chase, 1823	
First keeper:	William Porter,	
Rebuilt:	1840. Contractor John Bishop	

Land purchased from: (1840) James and Lucretia Morris
Land purchased from: (1840) James Morris and Peter Crary
Illuminating apparatus (IA): (1838) 10 lamps, parabolic reflectors
IA:	(1842) 8 lamps, 16" reflectors, fixed white light (FW)
Refitted:	1855, sixth-order Fresnel lens, FW
Fog signal:	none

Height of stone tower: (1838)   30 feet
Height of light above sea level: (1863)   50 feet
Discontinued:	November 1, 1889

Stonington Breakwater Light, east end of Inner Breakwater
Appropriation:	October 2, 1888	$8,000
Established:	1889	
First lighted:	November 1, 1889	
First keeper:	Benjamin F. Pendleton, appointed August 8, 1872	
IA:	1889, fourth-order Fresnel lens, fixed red (FR)	
Characteristic:	(1924) FR, 150-candlepower.	
Fog signal:	(1891) fog bell struck by machine, double blow every 30 seconds.	

Height of light above sea level: (1891) 35 feet.   (1924) 34 feet
Discontinued:	1926

I n March of 1822, Congress appropriated funds for establishing a lighthouse at the southernmost point of land in the
borough of Stonington. In that same year, the harbor's first
whaler, the *Hydaspe*, left to join the growing fleet of New England
vessels engaged in hunting down the gentle leviathans. Though the
port was dwarfed in the shadow of nearby New London Harbor,
Stonington had increasingly become a center of shipping and fishing
activities. In 1819, the nation's first sealer bound for Antarctic
waters had sailed from the harbor.

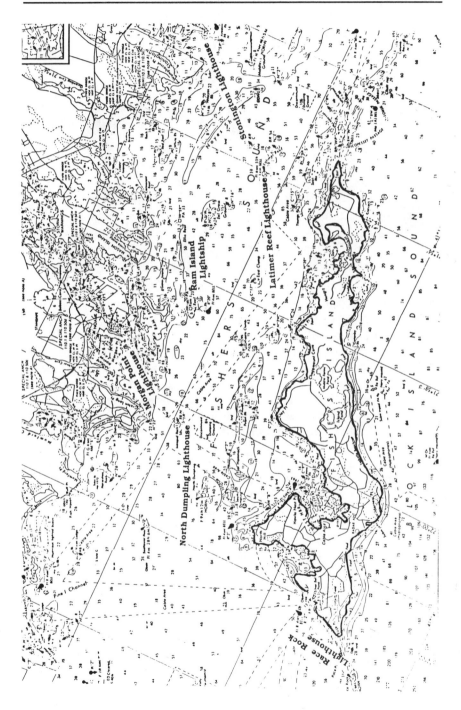

Adapted from chart #13214, Fishers Island Sound, 1987

Stonington Lighthouse Museum, 1980

The contract for construction of Stonington Harbor Light was awarded to Benjamin Chase, and he immediately began erecting a stone keeper's dwelling and thirty-foot stone cylindrical tower. Completed in 1824, the station had ten whale oil lamps with thirteen-inch reflectors, which were arranged on two horizontal tables in the form of an arc. On a clear night, the station's beacon was visible all along the shoreline for a distance of over twelve miles. During the day, mariners entering Stonington harbor were instructed to align themselves with the highest steeple in town and the lighthouse.

Over the next fourteen years, the sea gradually eroded the beach in front of the lighthouse to a point that the high tide line was only forty-five feet from the tower's base. Within two more years, the tower was found to be "in imminent danger of being washed away," and the decision was made to rebuild farther up from the point. Constructed of stones from the original buildings, a one and a half story dwelling was erected, with the tower rising from the front of the structure. The station's fixed white light, shown from sixty-two feet above sea level, was produced by eight lamps using sixteen-inch reflectors.

Stonington Breakwater Light.
National Archives, 26-LG-17-12

Stonington's first keeper, Capt. William Porter, tended the light until his death in the mid-1840s. As was customary, the keeper's widow was offered the post. She accepted the position, but when the station was inspected in October of 1848, officials had second thoughts concerning her appointment. After having visited Stonington, Capt. Howland reported that Patty Porter "kept the most filthy house he had ever visited; everything appeared to have been neglected." Subsequent inspections, however, must have been more favorable since the widow remained at Stonington for six additional years. She was succeeded by five more keepers before the lighthouse was discontinued on November 1, 1889.

Following the construction of a breakwater at the entrance of the harbor, the Stonington and Providence Steamboat Company built and maintained a light and fog signal at its east end. In time, it became apparent that the privately maintained beacon was much more effective than the lighthouse, and it was recommended that a government-maintained structure be erected there.

Work on the twenty-five-foot-high conical tower began in 1888, and it was completed on the following year. Rising from an octagonal base, the iron tower was equipped with a fog bell and a fourth-order lens that showed a fixed red light. Benjamin Pendleton, appointed the Harbor Light's keeper on August 8, 1872, was reassigned to the Breakwater Light, and, though he continued to live at the old lighthouse, a small shack was built on the breakwall, where he remained when conditions warranted it.

In 1901, inspection of the former lighthouse found living conditions there "so unhealthy as to menace the lives of its occupants, there having been more or less sickness in every family residing therein during the past twenty years." The house was deemed beyond repair, but it was nine years before a new dwelling was built; it was erected next to the old stone structure. In 1926, the Breakwall Light was dismantled and replaced by a skeleton tower.

The Secretary of Commerce in March of 1925 authorized the sale of the Stonington Harbor Light and its .725-acre property. The only bid received was that of Eugene Atwood, who had submitted it in behalf of the Stonington Historical Society. The bid was accepted, and the lighthouse was transferred to the society; the members refurbished the entire structure and converted it into a museum.

*The Stonington Lighthouse Museum is open to the public
from May to October, Tuesday to Sunday, and by appointment.
It is situated at the south end of Water Street in the borough
of Stonington.
NOAA chart #13214*

EEL GRASS SHOAL LIGHTSHIP
LATIMER REEF LIGHT (NY)

Eel Grass Lightship:
Established:	1849
First keeper:	Thomas Harris, appointed April 1, 1849
Lightship "L":	1849-
Lightship LV 12:	(?)1871-1872. Built 1846 (?)
Lightship LV 25:	1872-1878.
Lightship LV 17:	1878-1882. Built 1848, approx. $12,000
Lightship LV 12:	1882-1884.

Latimer Reef Lighthouse
Established:	1884
First lighted:	July 1, 1884
First keeper:	Charles E.P. Noyes, appointed June 12, 1884
Illuminating apparatus:	(1884) fifth-order Fresnel lens, flashing white light (Fl W)
Refitted:	1899, fourth-order Fresnel lens, Fl W every 10 seconds
IA:	(1924) 4-order, Fl W every 10 seconds, 1,800 cp.
Fog Signal:	(1891) fog bell struck by machine every 15 seconds
Height of light above sea level:	(1891) 56 feet

T he storm came out of the east on March 1, 1914, and began to batter Latimer Reef Light. "At 9:30 pm.," wrote Keeper William H. Smith, "the sea was so high that it broke over the Platform and Pier." Reportedly without assistance, the keeper tied down the station's two boats, and somehow they survived the relentless pounding, but his own skiff was smashed to pieces. A fence on the east side of the pier was washed away at 9:45 pm, and soon after, the woodshed and its contents were lost to the raging torrent. In a final blow, the outhouse gave way to a wall of water. The keeper listed the articles that had been lost, and he ended his letter to the inspector of the Third District by stating, "There is no wood at the station. The pier has been weakened."

Keeper Smith had been serving as assistant at Rockland Lake Light, NY, when he was transferred to Latimer Reef in March of 1909. The accommodations at the five-room cast-iron tower were adequate, but its walls were only partially brick-lined. As a result, the upper part of the tower was hot and damp in the summer and bone-chilling cold in the winter. The lantern, initially equipped with a fifth-order Fresnel lens, was refitted in 1899 with a fourth-order Fresnel lens. The rope and weights for the clockwork ran through the center of the tower; its mechanism had to be rewound every four hours.

Lighthouse Established, 1884

Latimer Reef Light began operating on July 1, 1884, replacing Eel Grass Lightship, which had been stationed there for thirty-five

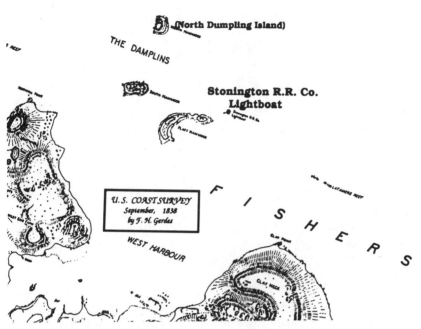

Site of Stonington Railroad and Steamboat Company's light boat.
Adapted from U. S. Coast Survey, September, 1838

years. From 1837 to 1849, the Stonington Railroad and Steamboat Company had maintained a light boat, which was anchored on the south side of Fishers Island Sound channel, a few hundred feet northeast of what is now known as Flat Hammock (NOAA chart #13214). An 1838 chart identifies four sites in Fishers Island Sound with the name of Latimer Reef (Pulpit Rock, Middle Clump, East Clump, and Latimer Reef), but it could have been considered as one continuous reef.

Lightship established, 1849

Established in 1849, Eel Grass Shoal's first government-operated lightship, L, was a forty-one-ton, wood-hull vessel. In 1863, the vessel was described as having its name painted on each quarter in large black letters, showing a fixed white light, and equipped with a fog bell and horn.

Prior to 1867, when the Light House Board adopted a numbering system to identify individual vessels, lightships simply took on the name of the station at which they were posted. The system was adequate in the beginning, but, as the number of lightship stations grew, it was difficult to keep track of vessels as they were transferred from one station to another. The use of alphabetical designations such as Eel Grass Shoal's lightship L, seems to have been applied in the 1860s, but only after some vessels had already been moved

Latimer Reef Lighthouse, 1988

several times.

Lightship *L* apparently remained at the shoal until 1872, when it was replaced by *LV 25*. The station's new vessel had been serving at Roanoke Sound, NC, but, with the construction of a screw-pile lighthouse at that site, the vessel was transferred to Eel Grass Shoal. Built in 1827, the sixty-one-foot vessel had a single lantern and a hand-operated fog bell.

With the exception of a minor collision with an unidentified vessel in 1874, life aboard *LV 25* seems to have been fairly uneventful. By 1878, the lightship was determined to be unfit for further duty, and it was replaced by *LV 17*. *LV 25* was returned to the light-house depot at New London and kept as a relief ship for emergencies only. At that time, the vessel was said to be barely serviceable, too old for rebuilding, and too small for general service. In January of 1885, *LV 25* was stripped and sold at public auction.

Lightship *LV 17*, remained posted at the shoal until 1882, when it was succeeded by *LV 12*; the replacement, a seventy-two-foot-long vessel, stayed there until establishment of the Latimer Reef Light. Charles E. P. Noyes, who had been master of the Eel Grass Shoal Lightship beginning in October of 1878, was put in charge of the new lighthouse.

In 1983, Latimer Reef Light's fourth-order Fresnel lens was removed and replaced by a more modern, 300-mm lens. The station's classic lens is said to have then been installed at the Elbow of Cross Ledge Light, in Delaware Bay, NJ. In 1988, the automated tower continued to flash a white light every six seconds and to sound its fog signal every fifteen seconds.

Latimer Reef Light stands at the east end of Fisher Island Sound, on the west end of the reef. It is accessible only by boat. NOAA chart #13214

RAM ISLAND REEF LIGHTSHIP (CT)

Established: 1886
First lighted: December 20, 1886
First keeper: E.A. Howell
Lightship LV 19: 1886-1894. Built 1845, *approximately $20,000*
Lightship LV 23: 1894-1925. Built 1857. *converted from brig*
Discontinued: April 4, 1925

I f a ship was ever capable of having feelings, one could only wonder what lightship *LV 19's* "state of mind" might have been as it was being towed away for use as a naval target. It had faithfully served navigators for fifty-five years.

The schooner-rigged, eighty-five-foot lightship *LV 19*, was built in 1845 by Henry Eckford at a cost of about $20,000. First posted at Cross Ledge, DE, from 1845 to 1875, it was then transferred to Fourteen Foot Bank, DE, where it remained until December 3, 1886. At that time, the lightship was taken to the Staten Island Depot and refitted. About two weeks later, it was moved to the newly established Ram Island Reef lightship station in Fishers Island Sound, and, once there, the vessel was placed under the command of Keeper E. H. Howell.

At its new station, the small lightship was equipped with a fog bell and with two lanterns shown from its two masts. The straw-colored hull had the words "Ram Island" painted in large black letters on each side.

Ice floes and heavy weather caused *LV 19* to part its moorings several times during its nearly eight years at Ram Island. The vessel had been rebuilt in 1876 at Wilmington, DE, but, for the next sixteen years, it received no major repairs; by 1892, it was found to be in very poor condition.

Cornfield Lightship Station was, at about the same time, preparing to take on a new vessel; the change made its old vessel, *LV 23*, available for transfer to Ram Island. In December of 1894, it permanently relieved Ram Island's *LV 19*.

Lightship *LV 19* spent the next six years as a relief vessel, and it was then transferred to the United States Navy to be blown out of the water. Its final role, however, may not have been that far removed from its original intent; the vessel's destruction may have saved the lives of naval gunners who were better trained because they had used it for target practice.

During the Civil War, vessel *LV 23* had served as a brig, the *A. J. W. Applegate*. When the conflict was over, it was converted for use

Ram Island Lightship, LV 19, replaced by LV 23 on December 8, 1894. National Archives, 26-LS-19-1

as a lightship. The ninety-four-foot, 186-ton sail-schooner was equipped with two lanterns, each having eight oil lamps, and a hand-operated fog bell. It was manned by a captain, a mate, four seamen, and a cook. The lightship's log indicated that, on average, its crewmen remained three weeks aboard, with one week off; provisions and mail were obtained in Noank.

Duty aboard Ram Island Reef Lightship was numbingly routine, and going to the aid of sailors in distress must have been a welcomed change. On December 21, 1900, the sloop *Lizzie A* went aground on a reef known as Middle Clump Rocks. With waves lashing at the sides of the stranded vessel, the lightship's crew launched a boat and picked up the sloop's three crewmen. In 1910, Keeper John Carlson and a crewman, saved the lives of a man and his son, whose small boat had capsized in mid-Fishers Island Sound.

Anchored in sixty feet of water on the south side of Ram Island Reef and about midway through Fishers Island Sound, the vessel was well protected in most storms. Unlike many other lightship stations, records seem to indicate that, throughout Ram Island's history, its ships were never rammed by another vessel.

On April 4, 1925, Ram Island's light vessel was discontinued, and it was replaced by an automatic gas lantern and bell buoy. Lightship *LV 23* was later surveyed and condemned.

MORGAN POINT (Noank) LIGHT (CT)

Appropriation: *March 3, 1831*   *$5,000*
Appropriation: *March 2, 1867*   *$12,000*
Established: *1831*
Land purchased from: Roswell Morgan
First keeper: *Eliza Daboll*
Illuminating apparatus (IA): (1838) 10 lamps, 13" reflectors, fixed white light (FW).
IA: *(1842) 10 lamps, 14" reflectors, FW*
Refitted: *1855, sixth-order steamer lens,*   225o and Argand lamp, FW*
Rebuilt: *1868*
Fog Signal: *none*
Height of light above sea level: (1863) 44 feet. (1873) 61 feet.
   *** The term, steamer lens, may refer to the type of light which was often
   shown from a ship's masthead.**

C aptain Mathers of the cutter *Madison* had been dispatched to Fishers Island Sound in 1843, to inspect the Morgan Point Light and review the site of a proposed beacon on North Dumpling Island; his report was not well received by Stephen Pleasonton of the Fifth Auditor's Office. "He recommends removal of the Morgan Point Light, or Mistic [Mystic], as he improperly calls it, to North Dumpling," wrote Pleasonton. "I do not concur with him. This is a small light intended mainly for the trade in Mistic River, and should be kept up for the accommodation of that trade."

Morgan Point's twenty-five-foot-tall stone tower, erected in 1831, was often referred to as an example of a "well-built" structure in Light House Establishment correspondence; however, its light, which was generated by ten lamps and reflectors, was inefficient. Lt. George Bache reported that in 1838, while at anchor at South Dumpling, two and a half miles away, the station's light was barely visible through the haze. At the same time and under the same conditions, Stonington Light, a distance of six miles, and New London Light, three and a half miles away, were both clearly visible. On two other occasions, Morgan Point Light was not visible from seven miles, though the nights were clear. The tower was refitted with a sixth-order lens and an Argand lamp in 1885.

The light station, which was erected on land purchased from Roswell Morgan in April of 1831, had a six-room stone dwelling that stood about eighty feet to the rear of the tower. In 1832, Morgan Point's first keeper, Ezra Daboll, built a kitchen and an addition described as a "wood house." The keeper's expenses of $100 were reimbursed, but he he was warned, as were all other keepers, that any further construction, without first obtaining prior authorization

Morgan Point Lighthouse, 1980

would not be paid for by the government.

The lighthouse was rebuilt between 1867 and 1868. The new two-story granite structure had eight rooms including an added-on kitchen; the tower, which rose from the front of the dwelling, was reached by a wooden stairway from the second floor. At the time of reconstruction, the wooden addition to the original dwelling was moved and converted into a barn. The remaining stone structure was then torn down, the cellar was filled, and the grounds were graded. In the late 1960s, the remains of the original tower's foundation could reportedly still be seen in dry weather.

In 1855, Jemina Morgan had granted the government the right-of-way across the family property for the sum of $1, but in 1916 a shipbuilding company that then owned the property erected a fence across the access road. Other stations had had right-of-way conflicts; at Morgan Point, the Light House Service was quick to respond to the challenge. The problem was easily resolved when the company agreed to allow unlimited access to the keeper and his family to and from the station.

When Keeper Daboll died in 1838, leaving his wife with six children, the government appointed the widow to the post. Commenting on conditions at the station in that same year, Lt. Bache wrote, "The establishment is kept in great neatness by the widow of the former keeper." She remained at the light until 1854, when Silas Spicer was named keeper. The station was maintained by another woman, Frances McDonald, from October of 1869 to November of 1871; she had also assumed the position following her keeper-husband's death.

Morgan Point Light was discontinued in 1919 and replaced with an automatic beacon tower which was erected in the channel east of the old structure. On June 25, 1922, the lighthouse and its property were sold at auction to Henry Hewitt for the sum of $8,625.

> *A private residence, the well-kept lighthouse stands at the tip of Morgan Point in Noank, CT. It still serves as an important landmark for sailors entering Mystic Harbor.*
> *NOAA chart #13214*

NORTH DUMPLING LIGHT (NY)

Appropriation:	March 3, 1847	$5,000
Appropriation:	July 15, 1870	$15,000
Established:	1849	
First keeper:	Alfred Clark, appointed December 8, 1848	
Illuminating apparatus (IA): (1849) 7 lamps, 14" reflectors, fixed red light (FR) -red shades.		
Refitted:	1855, sixth-order steamer lens, 225o, and Argand lamp, FR.	
Rebuilt:	1871	
IA:	(1907) fifth-order Fresnel lens, fixed white with fixed red sector.	
Fog signal:	1857, fog bell	
Fog signal:	(1873) bell struck by machine every 15 seconds.	
Height of light above sea level: (1863) 70 feet. (1873) 70 feet.		

W
here was Riley Clark? The resident of New York had been appointed keeper of the new light station at North Dumpling Island on October 18, 1848, but no one seemed to know "in what part of town he resided in."

Joseph Dayton, a local sea captain, was placed temporarily in charge of the light, and New London's collector of customs submitted the captain's name as replacement for the still-to-be-located appointee. In a letter to the Treasury Department, the collector wrote that Dayton intimately knew the waters surrounding North Dumpling Island. "The commercial community here and elsewhere has a deep interest in having a Light Keeper who is well acquainted with reefs, rocks and shoals in the neighborhood of the Light House." The

North Dumpling Lighthouse, 1980, before restoration.

collector went on by pointing out that another person, who was in charge of the New London Harbor Light, had rescued seven people from a single shipwreck and had also saved several reef-grounded vessels from destruction. He attributed these feats to that man's knowledge of the local waters. The collector's arguments in behalf of his candidate were unsuccessful. In December of that year, Alfred Clark was named keeper of the North Dumpling Light, and the appointment of the still missing Riley Clark, was revoked.

Ten years before establishment of the North Dumpling Light, area navigational charts indicated that a light boat had operated northeast of Flat Hammock and southeast of North Dumpling Island (see Eel Grass Lightship, page 93). From its position, the vessel marked the entrance to Fishers Island's West Harbor and served to direct mariners through Fishers Island Sound. When Alfred Clark arrived at North Dumpling in 1848, he found a fog bell which had been placed on the island some time before by the New York and Stonington Steamboat Line. In foggy weather, whenever the company's steamboats were expected to pass, the keeper sounded the bell. He was paid $32 per year for his services by the shipping company, but when he discovered that the keeper on Little Gull Island was receiving $43 more per year for the same type of effort, he refused to operate the fog signal any longer. The company petitioned to have

Clark removed, but the Light House Establishment ruled that, since it was a private arrangement between the two parties, the keeper had the right to decline. A few years later, the government installed a fog bell of its own on the island.

North Dumpling was originally purchased from the Pequot Indians in 1644 by John Winthrop, Jr., the colonial governor of Connecticut. On November 11, 1847, the entire island, which was still owned by the Winthrop family, was sold to the government for $600. Construction of the keeper's brick dwelling and a twenty-five-foot-high attached tower began shortly thereafter, and in late 1848 the station showed a red beacon for the first time. The light was generated by seven lamps with reflectors and red shades. In 1855, the lantern was refitted with a sixth-order lens.

Survey of the lighthouse property nineteen years after its establishment revealed the existence of a henhouse at the rear of the dwelling and a fog bell standing in front; all of the station's structures were described as being in an "advanced state of decay." In 1871, extensive repairs were made to the keeper's quarters, a new tower was erected on the front of the dwelling, and a barn was constructed for the convenience of the keeper.

During Prohibition, isolated coastal beaches and islands were often used as transfer points for illegal spirits. It was general knowledge that some of the Maynards, as the residents of nearby Fishers Island were called, were actively involved in bootlegging. In April of 1923, the yacht *Thelma-Phoebe* was engaged in smuggling Scotch when a storm swept it up on the south side of Fishers Island. By the time the Coast Guard arrived on the scene, most of the vessel's cargo had been "liberated" by enterprising Maynards. In December of that same year, whiskey from another vessel similarly disappeared when it too was shipwrecked in almost the same spot as the *Thelma-Phoebe*. It was not surprising, then, that after having received reports of "strange lights" in the vicinity of North Dumpling Island, the station's keeper came under close scrutiny. Keeper Burkhart was said to have been "running extra lights around the lighthouse, which were used as signals between main land, boats and Fishers Island." His accuser claimed that he had seen the keeper storing, delivering, and selling liquor to the citizens of Fishers Island "and receiving loads from ships at night." Though the Coast Guard did observe a green flare, a rocket, and sky signals from the island's vicinity, investigators never found any evidence that connected the keeper to smuggling activities.

In 1959, the Coast Guard erected a steel tower on the southwest section of the island and put the island up for auction. It was purchased for $18,000 by George Washburn, a New York City investment manager, who in turn sold it to David Levitt in 1980. By that time, the abandoned lighthouse with its broken windows and open doorways, had become a refuge for sea gulls and rodents. Levitt renovated the structure and made numerous changes before selling it to another New York resident, Dean Kamen, in 1986.

> *The North Dumpling Light stands facing toward the east, less than a mile off North Hill on Fishers Island. It can be seen and photographed from a boat, just off the island.*
> *NOAA chart #13214*

RACE ROCK LIGHT (NY)

Appropriation:	July 7, 1838	$3,000
Appropriation:	March 3, 1853	$7,000
Appropriation:	August 3, 1854	$8,000
Appropriation:	July 28, 1866	$90,000
Appropriation:	July 15, 1870	$10,000
Appropriation:	March 3, 1871	$150,000
Appropriation:	June 10, 1872	$40,000
Appropriation:	March 3, 1873	$75,000
Established:	1878	
First lighted:	January 1, 1879	
First keeper:	Neil Martin, appointed December 16, 1878	

Illuminating apparatus (IA): (1883) fourth-order Fresnel lens, alternating red and white, 10 second intervals.

IA: (1939) fourth-order, Fl W and R, 20 seconds. Incandescent oil vapor, W. 18,000-candlepower (cp), R. 16,000 cp

IA: (1988) DCB-24 lens, 1000 watt lamp, Fl R 10 sec.

Fog signal: (1883) fog bell by machine, double blow, every 20 seconds.

Fog signal: 1897, second-class siren.

Fog signal: (1907) third-class Daboll trumpet, blast 3 seconds. Emergency fog bell.

Fog signal: (1939) 1st-class siren, group 2 blast every 30 sec.

Height of light above sea level: (1891) 68.5 feet

Automated: November, 1978

Race Rock, located at the west end of Fishers Island and the eastern entrance to Long Island Sound, was considered "one of the most dangerous obstructions to navigation on the coast." Rising from a depth of seventy or more feet of water, several small spurs of rock broke the water's surface, while a large rock formation was covered with only three feet of water at low tide. Under normal weather conditions, the chief danger to sailing vessels entering the sound was mistaking the tides. If a mariner did not

Race Rock Lighthouse, 1879. National Archives, RG 26, 3-2-R-20

compensate for a flood (rising) tide, the strong incoming current could easily sweep the craft northeastward into Race Rock. During the early 1800s, there was hardly a summer month that a vessel did not strike the rock reef with sometimes disastrous results. Addressing the danger, Capt. Andrew Mather of the revenue cutter *Wolcott* recommended in 1837 that a second light be shown from Little Gull Island Light to alert mariners of incoming tides. As far as could be determined, his suggestion was never acted upon.

Documents indicate the Race Rock was marked with buoys sometime prior to 1795. In that year, a gale swept them away, and they were replaced at a cost of $213. Spindles driven into the rock reef were also attempted, but they were generally lost to floating ice fields each spring.

In July of 1866, Congress appropriated $90,000 for establishment of a beacon at Race Rock but made no provision for a keeper's quarters. The area had been surveyed in the 1850s and engineers returned again in 1868. During the second survey, soundings made with an iron rod determined that most of the reef surrounding the largest obstruction was seemingly flat. The survey, which had been made from a boat in strong currents proved, however, to have been inaccurate. The bottom was later found to be an aggregation of small boulders, making it impossible to use a cofferdam as had been planned. In the following year, a new proposal was made for a granite pier surmounted by a keeper's dwelling; its estimated cost was $200,000.

Construction of the riprap foundation began in the spring of 1870 with placement of 3,000 tons of rocks. By November of the following year, 10,000 tons of stones had been put into position, some weighing as much as 3 to 5 tons each. The riprap foundation was completed in 1873, but it was then determined that it was too unstable to proceed with erecting the lighthouse. Donning diving gear, contractor Francis Smith was said to have surveyed the bottom himself before deciding to replace the riprap with concrete. With the help of divers, rocks were removed from the center, the bottom was leveled, and an iron band, sixty-nine feet in diameter, was set in place. By 1875, the concrete foundation had been completed.

From plan by F. H. Smith, contractor Race Rock. National Archives, 3-2R

Weather, current, and an accident slowed progress. In 1874, the construction steamer blew up, killing four men and injuring five. Heavy wave activity twice destroyed the workmen's quarters, and each spring, as work resumed, a great deal of time was lost in repairing the past winter's storm damage. Charges were also made of unnecessary delays by the contractor, but the lighthouse was finally completed late in 1878. On January 1, 1879, Keeper Neil Martin lit the station's light for the first time.

The station's dwelling was built for a keeper and two assistants. Incorporated in the foundation was a 24,000-gallon cistern. The cellar, which was divided into two halves, had a large pantry and a cool closet. On the first floor, there were two separate kitchens, dining rooms, and sitting rooms; the second floor had five bedrooms. An iron spiral staircase, suspended by a central post with supports at each step, led to the lantern room. The tower, which rose to forty feet above sea level, displayed a flashing red and white light.

A fog siren was established at Race Rock in 1896. Though it helped many navigators find their way through the Race in heavy fog, it worked to their detriment in a few instances. In April of 1905, two vessels belonging to the Quartermaster Department grounded themselves within a short distance of the lighthouse. The station's fog signal was operating at the time, but it had not been heard   a tale reminiscent of other strandings at Little Gull Island and Bartlett Reef (see Bartlett Reef Lightship). The fog signal was malfunctioning when the steamer *Arizona* came to an abrupt halt on the station's "doorstep" in 1922. Fourteen years later, however, the signal was operating as the freighter *Willboro* went hard on the rocks, a "shouting distance" from the lighthouse. Capt. G. Grundy, the ship's master, reported that he had heard Little Gull Island's fog signal, but he had not used it for a bearing, nor had he availed himself to the use of its radiobeacon. The captain had instead "navigated by the Race Rock's Fog Signal, and," he added, "the accident was caused by an aberration of the sound of that signal." Somehow, the signal seemed to have been coming from a position southeast of the station's true location.

At 2:00 pm on April 26, 1931, Keeper George H. Tooker sighted a tug with four barges in tow. Caught up in the current, one of the four broke away and struck the lighthouse rocks. The keeper and his assistants worked their way hand-over-hand across the slippery rocks and managed to climb aboard the stranded craft. Using a line tied to the barge, they succeeded in rescuing its occupant, John Hazel. "Great credit is due the first and second asst. Keepers for their daring and promptly obeying orders," wrote Keeper Tooker in the log. "The barge has now gone to pieces at 4:30 pm."

George Tooker, who had been assigned to the post on September 1, 1930, tended to go into a great deal of detail in the log and in his correspondence to the Lighthouse Service. In a letter to the superintendent dated February 1, 1930, Keeper Tooker described a January gale. "The seas were coming over the dock, carrying small riprap on the dock, and freezing." By mid-day, the station's dock and boat had become ice sculptures. "The boat was covered with ice from 8 to 10 inches on the top cover, and from 18 to 20 inches on the stern and sides. Myself and the 1st Assistant worked all day of the 25th and 26th chopping out the boat."

Automated in November of 1978, Race Rock continues to contribute to safe navigation through the Race.

Race Rock stands about a half mile off the west end of Fishers Island. It can be approached only by boat.   *NOAA chart #13209*

4 *Long Island Sound Lights*

LITTLE GULL ISLAND LIGHT   (NY)

Appropriation:	*April 6, 1802*	*$8,000*
Appropriation:	*March 2, 1803*	*$1,000*
Appropriation:	*March 14, 1804*	*$3,500*
Appropriation:	*March 1, 1805*	*$7,000*
Appropriation:	*April 7, 1866*	*$3,000*
Appropriation:	*March 2, 1867*	*$14, 500*
Established:	*1806*	

Purchased land from: Benjamin Jerome, 1803. $800
First keeper: Israel Rogers, appointed July 1, 1805
Illuminating apparatus (IA): (1838)15 lamps, 13.5" parabolic reflectors,
*   fixed white light (FW)*

IA:	*(1850) 15 lamps, 15" reflectors, FW*
Refitted:	*1858, third-order Fresnel lens, FW*
Rebuilt:	*1869*
Refitted:	*1869, second-order Fresnel lens (2-order), FW*
IA:	*(1907) 2-order, FW, incandescent oil vapor lamp*
IA:	*(1939) 2-order, FW, electric lamp, 17,000 cp.*
IA:	*(1987) 2-order, FW, 1000 watt lamp.*
Fog signal:	*(1863) fog bell struck by machine every 10 sec.*
Fog signal:	*1870, second-class steam siren, Wilcox steam generator,*
	blast 5 seconds, interval 40 seconds.
Radiobeacon:	*(1939), 294 kc, dot and 3 dashes.*
Height of tower:	*(1838) 53 feet*

Height of light above sea level: (1863) 82 feet. (1873) 92 feet.

Automated:	*May, 1978*

The Fall River liner *Priscella* was bound from New York to Fall River, MA, in June of 1926 when it entered a dense fog bank near Orient Point. "Feeling" its way toward Little Gull Island Light, the vessel's paddlewheel struck a ledge off Great Gull Island. The force of the blow, the ship's momentum, and the area's unusually strong tidal currents turned the crippled vessel and hurled it head-on into the island's landing wharf. Plowing its way twenty-five feet into the pilings, the *Priscella's* 560 passengers were sent flying

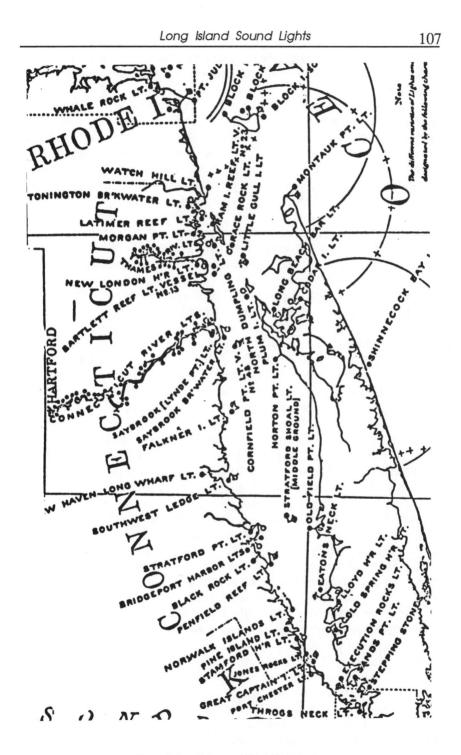

Long Island Sound Lights, 1895

out of their berths and sprawling on the decks. Somehow there were no serious injuries and despite damage to its hull, the disabled liner remained afloat.

Located at the eastern end of Long Island Sound, Little Gull Island marked the sound's access to the open sea. The four-mile expanse between Little Gull Island and Fishers Island, known as the Race, developed currents in excess of five knots. With opposing winds or heavy onshore seas on a falling tide, the portal to the sound sometimes became a caldron of twisting and churning waters that piled up into mountainous snow-capped peaks.

A survey of Little Gull Island in 1803 described it as having about one acre of land above high water. The report further indicated that the island had eroded very little over the years, and it was surrounded by rock reefs that would help prevent encroachment of the sea. Some stones were available on the island for the tower's foundation, but for the most part, the report concluded, materials had to be transported to the site by ship.

The tower, which was constructed of smooth hammered freestone laid in courses, rose to fifty-three feet above sea level; a wood spiral stairway led to the lantern. On July 1, 1805, Israel Rogers was appointed the station's first keeper, and the lighthouse became operational shortly thereafter. Though Little Gull Rock Light was often enveloped in dense haze or fog, it was fifty-one more years before a fog bell was installed.

On June 18, 1812, Congress declared war on Great Britain; it took four days for the news to reach Boston. Except for the occasionally passing warship, the struggle must have seemed particularly remote to Keeper Giles Holt, but on July 28, 1813, Little Gull Island Light was suddenly thrust into the conflict. The British landed a small force at the lighthouse, and though they did not destroy the station, they removed all of its lamps and reflectors. The incident left Commissioner of Revenues S. H. Smith in a quandary. "Whether under existing circumstances," he wrote, "the keeping of those lights would be promotive of public interests, and whether those removed should be replaced by new ones." Commissioner Smith instructed the superintendent of Little Gull Island Light to act as he saw fit, but it was not possible to determine exactly how long the station remained extinguished.

In January of 1838, the tower's original lighting apparatus was replaced with fifteen lamps and parabolic reflectors; twenty-one years later, it was changed to a third-order lens.

The decision to replace the original wood frame, seven-room dwelling and its stone tower was made in 1867. During construction, the station's light was shown from the fog bell tower. Completed in 1869, the new lighthouse rose to ninety-two feet above sea level

Little Gull Island Lighthouse, 1898. National Archives 26-LG-12-57

Little Gull Island Lighthouse, 1986

and was equipped with a second-order Fresnel lens. The two-story keeper's dwelling, connected to the tower, had three separate quarters to accommodate the three keepers and their families.

At the turn of the century, the light keepers at Execution Rocks, Stratford Shoals, Race Rock, and Little Gull Island allowed certain Long Island Sound pilots to wait for incoming steamers at their lighthouses. Regulations were specific concerning the practice: "Light-keeper's dwellings shall not be used as pilot stations, nor as boarding or lodging houses, except by special authority of the Board."

The arrangement came to an abrupt end when four Hell Gate pilots complained to the Light House Board that they had not been allowed to wait for ships at Execution Rocks or Little Gull Island. When confronted with the matter, Henry P. Field, keeper of Little Gull Island Light explained, "permit was given them [the pilots] by Captain Snow, in 1896, Aug. 29th, while inspecting the 3rd Light-House District. The pilot that is making the complaint, omits to inform you that two of them is owing me a board bill for the past ten years."

None of the keepers was disciplined in the affair, but all received a letter revoking the permission given by Captain Snow. "In the future you will be held strictly accountable," wrote Inspector William Folger.

On July 15, 1920, Head Keeper Eugene Merry and his family, and the wives of the two assistant keepers were at Great Gull Island, on their way back to the lighthouse from New London. Second assistant Douglas rowed to the island with Merry's personal boat in tow to bring the party back to the station. The head keeper started out for the light with his wife and child, but, encountering heavy seas, he immediately returned to the island, where he elected to remain for the night. Despite advice to the contrary, the assistant keeper left for the station with the other two women. Less than 200 feet short of their destination, their rowboat sprang a board, and it quickly filled with water. The first assistant launched a boat from the lighthouse and managed to bring the trio to safety, but Mrs. Douglas, who was described as a "very large" woman, collapsed and died almost as soon as she touched solid ground. The young woman apparently suffered a massive heart attack.

The Coast Guard automated Little Gull Island Light in 1978. The station's second-order "classic" Fresnel lens is expected to continue to cast a fixed white light for many more years to come.

Little Gull Island Light is accessible by boat only. It stands on the west side of the Race, seven miles from New London, CT. NOAA chart #13209

New London Harbor Lights (CT)

AVERY POINT LIGHT

Established: *1944*
Illuminating apparatus: 1944, cluster of 8 lights,
                        fixed white light, 100-candlepower.
Site's name from: James Avery
Previous owners: Morton F. Plant, State of Connecticut
Present owner: State of Connecticut
Fog signal: none
Height of light above sea level: (1946) 55 feet
Discontinued: 1967

The extinguished sentinel at the southeast point of the University of Connecticut's Avery Point campus was the last lighthouse to have been established in the Third District. Little is known of the octagonal, concrete tower that was erected in 1944 and operated until 1967. It first showed a flashing white light generated by a cluster of eight lights and was later changed to flashing green. The number of lights visible from the tower varied according to the direction of approach and the distance.

From 1942 to 1967, Avery Point's seventy-three acres were the site of the United States Coast Guard Training Center. The command, which was administered in 1964 by 60 officers and 437 enlisted men, graduated 2,355 men from various rating schools, advanced electronics, and specialty courses for officers.

Two years after the Coast Guard closed the center, the property was turned over to the State of Connecticut. Under the terms, the state agreed to maintain the site for educational purposes over a period of ten years. The property was obtained at no cost

Avery Point Lighthouse, 1987   to the state, but, had it not lived up the conditions, Connecticut would have been obliged to pay the federal government the full value of the property, less 10 percent per year for each year it had abided by the agreement.

Designated as Building #41 by the university, the former light-house has been used by the school as a physics laboratory and air sampling station.

> *Located in Groton, CT, Avery Point Light is easily*
> *accessible to visitors of the University of Connecticut*
> *campus at Avery Point.*   *NOAA chart #13213*

NEW LONDON LEDGE LIGHT
(Southwest Ledge, Black Ledge)

Appropriation:	*April 28, 1904,*	*$60,000*
Appropriation:		*$55,000*
Established:	*1910*	
Illuminating apparatus (IA):	*(1924) fourth-order Fresnel lens,*	
	group flash, white alternating with red	
	(Grp Fl W Alt R), 30 sec.	
IA:	*(1938) 4-order, Grp Fl W Alt R, 30 seconds.*	
	Incandescent oil vapor lamp, white light 24,000 cp	
	red light 660 cp.	
IA:	*(1988) FA-251 rotating, 150 watt lamp,*	
	Grp Fl W Alt R.	
Clock mechanism:	*1928, changed mechanism and installed*	
	mercury float pedestal	
Fog signal:	*(1924) first-class air siren, 3 second blast,*	
	17 second interval.	
Fog signal:	*(1939) air-diaphragm horn, 3 second blast,*	
	17 second interval.	
Height of light above sea level: (1924) 58 feet		
Automated:	*May 1, 1987*	

The feeling of being alone, truly alone, consumed the keeper as he climbed the metal stairs leading to the tower's balcony. Sliding under the railing, he walked to the edge of the roof, hesitated for a moment, and gave up his life to the darkened waters below. Ernie, a civilian keeper at the light, reportedly had received a letter from his wife earlier that day, informing him that she had left him for the captain of the Block Island Ferry. From that day on, keepers and Coast Guard personnel assigned to the lighthouse are said to have often felt the presence of Ernie's troubled spirit. There were chairs that moved on their own, doors that opened and closed, footsteps with no one there, and rooms that filled with a sudden chill despite the warmth of a summer's evening.[1]

---

1. No mention of a suicide at the lighthouse was found in the station's log, but longtime residents of New London and Coast Guardsmen stationed at New London Ledge feel that the often published story is indeed true.

New London (Harbor) Lighthouse, 1986 (see pages 115-117)

On January 12, 1913, George Hansen, one of New London Ledge's first keepers, was also feared lost after being seen drifting in stormy seas aboard a sixteen-foot boat. Early that morning, the thirty-five-year-old bachelor-keeper boarded the station's powerboat and started its engine. During his two and one-half years at the lighthouse, Keeper Hansen had consistently complained of difficulties with the outboard. Headed for New London, the 2 1/2 horsepower engine quit just as he was caught up in a sudden squall. Unable to restart it, Hansen was carried in his disabled boat by wind and currents until off North Dumpling Light. At that point, he was able to signal that station's keeper, who went to his aid.

Upon returning to New London Ledge, Keeper Hansen wrote a letter to the Light House Service requesting another engine. The service, reasoning that the same boat and engine had been in use at Romer Shoal for over three years, and had never given that station any trouble, concluded that the keeper just did not know how to maintain it. Their solution was simple; they reassigned the power-boat to another lighthouse and replaced it with a rowboat.

When New London Ledge was automated on May 1, 1987, it was the last manned lighthouse on Long Island Sound. The rock reef just southeast of the structure known as Black Ledge had claimed up to a vessel a month in 1853, prompting ships' captains to petition the Light House Board to establish a lighthouse to mark the site. "There have been a number of vessels wrecked on the ledge," wrote Andrew Mather, master of a revenue cutter, "and many of them have been a total loss of vessel and cargo; and in some instances lives were lost." Buoys did mark each end of the reef, but the navigational aids were so close together that sailors found them confusing. Furthermore, they were often swept off-station by ice flows or heavy seas. In 1856, an iron day-beacon was erected on Black Ledge, but it too was carried away by ice during the following winter. The beacon was replaced, but it soon became evident the it was not adequate as the harbor's commerce increased.

Established, 1910

On April 28, 1904, $60,000 was appropriated for the construction of a lighthouse at Black Ledge. An additional $55,000 was later allocated when it was decided that Southwest Ledge, a quarter mile away, was a better site for the beacon. A three-story brick lighthouse was constructed on a square pier, with a tower rising from the center of the roof. The station began to exhibit a light in 1910, using a Fresnel lens that was hand-built in Paris by Henry Lepaute.

During its last years in operation as a manned station, the four-man Coast Guard crew was assigned there for eighteen-month tours of duty. Daily routine consisted of twelve-hour watches, during which the guardsmen were expected to transmit weather informa-tion, wind the light's clockwork mechanism every six to eight hours, clean the lens, and maintain the station. For every one to two weeks at the lighthouse, the personnel were given six days ashore. Marking its final day as a manned lighthouse, the log read, "Rock of slow torture. Ernie's domain. Hell on earth — may New London Ledge's light shine on forever because I'm through. I will watch it from afar while drinking a brew."

A foundation, formed between Project Oceanology at Avery Point and the City of New London, operates the lighthouse as a maritime classroom. The Coast Guard continues to maintain its automated light.

> *New London Ledge Light is under the care of the New London Ledge Light Foundation.*
> *NOAA chart #13213, 12372*

NEW LONDON (HARBOR) LIGHT

Appropriation:	1760, Colonial Legislature,	500 pounds
Appropriation:	May 7, 1800	$15,700
Appropriation-fog signal: March 3, 1873		$4,500
Established:	1760	
Purchased land from:	State of Connecticut (1790) no cost.	
Purchased land from:	Daniel Harris (1801) $30, Griswold Harris (1817) $50, Charles Harris (1833) $650	
Rebuilt:	1801	
Illuminating apparatus (IA): (1838) 11 lamps, 13" reflectors, fixed white light (FW).		
IA:	(1842) 11 lamps, 14" reflectors, FW	
Refitted:	1857, fourth-order Fresnel lens (4- order) 315o FW.	
IA:	(1907) 4-order, FW with fixed red (FR) sector	
Illuminant:	June 10, 1912, changed from incandescent oil vapor to acetylene.	
IA:	(1924) 4-order, Fl W, 4 sec. FR sector, white light 2,200 cp, red light 660 cp.	
IA:	(1987) 4-order, 500 watt lamp. W, Isophase (Iso) every 6 seconds (equal light and dark period) R sector.	
Fog signal:	(1863) fog whistle, blast 6 seconds, every 14 seconds produced by caloric engine.	
Fog signal:	(1873) third-class Daboll trumpet, blast 6 sec.	
Fog signal:	(1883) first-class Daboll trumpet, blast 6 seconds, interval 30 sec.	
Height of light above sea level: (1863) 86 feet		

"**H**ow about that horrible shrieking and groaning siren that has been stuck up on top of the light house here? Our summer colony has begun to arrive for rest and recuperation and unless something is done pretty soon, this will be the best field of practice for a specialist of nervous disease that I know of."

Senator Frank Brandagee's letter of June 10, 1904, to the Light House Board expressed the sentiment of many New Londoners, but for sailors, the new fog signal was a welcome improvement.

It was not the first coastal community to pit landlubbers' discomfort against maritime interest. The citizens of Greenwich, CT, and Providence, RI, also shuddered at the sound of their area's newly installed fog signals. In New London, the pressure on both sides of the issue became intense. A local ship captain, T. A. Scott, argued that the fog horn had to stay. "If some of these persons who are protesting against the present horn had heard it with the welcome it gives mariners in a fog, they would see its necessity." Bryan Meahan, mayor of New London, and seventy-four other local citizens signed a petition for its removal. The problem was finally resolved in 1906, when the Light House Service substituted a Daboll trumpet for the siren. With the establishment of the New London Ledge Light in 1911, the Harbor Light's fog signal was discontinued.

Established, 1760

There is some evidence that a navigational beacon existed at New London Harbor as early as 1750. The sixty-four-foot high tower, erected in 1760, is recognized, however, as the harbor's first lighthouse and the nation's fourth.

In October of 1760, a group of New London merchants, led by Gurdon Saltonstall, petitioned the General Assembly of the Colony of Connecticut to erect a lighthouse. Stating that most of the shipping accidents and losses of life that had occurred on the area's rock reefs could have been prevented had there been a "good lighthouse," the petitioners requested authorization for its construction. They also asked that it be financed by means of a lottery and a tax on shipping. The assembly appropriated 500 pounds, a lottery was conducted, and construction began.

The stone tower was twenty-four feet in diameter at its base, and two feet in diameter at the top; it was lit for the first time in 1761.

Revenues proved to be insufficient to cover costs of operating the lighthouse. In 1774, the assembly was petitioned to repay the heirs of Nathaniel Shaw for money that he had spent out of his own pocket on behalf of the lighthouse. Ten years later, the colony had to increase taxes on shipping to keep up with expenses. Sometime after the formation of the Light House Service on August 7, 1789, its maintenance was taken over by the federal government.

By the turn of the century, a crack developed in the stone tower that extended ten feet down from the lantern. The light, which had never been very bright, was often difficult to distinguish from the lights of the surrounding homes, and from a westerly direction the beacon was completely obscured by a point of land. Recognizing all of its problems, Congress had no difficulty in making funds available for construction of a new lighthouse.

The contract for erecting the new tower was awarded to a New London resident, A. Woodward. Work on the eighty-foot high structure began in 1800. It was built of freestone, smooth hammered and laid in courses. A wood spiral stairway led to the lantern room.

New London Ledge Lighthouse, 1986 (see page 112-115)

Completed in 1801, the tower's flashing light was generated by oil lamps and an eclipser. In 1834, these were replaced by eleven lamps with fourteen-inch reflectors, and in the late 1850s, a fourth-order Fresnel lens was installed.

During the War of 1812, the New London Harbor Light was extinguished by order of Commodore Decatur. As the lighthouse was protected by a regiment of militia, the British chose not to raid it, but, at the unprotected Little Gull Island Light, the enemy struck and removed all of the station's lamps and reflectors (see Little Gull Island Light).

On May 12, 1912, an automatic acetylene flasher was installed in place of the incandescent oil vapor lamp that had been in use for about five years. With the change, the position of keeper was abolished and James Lynch was named custodian at a salary of "one dollar per annum." The lighthouse property, which had been divided by the construction of Pequot Avenue in the late 1860s, was sold at auction in 1928. Auctioned off as two separate parcels, the keeper's dwelling and its waterfront property was sold to James Saint Germain for $7,500, and the parcel across the street was sold to Alice Bunner for $21,110.

New London Light is one of the nation's most handsome lighthouses. It can be reached from Interstate 95 by taking the Colman Street exit and following it south to Montauk Avenue. Montauk ends on Pequot Avenue, four blocks from the lighthouse. NOAA chart #13213, 12372

BARTLETT REEF LIGHTSHIP (CT)

Established:	*1835*	
Keeper, pre-1846:	*William Young*	
Lightship LV "L":	*1835-1848*	
Lightship LV 17:	*1848(9?)-1867*	*Built 1848, $12,000*
Lightship LV 13:	*1867-1933.*	*Built 1954, $12,000*
Discontinued:	*May 19, 1933*	

B artlett Reef reaches out from the mainland near Seaside Park, Waterford, CT, to about one and a half miles offshore. Some of its rocks are awash at low tide, while others lurk just below the surface. One of its early victims, the privateer *Defense*, may also have been its richest.

The *Defense* had served as a West Indies trader before being made part of Connecticut's small Revolutionary War Navy. Outfitted with twenty swivel guns and sixteen, six-pounder cannons, the vessel weighed anchor at New London in the first week of March, 1779, and set out to patrol Long Island Sound. As Capt. Samuel Smedly sailed southwest of the Connecticut River, he encountered more than he had bargained for — a large British naval force. Making a hasty retreat, the captain tried to reach the protective cover of New London Harbor's guns, but he cut too close to shore and ran aground on Goshen Reef (Bartlett Reef). The vessel sank to the waterline, but all of its equipment above deck was saved. Some believe, however, that as much as $500,000 in gold and silver, which is thought to have been aboard and stored below deck, was lost with the ship.

The southernmost extension of Bartlett Reef was marked by a buoy as early as 1800, and in 1835 the Light House Service assigned a lightship, *LV L*, to warn mariners of the navigational hazard. Following its establishment, Long Island Sound pilots were generally satisfied with its performance and felt that it was one of the more important light boats on the sound. The 41-ton wooden vessel was, however, widely regarded as too small, thus unsafe for its crew. Nevertheless, it remained posted at Bartlett Reef until 1848. Its replacement, the 150-ton *LV 17*, was built at a Stonington shipyard. It had two lanterns that used eight oil lamps each, and a hand-operated fog bell.

The light vessel served for seventeen years at Bartlett Reef and was then assigned to Eel Grass Shoal and to relief duty. In 1890, *LV 17* was declared unfit for further duty and was transferred to the Navy

Bartlett Reef Lightship, LV 13, 1867-1933. National Archives, 26-LS-13-2

for use in target practice.

The lightship proved to be a more resilient target than had been anticipated. The white-oak vessel was subjected to intense gunfire for several hours from three Navy ships, yet it managed to remain afloat. Apparently exasperated by their inability to sink *LV 17*, the gunners resorted to attaching a torpedo to its sternpost, and it was finally blown out of the water.

Lightship *LV 13* was the third and last vessel to serve at Bartlett Reef. When it was posted there in 1867, it was already thirteen years old; it remained at the station until 1933, a total of sixty-six years. The seventy-nine-foot long vessel had a compliment of a master, one mate, four seamen, and one cook. It was equipped with a single lantern on its foremast and a hand-operated fog bell and horn. Under certain atmospheric conditions, however, its fog signal was barely audible, resulting in complaints by ships' captains.

The steamer *City of Worcester* was sailing from New York to New London on January 12, 1890, when it ran into a heavy fog off New Haven. The steamer slowed to half speed and, proceeding toward its destination, it had no difficulty in locating Cornfield Lightship. As it neared what was assumed to have been the site of the Bartlett Reef Lightship, the fog seemed to be even heavier. Captain Ward and his pilothouse crew strained to hear the light vessel's fog signal over the noise of their own engine, but nothing could be heard. A crewman checked the depth and recorded seventeen feet and then twenty-five feet just before the steamer came to a grinding halt. The pride of the Norwich Line's fleet had passed about a mile north of the lightship and had gone aground on Bartlett Reef.

Some of the 350-foot vessel's watertight compartments filled with water, but it was in no immediate danger of sinking. The *City of Worcester* was refloated, repaired, and put back into service. Eleven years later, it collided with the Cornfield Lightship.

In May of 1881, the steamer *Galatea* had also gone aground when it failed to detect a fog signal. Approaching the Race in a dead calm and fog-enshrouded sea, the vessel stranded itself just an eighth of a mile from the Little Gull Island Light Station. The captain accused the keepers of not operating their fog signal, but an investigation concluded that it had been working at the time of the accident. The fog siren was heard at Mystic, fifteen miles to the north, yet no one aboard the *Galatea*, on the south side of the station, had heard it.

Experiments with the signals at Beavertail and Little Gull Island demonstrated that humidity, pressure, temperature, winds, and even tidal conditions could influence the audible reach of a fog signal. The study concluded that mariners should, "in order to pick up sound of the fog-signal most quickly when approaching it from the windward, go aloft, and if when approaching it from the leeward

Bartlett Reef skeleton tower, 1988.
Site of the former lightship station.

the nearer he can get to the surface of the water the sooner he will
hear the sound." Also included
were instructions not to assume
that the signal was out of hearing
distance because it could not be
heard; it should not be expected
to be heard in a thunderstorm, a
fog signal usually could not be
heard if the upper and lower air
currents were running in different directions (upper sail fills and
lower sail flaps), and the sound
was likely to be muted when wind
and tide were running in opposite
directions.

In its last full year in operation,
the crewmen of the lightship *LV
13* were involved in saving the
lives of three men. It was 12:30
am on September 11, 1932, when
the man on watch thought he
heard a cry for help in the distance. Fighting choppy seas, the lightship's rowboat set out in that direction and located a small boat on
the verge of capsizing. The occupants had been adrift in the leaky
vessel for over four hours after their engine had broken down. They
were taken to the lightship, fed, and returned to New London.

The Bartlett Reef Lightship Station was discontinued on May 19,
1933. Since 1938, the south end of Bartlett Reef has been marked
by a square skeleton tower that displays a flashing white light every
five seconds and sounds a foghorn, two blasts every sixty seconds.

---

*The square skeleton tower with a triangular day-
mark stands the lonely vigil at Bartlett Reef. Power-
boaters approaching the beacon should be on the
lookout for lobster pots; the area is a "mine field" of
floats and lines waiting to become ensnared in
turning propellers.*
NOAA Chart 13211, 12354

LYNDE POINT LIGHT (CT)

Appropriation:	*April 6, 1802*	*$2,500*
Appropriation:	*March 3, 1837*	*$5,000*
Appropriation:	*July 7, 1838*	*$2,500*
Established:	*1803*	

Purchased land from: William Lynde $225
Contractor: *Abishai Woodward*
Illuminating apparatus (IA): (1838) 7 lamps, 6 plano-
                         convex lenses, 8.5" reflectors, fixed white light (FW)

Rebuilt:	*1839*
IA:	*(1842) 10 lamps, 9" reflectors, FW.*
IA:	*(1850) 10 lamps, 10" reflectors, FW.*
Refitted:	*1858, fourth-order Fresnel lens, 300o, FW*
Refitted:	*January 1, 1890, fifth-order Fresnel lens, FW*
IA:	*(1939) fifth-order, FW, oil lamp, 180 cp.*
IA:	*(1988) fifth-order, 1000 watt lamp, FW.*
Fog signal:	*(1863) fog bell*
Fog signal:	*(1883) fog bell struck by machine every 12 seconds*

Height of tower, base to focal plane: (1838) 35 feet. (1863) 70 feet.
Height of light above sea level: *(1863) 80 feet*

On November 3, 1802, a small parcel of land was purchased from William Lynde of Saybrook, CT, to erect a lighthouse at the mouth of the Connecticut River. Acquired at a cost of $225, the land was bordered by a large marsh on its west side and by the river on its east side. The light was established to serve as a leading light for mariners plying Long Island Sound and to mark the entrance to the Connecticut River, but the area was so hazardous that mariners were warned to avoid it. "Saybrook is no harbor for vessels either day or night, without it be those who are well acquainted," wrote the Blunts in *American Coast Pilot*, "it will be well to give Saybrook [Lynde] light a birth of 3 to 4 miles." Robert Mills, the author of *American Pharos*, complained in 1832 that the nearby salt marsh, "containing a pond of brackish water, which by its evaporation creates a mist, at times very much impedes the light, the weather at the same time being clear off shore."

The station's first tower, built in 1803 by Abishai Woodward, was constructed of wood. Its dim light and range were subject to a great deal of criticism by local sailors, and in 1833 a group led by Samuel Tudor petitioned to have the tower raised by twenty-five feet. "The present Light house at Lynde Point, will not admit of the increased elevation which the petitioners desire," wrote Fifth Auditor Steven

Lynde Point Lighthouse, 1988

Saybrook Breakwater Lighthouse, 1988

Pleasonton, "that Light house being thirty-five feet high, built upon a base of twenty feet diameter and graduated to eight feet at the top. No alteration can be made." Pleasonton thought that larger reflectors could be installed, but if that change did not solve "the evil complained of," then, he suggested, the petitioners should take their case to Congress for construction of a new tower.

In 1838, the station's lighting apparatus consisted of seven lamps, eight and a half-inch reflectors, and six plano-convex lenses arranged around a circular table. Though the light's maximum range was given as twelve miles, it was only infrequently seen by personnel aboard the Bartlett's Reef Lightship, a distance of about nine miles. The tower was refitted in the mid-1850s with a fourth-order lens, and changed again in January of 1890 to a fifth-order Fresnel lens.

Lt. George Bache described the keeper's dwelling during his 1838 inspection tour as a six-room frame structure, which was "in good order," but the tower, he found, was "very much decayed, and is about to be taken down." In the following year, the old tower was torn down, and an octagonal stone tower was erected that rose to seventy-three feet above sea level. The keeper's dwelling was rebuilt 1857-1858.

Erosion proved to be a continual problem at Lynde Point. In 1829, a seawall was built to protect the lighthouse from damage caused by the river's currents and onshore storms; two years later, it had to be enlarged. Because of the expense of fighting the erosion, criticism arose in 1840 over the station's location, but it was finally concluded that it could not have been placed anywhere else. Over the next three-quarters of a century, additional work had to be done, on at least seven separate occasions to prevent the lighthouse from being washed away.

In 1868, the tower was refurbished. The structure was brick-lined, its wooden spiral stairs were replaced with an iron stairway, and an iron deck plate was fitted in the lantern. The keeper's dwelling was torn down in 1966 and replaced with an unattractive duplex.

The lighthouse was automated in 1975, but the Coast Guard reassigned personnel to live at the station to help prevent vandalism. Still equipped with its classical fifth-order lens, the white tower has continued to show its fixed white light.

> *Lynde Point Light can be reached by taking the Old Saybrook exit off Interstate 95 and follow signs for Saybrook Point.*
> *NOAA chart #12354*

SAYBROOK BREAKWATER LIGHT (CT)

Appropriation:	*August 7, 1882*	*$20,000*
Appropriation:	*July 7, 1884*	*$18,000*
Established:	*1886*	
First lighted:	*June 15, 1886*	
First keeper:	*Frank W. Parmele, appointed June 2, 1886*	
Illuminating apparatus (IA):	*(1891) fourth-order Fresnel lens,*	
	fixed white with fixed red sector (FW w FR).	
Illuminant:	*1917, changed from oil to incandescent oil vapor*	
IA:	*(1939) fourth-order Fresnel lens, FW alternating with flashing green*	
	(Fl G), FR sector. Electric. W 2,900 cp, Fl G 12,000 cp, R 3,300 cp.	
IA:	*(1988) 300 mm lens, 1000 watt lamp. Fl G every 6 seconds.*	
Fog signal:	*(1891) fog bell struck by machine every 20 seconds*	
Fog signal:	*(1939) air-diaphragm horn, blast 2 seconds, interval 18 seconds.*	
Height of light above sea level: (1891) 60 feet		
Automated:	*1959*	

The seas on Long Island Sound were deceptively calm on the morning of September 21, 1938, as Keeper Sidney Gross and his assistant, S. L. Bennett, went about the station's duties. By 2:00 pm, a light breeze had picked up from the south, and, just one hour later, the lighthouse was being battered by gale-force winds. When Keeper Gross attempted to step outside to secure some articles on the platform, the wind prevented him from opening the door.

As the hurricane's fury increased, the platform encircling the tower was torn away, taking with it the station's boat and everything else attached to it. Fed by the rising tide, the storm waters rose rapidly and swept away breakwater rocks, some weighing as much as several tons. Fearing that the waves would break through the engine room's south window, the keepers began boarding it up. In the midst of their efforts, a huge wave crashed against the lighthouse, tearing away the window, its sash, and the boards. In the onslaught, the keepers were sent sprawling; both were slightly injured.

By 5:00 pm, the water level had risen to the level of the lower deck, and the cellar was flooded. The salt water disabled the station's engines and shorted out its batteries, putting the fog signal out of action. Efforts to continue showing a light were made even more difficult as the entire lighthouse shook from the constant pounding. Despite the difficulties, however, the keepers were able to maintain a light for the entire night.

When daylight came, the skies were clear; the nightmare had finally come to an end. Keeper Gross entered in the log, "everything was swept away by hurricane but the tower."

Saybrook Breakwater Light was regarded by the Lighthouse Service as a "relatively convenient" shore station, but keepers averaged only a little over two and one-half years at the post. In its earlier years, there were no assistant keepers at the lighthouse.

The cast-iron conical tower was cold and damp. Standing at the end of a one-half-mile-long breakwater, the structure was often flooded. "Everything moveable including the cord wood, had to be taken into the living room during heavy storms," complained one keeper. A ride to shore for supplies, aboard the station's twelve-foot rowboat often meant fighting the Connecticut River's strong currents. For a lone keeper returning to the lighthouse, onshore winds made getting out of the boat extremely difficult. Even when it was later possible to walk to shore along the breakwater, carrying supplies made the walk hazardous; in the winter, the ice-covered rocks made the trek out of the question.

In 1902, Keeper John Dahlman was assigned an assistant, but, five years later, when the next head keeper took over, the station once more reverted to a single keeper. In 1917, Keeper Joseph F. Woods made an impassioned plea for an assistant.

"I wish to inform you," wrote Keeper Woods, "of one instance that I have in mind at the present; the railroad round-house in the village near here, to cover about the same duties that I have to cover alone, has three watchmen for each twenty-four hours. Each man, in turn, is relieved, leaving each considerable time for rest and pleasure. The lowest paid of these three men gets more than this station pays its keeper. I am on duty twenty-four hours out of twenty-four hours, and the only relief I get is when my wife begs of me to rest while she stands watch." The keeper went on describing how his wife was in poor health and needed an operation; she could no longer help him. "This is a fog-signal station, and the signal must be going when I cannot see three miles regardless whether it is day or night." He complained of the new vapor lamp, which was difficult to adjust, and, "since the war, there has been a telescope, and other orders known to the Department, sent me with instructions for keeping a strict watch. I cannot see how the Department can possibly expect a man to cover such responsible matters without relief."

The keeper's request did not seem unreasonable. Similar Third District lighthouses at Sakonnet Point, Whale Rock, Plum Beach, Latimer Reef, Rockland Lake, Romer Shoal and Great Beds all had assistants, but District's Superintendent of Lighthouses, J. T. Yates, was not moved: "It is not considered that an additional keeper is necessary at this station and same is not recommended." Joseph Woods persisted in his request, and on December 4, 1917, Yates recommended his transfer to another station. A few years later, an assistant was assigned to the Saybrook Breakwater Light.

Established, 1886

Congress appropriated $20,000 on August 7, 1882, for the establishment of a lighthouse at the end of the Saybrook jetty. When it was determined that the amount was inadequate, a temporary stake-light was erected, and two years later an additional $18,000 was made available.

The foundation for the lighthouse was laid in 1885, and on June 15, 1886, the forty-four-foot tall tower showed a light for the first time. The station was initially equipped with a fifth-order lens, but in January of 1890, it was refitted with a fourth-order apparatus that displayed a fixed white light with a red sector; the station's fog signal consisted of a machine-struck bell.

Saybrook's fog signal had long been a source of complaint. In the late 1800s, steamboat companies provided Keeper Robert Bishop with a foghorn, which was sounded in addition to the station's bell, but the signal was still ineffective. A new striking machine was installed in 1899, but, under certain atmospheric conditions, the bell could not be heard until a short distance from the light. Petitioning for a new signal, J. H. Ross, president of the Inland Water Petroleum Carriers Association wrote in December of 1935, "To all intents and purposes, the bell is practically useless as an aid to navigation, for the reason that it cannot be heard by a vessel approaching Saybrook or the Connecticut River from the southeast with an easterly wind, until the vessel is practically within sight of the breakwater." Mariners had begun requesting a new signal in 1930, and, though the service recognized a need for change, the necessary funds did not become available until June of 1936. At that time, two diaphragm horns were installed.

Saybrook Breakwater Light was automated in 1959. Its flashing green light continues to direct large numbers of weekend sailors during the summer and a steady flow of commercial traffic throughout the year.

> *The Saybrook Breakwater Light stands at the end of the west jetty, at the mouth of the Connecticut River. Situated at the end of a private road, the light can only be reached on foot by non-residents. NOAA chart #12375, 12377*

CORNFIELD POINT LIGHTSHIP (CT)

Established: 1856
First keeper: Albert G. Crocker, appointed December 1, 1856
Ligthship LV 14: 1856-1872.   Built 1852,   approx. $15,000
Lightship LV 12: 1872-1882.   Built 1846(?)   at Philadelphia, PA
Lightship LV 23: 1882-1892.   Built 1857,   at Dorchester Ct, MD
Lightship LV 51: 1892-1894.   Built 1892, $53,325
Lightship LV 48: 1895-1925.   Built 1891, $57,280
Lightship LV 44: 1926-1938.   Built 1882, $49,999.58
Lightship LV 118/WAL 539 1939-1957. Built 1939, $223,900

T he bottom of Long Island Sound rises abruptly on the south side of Long Sand Shoal to a depth of less than seven feet. Located one and a half miles off Cornfield Point, the shallow sand bank extends westward from the mouth of the Connecticut River. In 1856, the sloop-rigged *LV 14*, under the command of Keeper Albert G. Crocker, was the first vessel posted at the newly established Cornfield Point Lightship Station. It was moored on the south side of the shoal, near its center. The ninety-one-foot lightship, which had previously served for three years at Brenton Reef Lightship Station, was equipped with a single lantern lit by eight lard lamps and a square cage day-mark. The ship's fog bell and horn were hand-operated.

During the history of the light station, Cornfield's lightships seemed to have had a special attraction for errant navigators. In 1866, *LV 14* was rammed and heavily damaged by a New London steamer. Over the next thirty-five years, there were at least three major incidents requiring injured lightships to be returned to port for repairs, but *LV 48*, posted at Cornfield from 1895 to 1925, had the dubious distinction of holding the record for collisions.

The fog that had begun to form before dusk on May 30, 1901, had, by dark, completely enveloped the 108-foot *LV 48*. Anyone standing at the ship's stern under those conditions, would have found it difficult, even in daylight, to discern who was standing at the bow. With visibility deteriorating rapidly, Capt. John A. Beede ordered a crewman to operate the vessel's steam fog signal, while the others wound down their day's activities.

The *City of Worcester* of the Norwich and New London Line had been making its way slowly up Long Island Sound when, just before midnight, the outline of the light vessel emerged from the fog. Too

LV 23, 1882-1892. (Also served as Wreck of the Scotland Lightship and Ram Island Reef Lightship). National Archives, 26-LS-1-23(1)

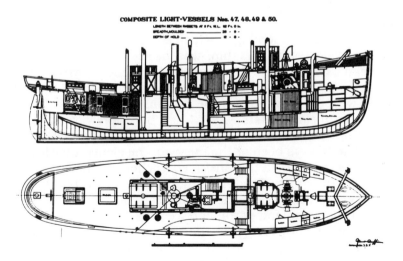

LV 48, 1895-1925, Light House Board, 1889

late to react, the steamer struck a glancing blow to the anchored ship. The crew of *LV 48* had just an hour to assess the damage before a second vessel, a barge in tow, struck the light vessel once again in almost exactly the same spot. Luckily neither collision produced much damage, but, six years later, history repeated itself.

It was barely an hour into the day of April 12, 1907, when the schooner *Rose Muller*, bound for Fishers Island Sound, ran broadside into *LV 48*. The captain and crew, who had been roused from their bunks by the lookout's warning shouts, arrived on deck in time to witness the accident. Just fifteen minutes later, while most of the ship's personnel were still on deck, a second schooner, the *Nat Neader*, rammed the light vessel on the same side. At the time of the collisions, the weather was clear, the seas were calm, and *LV 48's* lights were burning brightly. Neither schooner stopped to determine the amount of damage it might have inflicted, nor were the captains very cooperative in giving the names of their vessels; eventually, however, the owners paid for the damage. Over the next few years, *LV 48* had a few close calls, but fate saved it from being lost in a serious collision.

The steel-hull *LV 51*, built at West Bay City, MI, saw duty at Cornfield from 1892 to 1894. It then served at Sandy Hook for twelve years, and in 1908 it was designated relief vessel. On April 24, 1919, while acting as relief for *LV 48*, the lightship was rammed by a *Standard* oil barge. The force of collision was so great that *LV 51's* powerboat, which was resting on a cradle amidship, was totally destroyed. Capt. Ernest W. Borgstrom and his crew of six had but eight minutes to make their escape before the ill-fated ship sank to the bottom of Long Island Sound. Only the vessel's log and fog signal book were saved.

Saybrook Breakwater Light, which stood less than four miles from the Cornfield Point Lightship, was nearly destroyed in the 1938 hurricane. It is doubtful, however, that Saybrook's two keepers, who remained at their post throughout the storm, would have traded places with the crew aboard the lightship.

The Cornfield Lightship *LV 44* had been forewarned of the approaching hurricane. Built in 1882, the unpowered, steel-hull vessel had always been at the mercy of the elements; with insufficient time to be towed to a sheltered anchorage, the crew prepared to ride out the storm. They let out more scope on the mooring chains, moved equipment below the decks, battened down the hatches, secured the doors and ports, and went to the cabins below deck.

As the hurricane's fury grew, the 197-ton ship was lifted to the top of the waves, only to plunge to their depths with such force that each of the vessel's rivets creaked under the tremendous strain. Thrashing wildly at its moorings like a trapped animal, the lightship

LV 44, 1926-1938 (Also served as Northeast End Lightship)
National Archives, 26-LS-1-44-1

LV 118/WAL 539, 1939-1957. National Archives, 26-G-126-21134

dragged its mushroom anchors across the sandy bottom. For five hours, the vessel continued to move westward toward shore. At some point, a massive wave broke the cabin's skylight, and water rushed in. The crew managed to hold back the torrents, and as the night finally gave way to the new day, the seas grew calm. When they emerged, the crew discovered that the lightship had been dragged off-station for nearly a mile, but they were thankful to be still alive.

Cornfield's first lightship, *LV 14*, served from 1856 to 1872, when it was replaced by *LV 12*. It was then decommissioned and sold at auction in New London, CT, for $615. A succession of four more vessels (*LV 23, LV 51, LV 48, LV 44*) were posted at Cornfield until April 25, 1939, when the *LV 118 (WAL 539)* was placed on station.

The last of Cornfield's lightships, *LV 118*, was specially built for the station. Designed to prevent flooding of the main compartments in the event of a collision, the all-steel, 115-foot vessel had a cont-inuous series of wing tanks along both sides that formed an inner and outer hull. Each of the ship's compartments was provided with at least two escape routes. The vessel was powered by diesel engine, allowing it to place itself on station and seek shelter in the event of a severe storm. Diesel generators produced power for the ship's masthead light, its radiobeacon, and auxiliaries. Diesel-driven air compressors provided air for the foghorn, and for operating the anchor windlass and boat hoist.

The Coast Guard discontinued the lightship station at Cornfield Point in 1957, transferring *LV 118* to Cross Rip, MA. It remained there for five years, spent its next ten years at Boston, MA, and was decommissioned in 1972.

LV 118/WAL 539 was donated to the Lewes Delaware Historical Society in August of 1972. Open to the public during the summer season, the vessel is located on the water, at the end of Shipcarpenter Street, in Lewes, DE.
NOAA chart #12354 (Long Sand Shoal)

HORTON POINT LIGHT (NY)

Appropriation: *August 3, 1854*   *$4,000*
Appropriation: *August 18, 1856*   *$3,500*
Established: *1857*
Purchased land from: *Charles and Hannah Paine, 1855*
First keeper: *William Sinclair, appointed June 4, 1857*
Illuminating apparatus (IA): 1857, third-order Fresnel lens, fixed white light (FW)
Illuminant: *1907, changed from 2-wick oil to incandescent oil vapor. Power increase from 1,782 candlepower (cp) to 22,720 cp.* *
Fog signal: *none*
Height of light above sea level: (1891) 105 feet
Discontinued: *1933, replaced by skeleton tower.*
IA: *(1939) electric, flashing green 0.5 seconds, eclipse 14.5 seconds, 90,000 cp.*

* Later official documents indicate that the increase may had been to only 12,000 cp.

"Gentlemen," began Capt. William Brown's letter of November 22, 1853, to the Light House Board, "I would suggest that a fixed light upon Horton's point would be of great value to those who navigate Long Island sound, supplying, as it would, the existing deficiency of lights upon the Long Island shore between Old field Point light and Plum Island light." In the same letter, the captain of the steamer *Bay State*, argued for a lighthouse at Bristol Ferry, RI. At that site, the steamship company had been maintaining its own light, but it was widely regarded as inadequate.

It is often said that, when George Washington visited Horton Point in 1757, he proposed erecting a lighthouse at the site. As president, he commissioned its construction in 1790, but as things sometimes go in Washington, DC, Congress did not get around to appropriating the necessary funds for another sixty-seven years.

Looking out from a steep promontory, seventy-five feet above the beach, the station's tower rose from the end of a brick dwelling to a total of 110 feet above sea level. The lighthouse, which was equipped with a third-order lens, showed a fixed white light for the first time in 1857.

Unlike its neighbor to the west at Old Field Point, the light station at Horton Point only briefly had a female keeper. While washing down the tower in May of 1903, Keeper Robert Ebbitts fell thirty feet to the ground when his ladder collapsed. Left immobile with a dual fracture of his left leg, the keeper requested that Stella M. Price be named acting assistant keeper until he had recovered. Price, whose father had been keeper at Horton Point, received the temporary appointment; she remained in that capacity for about two months.

Canadian-born Robert Ebbitts had been appointed to the post on September 10, 1896; he was the seventh of eight keepers stationed at Horton Point. After his accident, his spotless inspection record was twice marred. In 1907, he was admonished for having left "greasy rags in the lantern and watch rooms," and in the following year, he was informed that he had not properly cleaned the lantern. "The Board notes that you have before been warned for neglect of duty," read the letter from the Light House Board, "but it appears that this warning was unheeded. If future inspections of your station do not show better results, the Board may be called upon to take more drastic measures than reprimanding you." Keeper Ebbitts remained at Horton Point until May 1, 1919.

George Ehrhardt succeeded Ebbitts and was still the keeper when it was announced in 1933 that the Horton Point Light was to be discontinued. From about 1907, the station's light had been generated by an incandescent oil vapor lamp that produced 12,000 candlepower. It was replaced by an automatic 90,000-candlepower electric light, shown from a skeleton tower; it became operational in June of 1933.

The entire lighthouse property, which had been deeded to the

Horton Point Lighthouse, 1986

government in 1855 by Charles and Hanaah Paine, was turned over to the town of Southhold in January of 1934. Under the terms of the transfer, the federal government retained the right to repossess the property at any time it deemed necessary.

Southhold at one point considered tearing down the lighthouse, but local opposition saved the structure. Work was begun on refurbishing the structure in the late 1970s and it was converted into a museum that exhibits a variety of boat models, scrimshaw, artifacts related to ships, and lighthouse documents and its Fresnel lens.

Horton Point Light is located on Lighthouse Road in Southhold, NY. From the water, the structure is partially hidden behind the surrounding trees. The museum is open to the public during the months of July and August and by appointment. (516) 765-5500 NOAA chart #12354

FALKNER (Faulkner) ISLAND LIGHT (CT)

Appropriation:	*March 3, 1801 $6,000*
Established:	*1802*
Purchased land from:	*Medad Stone, May 12, 1801*
Contractor:	*Abishow Woodward*
Tower completed:	*July 29, 1802*
First keeper:	*Joseph Griffing, acting, 1802*
Illuminating apparatus (IA):	*(1838) 12 lamps, reflectors and 8 lenses. Fixed white light*
Refitted:	*1840, 9 lamps, 16" reflectors, fixed white light (FW).*
Refitted:	*1856, fourth-order Fresnel lens, 360o, fixed white light varied by white flash (FW W Fl), interval 1.3 seconds.*
Illuminant:	*1876, changed to kerosene.*
IA:	*(1883) fourth-order Fresnel lens(4-order), FW W Fl every 90 seconds.*
IA:	*(1907) 4-order, Fl W, every 15 seconds.*
IA:	*(1939) 4-order, Fl W, every 15 seconds, incandescent oil vapor lamp, 24,000-candlepower (cp).*
IA:	*(1988) 190 mm lens .77 amp lamp, Fl W every 10 sec*
Fog signal:	*(1873) fog bell struck by machine every 15 seconds*
Fog signal:	*1880, first-class steam whistle, 8 second blast, interval 52 seconds.*
Fog signal:	*October 15, 1902, first-class compressed-air siren Fog signal:*
Fog signal:	*(1939) air-diaphragm horn.*
Height of light above sea level:	*(1842) 93 feet. (1863) 98 feet*
Automated:	*March 17, 1978*

Congress appropriated $6,000 on March 3, 1801, for the establishment of a lighthouse on Falkner Island, but, when the contractors' proposals were received, all of them exceeded the available funds.

Some thought was given to changing the building materials from stone to brick or wood. Or, asked Commissioner of Revenue William Miller, could the plan be somehow altered without "effecting its utility or stability," thereby bringing down the cost to the level of the appropriation? The latter course was followed. A forty-foot octagonal tower was erected, using cut sandstone and rough stone backing, which were laid in lime mortar; it became operational in 1802. A wood spiral stairway led to the lantern room.

Falkner Island, once known as Falcon and Fortune Island, lies about two and a half miles offshore of Guilford, CT. In the early history of navigation on Long Island Sound, countless vessels ran themselves up on the rock reefs surrounding the island. Having noted both the site's importance as a way-point for sailors plying the sound and the need to mark the area's dangerous reefs, the Light House Establishment in 1801 requested funds for construction of a lighthouse. Two months after the monies became available, the island was purchased by the government from Medad Stone for $325.[1]

In 1838, the station was listed as having twelve lamps and reflectors that showed a fixed light. Arranged on two separate tables, the upper one held eight lamps, and the lower had four. It was refitted in 1840 with nine lamps and parabolic reflectors, and sixteen years later the station was equipped with a fourth-order Fresnel lens that varied its fixed light with a flash every two seconds.

The keeper's dwelling had eight rooms; by 1855, the structure had deteriorated to such an extent that it was pronounced unworthy of repair, and it was rebuilt three years later.

The second dwelling was one and a half stories high with a kitchen attached; a covered walkway connected the kitchen to the tower. The quarters had a dining room, sitting room, and three bedrooms. The entire structure, however, proved to have been so poorly constructed that, in the winter, open spaces in the walls and roof allowed large quantities of snow to enter. It was rebuilt in 1871, and at the same time, the tower was refurbished, and an iron spiral stairway was installed.

Establishment of a lighthouse on Falkner Island did not prevent further shipwrecks. One cold winter morning, the station's first keeper, Joseph Griffing, discovered the frozen bodies of seven sailors whose vessel had struck area reefs on the previous night; the keeper buried them on nearby Goose Island. During the War of 1812, Griffing's successor, Solomon Stone, was "visited" by British troops. His wife, seeing the British approaching, is said to have hidden her children in fear that they might be harmed. The precaution proved unnecessary. The British, it seems, needed the light station and its

1. Local historians often refer to Noah Stone as the property's seller, but it is Medad Stone whose signature appears on the government deed.

Falkner Island Lighthouse, circa 1890.   National Archives, 26-LG-11-55

Falkner Island Lighthouse, 1988

keeper as much as the American revolutionaries needed them.

During Oliver N. Brooks' thirty-one years as keeper, 1851 to 1882, there may have been as many as 101 ships wrecked in the vicinity of the island. On November 23, 1858, the schooner *Moses F. Webb* ran up on the rocks at Goose Island. Keeper Brooks launched his small sailboat in heavy seas and managed to rescue all but one of the ill-fated ship's occupants. For his efforts, he received a gold medal from the New York Life Saving Society and the admiration of area citizens.

Relationships of keepers with the local population, however, were not always as good as they might have been. Fishermen sometimes viewed light keepers' fishing activities as competition for their own livelihood, and conflicts arose. In May of 1925, three Guilford lobster fishermen complained in a letter to the Connecticut Department of Fish and Game that the keepers on Falkner Island were stealing from their lobster traps. The allegations proved false, but similar accusations concerning keepers at other stations prompted Superintendent J. T. Yates of the Third District Light House Service to warn his personnel that they could take fish and lobster for personal consumption only. Selling the catch, a practice that had been, for some, a means of increasing the family income, was strictly forbidden.

Two Coast Guardsmen were on duty in the late afternoon of March 15, 1976, when a fire suddenly broke out in the station's three-story keeper's dwelling. Fire fighters from Guilford, CT, made it out to the island in time to see the blaze engulfing the entire dwelling and sending searing flames up the stone tower. Under the darkened sky, crowds of onlookers watched from the Guilford shoreline as the whole island appeared to be in flames. When it was over, only the scorched tower and the fog signal building were left standing. An emergency light was immediately erected on the island, and later, when the tower had been repaired, the light was automated. In the late 1980s, the lighthouse continued to flash its white light every ten seconds, but the station fog signal had been discontinued.

Falkner Island, a major site for nesting roseate and common terns, was made part of the Connecticut Coastal Wildlife Refuge in 1985. Administered by the U.S. Fish and Wildlife Service, the refuge includes Chimon Island and Sheffield Island off Norwalk, CT, and Milford Point, CT.

> *The lighthouse can be safely approached for a closer look on the island's south side, but the island itself is off limits during the nesting season. NOAA chart #12354*

New Haven Harbor's Lights (CT)

FIVE MILE POINT LIGHT (New Haven Light)

Appropriation: March 16, 1804 $2,500
Established: 1805
Purchased land from: Amos Morris, May 5, 1804
Contractor: A. Woodward
First keeper: Jonathan Fitch(?), appointed December 19, 1805
Illuminating apparatus (IA): (1838) 8 lamps, 13" parabolic reflectors,
                      fixed white light (FW).
IA: (1842) 8 lamps, 9" reflectors, FW
Rebuilt: 1847
IA: 1847, 12 lamps, 21" reflectors, FW
Refitted: 1855, fourth-order Fresnel lens, FW
Fog signal: (1863) fog bell operated by caloric engine.
Fog signal: 1871, bell mechanism replace by Steven's striking apparatus,
                      sounded every 15 seconds.
Height of tower: (1838) 30 feet.   (1863) 70 feet
Height of light above sea level: (1838) 50 feet. (1863) 93 feet
Discontinued: 1877

U nder the best of conditions, sailors approaching New Haven Harbor during the early 1800s, could barely make out the beacon shown from the lighthouse at Five Mile Point. Vessels sailing in a westward direction along Long Island Sound were instructed to give the light a berth of at least two miles to avoid a ledge to its southwest; it was marked by a black buoy. The lighthouse stood at the extreme southeast corner of the harbor on land purchased from Amos Morris of East Haven. Established in 1805, the wooden octagonal lighthouse was eighteen feet in diameter at its base and thirty feet tall; an iron lantern surmounted the tower. Lt. George Bache found the lighthouse in 1838 to be "very much decayed, the sides and deck in a leaky condition." The dwelling, originally a one and a half-story, sixteen-foot square structure, was expanded by the keepers to a six-room residence; it was described as leaking "where different portions had been joined together."

The lieutenant's report indicated that the station's fixed light was generated by eight lamps and thirteen-inch reflectors, arranged on a circular table; it was said to have a range of over twelve miles. Mariners, however, were generally unhappy with the light; it was considered neither bright enough, nor high enough. Recommending a new tower in November of 1845, Fifth Auditor Steven Pleasonton wrote: "It would probably be a better plan to build a Light House on the Southwest Ledge, at the entrance of New Haven harbor, and to abandon the Light at Five Mile Point, but a Light House on the Ledge would be so expensive that I have no hope of getting an appropriation for it. We must therefore rebuild the Five Mile Point Light and put a large Buoy on the South West Ledge." The new tower operated for only thirty years, before being replaced by a lighthouse on Southwest Ledge.

On March 3, 1847, Congress appropriated $10,000 for the construction of the sixty-five-foot tower. The exterior of the lighthouse was built from hewn stone by Marcus Bassett of East Haven, and the inner walls were lined with brick; a spiral stairway led to the lantern. The keeper's dwelling was attached to the tower.

Initially, the lighting apparatus consisted of twelve lamps and twenty-one-inch reflectors, but in 1855 it was updated to a fourth-order Fresnel lens. During the 1860s, the stations fog signal was a bell operated by caloric engine; in 1871, its mechanism was replaced by a Steven's striking apparatus.

In 1872, the possibility of erecting a lighthouse at Southwest Ledge and discontinuing the one at Five Mile Point, was reexamined. The ledge, which was located in the center of New Haven Harbor's main shipping channel, was covered with a little more than seven and a half feet of water at low tide. Army engineers had proposed blasting the rock reef, but later, it was felt that maritime interests would be better served if a light and fog signal were established there. The harbor's main light at Five Mile Point, was located one and a half miles inside of Southwest Ledge. Since vessels tended to run for a light, it was reasoned that marking the ledge with a lighthouse and a fog signal, would serve to direct mariners into the harbor and help them avoid the serious navigational hazard. Construction of a lighthouse, however, had always been recognized as being an expensive project; the structure had to be especially strong to resist the winters' heavy ice floes. Its estimated cost was $117,800.

An initial appropriation of $50,000 was made, and the foundation was completed in 1874. Southwest Ledge Light exhibited its light for the first time on January 1, 1877, and at that time the Five Mile Point Light was discontinued. On November 13, 1896, the old light station was transferred to the War Department.

At the turn of the century, the War Department leased the one-acre lighthouse reservation to Albert Widmann for $100 per year. The enterprising man spent about $3,000 making improvements, which included a boat landing. Patrons of a nearby amusement park were ferried to the site, and allowed to climb the old tower for a small fee.

Widmann's lease expired on January 1, 1922. Under the bill

Five Mile Point Lighthouse, 1986

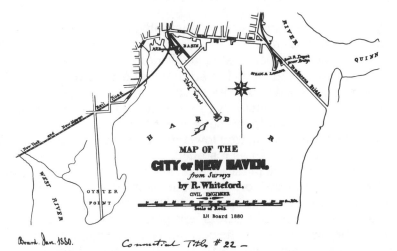

New Haven Long Wharf, Light House Board, 1880

H.R. 11346, dated April 18, 1922, the property was transferred to the state of Connecticut, and the buildings went to the city of New Haven; the bill stipulated that the site was to be used solely as a public park.

> *Five Mile Point Light (New Haven Light), locally known as Lighthouse Point, is a public park; an admission fee is charged during the summer season. It can be reached from Interstate 95 by taking exit 50 and following signs south to Lighthouse Point.*
> *NOAA chart #12354, 12371*

NEW HAVEN LONG WHARF LIGHT

Appropriation: *August 31, 1852*   *$500*
Appropriation: *June 20, 1860*   *$2,000*
Established: *1854*
First keeper: *John Wood, appointed January, 1854*
Illuminating apparatus (IA): French dioptric "steamer" lantern
Discontinued: *1859*
Re-established: *1861*
IA: *1861, sixth-order tubular lantern, fixed red light (FR).*
Refitted: *July 24, 1901, locomotive headlight lantern, FR*
Fog signal: *1900, 160-pound bell, 10,000-blow striking machine struck every 10 seconds.*
Fog signal: *(1907) fog bell struck by machine every 10 sec*
Height of light above sea level: (1861) 21 feet

A cast-iron beacon post was established at New Haven Long Wharf in January of 1854, and John Wood was appointed its first keeper. Using a French dioptric lantern, the beacon showed a fixed light. The station was discontinued in 1859 but was reestablished two years later.

The original site, purchased by the government for the Long Wharf Light, was an area of only two square feet; it was later expanded to six square feet. In 1900, an iron tower was erected in place of the old structure, and a fog bell was installed.

There was no provision made for a keeper's dwelling at Long Wharf, and the unwatched beacon was often defaced by boys who frequented the area. The youngsters climbed the tower. On several occasions they tampered with its equipment, and, at least in one instance, they extinguished the beacon. The owner of the wharf, the New York, New Haven, and Hartford Railroad, had abandoned the property, and the nearest building was eighteen hundred feet away.

When the keeper requested assistance from the local police, they responded that the station was out of their jurisdiction. In July of 1912, vandals set fire to the station's oil and supply shack. The blaze spread quickly to the wood platform and shed directly above and badly damaged the fog signal housed there.

From 1914 to 1917, the keeper of Sandy Point Jetty Light, located less than a mile away, was also made responsible for Long Wharf. That arrangement proved to be unworkable, however, and a keeper was reassigned to Long Wharf. George B. Keller, who retired in 1923, was the last to hold the position of keeper at the station. The designation was then changed to that of a light attendant, and it remained as such until the beacon was made automatic.

Standing at the end of a pier, Long Wharf Light
displays a flashing green light from a pipe tower.
It can be reached from the access road, Long Wharf Drive,
off Interstate 95 in New Haven, CT.
NOAA chart #12371

SOUTHWEST LEDGE LIGHT

Appropriation:	August 12, 1848 (for removal of ledge)	
Appropriation:	March 3, 1873	$50,000
Appropriation:	June 23, 1874	$50,000
Established:	1877	
First lighted:	January 1, 1877	
First keeper:	Eljur Thompson, appointed January 3, 1877	
Illuminating apparatus (IA):	(1883) fourth-order Fresnel lens (4-order), fixed white light (FW).	
IA:	May 15, 1889, 4-order, FW with fixed red sector	
IA:	(1932) 4-order, FW R sector, incandescent oil vapor (iov), white light 2,900 cp, red 870 cp.	
IA:	(1939) 4-order, iov, Fl R 5 seconds, 11,000 cp.	
IA:	(1988) FA-251 lens, 150 watt lamp, Fl R, 5 sec.	
Fog signal:	(1883) fog bell struck by machine every 15 sec.	
Fog signal:	August 20, 1888, Daboll hot-air fog signal	
Fog signal:	March 30, 1897, second-class compressed air Daboll trumpet, blast 3 sec.	
Fog signal:	(1939) air diaphragm horn.	
Height of light above sea level:	(1891) 55 feet	
Automated:	1953	

I n the endless confinement of the breakwall tower, an insidious madness crept over the one-time hero. Nils Nelson had served at a Rhode Island lighthouse prior to being assigned to Southwest Ledge Light. At his former post, the assistant keeper had made a daring rescue for which Congress awarded him a medal, but, over a period of several months, he had become moody and prone to unrestrained anger. When a minor disagreement arose between the assistant and Head Keeper Jorgen Jonnesen, Nilson became enraged. In a scene resembling the plot of a grade-B horror movie, the assistant reportedly picked up a fire axe and chased his coworker around the lighthouse, fully convincing him that he was about to be reduced to kindling. The head keeper was finally able to barricade himself in a storage room, and, upon emerging some time later, he found that his assailant had left the lighthouse in the station's rowboat.

Intimidated by the "strapping big fellow," the small-frame Jonnesen did not report the assistant's behavior to the Light House Service. Rather, he sent for his brother-in-law and asked him to remain with him at the light. In mid-January of 1908, Nilson was again consumed by anger. He pinned the keeper against the wall and threatened to cut his throat with a butcher knife, but, before harm was done, the brother-in-law was able to intervene. Shortly thereafter, the assistant went to shore and took his own life; the troubled man was finally at peace.

Established, 1877

Construction of the Southwest Light began in 1873. Riprap stones were placed in a circle, with a central core prepared to receive the foundation cylinder, but, before much progress had been made, a winter storm struck. It caused so much damage that the project had to be temporarily abandoned. Work was resumed in the spring; first boulders that had rolled into the center during the storms were removed. An iron tube was then sunk into place and filled with concrete, making the tube approximately level with the top of the ledge. Additional tubes were set in position, filled with concrete, and an area was left opened in the top of the foundation for a cistern. By the summer of 1876, the superstructure had been installed, and the lighthouse became operational on January 1, 1877. Equipped with a fourth-order Fresnel lens, the station showed a fixed white light, and in the following year a Daboll hot-air fog signal was installed. The lighthouse was later incorporated into the harbor's east breakwall at the time of that structure's construction.

Life at the new lighthouse for Keeper Elizur Thompson and his assistant was anything but pleasant. The roof leaked and the tower was described as "very damp and uninhabitable." Rainwater collected in the cistern was said to be undrinkable, and the boat landing filled up with riprap stones with every storm. Though the lighthouse survived the hurricane of 1888, the foundation was unstable, and the tower shook in strong winds and heavy seas. After the cistern had cracked on several occasions, the Light House Service, in 1911, shored up the foundation sufficiently to increase its stability. The

Southwest Ledge Lighthouse, 1987

*New Haven Breakwall Lighthouse, foundation cylinder, 1899.
National Archives, 26-LG-13-15*

damp, wood-lined iron tower, however, continued to be a problem for the personnel stationed there.

In 1916, Assistant Keeper Edward Grime resigned his appointment to Southwest Ledge, complaining of the constant dampness, the poor quality of water, and the infestation of the tower with cockroaches. The station had only one cistern, and the water was used for cooling the fog signal engines. In the wake of the assistant's resignation, the service pointed out that the lighthouse had barrels for holding a limited amount of drinking water and that a boat from New Haven had a contract with the station to supply water upon request. Inspection of the station did confirm the presence of the nasty little urban-critters, but it was said that there were "very few." The inspector concluded that "the present keeper has the station in better order that it has been for some time, and that he is continually making improvements."

With the onset of the Spanish-American War, Southwest Ledge Light was not ignored by the War Department. In what was then the Third Lighthouse District, preparations had already been made to install gun batteries at the Bridgeport Harbor Light and at the abandoned Gardiners Island Light; many of the lights marking the approaches to the port of New York were temporarily extinguished. On May 20, 1898, Southwest Ledge was ordered to discontinue its foghorn, and empty its cistern to receive electric batteries for a "torpedo system." Whether or not such a system was ever installed was impossible to determine. It would seem, however, that using that type of armament from a fixed structure, even if it were aimed at the main ship channel, would have been highly impractical. One can imagine an officer at the lighthouse signaling the captain of an enemy vessel to please move his vessel over a bit, so that it would be in the line of fire!

Rescues from the Southwest Ledge Light were common. Shortly after it became operational, Assistant Keeper Sidney Thompson saved four people in an action described as "at great personal risk." During a ten year period from 1914 to 1924, at least twenty people owed their lives to the station's vigilant keepers. The light was manned until 1953, when the Coast Guard automated the old tower. Equipped with a foghorn and flashing red light, the beacon is expected to continue marking Long Island Sound's busiest commercial port for many more years to come.

> Southwest Ledge Light can safely be approached
> by boat, to within less than fifty feet. It can
> also be seen in the distance from Long Wharf,
> off Interstate 95, in New Haven, CT.

NEW HAVEN OUTER BREAKWALL LIGHT
(New Haven Light, Sperry Light)

Appropriation:	*June 4, 1897*	*$25,000*
Appropriation:	*July 1, 1898*	*$50,000*
Established:	*1899*	
Contractors:	*Toomey Brothers*	
Tower completed:	*November, 1889*	
First keeper:	*William H. DeLuce (?) head keeper*	
First assistant keeper:	*Bernice A. Francisco*	
Illuminating apparatus (IA):	*1900, fourth-order Fresnel lens (4-order),*	
	flashing red light (Fl R)	
IA:	*(1907) 4-order, Fl R every 5 seconds*	
Name change:	*1912, to "New Haven Light."*	
IA:	*(1932) 4-order, Fl R, 5 seconds. Incandescent oil vapor lamp,*	
	11,000-candlepower (cp).	
Fog signal:	*1900, second-class compressed air siren*	
Fog signal:	*February 2, 1903, blower siren*	
Fog signal:	*(1924) 10-inch air whistle, blast 2 seconds, interval 18 seconds.*	
Height of light above sea level:	*(1907) 61 feet*	
Discontinued:	*1933, replaced by black skeleton tower,*	
IA:	*(1939) skeleton tower, Fl W, 2.5 seconds,*	
	375 mm lens, acetylene, 390 cp.	

C apt. Coffey strained to hear the station's foghorn as his tug, *Frederick Ives*, approached the passage between the outer and middle breakwalls. Advancing slowly, he thought he heard the signal's engine just before the lighthouse emerged from the misty envelope. The helmsman reacted quickly. The vessel narrowly missed the end of the west breakwall, but the six barges that it was towing slammed sideways into the jagged stone structure. Three of the barges sank; the others, though damaged, remained afloat.

Immediately following the accident, the Outer Breakwall Light's keeper, William Tuddy, walked 100 feet out along the breakwall. At that point, "he could not hear the horn and thought that it had stopped. He then walked back to the lighthouse and discovered it was working."

When the Outer Breakwall Light was first established, it had been equipped with a powerful second-class fog siren. Its thirteen-horsepower engines however, vibrated the unstable tower to such an extent, that in 1903 the entire system had to be replaced with a smaller, less effective fog signal.

For a time, the breakwalls at New Haven seemed to act as a magnet to errant navigators. During a 1906 snowstorm two years before the mishap of the *Frederick Ives* the canal-boat *C. H. French* had run up on the middle breakwall, near its west end. Separated by water from both of the breakwall lighthouses, the crew took down the light from one of the post-lanterns, broke into its oil storage shed, and they spent the night there. Had it not been for the heat of the lantern, the men would probably have frozen to death. In November of 1911, the schooner *Witch Hazel* crashed into the outer breakwall and sank within minutes. Two of the schooner's crewmen were rescued from its rigging; four perished. Earlier that very night, Keeper Tuddy had gone to the assistance of six fishermen whose vessel, *Busy B*, had also sunk at the breakwall.

Established, 1899

From the beginning, the Outer Breakwall Light was haunted by structural problems. Work on the cylindrical tower had begun in 1899, but, when pilings were driven into the sea floor for a construction wharf, the contractor discovered sticky clay to a depth of seven feet. The plans had called for sinking the caisson to that depth, and, using an air-lock system, bottom materials were to have been removed. The soft sediment, however, forced a change of plans. The site was dredged to eight feet and filled with gravel, which, it was hoped, would provide a stable base for the iron tower.

Fabricated by a West Haven shipyard, the foundation cylinder was made watertight at its base, and the structure was filled with cement to overcome its buoyancy. As the section was being lowered into position, trapped air ruptured the bottom seal. Workmen then watched helplessly as the cylinder filled with water, sank, and landed on the gravel bed at a definite tilt.

As a hard-hat diver inspected progress, gravel was removed from under the cylinder's high side, and as additional weight was directed to that side inside the structure, it was finally righted. Several months later, as the lighthouse neared completion, it was equipped with a fourth-order, fixed red light and a fog signal; it exhibited a light for the first time in January of 1900.

Seven years after becoming operational, the tower's foundation cylinder was found cracked in several places, the tower had tipped slightly, and concrete was reported to be washing out at an "alarming rate." Iron straps were bolted over the cracks, and the voids were filled with grout. With other improvements, the light station was able continue to operate until 1933, when it was torn down and replaced with a skeleton tower.

The name of the Outer Breakwall Light was officially changed in 1912 to the New Haven Light. Local historians, however, usually refer to the lighthouse as the Sperry Light, after Congressman Nehemiah Sperry, through whose efforts many improvements were made in New Haven Harbor.

NOAA Chart #12371

STRATFORD POINT LIGHT (CT)

Appropriation:	March 3, 1821	$4,000
Appropriation:	May 7, 1822	$500
Appropriation:	June 20, 1860 (for fog bell)	$1,200
Established:	1822	
Contractor:	Judson Curtis	

Illuminating apparatus (IA): (1838) 10 lamps, 15" reflectors, revolving white light (Rv W)
IA: (1842) 10 lamps, 14" reflectors, Rv W, 2.15 min
Refitted: 1855, six Argand lamps, 21" reflectors, new clock machinery.
IA: (1863) third-order Fresnel lens (3-order), Rv W
Rebuilt: 1881
IA: 1881, 3-order, flashing white (Fl W) every 45 sec
IA: (1932) fourth-order Fresnel lens, Fl W 30 sec., incandescent oil vapor 290,000-candlepower (cp).
IA: (1939) 4-order, Fl W 30 sec., electric 290,000 cp.
IA: (1988) DCB-224 lens, 1000 watt lamp.
Fog signal: 1864, fog bell, clock-work machinery.
Fog signal: (1932) Tyfon air, 2 blasts every 30 seconds:
Height of light above sea level: (1838) 44 feet. (1883) 55 feet

T he wood tower was old and frail, and though, it was covered with shingles on the outside, the cold night wind blew freely through the cracks of its unfinished interior. As twelve-year-old Lottie Lillingston climbed the steep ladder with the small brass lantern in hand, she dared not look down; she had never been to the top of the twenty-eight-foot lighthouse.

Lottie's grandfather, Keeper Benedict Lillingston, and her uncle, Assistant Frederick Lillingston, had gone to the aid of a disabled vessel on that October night of 1871, when the young girl noticed that the station's beacon was extinguished. She located the brass safety lamp, lit it, and carrying it carefully lest it blow out, she made her way to the tower. Inside the lantern room, Lottie stopped the light's clockwork, suspended the dimly-lit safety lamp, and re-started the mechanism. At about the same time, the steamer *Elm City* was approaching Stratford Point; the vessel's captain later reported that only a very dim light had been showing as he passed the lighthouse.

Benedict Lillingston was appointed to the light station in August of 1869, and Lottie joined her grandparents and uncle at the light-house shortly thereafter. The girl found the station's one and a half-story dwelling old but comfortable. It had a kitchen, pantry, living room, and two bedrooms on the ground floor and a single room in the attic; a covered walkway led from the dwelling to the tower.

Many years later, Lottie was interviewed by a *Bridgeport Sunday Post* reporter at her Stratford home. It was only then that it was learned why the captain of the steamer *Elm City* had observed such a dim light, showing from Stratford Point lighthouse on that October night.

Established, 1822

Stratford Point's original tower was built by a local contractor, Judson Curtis, on land sold to the government by Betsy Walker. Established in 1822, the beacon was equipped with ten lamps and reflectors, arranged on two separate tables having five lamps each. The machinery for revolving the light was similar to that at Point Judith (see Point Judith Light). In 1855, the station's lantern was refitted with a new clockwork, and the illuminating apparatus was upgraded to six Argand lamps with reflectors.

In 1867, the tower was said to be "showing signs of decay." The lighting apparatus, which consisted of two range lights supported by an iron frame, gave flashes that were too short in duration; the intervals between flashes were too long. The station's dwelling was reported in better condition, but it was in need of constant repair. It was also, apparently, too small for both a keeper and an assistant.

Perhaps unintentionally, the Light House Establishment solved Stratford Point's crowded housing problem in 1878 by appointing Jerome and Mary Tuttle as keeper and assistant. Though they seemed to have had a decent combined salary of $985 per year, the Tuttles remained at the station for only one year. Their successors were also a husband-wife team, Theodore and Kate Judson.

In 1881, a new eight-room dwelling was erected along with a thirty-five-foot tall, cast-iron tower; equipped with a third-order lens, the tower flashed a white light every forty-five seconds. The station's machine-operated fog bell, installed in 1864, was, at the same time, replaced by a more efficient bell. At the urging of the American Association of Masters, Mates, and Pilots, the bell gave way to a horn operated by compressed air in 1911.

William F. Petzolt was assistant keeper of Stratford Point when he rescued two boys who were being swept toward the open water aboard their disabled boat. At a later time, in August of 1922, Petzolt, who had been promoted to head keeper, set out with his assistant to the grounded power launch, *Ellen May*. The keepers ferried the vessel's thirty passengers in their small boat, a few at a time. They fed their guests, helped dry their clothes, and put them on a trolley for New Haven. The two then returned to the *Ellen May* and helped move the stranded vessel off the sandbar.

Stratford Point Lighthouse, pre-1881. National Archives, 26-LG-17-13

Stratford Point Lighthouse, 1987

During the 1970s, the Coast Guard automated Stratford Point Light. To protect the site from vandalism, a Coast Guard family reoccupied the keeper's dwelling in 1982.

> *Stratford Point Light stands on the west side of the Housatonic River. The station is located at the end of Prospect Drive in the Lordship section of Stratford, CT. Though closed to the public, the structures can be seen from outside the fenced-in property. NOAA chart #12354*

STRATFORD SHOAL (Middle Ground) LIGHT (NY)

Stratford Shoal Lightship

Appropriation:	(floating beacon) March 3, 1837	$10,000
Established:	1837	
Lightship:	LV 15 1837-1877	
Discontinued:	1877	

LV 15 used as barracks during construction of Great Beds Light, 1880-1881.

Stratford Shoal Lighthouse

Appropriation:	March 3, 1873	$50,000
Appropriation:	June 23, 1874	$50,000
Appropriation:	March 3, 1875	
Established:	1877	
First keeper:	William McGloin, transferred from lighship December 4, 1877	
First lighted:	December 15, 1877	
Illuminating apparatus(IA):	(1879) fourth-order Fresnel lens, flashing white (Fl W) every 10 seconds.	
Illuminant:	November 12, 1912, changed from oil to incandescent oil vapor, 40,000-candelpower (cp).	
IA:	(1988) 300 mm lens, 3.05 amp lamp, Fl W 6 sec	
Fog signal:	(1879) 1,144-pound bell, Stevens striker	
Fog signal:	(1883) second-class Daboll trumpet, blast 6 sec. interval 21 sec. Emergency fog bell.	
Fog signal:	(1891) third-class Daboll trumpet	
Fog signal:	(1932) first-class siren, blast 2 sec. silent 13 sec.	
Radiobeacon:	(1932) 1 dot, 2 dashes, 1 dot, 310 kc.	
Height of light above sea level: (1883) 63 feet		
Automated:	Summer 1970	

When Adrian Block made his voyage of exploration up Long Island Sound in 1614, he charted two islands where Stratford Shoal Light now stands. Over the next one hundred years or so, the action of the sea washed away the low-lying land, leaving a dangerous shoal of about three-quarters of a mile in length. Located midway between the shores of New York and

Laying foundation for Stratford Shoal Light, July 29, 1875.
National Archives, 26-LG-17-15

Stratford Shoal Lighthouse, 1988

Connecticut, the rock reef was covered with less than two feet of water, making it a constant threat to vessels plying the sound.

The earliest effort to mark the navigational hazard may have been around 1820, when spar buoys were placed on the north and south sides of the shoal. In May of 1831, a proposal was made to erect an iron spindle at a cost of $1,000, and the contract was awarded to a man named Wicks. It was impossible, however, to determine whether or not it was ever built.

The Light House Board established a lightship, *LV 15*, at the southeast extremity of Stratford Shoal on January 12, 1838. Built during the preceding year at Norfolk, VA, the one hundred-ton vessel was manned by two officers and four crewmen. It showed lights from two masts, each having a compass lamp fitted with ten wicks.

The single 1,200-pound anchor that held the lightship in position, proved to be inadequate; just eight days after *LV 15* became operational, it was driven off station. The vessel lost anchorage several more times before better moorings were sunk into place, but, even with two larger anchors, the problem persisted. On February 9, 1875, *LV 15* was dragged from its mooring by pack ice, and it went aground at Orient Point. It was hauled off by the tenders *Cactus* and *Mistletoe* and taken to New London for repairs. In February of the following year, the ship again parted its mooring and was reported missing by a passing vessel. A search was initiated, and the lost vessel was located twenty-three miles to the northeast, off Faulkner Island.

In 1872, the Light House Board proposed replacing the aging vessel with a lighthouse, which, it was felt, would be more economical and durable. Construction began two years later with the placement of several tons of riprap (stones) in the form of a ring, within which the foundation was to be laid. Winter storms, however, filled the prepared ring with gravel and the center had to be re-excavated. More riprap was brought in, and well over 5000 tons were put into place by the time the station became operational on December 15, 1877. Just one month before completion, a severe storm moved into the area, and the construction schooner *Mignonette* was driven up on the lighthouse rocks. The stricken vessel sank within a short time, but none of the crew was lost, and most of the supplies were saved.

The dwelling, which accommodated one keeper and two assistants, had a kitchen, living room, sitting room, supply room, and five bedrooms. An iron spiral staircase, supported by a central post, led to the foot of the lantern. The clockwork mechanism for the fourth-order Fresnel lens was located on the underside of the lens. Its chain passed through the deck to one corner, where an open channel in the brick face led it down twenty-four feet to the floors below.

After the completion of the Stratford Shoal Light, *LV 15* was transferred to the Light House Depot at Staten Island. For its last two years before being decommissioned, the vessel suffered the indignity of being reduced to the role of a floating barracks for the men employed in construction of the Great Beds Light, Raritan Bay, NJ. The forty-four year old vessel was sold at auction in 1881 for $1,010.

There was little to break up the monotony at Stratford Shoals. When not busy with lighthouse duties, the keepers fished, trapped lobster, or read books. For at least one keeper at the station, the secluded existence brought about a personal tragedy.

Julius Koster had scored well on the exam given to prospective keepers, and in September of 1904 he received an appointment to Sakonnet Point Light at Little Compton, RI. He proceeded from his home in New York City to Grand Central Station, where he later wrote to the Light House Board: "Everyone said they never heard of such a place. It must be in the woods for sure." Koster never made his way to Little Compton but was reassigned to the Stratford Shoal Light.

From the isolation at Stratford Shoal emerged a hidden pathology in the new second assistant keeper. The head keeper had left for the mainland in early May of 1905, leaving his two assistants in charge of the light. First Assistant Morrell Hulse noted that his companion had become unusually moody and uncommunicative, but he did not think much of it. On the following evening, something within Assistant Koster triggered an unbridled rage. He charged up to the tower, locked himself in, and threatened to destroy the light. For at least twenty minutes he stopped the lens' rotation and did not respond to calls from Assistant Hulse. When finally coaxed out of the tower, the distraught man turned his rage on himself and tried to take his own life. Luckily however, Hulse was able to block the attempt and a few days later, Koster was dismissed from the service.

Fearsome storms sometimes struck the lighthouse and there were occasions that keepers went out to rescue hapless sailors at great personal risk. In 1915, Assistant Keeper Emil Usinger rescued three men and two women in a disabled boat during a gale. While posted at Great Captains Light a few years earlier, the assistant had saved the lives of two other sailors.

The auxiliary cruiser *Saugatuck* set out in a winter storm on the evening of February 8, 1933, in search of a youth who had apparently become lost on Long Island Sound. When the vessel arrived at Cockenoe Island, three of the crew of thirteen disembarked to search the island while the others remained aboard. The wind picked up, and, as the seas increased in height, the *Saugatuck's* tiller broke; it then lost anchorage. With the crew unable to call for help, the vessel began a slow drift eastward that was to last sixty-two hours. Just off

Stratford Shoal, the crew managed to signal the lighthouse. Keeper Lewis J. Allen, a former Mississippi River pilot, and his assistant, Alfred Auger, chopped away at the thick ice coating their powerboat and set out for the disabled cruiser in sub zero temperatures and heavy seas. They took it into tow and brought in the occupants, all of whom were suffering from various degrees of exposure and frost-bite. The youth that had been sought, had made his way to Pecks Ledge Light, where he had remained for the night.

Stratford Shoals continued to be manned until July of 1970, when it was made automatic.

> *Standing in mid-sound, between Port Jefferson, NY, and Bridgeport, CT, the lighthouse is a favorite fishing spot for many local enthusiasts. The light can be seen from a distance while crossing Long Island Sound aboard the Port Jefferson ferry. NOAA chart #12354*

OLD FIELD POINT LIGHT (NY)

Appropriation: *May 7, 1822*   *$2,500*
Appropriation: *March 3, 1823*   *$1,500*
Established: *1824*
Purchased land from: Ludlow and Ruth Thompson, $600.
Contractors: *Timothy, Ezra and Elisha Daboll , 1823*
First keeper: *Edward Shoemaker, appointed October 10, 1823*
Lighting apparatus furnished by: Winslow Lewis, $900
Illuminating apparatus (IA): (1838) 9 lamps, parabolic reflectors
Refitted: *1839, 10 lamps, 14" reflectors, fixed white light (FW)*
Refitted: *1855, fourth-order Fresnel lens (4-order), FW*
Rebuilt: *1869, 4-order, FW*
IA: *(1932) 4-order FW, incandescent oil vapor, 2,900 cp*
Fog Signal: *none*
Height of tower: *(1838) 30 feet*
Height of light above sea level: (1873) 67 feet
Discontinued: *1933*

The female keepers of Old Field Point Light never attained the fame of Ida Lewis (see Lime Rock, RI), but on December 21, 1826, the widow of Edward Shoemaker became the first female keeper in the Third District and certainly one of the first in the nation. She assumed the post following her keeper-husband's death and remained there for six months.

Old Field Point Lighthouse, 1988

Walter Smith succeeded the widow on June 5, 1827, and he kept the light until his death in April of 1830. His wife, Elizabeth, who had assisted with the station's duties, made an easy transition into the role of keeper. She operated the station for twenty-six years and was replaced by yet another woman, Mary A. Foster.

In June of 1833, Keeper Elizabeth Smith wrote to the Light House Establishment asking that a small barn be built on the station's property. The structure was erected, and nearly a half century later there was another urgent appeal for a barn. By that time, the existing structure was described as "ready to go to pieces." As it was at Montauk Point, the distance and difficulty of travel to the nearest supply depot made a horse and wagon indispensable; the barn was equally necessary to house any horses.

Established, 1824

First established in 1824, the light tower stood separate and seaward of the station's five-room dwelling. The contract for erecting the two rough-cast stone structures and for digging a well, was awarded to Timothy, Ezra, and Elishia Daboll; they had submitted the low bid of $2,980. Winslow Lewis was given the contract for furnishing the illuminating apparatus.

During its early operation, the station's fixed light was generated by ten oil lamps, but by 1838 it was listed as having nine lamps with parabolic reflectors. They were arranged around two circular iron bars, so as to be visible along the entire shoreline. In the mid-1850s, the lantern was refitted with a fourth-order lens, but the station was never equipped with a fog signal.

Prior to the establishment of a lightship station off Stratford Shoal in 1837, mariners were instructed to steer from Falkner's Island "S.W. by W. 3/4 W. for Old Field Point, 8 leagues," which took them south of the dangerous shoal. They were reminded however, to "come no nearer Old Field Point than 8 fathoms (distant half a mile,) in the night." Large rocks lined the bottom directly off the point.

Lt. George Bache's 1838 report on the area's lighthouses indicated that, though a lightship had been operating for about a year off Stratford Shoal, the lights at Stratford Point and Old Field were still very important. Located on opposite sides of Long Island Sound, these beacons helped mark the shoal when the lightship lost anchorage —as it often did. Lt. Bache felt, however, that when and if a lighthouse was built on the shoal, one or both of the shore lights could be discontinued. Luckily for those mariners plying area waters, the two continued to operate after Stratford Shoals Light was erected in 1877; they no doubt helped many who strained to see the brief flicker of their life-saving beacons in heavy fog or on a moonless night. The lighthouse was rebuilt in 1868-1869, using plans similar to those of other area lighthouses (see Norwalk Island Light). In 1888, part of the original keeper's dwelling was converted into a barn.

Two years earlier, the Light House Board had received a complaint from Capt. Francis Weller of the schooner *Stony Brook*. He charged that Keeper Charles F. Jayne had refused to go to his vessel's aid when it had gone aground and broken up in the vicinity of the lighthouse. Shipwrecked captains had been known to accuse keepers of not sounding their fog signals or of not keeping up their lights. Such accusations might sometimes have been convenient excuses for their own negligence, as few keepers were ever said to have refused aid.

The Light House Board investigated the *Stony Brook* incident and concluded that the charges had been "frivolous and made for an interested motive." It seems that the captain may have wanted to leave the rigors of the sea for keeping the light at Old Field Point himself.

Rescues were made from the station. Keeper Richard Ray in 1923, went to the aid of two men whose powerboat had drifted up on the rock reef in front of the lighthouse. Following their rescue, the keeper brought the men to the station, and for the next two days he furnished them with food, clothing, and shelter. Old Field Point

Light continued to operate until 1933, when it was replaced by a steel tower, which was erected next to the lighthouse. The village of Old Field had purchased part of the lighthouse reservation from the govenrment in February of 1929, at a cost of $2,405. Under the terms of the sale, the village agreed to construct and maintain an access road connecting the light station to the main highway, not to allow trees to grow so as to obstruct the light, and not to erect any structures on the parcel. Two years after the lighthouse was discontinued, the village was granted a revokable license to occupy the remaining grounds and its buildings.

After the Japanese attack on Pearl Harbor, Mayor Marco Smith received notice that the village had to vacate Old Field Point; the site was needed for national defense. Southhold, NY, which had a revokable license for the Horton Point Light, received the same notification. The Coast Guard maintained a small contingent at Old Field, and Horton Point was used for aircraft spotters. The lighthouses were returned to their communities at the end of the war.

In the late 1980s, the lighthouse was occupied by the village police chief, Robert E. Cummings, and his family. On the first floor were a living room, dining room, kitchen, and laundry; the entrance room served as a den. The second floor had three bedrooms and a bath, and the third floor attic was used for storage. The original keeper's dwelling, behind the lighthouse, served as Old Field Village Hall.

Old Field Light, a private residence, is located at 207 Old Field Road in the Village of Old Field, NY. Boaters approaching the lighthouse should stay at least 750 yards off the point. NOAA chart #12363

BRIDGEPORT HARBOR BEACONS (CT)

BRIDGEPORT'S BELL BOAT

Bridgeport Harbor Light
Appropriation: April 21, 1806 (for beacon or pier) $1,000
Appropriation: September 28, 1850 $3,500
Appropriation: July 15, 1870 $45,000
Established: 1851
First keeper: A.A. McNeil, appointed December 17, 1851
Refitted: 1854, sixth-order lens, fixed red light (FR)
Rebuilt: 1871, operational November 1871
Refitted: 1871, fourth-order Fresnel lens (4-order), FR
Illuminating apparatus: (1939), 4-order, FR, incandescent oil vapor, 870 cp.
Fog signal: (1873) cast-steel bell struck by machinery every 15 seconds.
Fog signal: (1907) fog bell
Height of light above sea level: (1863) 23 feet. (1883) 56 feet
Discontinued: 1954

Bridgeport Breakwater Light
Appropriation: March 3, 1893 $2,000
Approrpriation: August 18, 1894 $2,500
Established: 1894
Lantern light: January, 1894
Tower first lighted: March 1, 1895
First keeper: Stephen A. McNeil
Illuminating apparatus (IA): (1907) lens lantern, fixed white light (FW).
IA: (1939) fifth-order, flashing green, acetylene, 130 cp.
IA: (1988) 155 mm lens, 1.15 amp lamp
Fog signal: (1939) fog bell, 1 stroke every 20 seconds.
Height of light above sea level: (1939) 31 feet

T he story of Bridgeport Harbor's beacons began sometime after the creation of a channel across the port's outer sandbar in 1844. Steamboat service to Bridgeport had been established about twenty years earlier, but, prior to dredging, large vessels could cross the sand obstruction only at high tide. Though the new waterway was a great improvement, it was less than sixty feet wide and was difficult to locate even on the clearest night. At the urging of Capt. John Brooks of the steam vessel *Nimrod*, a small rowboat was equipped with a navigational light, which was hung from a rigged-up mast. In the evening, when a steamboat was spotted heading for the harbor, the light boat set out for the channel's spar buoy, and was secured there until the approaching vessel had crossed the sandbar. The steamer then stopped, tied the

Bridgeport Harbor's Bell Boat, circa 1846.
Courtesy of Bridgeport Public Library

Bridgeport Harbor Lighthouse, circa 1875. National Archives, 26-LG-11-22

light boat to its stern, and towed it back to the dock.

On the following season, a long boat was purchased from the whaling ship *Steeglets* and it was modified with a deck and a five-foot high mast. From the mast was hung a light and seven cow bells. The bell boat, with the top of its deck barely two feet above the water line, was easily awash; it was usually wet and slippery in the summer and ice-covered in the winter. Despite its difficulties however, Keeper Abraham A. McNeil is reported to have made his way out from shore twice daily and successfully maintained his charge under the most adverse of conditions.

It easily can be imagined that the bell boat's fog signal, that was sounded by wave action on the anchored vessel, was of little use in calm, fog-enshrouded seas. Nevertheless, it continued to operate until 1848 when in a heavy gale, the vessel parted its mooring, drifted, and broke-up on the shores of Orient Point.

BRIDGEPORT HARBOR LIGHT

I n 1849, five pilings, surmounted by an iron cage, served as the harbor's beacon. Driven into the sand bottom, the pilings were held together by cross pieces, that gave the structure a measure of stability and served as a crude ladder.

The pilings beacon proved to be less than adequate, and on the following year, Congress appropriated $3,500 for construction of Bridgeport's first lighthouse. The new beacon, a box-like structure, was erected on the west side of the harbor's entrance. It stood on four iron piles, and from its center arose an octagonal cupola which housed a sixth-order, fixed red light. The light station became operational in 1851.

Exposed on all sides, the spindle lighthouse was subject to damage from wind, waves, ice, and on at least one occasion, collision with a vessel. The structure was too small to house a keeper, and, because the beacon had to be attended from shore, it sometimes went unlit for extended periods. With an increase in port traffic and with the reliability of the beacon in question, the decision was made to replace the small lighthouse.

Construction of Bridgeport's second lighthouse began in 1870. Built of wood, the structure stood on iron screw-piles and was a near duplicate of the Long Beach Bar Light. The tower, which rose from the front of the dwelling, was equipped with a fourth-order lens displaying a fixed red light. It was lit for the first time in November of 1871.

The lighthouse stood at the mouth of the harbor, a little more than a mile offshore. Visitors frequently made their way out to it during the summer, but in the winter, the station must have been a lonely place to be. (One notable exception was the winter of 1893, when the entire harbor was frozen over; that year, hoards of sightseers walked out to the lighthouse on the ice). For the most part, Bridgeport Harbor Light was remote from world events, but, the sinking of the Battleship *Maine* in Havana, Cuba, on February 15, 1898, suddenly immersed it in preparations for the war with Spain.

The War Department secured permission to "arm" the lighthouse on April 7, 1898, and ten days later Keeper Stephen A. McNeil received word that a battery of ten-inch guns would soon be installed. The schooners *Tom Beattie* and *Mary Beattie* brought loads of stones and cement to increase the size of the station's foundation, and by May 9, 1898, the guns had been mounted. Though the armaments were later removed, their wooden cradles were still in place at the time Dan McCoart was the station's keeper in 1935.

The station's personnel were often credited with saving lives, but perhaps the most dramatic incident involved Keeper William Harwick. A fierce storm had developed over the northeast on December 14, 1920, as the 187-ton steam lighter *Calvin Tompkins* made its way up the sound. Loaded with 130 tons of iron castings, the vessel sprang a leak and soon began taking on water over its sides. Finding that the pumps were no longer able to keep up with the incoming water, Capt. William LaCompte lashed down the ship's whistle valve and gave the order to abandon ship; no one responded to its desperate call for help as the vessel went to the bottom. Seven crewmen had boarded one rowboat, while the captain and four others set off in another. As the two boats made their way toward the Connecticut coast, they became separated by a few hundred yards. At that point, the captain's boat was swamped, and it disappeared below the surface. The seven in the other boat searched for survivors, but, after finding themselves also on the verge of sinking, they turned again north. Bailing continuously, the crew rowed for nearly four hours, making some progress only to lose most of their gains to the fury of the sea. As they neared Seaside Park, their boat struck a rock and broke up.

From the lighthouse, Keeper William Harwick spotted the seven battling their way to shore. Realizing that they were in trouble, the keeper launched his boat and reached the rocks just in time to rescue them. For his efforts, Keeper Harwick received a Letter of Commendation from Secretary of Commerce Herbert Hoover.

After Capt. LaCompte's lifeboat had capsized, he and his mate managed to climb aboard a raft that had broken loose from the *Calvin Tompkins*. There they clung for twenty hours until picked up by the tug *John Gaynor*. Though near death from exposure, both men survived; the other two crewmen were lost.

In 1953, the Coast Guard announced plans to replace the familiar landmark with a skeleton tower. Because of its poor condition and the high cost of tearing it down, the service decided to burn it. Its fate, however, was temporarily postponed when it was instead sold to the Fairfield Dock Company. The company's owner, a man named Burroughs, had a special affection for the lighthouse; he planned to use jacks to move it off its foundation, and float it to city park land. Unfortunately, local officials refused him permission and, unable to find any other site for the old beacon, he was forced to have it dismantled. While the workmen were in the process of tearing it down, sparks from a bonfire set to burn unsalveageable wood ignited the entire structure. Within an hour, the Bridgeport Harbor Light had been reduced to ashes.

BRIDGEPORT BREAKWATER LIGHT
(Bug Light, Tongue Point Light)

Bridgeport's inner breakwater was erected in 1891 to provide safe anchorage and protection for harbor facilities, but at night the unlit structure presented a dangerous obstruction. In January of 1894, a lantern light was erected to mark the breakwater, and it was replaced in the following year with a thirty-one-foot tall, cast-iron lighthouse. Nicknamed Bug Light, the beacon stood about 500 feet offshore, at the end of the breakwater. There were no accommodations for a keeper at the lighthouse.

At the time of its establishment, Stephen A. McNeil, who was keeper of the Harbor Light, was made also responsible for the care of the new lighthouse. For a few years, the keeper did manage to maintain both lights and their fog signals, but, as he advanced in age, he found himself no longer able to do so. He hired a laborer, paid him out of his own wages, and placed him in charge of the Harbor Light. He then moved to his home in Bridgeport and continued keeping the light at the breakwater.

In June of 1901, an inspection of the Harbor Light revealed that it was "badly cared for." McNeil had hired the assistant without obtaining the approval of the Light House Board, an action that could have resulted in his dismissal. Recognizing his years of faithful service, however, the inspector recommended that no

Bridgeport Breakwater (Tongue Point) Lighthouse, 1988

charges be brought against him and that he be made solely responsible for the Breakwater Light. Keeper McNeil was appointed to the
post later that month, and Ole Andersen was made keeper of the
Harbor Light.

In 1902, McNeil built himself a shack next to the tiny lighthouse
which allowed him to start the fog signal at a moment's notice. The
keeper continued to tend the light, as he had done for twenty-eight
years, until his death in December of 1904. His widow, Flora,
assumed his duties and was later appointed to the post; she was
Bridgeport's only female keeper.

The inner breakwater proved to be effective in protecting the
harbor, but tugboats entering with barges in tow encountered a
great deal of difficulty in negotiating the sharp turn around its end.
Thus, in 1920, the lighthouse was moved shoreward a distance of
275 feet, the outer part of the breakwall was dismantled, and the
channel was widened and dug to a depth of 18 feet. When the Coast
Guard proposed removing the tower in 1967, the Bug Light found a
vocal constituency among area boat owners and yacht clubs. Their
protest saved the tiny beacon, and it has continued to operate. Listed
as Tongue Point Light, the automated lighthouse displays a flashing
green light, every four seconds.

> *The Bug Light, stands at the southeast end of the United
> Illuminating Company's property. It can be approached by water,
> or seen from a distance at the eastern end of Sound View Drive,
> Seaside Park in Bridgeport. NOAA chart #12369*

FAIRWEATHER ISLAND LIGHT (CT)
(Fayerweather, Black Rock Light)

Appropriation: February 10, 1807 $5,000
Appropriation: April 30, 1822 $3,000
Established: 1809
First keeper: John Maltbee, appointed October 14, 1808
Rebuilt: 1823
Illuminating apparatus (IA):(1838) 8 lamps, 14" parabolic reflectors, fixed white light (FW)
Refitted: 1854, fifth-order Fresnel lens, FW
Refitted: 1899, fifth-order lamps
IA: (1924) fifth-order Fresnel lens, FW, 350 cp.
Fog signal: none
Height of tower, base to top of lantern: (1809) 47 feet (wooden)
Height of light above sea level: (1891) 43 feet
Discontinued: March 3, 1933

T he storm came out of the east on September 3, 1821, sending wave after wave cascading across the low-lying island. A four-foot-deep stone foundation had been laid to support the oak and pine tower, but it could not stand up to the sea. In an avalanche of water, the wooden structure gave way, and its parts were carried away in the grasp of the raging torrents.

Erected in 1808, Fairweather Island's octagonal tower was twenty-four feet in diameter at its base and tapered to nine feet at the bottom of the lantern; it rose forty feet to the bottom of the lantern. The keeper's dwelling, a one and a half-story wooden structure, had a kitchen, living room, and one bedroom. It stood about 700 feet from the tower, across a tidal marsh, which was generally awash during spring tides and storms.

When the lighthouse was rebuilt in 1823, the contractor wrote of his work in a local newspaper, stating that the structure was "prepared to withstand the storm of ages, and reflects no little credit on the faithfulness and skill of its enterprising builders." Edmund Blunt, publisher of the *American Coast Pilot,* was not impressed: "A more contemptible Lighthouse does not disgrace Long Island Sound, most shamefully erected and badly kept." The new tower had been erected using freestone on its exterior, laid in courses, but it was filled in with small rubble stone, and timbers. "These pieces of timber," wrote Lt. Bache in 1838, "are about eight inches square, and average four feet in length; they are inserted horizontally in the masonry, in lieu of stone, at a distance of four feet or less apart, and

Fairweather Island Lighthouse, 1986

are now in a state of decay." Some repairs were made to the tower and dwelling, and, over the next forty-two years, proposals were made to rebuild them. It was not until 1880, however, that the keeper's dwelling was rebuilt and the tower was refurbished.

The lamps in the original tower were suspended from chains that dropped from the roof of the lantern. In 1823, Stratford Point, which had recently installed a revolving lighting apparatus, transferred its old device to Fairweather Island. Seven years later, the island lighting system was updated to eight lamps and parabolic reflectors, but, despite the improvement, its light was barely visible when the weather was the least hazy. In 1855, Fairweather was furnished with a fifth-order Fresnel lens but the station was never equipped with a fog signal.

John Maltbie of Fairfield was appointed first keeper in October of 1808. The station's third keeper, Stephen Moore, assumed the post on November 3, 1817. Over the years, he and perhaps his predecessor, Isaac Judson, expanded the original dwelling to eleven rooms. Apparently the two were better keepers than carpenters. An 1838 inspection of the station indicated that the building leaked badly where new sections were connected to the old structure.

Kate Moore, the keeper's daughter, began assisting in trimming the wicks at age twelve. She gradually assumed all of the lighthouse duties as the elder Moore's health began to fail. Never married, Kate was appointed keeper when her father passed away on December 13, 1871. She remained at the station for seven more years, resigning her post at the age of eighty-four.

In an interview with a *New York World* reporter, Kate related that she had saved the lives of up to twenty-one persons while at Fairweather Island. Describing the care for the station's lamps, she recounted: "It was a miserable one to keep going, too; nothing like those in use nowadays. It consisted of eight oil lamps which took four gallons of oil each night, and if they were not replenished at stated intervals all through the night, they went out. During very windy nights it was impossible to keep them burning at all, and I had to stay there all night."

Away from the lighthouse duties, Kate Moore stayed busy by keeping a small flock of sheep, two cows, chickens, and a garden. In her "spare time," she carved wood duck decoys, for which she never seemed to lack customers.

Fairweather had a second female keeper, Mary Elizabeth Clark. She assumed the position following her husband's death on March 14, 1906. Two months later, John D. Davis succeeded Mrs. Clark and remained at the station until it was discontinued.

The new keeper, a native of Ireland, had served in the Irish Light Department prior to joining the U.S. Lighthouse Board. Life for Keeper Davis was much more tranquil at the island station than it apparently had been for Kate Moore. For him, there were no rescues from shipwrecks. Rather, he occupied himself with lighthouse tasks and raising a family. For his faithful service, Keeper Davis received the Light House Efficiency Star.

Noting that Fairweather Island Light was at a considerable distance from the channel, the Light House Service, in 1931, proposed the establishment of two acetylene lights offshore of the island. The lighthouse was officially discontinued on March 3, 1933, and shortly thereafter, the Department of Commerce granted the city of Bridgeport a revocable license to occupy the lighthouse reservation for use as a public park.

> *Fairweather Island Light can be reached from the western end of Barnum Boulevard at Seaside Park Bridgeport, CT.*
> *NOAA chart #12363, 12369*

PENFIELD REEF LIGHT (CT)

Appropriation:	July 15, 1870	$30,000
Appropriation:	March 3, 1871	$25,000
Established:	1874	
First lighted:	January 16, 1874	
First keeper:	George Tomlinson, appointed January 5, 1874	

Illuminating apparatus (IA): 1874, fourth-order Fresnel lens, flashing red light (Fl R), every 5 seconds.

IA:	(1932) fourth-order Fresnel lens, Fl R, 5 seconds, incandescent oil vapor, 4,300 cp.
IA:	DCB-24, 1000 watt lamp, Fl R every 6 seconds
Fog signal:	1874, fog bell struck by machine, double blow every 20 seconds.
Fog signal:	(1924) second-class reed horn, blast 3 seconds, interval 17 seconds.

Height of light above sea level: 1874, 54 feet

Automated:	September 4, 1971

T he assistant keeper watched as Head Keeper Frederick A. Jordan swung away from the dock in choppy seas and began rowing his dory toward the mainland. It was December 22, 1916, and Jordan planned to spend Christmas with his family. What happened next was recorded in the station's log by assistant keeper Rudolph Iten.

> *Keeper left station at 12:20 pm and when about 150 yards NW of the light, his boat capsized, but he managed to cling to the overturned boat. He motioned to me to lower the sailboat but on account of the heavy seas running from the NE, it was impossible to launch the boat alone. At 1:00 pm, the wind died down a bit and shifted to the south. I then lowered the boat safely and started off after the keeper who had by this time drifted about one and a half miles to the SW. When about a one half miles from the light, the wind shifted to SW making a headwind and an outgoing tide which proved too much for me to pull with the heavy boat. I had to give up and returned to the station with the wind now blowing a gale from the WSW. Sent distress signals to several ships but none answered. Lost tract of the keeper at 3:00 pm. He is probably lost.*   R. J. Iten, asst. keeper.

Jordan is often said to have returned on several occasions to haunt the station. One evening, Head Keeper Iten (perhaps out of a

Penfield Reef Lighthouse, 1988

sense of guilt) felt a chill as an unearthly figure emerged from the room once occupied by the drowned keeper. Stopping for a moment at the top of the stairs, the specter melted into the darkness below. Gathering his wits, the keeper went to investigate and found that the logbook had been taken off the shelf; it was opened to the very page that described Jordan's accident! Years later, following the light station's automation, the beacon began to operate erratically. Whenever someone went out to investigate, the light was found to be in good working order. A Coast Guard spokesman placed the blame on "atmospheric conditions," but old-timers blamed it to the mischievous spirit of Fred Jordan.

After the unfortunate keeper had succumbed to the cold waters, his boat, marked *US LHS #231*, drifted in an easterly direction and was beached at Mattituck, NY. Frank Blasick of Mattituck found the boat three days after Christmas, loaded it up on his wagon, and stowed it in his backyard. Boasting of his find to friends, he planned to use it for fishing in the spring, but someone notified the authorities. The much chagrined Blasick then tried to claim salvage, but the boat was reclaimed and returned to Penfield Reef.

The Light House Service was slow to equip light stations with two-way radios, and their need was most apparent in times of crisis. On the morning of October 19, 1930, four fishermen set out from Fairfield, CT, despite strong winds and four-foot waves. Two miles offshore, their sixteen-foot boat capsized, sending the occupants into the cold water. One of the men began swimming to shore while the others clung to the overturned boat. Assistant Keeper E. T. Pastorini spotted the three, rescued them, and brought them to the lighthouse, where they remained for the night. When their companion made it to shore, he alerted the authorities, who set out to search for the trio but found only the abandoned boat. Having no means of communicating with the mainland, the keeper was unable to make the rescue known. Until the next day, the distraught families were left to assume that their loved ones had surely perished.

Established, 1874

Penfield Reef Light's first keeper, George Tomlinson, was appointed to the post on January 5, 1874, eleven days before the station became operational. The station's history includes two women who were appointed assistant keepers, Pauline Jones and June Martin; their husbands were the head keepers.

Standing on a riprap foundation, 108 feet in diameter at its base, the Penfield Reef's wooden tower rose to 54 feet above sea level. The lantern was equipped with a fourth-order Fresnel lens, which displayed a flashing red light; the station's fog bell was operated by machine. The granite, two-story dwelling had a kitchen, sitting room, and oil room on the first floor, and four bedrooms on the second; a wooden stairway connected the floors. The clockwork's weight hung on a rope through the floor and stairwell of the second floor; it had to be rewound every four hours.

In 1969, the Coast Guard announced its intentions to tear down the granite structure and replace it with a pipe tower. Local citizens came to Penfield's rescue, and, with the help of then Congressman Lowell P. Weicker and State Representative Stewart McKinney, the lighthouse was saved. The beacon was automated on December 3, 1971.

> *Penfield Reef Light is a favorite site for local fisher-*
> *men and scuba divers. Standing over two miles offshore,*
> *it is accessible only by boat.*
> *NOAA chart #12368*

Norwalk Island Lights (CT)

PECK('s) LEDGE LIGHT

Appropriation:	*March 3, 1901 $10,000*
Total cost:	*approximately $40,000*
Established:	*1906*
Site:	*7 feet of water, 600 feet NE of Peck Ledge Rock*
Contractor:	*Daniel F. Toomey*
First lighted:	*July 10, 1906*
First keeper:	*George W. Bardwell, appointed July 15, 1906*
Illuminating apparatus (IA): 1906, fourth-order Fresnel lens,	
	flashing white (Fl W), every 10 seconds.
IA:	*(1932) fourth-order Fresnel lens, group Fl W, 30 seconds,*
	incandescent oil vapor, 37,000 cp.
IA:	*(1939) 375 mm lens, flashing green (FL G),*
	2.5 seconds, acetylene, 210 cp.
IA:	*(1988) 250 mm lens. Fl W every 4 seconds*
Fog signal:	*July 17, 1906, compressed air siren, blast 2 seconds,*
	interval 6 seconds.
Fog signal:	*removed when automated*
Height of light above sea level: 1906, 54 feet	
Automated:	*1933*

T he steam canalier *J. C. Austin* was battling heavy seas in Long Island Sound on December 5, 1921, when, just south of Greens Ledge Light, the vessel sprang a leak. The ship's pumps could not keep up with the rising water; a pipe from its boiler burst, and the *Austin's* fate was sealed. The four crewmen took to a lifeboat, but, lacking oars they began drifting helplessly in an easterly direction.

At Peck Ledge Light, Keeper Charles J. Kenny was looking out toward the southwest when he spotted the hapless sailors. The keeper and his assistant launched the station's small boat, and, fighting waves of up to five feet, they reached the lifeboat. The four were taken to the lighthouse, where they were given first aid, food, dry clothes, and shelter for the night. On the following morning a distress signal was displayed from the lighthouse, and at least two vessels passed nearby, but either they did not see the signal or they simply ignored it. Finally, in late morning, an oyster boat responded and picked up the *Austin's* crew.

Established, 1906

A lighthouse was first proposed for Peck Ledge in 1896, along with a light for Greens Ledge and a list of other harbor beacons. By 1902, the harbor beacons and Greens Ledge Light were operational but it was another three years before construction of Peck Ledge was begun. Not all of Norwalk's citizens were in favor of a lighthouse on the site. Victor Ferris, manager of the *Norwalk Hour*, a local newspaper, sent a letter to the Light House Board, echoing the feelings of many others. He argued that mariners would be better served if the lighthouse was established at George's Rock, located at the southeast end of the reef that extended from Cockenoe Island. From there, he stated, the beacon would serve vessels plying the sound, warn of the reef, and help point the way to Norwalk Harbor. His arguments fell on deaf ears. On July 10, 1906, Keeper George W. Bardwell lit Peck Ledge Light for the first time as crowds of onlookers watched from a nearby beach.

A fire broke out at Peck Ledge on February 17, 1913, almost destroying the lighthouse. Intending to tar some lobster trap funnels, Keeper Conrad Hawk placed a tub of tar on a piece of newspaper near the kitchen stove. At some point, he noticed that the post lantern at Grassy Hammock was not functioning properly, and he set out for it in a rowboat. He made the necessary adjustments, and, as he began the return trip, to his horror he saw smoke billowing from the lighthouse windows. The keeper first tried to smother the tar fire with a blanket, but he was driven off by the intense heat. Using a clam rake, he dragged the tub across the floor and out of the door and pushed it into the water. He then climbed up the boat davit to the porch roof. From there, the energetic keeper entered the bedroom and retrieved a quilt, which he placed over the kitchen's east window to slow the draft. Drawing seawater with a rope and pail, Hawk finally succeeded in extinguishing the remaining flames.

Though the superintendent of lighthouses reprimanded Keeper Hawk for having caused the fire, he also commended him for his extraordinary courage and determination in fighting the blaze.

Reminded of the many times that the keepers at Peck Ledge rendered assistance to sailors, the citizens of Norwalk voiced protest in 1933 when it was announced that the station's personnel were to be removed in favor of automation; "progress," however, won out.

The conical tower continues to operate but against the bright lights of Norwalk's Calf Pasture Beach, its flashing light is often barely discernable.

Standing offshore to the east of Calf Pasture Beach, Peck Ledge Light can easily be seen from any point along the beach.
NOAA chart #12363, 12368

NORWALK (Sheffield) ISLAND LIGHT

Appropriation: *May 18, 1826*   *$4,000*
Appropriation: *March 2, 1867*   *$12,000*
Established: *1828*
First keeper: *Gershom B. Smith, appointed June 4, 1827*
Illuminating apparatus (IA):(1838) 10 lamps, 14" parabolic reflectors,
                 revolving light (Rv).
IA: *(1848) 10 lamps, 14" reflectors, Rv -red shades on one side.*
Refitted: *1855, 6 Argand lamps, 21" reflectors, new clockwork machinery.*
Refitted: *1857, fourth-order Fresnel lens (4-order), fixed white light varied by*
red flashes (FW v R Fl).
Rebuilt: *1869*
IA: *(1883), 4-order, FW v R Fl, every minute*
Fog signal: *none*
Height of light above sea level: (1842) 40 feet. (1891) 52 feet
Discontinued: *February 15, 1902*

I n June of 1826, the Treasury Department, then in charge of lighthouses, dispatched two of its personnel to survey Routon Neck and the west end of Sheffield Island as possible sites for a Norwalk Harbor light. The men were also instructed to ascertain the expense of erecting beacons at Shipman's Reef off Stamford, Smith's Ledge off Darien, and a reef "known by the name of Patrick's Horse, at the western extremity of Norwalk Harbor."

Routon (Roton Point) Neck stood isolated at the end of a mile-wide tidal marsh, and it was too far from the channel to be a good site; the western end of Sheffield, situated near the harbor's entrance, proved to be the best choice. By June of the following year, a thirty-foot-high stone tower had been erected on the island, and Gershom Smith, selected from a list of eight applicants, was appointed keeper. Earlier that year, the government had entered into negotiations with Norwalk to purchase Patrick's Horse (Patrick's Reef). In a deed signed by four Norwalk selectmen, the 165-foot-long reef was transferred to the United States Government for a sum of $1. One hundred and twenty-seven years later, the General Services Administration declared Patrick's Horse surplus property and attempted to sell it. The agency sent inquiries to local historians and searched through the National Archives, but it was to no avail. Area charts and records of the time failed in both pinpointing the site and identifying the type of beacon that might have stood there.

Peck Ledge Lighthouse, 1988

Norwalk Island (Sheffield Island) Lighthouse, 1987

Gershom Smith, who owned Sheffield Island, sold three acres to the government for the purpose of erecting the lighthouse. After assuming the position of keeper, he built a barn and corn storage shed near the light tower, and, when not occupied with his station duties, he raised farm animals, grew crops, and collected oysters. For the most part, the keeper seemed to have maintained the station satisfactorily, but in the last of his eighteen years, he had apparently let things go. When Lewis Whitlock arrived at the Norwalk Island Light in January of 1845, the new keeper was dismayed by the condition of the lighthouse's equipment. In lengthy letters to the superintendent of lighthouses, Whitlock complained that the station's boat had no sail or rigging and that the tower's clockwork mechanism was "good for nothing."

The light shown from the tower was generated by ten lamps and parabolic reflectors, which were arranged on two separate tables, having five lamps each. Operating like a grandfather clock, a weight attached to a rope turned the tables a half rotation every two and three-quarter minutes. With panes of red-colored glass placed in front of each lamp on one table, the tower exhibited alternating white and red lights. In 1857, the tower was refitted with a fourth-order Fresnel lens, which was later used in the new structure.

Congress appropriated funds for the construction of a new lighthouse at Sheffield on March 2, 1867. Completed in 1868, the structure resembled five other area lighthouses built within a three-year period (see Block Island North). The tower rose from the front of the keeper's dwelling, and it was accessible from the second floor hallway. The original one-story keeper's dwelling, built of stone, was then used as a stable, pigpen, and henhouse. By the time the light station was discontinued in 1902, the floor of the old facility had rotted away, and "its condition was precisely as would be expected for the use to which it had been put."

Unlike nearby Chimon Island, Sheffield had no source of fresh water. Rainwater, collected in a cistern, was drawn by hand pump into the kitchen. In August of 1901, the station's water supply became contaminated by the privy, and Keeper Samuel Armour fell victim to typhoid fever. Unable to continue with his duties, his wife took over the care of the light. As the keeper's illness continued into its third month, the Light House Establishment hired a laborer as temporary assistant. Armour did make a full recovery, and, when the lighthouse was deactivated on February 15, 1902, he was transferred to the New Haven Outer Breakwall Light.

For a time, the abandoned light was used as a shore station by William deLuce and Henry Beurdet, keepers of Greens Ledge Light. At some point, Emma Lassen, laborer-in-charge of the Grassy Hammock post-lamp, was appointed custodian of the island station.

In her new position, she received $15 per month in addition to $5 per month salary for maintaining the lamp. In 1911, however, the Light House Service found her pay excessive in comparison to similarly held positions at other stations. Her salary as custodian was thus reduced to $1 per annum, and the responsibility of keeping the Grassy Hammock beacon was turned over to the keepers of Peck Ledge. Shortly thereafter, Emma Lassen left Sheffield, and she was replaced by Ole Olson, who remained there until the station was sold.

On February 11, 1914, the Light House Service, having found that the light station on Sheffield was no longer of value to the government, put it up for sale. Five sealed bids were received, and Thorsten O. Stabell of South Norwalk, whose offer was $2000 greater than the next highest bid, was awarded the property. Used as a summer residence, the lighthouse remained in the Stabell family until December of 1986, when it was purchased by the Norwalk Seaport Association for $700,000. After completing its restoration, the not-for-profit group intends to use the lighthouse for educational programs.

The lighthouse may be visited by contacting the Norwalk Seaport Association, Norwalk, CT.   *NOAA chart #12368, 12363*

GREENS LEDGE LIGHT

Appropriation:	March 3, 1899	*$60,000*
Established:	1902	
First lighted:	February 15, 1902	
First keeper:	William H. deLuce, appointed February 15, 1902	

Illuminating apparatus (IA): 1902, fifth-order Fresnel lens, flashing red every 15 seconds.

Refitted:	May, 1902, fourth-order Fresnel lens (4-order), fixed white light varied by red flashes (FW v Fl R) every 15 seconds.
IA:	(1932) 4-order, FW v Fl R, incandescent oil vapor, W 2,900 cp, R 7,200 cp.
IA:	(1987) FA 251 lens, 150 watt lamp, alternating white and red flashes.
Fog signal:	1907, third-class Daboll trumpet, blast 3 seconds, interval alternating 2 and 32 seconds.
Fog signal:	(1932) second-class reed horn.

Height of light above sea level: (1907) 62 feet

A ny weekend sailor who has run aground on the shoal between the west end of Sheffield Island and Greens Ledge understands why a lighthouse was established there. In 1889, nearly 100,000 tons of coal and an even greater amount of general merchandise passed through Sheffield Harbor. The New

England Terminal Railroad had already begun to transport railroad cars on the decks of car-floats and transfer steamers from Wilson Point. With an anticipated doubling of harbor tonnage, the Light House Board recommended erecting a lighthouse to replace the buoy marking the "4-foot spot" off Noroton Point. Equipped with a light and fog bell, the structure was to have been an iron caisson filled with concrete and surmounted by a wooden tower.

More pressing commitments prevented Congress from appropriating the necessary funds, but in 1896 a new proposal was put forward for lighthouses at Greens Ledge and Peck Ledge and for five post lanterns to mark the harbor's channel. Construction of Greens Ledge began about four years later, and, on February 15, 1902, a light was shown for the first time. The tower was fitted with a fifth-order Fresnel lens which was replaced with a more powerful fourth-order Fresenl lens just a few months later.

William deLuce, appointed Greens Ledge's first keeper, remained at the station for six years before being transferred to Fort Wadsworth, Staten Island. The harbor's post lanterns, completed six months before the lighthouse, were tended by Francis and Emma Lassen. A later keeper of these beacons, R. G. Hendrick, became a local hero when he pulled two men from the freezing waters in April of 1922. For his efforts, he received a commendation from Herbert Hoover.

William Rhodes, Greens Ledge's keeper, and his assistant, Frank Thompson, were also involved in a number of daring rescues, but, on February 15, 1917, the assistant was himself subject of a desperate search. Having gone to South Norwalk for supplies by rowboat, the assistant keeper began his return journey at about 1:00 pm. Forced to row around ice floes, Thompson found himself only halfway to the lighthouse as darkness fell. Groping in the waning light, he became trapped in a large ice field. As the assistant began drifting with the tide toward the open sound, he huddled at the bottom of the small boat and desperately tried to find relief from the biting cold.

Charles Mills, a resident of South Norwalk, had watched from the shoreline as the unlit boat became trapped in ice. He made some frantic calls to the Light House Service and local port authorities, but by then the harbor had become totally ice bound, and no boat could get out. The service contacted the Bridgeport Towing Company, and they consented to send a tug to look for the lost keeper, though only after a fee of $50 had been agreed upon. The tug did finally locate the Thompson at 10:30 pm, and the cold, hungry, but happy-to-be-alive keeper was returned to Greens Ledge.

Over the years, the sixty-two-foot conical tower settled and developed a slight tilt. After the Coast Guard took over the responsibility

Greens Ledge Lighthouse under construction, August 1901,
National Archives, 26-LG-12-12A

Greens Ledge Lighthouse, 1988

for keeping the light, the station's personnel began complaining that the dynamos were producing so much vibration that the furniture gradually walked across the room to the lowest point. From that time on, the guardsmen simply kept the furniture to that side of the room.

As part of a Coast Guard economy measure, the station's light and fog signal were automated in the 1960s.

Greens Ledge Light is surrounded by large riprap boulders that are a haven for lobster and blackfish. The site, which is a favorite for fishermen and scuba divers, is accessible only by boat. NOAA chart #12368

EATONS NECK LIGHT (NY)

Appropriation: March 14, 1798 $13,250
Established: 1799
Contractor: John McComb, Jr
Purchased land from: John and Johanna Gardiner, $500
First keeper: John Squire, appointed December 11, 1798
Illuminating apparatus (IA): (1838) 12 lamps, 13" reflectors, fixed white light (FW)
IA: (1842) 12 lamps, 9" reflectors, FW
IA: (1850) 13 lamps, 15" reflectors, FW
Refitted: 1858, third-order Fresnel lens, FW
Illuminant: 1907, change from 2-wick oil to incandescent oil vapor. Power increase from 1,782 cp to 22,720 cp.
IA: (1988) third-order Fresnel lens, FW, 1000 watt lamp, 150,000 cp.
Fog signal: 1868, steam siren
Fog signal: (1873) second-class steam fog siren, 12 hp steam-engine, blasts 9 seconds, interval 35 seconds.
Fog signal: (1907) first-class automatic compressed air siren
Height of light above sea level: (1891) 147 feet

"T his light house stands on an eminence, about 73 feet high," wrote Edmund and George Blunt in their 1800 edition of *American Coast Pilot,* "the height of the walls is 50 feet more." Describing the tower, they wrote, "it is a single light, and is painted black and white in stripes from the top to the bottom."

Long Island Sound's second lighthouse was established at Eatons Neck; it served as a guide to mariners plying the sound and directed those entering Huntington Harbor. Sailors approaching the light were warned of a shoal off the point. Countless mishaps occurred on those very shallows, which reached out northward and eastward for three-quarters of a mile.

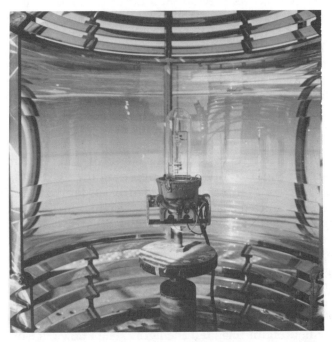

Inside of Fresnel lens, Eatons Neck Lighthouse, 1986

Eatons Neck Lighthouse, 1988

The lighthouse was erected on land purchased from John Gardiner, and the station's contractor was John J. McComb, the same individual who had constructed the lighthouse at Montauk Point. Eatons Neck's tower was built of freestone and laid in courses, with a wood spiral stairway leading to the lantern. On December 6, 1798, John Squire was notified that he had been appointed keeper, but he immediately declined the position. A week later, Thomas Burgher, a resident of New York City, accepted the post; the lighthouse became operational shortly thereafter.

In 1837, Eatons Neck Light was inspected by Lieutenant Blake, who was, at the time, surveying Long Island Sound. The Army officer had heard frequent complaints concerning the light and, when he entered the tower's lantern, he found all of the lamps to be defective. "The keeper admitted that the lights were bad, and he was censured for keeping a bad light." In a November 30, 1837, letter that was critical of the Light House Establishment, the Blunts described how the keeper had referred the matter of the defective lamps to Fifth Auditor Stephen Pleasonton, but Pleasonton apparently had done nothing. When Lt. Blake arrived at the Fifth Auditor's office, he informed him of the situation, and Pleasonton said that he would "immediately take steps to redress the evils complained of." A year later, the lieutenant revisited the light. "The knowledge of this light being so defective was so clearly brought to the notice of the superintendent," the Blunts complained, "[but] the light still remains unaltered, and Lieutenant Blake, in visiting it the last summer, a year after his notice, found everything as formerly. Most, if not all, the lamps of this house should have been condemned many years since; the light, for the most part, cannot be seen more than 7 or 8 miles." In a lengthy point-by-point letter, Pleasonton retorted that he did not recollect a visit from Lt. Blake concerning Eatons Neck and that he had never received any form of communications from the keeper. Over the next few years, there were many more complaints of bad management by Pleasonton.

In 1838, the tower was refitted with twelve lamps and reflectors arranged around two circular tables; the light was visible at a maximum distance of seventeen and a half miles. Twenty years later, part of the tower's stonework was torn down, and it was then rebuilt to receive a new lantern and a third-order lens. In 1868, along with a host of other improvements, the tower's wooden stairs were replaced with iron steps and landings, and the walls were lined with bricks. The keeper's dwelling, which was apparently a one and a half-story structure, was partially torn down and expanded. Extensive repairs and further expansion were made around 1880 to accommodate three keepers. Upon completion of the renovations, the residence consisted of a kitchen, a pantry, two storerooms, three sitting rooms, and five bedrooms. It was connected to the tower via a brick gallery, and a privy stood behind them. The station's other structures consisted of a shop, a barn, a coal bin, and a fog signal building.

On January 26, 1926, the barge *Planet*, with one crewman aboard, parted its towline and began drifting toward shore. At the time, the Coast Guard had only one man stationed at Eatons Neck, and, when he spotted the drifting barge, he called for a tug and notified Assistant Keeper Ole Anderson. While the guardsman was busy on the phone trying to get more help, the assistant set out by himself in rough seas. Anderson managed to reach the barge which by then was up against the rock reef. He rescued the crewman, and, somehow avoiding the rocks himself, he rowed to the safety of a nearby beach.

On the same day, another barge, *Murray Valley*, broke loose from its tug and began drifting helplessly. Head Keeper Arthur Jensen left in his own rowboat and was able to move the stranded crewman off the barge; both keepers received a letter of commendation for their efforts.

The Life Saving Benevolent Association of New York, whose purpose was to save lives from shipwrecked vessels, was chartered by the legislature on March 29, 1849. Funded by private donations and the federal government, the association had, by 1857, two stations on Long Island Sound: one was located at Eatons Neck, the other at Sands Point. On September 16, 1875, the Coast Guard received authorization to occupy a small portion of the Eatons Neck property for the establishment of its own lifesaving station. In 1936, the guardsmen took over a larger section, and erected a frame building southwest of the lighthouse and a boathouse at the water's edge. During that time, the Coast Guard covered the entire length of Long Island Sound, from Hells Gate to Plum Gut, from the one station. Three years later, as part of the reorganization of the Light House Service, the guardsmen took over the whole ten-acre lighthouse reservation and the responsibility for all aids to navigation.

In 1973, Eatons Neck Light was entered in the National Register of Historical Places, making it eligible for federal funds for its maintenance. Still using the third-order classical Fresnel lens, installed in 1858, Eatons Neck continues to show a flashing white light. Its foghorn is sounded every thirty seconds, for a three-second period.

Access to the lighthouse at Eatons Neck, is by permission only. Those wishing to visit the white tower should contact the station's Coast Guard duty officer.
NOAA chart #12363

LLOYD HARBOR LIGHT —
HUNTINGTON HARBOR LIGHT

Appropriation: August 3, 1854 $4,000 (first site)
Appropriation: March 4, 1907 $40,000, expended $32,551.41
Established: 1857
Purchased land from: Samuel Donton, July 24, 1855, $250
First keeper: John S. Wood, appointed June 4, 1857
                     A. Johnson, appointed August 11, 1857
Illuminating apparatus (IA): 1857, fifth-order Fresnel lens (5-order), fixed white light (FW).
IA: (1883) 5-order, fixed red light (FR).
Rebuilt: June 16, 1912
IA: 1912, 5-order, FR
IA: (1987) 300 mm lens, 3.05 amp lamp, isophase (iso)
                     equal dark and light period every 6 seconds.
Fog signal: 1857-1912 none
Fog signal: 1912, 1,000 fog bell, no. 4 striker
Fog signal: (1986) horn, 1 blast every 15 seconds
Height of light above sea level: (1857) 48 feet. (1912) 42 feet
Automated: 1949

D uring the early 1800s, Huntington Harbor often served as protective anchorage for vessels plying Long Island Sound. With onshore winds, however, the harbor offered only limited refuge, sending ships to seek safety at nearby Lloyd Harbor. In 1838, as many as seventy sailing vessels could be seen there, lying at anchor. During that year, Lt. George M. Bache recommended the establishment of a lighthouse for Lloyd's Harbor. His views were echoed by Capt. H. Paulding, USN, after he had inspected the site in 1853: "Lloyd's Harbor, on Long Island sound, is the only refuge in stormy weather, for many miles, for the numerous coasting and other vessels that navigate the sound in all seasons. The light on Eaton's neck guides them into the bay of Huntington; but the approach to Lloyd's harbor, where alone they can find a safe anchorage, is dangerous." Vessels entering Lloyd Harbor had to avoid a sand spit that reached out into the channel and rock reefs that lay on the opposite side. The approach was difficult at the best of times; at night or in low visibility, the obstructions made it nearly impossible. Capt. Paulding strongly recommended a beacon or some other conspicuous landmark for the site.

On August 3, 1854, Congress appropriated $4,000 for the establishment of a lighthouse at Lloyd Harbor; construction began two years later.

Lloyd Harbor Lighthouse, September, 1935 . National Archives, 26-LG-12-62

Remnants of original Lloyd Harbor Lighthouse, 1987

The light station consisted of a white, square brick tower and an attached frame keeper's dwelling. The tower, which was located on the northeast side of the residence, rose to forty-eight feet above sea level. The first floor had a kitchen, dining room, and sitting room, and the second floor had three bedrooms. Access to the tower was from the second floor; wooden stairs led to the lantern.

The station, which began operating in 1857, showed a fifth-order, fixed white light. A survey of the property in 1895 revealed three jetties protecting the site. A barn was located southwest of the dwelling, and a privy stood to the northwest.

In January of 1905, Representative Scudder presented a petition, signed by Huntington residents, asking for the establishment of a lighthouse at the entrance of Huntington and Lloyd Harbors. Approved in March of 1907, the new structure, it was felt would "serve every purpose now served by Lloyd's Harbor light." With its construction, the old facility was discontinued.

The new structure was located in six feet of water, one-third of a mile from the original lighthouse. A reinforced concrete crib, twenty by thirty feet in diameter, and sixteen feet in height, was constructed on shore, towed out to the site, and sunk into position. A concrete pier was then built on top of the crib, followed by the erection of a one-story concrete dwelling and tower. The quarters had a kitchen, sitting room, and one bedroom, and the cellar housed a 2,000-gallon cistern, an oil room, and a coal room. Water was drawn from the cistern by means of a pump in the kitchen. The residence was regarded as appropriate for a keeper and wife only or for a keeper without a family.

The station's tower rose from the front of the structure to a height of forty-two feet above sea level. Its illuminating apparatus consisted of a fourth-order Fresnel lens, with a single-wick mineral oil lamp; a ruby chimney produced the station's fixed red light. The station was also equipped with a clockwork-operated, 1000-pound fog bell, which had to be rewound every three and a half hours.

Lloyd Harbor Light's first keeper, John S. Wood, took over the post in 1857 but remained for only two months. He was succeeded by six more keepers until the station was discontinued on June 16, 1912. Robert McGlone had kept the light for nearly twenty-four years, when the new station became operational. After his wife's death in 1900, the keeper hired Agnes Harrington to help raise his five children and keep up his home. When Keeper McGlone was transferred to the new lighthouse in 1912, Harrington remained on at the old facility in the capacity of caretaker. Living alone after the last of the McGlone children had moved away, she rowed her boat to the mainland to get her mail and supplies several times a week. In the winter, when the water was too rough, she walked along the beach

Lloyd (Huntington) Harbor Light, 1986

to get to her mailbox, a distance of about two miles. Owning neither a radio nor a telephone, Harrington resided there for about thirty-five years.

On June 7, 1924, the original lighthouse and its property were deeded to the state of New York, which, four years later, turned them over to the town of Huntington. On November 12, 1947, a fire, thought to have been set by hunters, destroyed the keeper's dwelling and severely damaged the tower. Storms and vandalism finally toppled the structure a few years later, leaving only its foundation and some brickwork.

The Huntington Harbor Light was automated in 1949. In the late 1960s, the Coast Guard announced plans to discontinue the light, but protests reversed its decision. Over the next years, the tower developed a large crack along its north wall. The Coast Guard again considered demolishing the structure, but Save the Huntington Lighthouse, a not-for-profit group, proposed its restoration. In 1986, estimates for refurbishing the lighthouse's exterior were $350,000 and for its interior, $200,000.

Remnants of the original light can be seen standing on the beach, northwest of the Huntington Harbor Light. Both sites can be reached by boat.   *NOAA chart #12363*

STAMFORD HARBOR LIGHT (CT)
(Chatham Ledge Light)

Appropriation:	*June 16, 1880*	*$7,000*
Appropriation:	*March 3, 1881*	*$23,000*
Established:	*1882*	
First lighted:	*February 10, 1882*	
First keeper:	*Neil Martin, appointed January 14, 1882*	

Illuminating apparatus (IA): (1883) fourth-order Fresnel lens (4-order), fixed red light (FR)

IA:	*(1932) 4-order, FR, incandescent oil vapor, 870 cp*
IA:	*(1939) 4-order, FR, electric, 1,600 cp.*
IA:	*(1986) flashing white, 4 seconds. Private aid*
Fog signal:	*1882, fog bell struck by machine every 20 seconds.*
Fog signal:	*(1939) air-diaphragm horn, blast 2 seconds, silent 18 seconds.*

Height of light above sea level: 1882, 60 feet

Stamford Harbor Light's second keeper, Naylor Jones, was determined to retain some of the amenities lost in making a home surrounded by water. His predecessor, Neil Martin, had apparently not been pleased with the post. Ten months after arriving at the station he asked for, and was granted, a transfer to the more spacious Penfield Reef Light.

Keeper Jones moved his furniture and belongings out to the light, built a dock, and erected a chicken coop, but he and his family had barely settled into a normal routine when the lighthouse was struck by a strong northeaster. The dock, chicken coop, and station's boat were all carried out to the open sound. The keeper's family returned to live on shore, and for his remaining four years at the light, Jones commuted by rowboat from his home at Shippan Point.

The original location for the lighthouse was to have been at Forked Rock, but, after a survey of the area, it was decided to build at Chatham Ledge. Fabrication of the conical tower began in 1881 at a Boston foundry. Transported to the ledge, the cast-iron sections were bolted together on site. The completed tower, equipped with fourth-order fixed red light and a foghorn that worked by means of a clockwork mechanism, became operational on February 10, 1882.

Following keeper Naylor Jones, there was a succession of ten keepers over a period of twenty-five years. Cramped quarters and the relative isolation of the station probably accounted for the high turnover of personnel. The long and lonely nights at Chatham Ledge, however, did not seem to be a problem for Keeper Robert M. Fitten;

Stamford Harbor Lighthouse, 1882. National Archives, 26-LG-15-40

Stamford Harbor Lighthouse, 1987

his wife gave birth at the lighthouse on December 9, 1929. Recording the event in the station's log, the keeper wrote, "WOW! A son born, all ok now."

Tragedy was not a stranger at Stamford Light. On August 11, 1931, entries made in the lighthouse log suddenly ceased. Keeper Raymond Bliven had left the light station in mid-afternoon of that day to pick up supplies, and he started back at 10:30 pm. Three days later, at 10:30 pm, a resident of Old Greenwich reported that the station was showing no light. Harbormaster Clarence Muzzio left immediately for the lighthouse, and, finding no one there, he relit the lamp.

The body of the thirty-four year old keeper was found floating a half mile southeast of the light. Autopsy established that he had deep cuts on his forehead and scalp and that death was due to drowning. The keeper had been in good health, and he had not been drinking. The coroner felt that Bliven had run into the rocks with his boat or had somehow slipped on the ladder leading to the lighthouse. The vapor lamp had enough fuel to burn for a little more than two days. Knowing this fact, others believed that the keeper might have had time to refuel the lamp before being confronted by someone, who then pushed him from the lighthouse balcony.

An equally bizarre incident at Stamford Harbor Light occurred after a keeper's daughter, having been recently married, went out to the lighthouse and then refused to rejoin her husband. Persuaded to return to shore to talk things out, the young bride scarcely had time to step out of the boat when her husband shot and killed her.

Marty L. Sowle was retained as the station's civilian keeper after the Coast Guard took over the Light House Service in 1939. During a severe storm in October of that year, the keeper spotted a sinking boat between the lighthouse and shoreline. The two occupants abandoned their boat and began swimming for shore. Keeper Sowle set out in his sixteen-foot boat and rescued one of the men, but, before he was able to reach the other one, the exhausted swimmer sank below the surface. For his heroic efforts, Sowle received a Congressional Silver Medal.

In 1949, the Coast Guard began to consider ceasing operation of the Stamford Harbor Light. The mere suggestion was met by strong protests from area sailors, but they were eventually to no avail. In 1953, the extinguished light was transferred to the General Services Administration (GSA), which then offered it for sale. Mayor Thomas Quigley of Stamford was able to persuade GSA to transfer the structure to the city, with the provision that it would be used as a historical monument for at least twenty years. Eight years later the city, having failed to care for the lighthouse, agreed to return it to the government. In 1967, the light was sold to three investors for

$10,000, and it was later acquired by Northeast Utilities. In 1984, Eryh Spektor, a native of Poland and chairman of the First Women's Bank of New York, paid $230,000 for the 103-year-old structure. With the lighthouse came title to ten acres of land, all of it underwater!

> The restored Stamford Harbor Light stands on the west side of the entrance to Stamford Harbor. It can be seen best from the water.
> NOAA Chart #12368, 12363

GREAT CAPTAIN ISLAND LIGHT (CT)

Appropriation:	*March 2, 1829*	*$5,000*
Appropriation:	*March 2, 1867*	*$12,000*
Established:	*1829*	
Purchased land from: Samuel Lyon, May 19, 1829		
Contractor:	*John H. Smith*	
First keeper:	*John W. Smith (?) -appointed May 24, 1830*	
Illuminating apparatus (IA): (1838) 10 lamps, 14.5" reflectors, fixed white light (FW)		
Refitted:	*1858, fourth-order Fresnel lens (4-order), FW*	
Rebuilt:	*1868*	
Illuminant:	*1907, changed from 1-wick oil lamp to incandescent oil vapor (iov). Power increase from 475-candlepower (cp) to 4,308 cp*	
IA:	*(1932) 4-order, FW, alternating group flashing red, 10 sec, 2 flashes. iov, white light 2,900 cp, red light 7,200 cp.*	
IA:	*(1986) 4-order, alternate occulting white and group flashing red, W 100,000 cp, R 25,000 cp.*	
Fog signal:	*1890, 10-inch steam whistle, Crosby automatic*	
Fog signal:	*(1907) first-class compressed-air siren, blast 3 seconds, interval 27 seconds.*	
Height of light above sea level: (1838) 62 feet. (1891) 74 feet		
Automated:	*January 30, 1970*	

On May 23, 1925, Coast Guard Cutter #175 anchored off Great Captain Island to investigate reports of suspicious activities in the vicinity of the island. A reliable source had informed the Coast Guard "that the liquor had been landed on the island and then repacked in sacks for redistribution." Searching the southwest end of the island, a quarter mile from the lighthouse, the guardsmen found seventy-five empty whiskey cases and several empty alcohol cans. The cases and cans were said to have been found well inshore, and, from their appearance, they had been landed and not washed ashore.

Several months earlier, Great Captain's keeper had piloted the Coast Guard cutter into Port Chester and Byram Shore to aid in an investigation. On another occasion, he had phoned the New York Custom House to inform it of a four-masted schooner that was discharging its illegal spirits to two smaller boats in broad daylight. In the hysteria of the Prohibition era, he nonetheless came under suspicion. The keeper was taken out to the cutter and asked to explain an empty champagne case found on the island. "It could not have washed ashore on the island," he was told, "as test [silver nitrate] of same failed to reveal any trace of salt."

In January of that same year, two fishing boats loaded with liquor had become stranded southwest of the Montauk Point Light. Though the wrecks were out of sight of the lighthouse, the actions of the keepers came under close scrutiny (see Montauk Point Light). Investigation in both instances proved that there had been no complicity on the part of the staff at either lighthouse, but similar incidents continued to surface at other stations along the coast.

Established, 1829

Congress had appropriated funds on March 2, 1829, for the establishment of a lighthouse in the vicinity of Great Captain Island. A few weeks later, Fifth Auditor and Superintendent of Lights, Stephen Pleasonton, instructed New London's Collector of Customs, Richard Law to inspect Great Captain Island and Greenwich Point as possible sites for the lighthouse. Law strongly favored the island, while the citizens of Stamford made it known that they much preferred Greenwich Point. To help resolve the differences in opinion, Pleasonton decided that experts, who were acquainted with the coastline and "entirely unconnected with the inhabitants of the place" be appointed to make the selection. In early August of that year, naval officers George W. Rogers and Francis Gregory made their way to the sites and selected Great Captain Island; Law was directed to see to the officers transportation, and to pay for all of their expenses.

The fifth auditor lost no time in preparing the way for establishing the island's beacon. In September of 1829, he accepted Charles H. Smith's low bid of $2,450 for erecting the lighthouse and an additional $500 for fitting it with patent lamps and reflectors. Three acres of land on the southeast part of the island had been purchased on May 19, 1829, from Samuel Lyon, three months before the final site selection! Apparently, someone had been a little hasty in purchasing the property, or the location of the beacon had been a foregone conclusion.

In May of 1830, Pleasonton received the deed of jurisdiction for the parcel, ceded by the state of Connecticut. He then discovered, however, that New York also claimed the island as being within its

Great Captain Island Lighthouse, 1988

own borders. "As it appears that the Island lies in the state of New York, you will apply to the Legislature of that state for a cession of jurisdiction," he instructed the collector of customs. It was over a half-century later before the disputed jurisdiction was finally settled in favor of Connecticut.

Great Captain's tower, built of rough stone, was described by Lt. Bache in 1838 as "badly constructed." The mortar used in the masonry had not hardened, and the walls were cracked in several places. The keeper's five-room stone dwelling, which stood separate from the tower, was, however, said to be "in good order."

During the lieutenant's inspection tour, the station's lighting apparatus was reported to have consisted of ten lamps and parabolic reflectors, grouped so as to show a light from every direction. In 1858, the lighthouse was refitted with a fourth-order Fresnel lens, showing a fixed white light.

John W. Smith appears to have been the station's first keeper. He was followed by James Merritt, who was appointed to the post on June 20, 1834. The island lighthouse was a family station, but there is no record of a woman ever taking over the facility, even temporarily. From 1830 to 1907, there was a succession of fifteen keepers.

With the original tower steadily deteriorating, Congress appropriated funds for a new lighthouse in March of 1867. Rebuilt in the following year, the tower rose from the front of the two-story, granite dwelling. Designed for one keeper and his family, the quarters had eight rooms. Its 4,226-gallon cistern was located at the north corner of the house; a barn stood to the rear of the property. Access to the tower was by means of a wooden stairway from the second floor. In 1916, another kitchen and a separate entrance were built for the station's assistant keeper.

The station's fourth-order lens, which had been installed in the old tower in 1858, was transferred to the new lighthouse; it continued to show a fixed white light. In 1890, the station was equipped with a ten-inch steam fog whistle. Citizens of Belle Haven and adjacent areas had become accustomed to the Great Captain Island's signal, but, when a new fog siren was installed in 1905, it was greeted with the headlines, "SIREN IS BREAKING UP HAPPY HOMES." The newpaper reported that the population of Greenwich and other places had, "petition[ed] Uncle Sam to seal the lips of a fog horn. If you see a shrinking looking man or woman, whose hands clasp and unclasp nervously, who shivers every half minute as if from a blow, whose lips twitch and eyes roll, while the hair shown a tendency to uplift at regular intervals, it is safe to put either of them down as from one of those ports within hearing distance of the fog horn on Great Captain's Island." A local newspaper asked, "What has Greenwich done that the government inflicts such severe punishment on this community?" Answering a protest from the president of Greenwich Board of Trade, Capt. R. S. Mackenzie of the Light House Establishment wrote, "It is impossible to make a fog-signal that can be heard which is not a nuisance to those who do not need it." The instrument was eventually adjusted, making it more acceptable to the local population.

In 1968, the Coast Guard announced its plans to abandon the 100-year-old lighthouse and replace it with a steel tower. The new structure was surmounted with a diamond-shaped day-mark, and it showed red and white flashing lights; it became operational on January 30, 1970.

In October of 1966, the town of Greenwich acquired 13.7 acres of Great Captain Island from the Aerotec Corporation; they had used the site as a recreation area for its employees. In June of 1973, the town purchased the lighthouse and its 2.6-acre reservation from the federal government for $42,500.

> *The Great Captain Light can be approached from on the water, on the south side of the island. The lighthouse and its property are open to Greenwich residents only.*
> *NOAA chart #12367*

EXECUTION ROCKS LIGHT (NY)

Appropriation:	*March 3, 1837*	*$5,000*
Appropriation:	*March 3, 1847*	*$25,000, expended $24,317.50*
Established:	*1850*	
First keeper:	*Daniel L. Caulkins*	
Illuminating apparatus (IA): June 15, 1850, 15 lamps, 21" parabolic reflectors		
Refitted:	*1856, fourth-order Fresnel lens (4-order), fixed white light (FW)*	
IA:	*(1891) 4-order, FW with fixed red (FR) sector*	
IA:	*(1907) flashing white with flashing red sector*	
	(Fl W Fl R sector), flashes every 10 seconds	
Illuminant:	*December 1, 1912, oil to incandescent oil vapor. Power increased, white light 9,000 to 40,000 cp, red sector 2,300 to 10,000 cp.*	
IA:	*(1988) DCB-10 lens, 500 watt lamp, flashing white every 10 seconds.*	
Fog signal:	*1850, fog bell, machine operated*	
Fog signal:	*(1873) third-class fog trumpet, blast 7 seconds every 15 seconds. Emergency Anderson's fog horn.*	
Fog signal:	*(1883) first-class Daboll trumpet, blast 7 seconds, interval 43 sec.*	
Fog signal:	*1905, first-class compressed air sirens, blast 3 seconds, interval 17 seconds.*	
Radiobeacon:	*(1934) 1 dash, 1 dot, 1 dash, 310 kc*	
Height of light above sea level: (1891) 58 feet		
Automated:	*December 5, 1979.*	

xecution Rocks Light was erected about three-quarters of a mile northwest of Sands Point at the western end of Long Island Sound. An often told legend attributes the site's name to the execution of American revolutionaries at the hands of British soldiers. The unfortunates were said to have been shackled to rocks that were exposed at low tide; death came slowly on a rising tide. There is no proof for the tale, and it is more likely that the name was testament to the great number of ships lost to the treacherous reefs.

During the summer of 1837, it was estimated that up to one hundred ships sailed past Execution Rocks each day. For the most part, the nearby Sands Point Light guided mariners clear of the reefs, but, in fog or heavy weather, it was of little use. At various times, a light vessel and a lighthouse were recommended to mark the dangerous obstructions, and funds for a light vessel were appropriated in 1837. The Light House Establishment, however, became gradually convinced that in the long run, a lighthouse would be less costly. The structure, it was reasoned, would also be able to maintain a brighter light and, unlike a ship, it would not change position in a storm.

Two very different plans were proposed for the lighthouse. One called for a boiler-plate iron structure that was to stand on iron piles; the other was a stone tower designed by Alexander Parris, a Boston civil engineer. On March 3, 1847, Congress appropriated $25,000 for construction of the latter.

Selection of a site for the lighthouse proved to be a difficult process. Parris was asked to survey the extensive reefs, and make his recommendation. He chose the largest boulder he could find near the natural channel, but local mariners disapproved; they wanted another location.

Fifth Auditor Steven Pleasonton dispatched New York's Collector of Customs to the area, along with the most experienced captains and pilots; he wanted their opinion as to the best location. "They fixed upon a place," Pleasonton wrote, "different from all of the others who had expressed an opinion on the subject, in water 7 feet deep at low tide." When queried as to the possibility of erecting the light-house at that site, Mr. Parris answered that it could be done, but at a greater cost, "4 to 5 times as much [about 50,000 dollars] in addition to the tower." The lighthouse was erected at the location first selected by Parris.

The contract for erecting Execution Rocks Light was awarded to the lowest bidder, a little-known New York man by the name of Thomas Butler. Under a 1809 law, the government was required to accept the lowest bid, but officials had not carefully examined Butler's credentials. It soon became evident that he had "neither the necessary skills nor the means to carry out the contract," and the project could not possibly be completed by the agreed upon date. Work went on with much of it done by subcontractors, and the project was finally completed in May of 1849, almost a year behind schedule.

To distinguish the station's beacon from Sands Point's fixed white light, Execution Rocks exhibited a red light, using thirteen lamps with red shades, and reflectors. In 1856, the lighting apparatus was replaced with a fourth-order lens that displayed a fixed white light, and Sands Point was refitted with a fourth-order, revolving white light.

There was no provision made for keeper's quarters at the new lighthouse; thus Daniel H. Caulkins, keeper of the Sands Point Light, was placed in charge of both beacons. He then appointed two assistants to look after Execution Rocks. Despite the lack of accommodations, one assistant remained there most of the time with his wife, while the second assistant was employed principally in re-supplying the station. That type of arrangement continued until April 1, 1851, when William Craft was appointed head keeper of Execution Rocks. He hired an assistant, and both resided at the

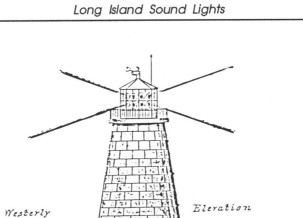

Westerly *Elevation*

*From plans for Execution Rocks Lighthouse, A. Parris, April 14, 1847.
National Archives, 3-2E-16*

Execution Rocks Lighthouse, 1987

lighthouse.

Eight years after becoming operational, the east side of the tower's foundation was found to be rapidly eroding. Riprap was placed on that side, but a gale washed the huge boulders to the opposite side. A barge filled with stones was then sunk into position to act as a breakwall, but it too began to break up within a short time. Winter ice and storms continued to threaten the station until, a number of years later, large blocks of granite were placed around its base.

The keepers of Execution Rocks Light finally found relief from their cramped quarters when a keeper's dwelling was erected in 1867. The tower was refurbished and connected to the dwelling by a barely noticeable passageway. Stephen Miller, who had been keeper during construction of the new quarters, was relieved in 1869 by a husband-and-wife team, William and Jane Williams. They remained there for two years and were replaced by another like pair, the Frazers, who also served for about two years.

On December 8, 1918, the lighthouse was wrapped in a dense cloak of haze as Keeper Peter Forget strained to see the faint outline of Sands Point less than a mile away. The fog signal had been running continuously from 7:00 am, and at 11:50 am, Forget decided to go to lunch. While preparing his food, he noticed the engine, which provided power to both the light and the foghorn, had slowed down. The keeper walked out to the engine house that stood a short distance away, and, when he opened its door, he was met by a solid a wall of flames!

Forget's radio distress call was picked up by the newly installed radio at Manhattan's Police Headquarters. They relayed the information to the Lighthouse Service on Staten Island and dispatched the city's fireboat, *Cornelius W. Lawrence*.

Using buckets and fire extinguishers, the keepers and two young Navy men assigned to the lighthouse began to fight the blaze. About an hour later, Navy patrol boats came on the scene, and they were soon joined by soldiers who had made their way out from Fort Slocum aboard commandeered rowboats. Risking their lives, the men removed barrels of kerosene from a storage shed, which was about to be engulfed in the spreading inferno. At 2:00 pm, the *Cornelius W. Lawrence* arrived, and, a fireboat's hose was gingerly carried to shore across the makeshift platform of rowboats strung together. The unlimited supply of water soon had the fire under control, and though badly scorched on its outside walls, the lighthouse was saved.

Three years after the engine room blaze, fire again threatened the station. An overheated exhaust pipe set a fire in the engine room's roof and sent smoke billowing up the tower. The Fresnel lens and the clockwork were darkened, but the flames were quickly contained,

Fourth-order Fresnel lens, Execution Rocks Lighthouse, August, 1979

and damage was minor.

The light station continued to be manned until December 5, 1979, when the station was automated. Much to the chagrin of many Coast Guardsmen, the classic Fresnel lens was removed and replaced by a "modern," small plastic lens.

Execution Rocks Light can be safely approached by boat, being careful to avoid reefs north and west of the light.
NOAA chart #12363, 12366

SANDS POINT LIGHT (NY)

Appropriation:	*January 22, 1806*	*$6,000*
Appropriation:	*February 10, 1808*	*$1,000*
Appropriation:	*February 17, 1809*	*$8,337.50*
Established:	*1809*	
Contractor:	*Abishow Woodward*	
First keeper:	*Noah Mason, appointed September 5, 1809*	
Illuminating apparatus (IA): (1838) 11 lamps, 9" parabolic reflectors		
IA:	*(1842) 11 lamps, 14" reflectors, fixed white light (FW).*	
Refitted:	*1856, fourth-order Fresnel lens (4-order), revolving white light (Rv W).*	
IA:	*(1883) 4-order, Fl W every 30 seconds.*	
IA:	*(1907) 4-order, FW*	
Fog signal:	*none*	
Height of light above sea level: (1891) 68 feet		
Discontinued:	*December 15, 1922*	

B enjamin Hewlett was somewhat of a shrewd negotiator; his land, which stood on a point at the western end of Long Island Sound, was an ideal site for the proposed beacon. When approached by the Light House Establishment, Hewlett asked $500 for one acre of land. In addition, he wanted the deed to include a clause that would allow the position of keeper to be left in perpetuity for the Hewlett family. "The appointment is vested in the President," was the Treasury Department's answer. Five acres of land were obtained for $512.50.

A New London builder, A. Woodward, was awarded the contract to erect the Sands Point Light in March of 1809. Work on the forty-foot freestone tower progressed rapidly, and on September 11 of that year, Noah Mason was appointed the station's first keeper.

For more than a century, Sands Point Light helped guide ships past dangerous rock reefs, 1500-yards north of the station. Records show that, when first established, the station showed a fixed white light. The lighting apparatus in 1838 consisted of eleven lamps and nine-inch parabolic reflectors, which were arranged on two tables so as to cast light toward vessels entering and exiting the sound. In 1856, the tower was refitted with a fifth-order Fresnel lens that produced a flash every thirty seconds.

The keeper had added onto the station's frame dwelling at different times, and in 1838, according to Lt. Bache's report, it had been expanded to twenty-three rooms! (If that was not a misprint in his report, the keeper certainly had created himself a mansion!)

In 1864, a request was made to Congress for funds to renovate the lighthouse and rebuild the dwelling which had been deemed beyond

Sands Point Lighthouse, 1884. National Archives, 26-LG-14-63

Sands Point Lighthouse, 1988

repair. Three years later, $9,400 was appropriated, and work began. The tower was repaired and renovated; its wood spiral stairs and window frames were replaced by iron. A new brick dwelling was built to connect with the light tower, and the old quarters were torn down; its lumber was used to build a barn, shed, and outhouse.

John Seaman was appointed keeper on March 12, 1866. During a July 1881 inspection of Sands Point, the "dwelling was crowded with boarders, which the Keeper had received in violation of the Regulations, and after having been heretofore informed that he could not do so without the authority of the Board." The author of the letter to the Treasury Department, Comdr. George Dewey, demanded Keeper Seaman's immediate dismissal, but Seaman apparently "weathered the storm." He remained at the station until his death in the summer of 1895. During his time at Sands Point, the light was determined to be no longer necessary, and it was discontinued. The October 31, 1894, action was met with so much opposition that the light was reestablished three months later.

As far as can be determined, life for the most part was quite routine at Sands Point. The station's personnel divided their time between lighthouse and domestic chores. The keepers went to the aid of some mariners in distress, and on one occasion, in 1913, they assisted a woman who had been shot on a neighboring beach. Most area rescue efforts however, originated from the nearby Execution Rocks Light. Keepers' salaries at the station were generally about $100 per year less than the more isolated Execution Rocks; Sands Point's keepers drew $400 per year from 1840 to 1866.

On December 15, 1922, the Light House Service abandoned Sands Point Light. It was replaced with an automatic acetylene light on top of a skeleton tower, which was erected 800 feet offshore. A little over a year later, the lighthouse and its five acres of land were sold at public auction to Mrs. Alva E. Belmont. Her country estate, which bordered the lighthouse reservation, had a twelve-foot right-of-way that lead to the lighthouse; it ran through a corner of her property. She paid $100,000 for her privacy.

> *Since 1924, the lighthouse has remained private property; it can only be seen from on the water. NOAA chart #12363, 12366*

STEPPING STONES LIGHT (NY)

Appropriation:	April 7, 1866 *(Hart Is.)*	$6,600
Appropriation:	June 10, 1872	$50,000
Appropriation:	June 23, 1874	$6,000
Established:	1877	
First lighted:	March 1, 1877	
First keeper:	Findlay Fraser, appointed January 3, 1877	

Illuminating apparatus (IA): (1883) fifth-order Fresnel lens (5-order), fixed red light (FR).
IA: *(1932) 4-order, fixed green (FG), incandescent oil vapor, 870 cp.*
IA: *(1986) 4-order, FG, electric.*
Fog signal: *(1883) fog bell struck by machine, double blow, interval 20 seconds.*
Height of light above sea level: (1891) 49 feet

T he groundhog could not have been more accurate when he emerged for his annual appearance on February 2, 1934. It was later said that he had not linger long before returning to the depth of his den, predicting six more weeks of hard winter.

The month of January had been relatively mild, but on February 9, the temperature dropped to a seventeen-year low. In New York City, the thermometer registered fourteen degrees below zero; in one upper New York State community, it was fifty below! Ice hampered ship movement in New Haven Harbor, and farther west, all but mid-Long Island Sound was iced over. On February 20, 1934, a blizzard hit the area, dumping seventeen inches of snow overnight; it was headlined as the worst snowstorm since 1888.

Keeper Charles A. Rogers of Stepping Stones Light, who had perhaps become a bit complacent after the January winter lull, had not properly supplied himself for the long February siege. With his lighthouse completely surrounded by ice, he could not get ashore to purchase supplies. By March 1, the keeper, with his wife and child at the station, was running short of food.

An unidentified person at City Island's pilot station was the first to spot Stepping Stone's American flag being flown upside down on that March 1 morning. He contacted the police, but its launch was ice-locked at its City Island dock. At about the same time, the tug *Mexpet*, which was making its way out of Long Island Sound, spotted the distress flag. Capt. Sioss broke through some of the ice and then sent a man to investigate. He was met by Keeper Rogers, who related that it had been impossible to get to shore with his rowboat; he was down to two days supply of food. The tug's captain offered him some food, but he refused; he asked only that the Light House Depot at St. George, Staten Island, be notified of his situation. When the tug docked in New York, the Light House Service was notified; that afternoon, the tender *Hickory* made its way to the lighthouse.

Stepping Stones Lighthouse, 1987

Established. 1877

In April of 1866, Congress had appropriated $6,600 for establishment of a lighthouse at Hart Island. The island was located about one mile north of Stepping Stones, a rock reef that had been marked with a buoy from about the early 1800s. Preliminary examination and survey of Hart Island were made in 1871, and plans were made for a foundation, pier, and dwelling, but difficulties in obtaining the necessary parcel of land forced a change of site. In 1874, the Light House Board opted to erect the lighthouse on Stepping Stone's rock reef.

Construction of the lighthouse began in the summer of 1875 and continued uninterrupted until late December. Contractor A. D. Cook resumed work in May, and, by the first of the next year, the red-brick dwelling with its mansard roof was completed. Findlay Fraser was appointed keeper, and on March 1, 1877, the station's fifth-order, fixed red light was shown for the first time.

Ernest Bloom, appointed to the post on April 20, 1910, was awarded the Efficiency Pennant in 1911. The pennant, which was flown over the lighthouse for the entire following year, was awarded to the station with the highest general efficiency.

Using a classical, fourth-order lens and an electric bulb, the automated lighthouse, in the late 1980s, showed a flashing green light; its fog bell had long ago been displaced for the sound of a foghorn.

> *Standing totally surrounded by water, just east of the Throgs Neck Bridge, Stepping Stones Light can be seen from the bridge, or better from on the water.*   NOAA chart #12363

5 *East River Lights*

THROGS NECK LIGHT (NY)

Appropriation:	March 3, 1821	$4,000
Appropriation:	May 7, 1822	$500
Appropriation:	March 3, 1825	$7,000
Appropriation:	August 7, 1882	$10,000
Established:	1827	
Contractors:	Timothy, Ezra, and Elisha Daboll	
First keeper:	Samuel Young, appointed December 12, 1826	
Rebuilt:	1835	

Illuminating apparatus (IA): (1838) 11 lamps, 9" reflectors
IA: 1842) 10 lamps, 14" reflectors, fixed white light (FW).
Refitted: 1855, sixth-order Fresnel lens, FW.
Rebuilt: 1890
Refitted: 1890, fifth-order Fresnel lens, FW.
Rebuilt: 1905
Refitted: 1906, fourth-order Fresnel lens, FW.
Fog signal: (1863) fog bell.
Fog signal: (1907) bell struck by machine every 15 seconds.
Fog signal: (1939) bell, electric. 1 stroke every 10 seconds.
Height of tower --base to center of lantern: (1842) 40 feet
Height of light above sea level: (1891) 72.5 feet
Discontinued: 1934

T he point of land projecting out into Long Island Sound known as Throgs Neck marked the eastern entrance to the East River. Forming a natural pier, the area was used, early on, as a transfer site for river pilots. During that same time, it was also a favorite meeting place for sportsmen from the city, who hunted ducks in East Chester. Keeper Samuel Young, the station's first keeper, and one of his successors, Jeth Bayles, kept a bar on the premises, from which they reportedly served rum to hunters, sailors, and soldiers. Possibly because of low pay or simply because of a lack of professionalism during the lighthouse system's infancy, it was not unusual for certain keepers to spend a minimum of time with their charge while pursuing other trades or interests. Some were known

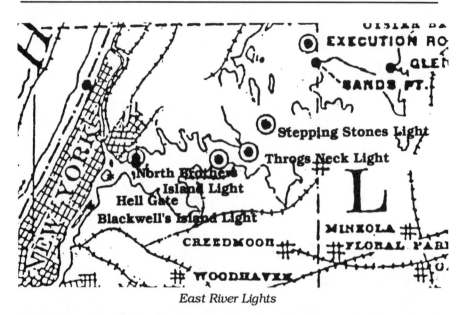

East River Lights

to remain away for several days, leaving the beacon in the care of family members or a hired hand.

Throgs Neck Light had nearly always stood in the shadow of Fort Schuyler. The lighthouse property is believed to have been obtained through an 1823 state of New York condemnation procedure. The beacon's location, however, was also regarded as an important strategic site by the military, and on July 26, 1826, the same year that construction of the lighthouse was begun, the government purchased the remaining portion of the point to build a defensive fort.

The contract for construction of the tower and dwelling was awarded to Timothy, Ezra, and Elisha Daboll; George W. Thompson was engaged to fit the lighthouse with an illuminating apparatus. In 1828, Keeper Young erected some sort of barricade in front of the dwelling, "in order to prevent the water of the sound from entering the lower rooms and cellar;" he also built himself a barn to house his cow. The original tower and residence did not last long; they were torn down in 1835 to make way for the ongoing construction of Fort Schuyler. As the buildings were being dismantled, some of their stones were used in erecting the fort.

To replace the dismantled beacon, a temporary wooden tower was erected. Its lighting apparatus consisted of eleven lamps with spherical reflectors that were arranged around two horizontal tables. Described as very feeble, even on a clear day, the fixed light could be seen at a maximum distance of only four and a half miles. In 1855, the lantern was refitted with a sixth-order lens, and the station was furnished with a fog bell.

Throgs Neck Lighthouse, 1884. National Archives, 26-LG-17-30

Throgs Neck Lighthouse, 1894. National Archives, 26-LG-17-29

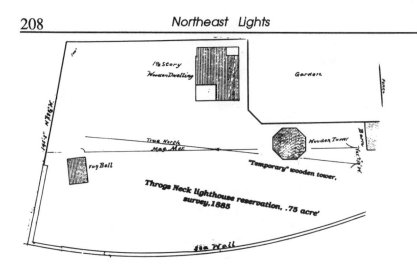

Throgs Neck light station, survey 1885

The "temporary" tower gave new meaning to the word temporary; it was to remain in continual use for over a half-century! In 1838, Lt. George Bache had found the then three-year-old structure "in a leaky condition." Twenty years later, it was said to be "old, leaky, shaky, and requiring immediate and thorough repairs." The nine-room frame dwelling, which had been built at the same time, was also in dire need of refurbishing. Repairs were made to both structures, but it was felt that only a "temporary" tower could be used in front of the fort's walls. To give Army gunners a clear field of fire in time of national emergency, the structure had to be easily moveable.

In 1874, the dwelling's sills had rotted to such an extent that the entire structure leaned to one side; doors and windows were ajar, and large pieces of plaster broke away from the walls and ceilings. "It would seem more judicious to build a new dwelling," the Light House Board reported, but nothing was done but patchwork repairs for nearly another decade. In 1883, construction of a new, one and a half-story residence was begun, and it was completed in the following year.

In 1890, an iron skeleton tower, resembling the structure still standing in the late 1980s at Coney Island, replaced the "temporary" wood tower. Equipped with a fifth-order lens, the new structure rose sixty-one and a half feet from its base to the center of its lantern.

At the request of Major William Marshall, Fort Schuyler's commanding officer, the Light House Establishment made an inspection tour of the Throgs Neck light station in July of 1900. "We find," read the joint report of the Light House Establishment and Corps of Engineers, dated September 24, 1900, "that the present location of the tower and Keeper's dwelling is objectionable from a military point of view, as they are in the field of fire of batteries constructed." Firing the newly installed five-inch guns would have blown the top off the lighthouse! Plans called for building a small tower on one of the fort's bastions, with an iron stairway to be erected along the face of the wall to allow access. The keeper's dwelling was to be torn down, and a smaller building was to be converted into new quarters. The proposal was reintroduced over the next three years, but in 1905 there was a change in plans. In its place, a red brick tower was erected 700 feet southwest of the iron tower, and the keeper's dwelling was left intact. The new structure stood thirty-five feet high from its base to the focal plane and was equipped with a fourth-order lens; it became operational on July 25, 1906.

The station was continually manned until 1934, when the lighthouse was discontinued and replaced with an automatic light shown from a skeleton tower. In the late 1980s, the former keeper's dwelling was still occupied by a Coast Guard family.

> *Throgs Neck Light stands under the Throgs Neck Bridge on the campus of New York State Maritime College. The site can be visited by appointment only, (212) 409-7200.*   NOAA chart #12363

NORTH BROTHER ISLAND LIGHT

Appropriation:	1829	$5,000
Appropriation:	August 14, 1848	$10,000
Appropriation:	April 7, 1866	$8,500
Appropriation:	March 2, 1867	$7,500
Established:	1869	
First lighted:	November, 1869	
Illuminating apparatus (IA):	(1873) sixth-order lens, fixed white light (FW).	
IA:	(1891) sixth-order lens. FW.	
Refitted:	1900, fourth-order Fresnel lens (4-order), FW 5 seconds, eclipse 5 seconds (Occ W).	
IA:	(1933) 4-order, Occ W, electric, 6,000-candlepower (cp).	
Fog signal:	1889, fog bell struck by machine every 15 seconds	
Height of light above sea level:	(1873) 50 feet	
Discontinued:	1953	

In 1829, Congress appropriated $5,000 "for building a lighthouse on or near one of the islands called Brothers at the narrows of Long Island Sound." Thus began a long process that spanned four decades before a light station was finally established at North Brother Island.

New York's Superintendent of Lights attached a great deal of importance to establishing a light marking the northern approach to Hell Gate; the dangerous waterway had claimed a countless number of vessels.

There was little discussion over the most suitable site for the lighthouse; North Brother Island was ideal, but the land's owner, Edward Ackerman, refused to sell on any terms. After attempting to purchase the site over a period of three years, Fifth Auditor Stephen Pleasonton asked the legislature of New York to begin condemnation procedures on the property. Two years later however, the state of New York had yet to act, and the funds reverted back to the Treasury.

Money was reappropriated in 1848. Navy Commander Pearson was dispatched to reexamine the North Brother Island site, and enter into negotiation for a two-acre parcel. He reported that the owner "was indisposed to sell less than the whole island for which he asked 9,000 Dollars but would take 5,000 Dollars for two acres." The price was considered unreasonable, and the funds were transferred to support and maintain other lighthouses.

In 1868, the state of New York was again asked to intercede, and the necessary parcel was finally obtained. In November of the following year, the station became operational.

The keeper's residence had a pantry, kitchen, dining room, sitting room, and oil room on the first floor, and four bedrooms on the second. The octagonal tower, which rose from the front of the dwelling to fifty feet above sea level, was equipped with a sixth-order lens, showing a fixed white light. In 1889, a fog bell was established at the station, and the illuminating apparatus was increased in strength to a fourth-order Fresnel lens in 1900.

A boundary fence was erected on North Brother Island in 1883 to separate the lighthouse reservation from the grounds of its neighbor, Riverside Hospital. The institution was operated by the city of New York for the treatment of infectious diseases. The hospital's most famous patient, Mary Mallon, was housed there for a total of twenty-three years; she was best known as Typhoid Mary.

Mary Mallon was outwardly the picture of health, but she carried a bacteria in her intestines that caused typhoid fever. The robust woman was not careful with her personal hygiene, and, working as a cook, she spread the disease from one household to another. Health authorities finally identified Mary as a carrier of the disease, and in 1907 she was confined to the island's hospital. Public pressure obtained her release in 1910, and, though she had promised not to cook for others again, she soon returned to the only trade she knew. In 1915, Mary was rearrested and remanded to Riverside Hospital, where she died of a stroke on November 16, 1938; she was buried at Saint Raymond's Cemetery, Bronx, NY. Fifty-one cases of typhoid fever and three deaths were attributed to Mary Mallon.

Joseph D. Meade was appointed keeper of North Brother Island Light on October 1, 1902. Before this date, he had been keeper of

North Brothers Island Lighthouse, undated. National Archives, 26-LG-13-28

Abandoned lighthouse on North Brothers Island, 1988

Whale Rock Light, RI, for less than six months, when, on December 1, 1901, he attempted to rescue his assistant, Martin W. Eckman; the assistant's boat had capsized. Though unsuccessful, Keeper Meade received a letter of commendation from the Light House Board for his heroic efforts.

On January 5, 1903, Keeper Meade left North Brother Island for his mother's home in New York City; his two brothers, who were living with him at the lighthouse, remained behind to look after the station. When he had not yet arrived at his parent's residence on January 7, the police were called in. The keeper's boat was immediately located tied up at a city dock, but his body was never found; the police later attributed the disappearance to foul play. On February 20, 1903, J. T. P. Jacobs was named North Brother Island's new keeper; it was during his tenure that New York's worst maritime disaster occurred on the shores of the island.

It was 9:30 am on Wednesday, June 15, 1904, when the excursion vessel, *General Slocum*, left its East Third Street dock. Very few of the 1500 passengers aboard were men; most were women and their children, bound for a Sunday school picnic. At 10:00 am, with the band playing, the 280-foot-long vessel passed Hell Gate. Just opposite 130th Street (or 113th Street according to other accounts), smoke began pouring from the bow on the port side of the ship. "We had fires on the *General Slocum* before, but we always had been able to handle them," Capt. Van Schaick reported. "The first thing which I did was to call upon the men to take steps necessary according to the fire drill. They were twenty-three of our men on board. They were set to work, but as I looked back I already saw a fierce blaze   the wildest I have ever seen."

The fire spread quickly and sent the passengers scurrying for the stern. For some reason, Capt. Schaick chose not to beach his blazing vessel on the shore, a distance of only 300 feet away. Instead, he headed at full speed toward North Brother Island, fanning the flames as he went. The frantic women fought over the life preservers, but they were rotten and fell apart in their hands. Some crewmen tried to control the fire with their hoses, but the men were poorly trained, and the majority of the hoses did not work. Nicholas Belzer tried to release a lifeboat, but he discovered that it had been wired in place. The passengers, most of whom could not swim, began to jump overboard as the vessel neared the south end of the island. Instead of landing there, however, the captain chose to go completely to the other side, where he ran his ship up on shore in a small cove. Though beached, the vessel's stern stood in deep water.

Lulu McKibben saw the blazing vessel coming up the East River toward the island. She notified the police, fire department, and several hospitals. The twenty-year-old woman then ran out to the point and saw the boat round the bar. "In a minute," she said, "the water was full of struggling women and children." She ran into the water and began pulling some people in.

When the *General Slocum* finally ran aground, the impact sent the hurricane deck crashing down through the lower decks; passengers were hurled into the water, while others fell into the throat of the flaming abyss. Doctors, nurses, and employees of the island's hospital formed a human chain and began to bring in victims. The tug *Wade*, saved 155 persons, and a doctor from the hospital, saved six with his small boat. There was no record of Keeper Jacob's role in the disaster, but he no doubt joined the many other unsung heroes of the disaster. Over 1000 persons perished aboard the *General Slocum.*

The burned wreck was raised later that month to check for the remains of other victims. In June of 1905, the vessel's hulk was converted into a coal barge, which was then used on the Delaware River; it is said to have sunk some years later.

In 1953, the lighthouse was discontinued and replaced with a white skeleton tower. The abandoned and deteriorating keeper's dwelling, with its tower removed, was, in 1988, completely surrounded by tall, salt-tolerant plants.

> *The badly deteriorated dwelling stands on the south side of the island. It can be seen only by boat.*
> *NOAA chart #12339*

HELL GATE (Hurl Gate) ELECTRIC LIGHTS

Appropriation: August 7, 1882 $20,000
Appropriation: March 30, 1888 $1,350 (Hallets Point)
Established: 1884
First lighted: October 20, 1884
Illuminating apparatus: 9 electric lights, 6,000-candlepower each
Height of light above sea level: 255 feet
Discontinued: 1886

I t was mid-autumn of 1760 when the British pay ship HMS *Hussar* entered Hell Gate, bound for Long Island Sound. As it was sailing toward Pot Rock, the pilot misread the currents, and the vessel was swept up against the cone-shaped rock, the top of which was about the size of a barrel's lid. Within a short time the

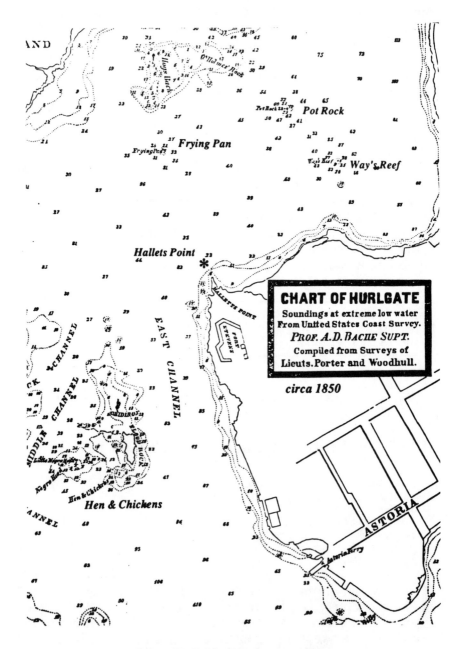

AND

D.Holmes' Rock

Huge Rock

Frying Pan

FryingPan

Pot Rock

Pot Rock

West Reef

Way's Reef

Hallets Point

HALLETTS POINT

FORT STEVENS

CHART OF HURLGATE
Soundings at extreme low water
From United States Coast Survey.
PROF. A.D. BACHE SUPT.
Compiled from Surveys of
Lieuts. Porter and Woodhull.

circa 1850

EAST CHANNEL

MIDDLE CHANNEL

SQUADRON

Hen & Chickens

Negro

Hen & Chickens

ASTORIA

Astoria Ferry

CHANNEL

Chart of Hell (Hurl) Gate, circa 1850

114-foot frigate had sunk to the bottom, taking with it an estimated $4 million worth of gold and silver.

Pot Rock lay eight feet below the surface at low tide. During Lt. David Porter's 1848 survey of Hell Gate, the naval officer observed eight wrecks in a single day, all of which he attributed to the eddies caused by Pot Rock. The narrow passage's strong currents, whirlpools, and many rock reefs claimed an unknown number of ships. Of the sailing vessels entering Hell Gate in that same year, it was estimated "that one in fifty sustained more or less injury by being forced by the violence of the currents on the rocks or shoals."

In 1851, Mons Maillefert was hired to blast away Pot Rock, Way's Reef, and Frying Pan, all of which lay within a short distance of one another. In examining Way's Reef, the surveyor had recovered several pounds of copper surrounding it, which had been scraped from the bottoms of ships!

Working from a small boat, an operator first found a crevice on Pot Rock, within which the pole could be solidly wedged. Canisters, filled with sixty-two to eighty-two pounds of powder, were then guided down the pole by means of rings; a wire ran from the charges to batteries aboard a barge. "The first two charges removed four feet from the top of Pot Rock," it was reported, "and these with the subsequent charges have already nearly quieted the whirlpool." The rock was eventually reduced to twenty-four feet below mean low water.

Pot Rock, after New York Municipal Gazette, 1850

The top of Way's Reef was blasted, and then a four-ton tripod was erected over it. From that platform, a shaft was drilled into the rock, eight inches in diameter and nine and a half feet deep. A seven-foot long canister of powder was fitted in the shaft, and was then fired by battery. When the charge was set off, a column of water was said to have risen to a height of 140 feet!

The elimination of the three obstructions was hailed as a major improvement in navigating Hell Gate, but it was still fraught with

Hell Gate Electric Lights, 1884-1886. National Archives, 3-9H-B-6

danger. In 1865, a New York State law addressed the waterway's hazards by forbidding vessels of over fifty tons, except for regularly scheduled steamboats, to pass through Hurl Gate unless manned by a qualified pilot. Amended in 1871, the law compelled sailing vessels of 100 tons or more to pay one half of the $5 pilotage fee if the master of a ship refused the services of a pilot. At the time, there were forty-two Hell Gate pilots.

Ships preparing to make the perilous passage were instructed to make their anchors "ready for letting go, and chains ranged and stoppered at 10 or 12 fathoms." Sailing vessels bound for Long Island Sound could set out only on a flood tide, being sure to keep south of Flood Rock, the southernmost point of a group of three large rocks. Those leaving the Sound had to sail on an ebb tide, following a course that took them to the north side of Mill Rock. Though many more of the rock obstructions were cleared during the mid-1870s, navigating Hell Gate at night still posed considerable danger.

In 1883, construction began on a 255-foot iron skeleton tower, from which were shown nine electric lights of 6,000-candlepower each. Becoming operational on October 20, 1884, the beacon was described as bright as a full moon on a clear night and "sufficient to enable even sailing vessels to go through the gate in safety." River pilots soon found, however, that the illumination produced was so bright that it blinded them; the shadows were so dark that they were sometimes mistaken for obstacles.

Problems plagued the tower from the start. As its third section was being lifted into place, the derrick's cable parted, and the section dropped; the entire structure was damaged. Also the light did not always function properly. In the first three months of 1886, Keeper Daniel Fox reported that, because of malfunctioning boilers, the beacon had been out on a number of occasions. Matters became further complicated when, in that same year, the lease for the land upon which the tower stood ran out. Congress had failed to pass an appropriation for payment of the rent.

Hell Gate Electric Light was discontinued in 1888, and replaced by a wooden tower, to which a fog bell was later added. Equipment removed from the tower that was still of use was stored at the General Depot; the remaining materials and buildings were disposed of at auction. The iron structure, which had been the tallest skeleton tower built by the Light House Service, was torn down and sold for scrap, and the landowner finally received his back rent.

BLACKWELL'S ISLAND LIGHT

Motorists traveling along the Franklin D. Roosevelt (FDR) Drive, can see a slender black lighthouse standing at the north end of Roosevelt (Welfare) Island. Established in 1872, the forty-eight-foot stone tower was erected on the what was then called Blackwell's Island; it marked the entrance to Hell Gate. A reef known as Bread and Cheese, was located on the eastern end of Blackwell's Island. Reporting to the New York Chamber of Commerce on May 14, 1848, Lt. Comdr. Charles H. Davis stated: "Vessels are liable to go on it on the flood when it is covered, by getting into the eddy near it, with a light wind. The chief danger is ebb." An outgoing tide could carry an unfortunate vessel directly onto the dangerous reef. In 1872, ships caught in its eddies received specific instructions: "the only chance of avoiding the rocks is to stand through between Bread and Cheese and Blackwell's point, a good 7-foot channel at low water, and about 50 yards wide."

Blackwell's Island Lighthouse, 1987

Built and maintained by the City of New York, Blackwell's Island Light was constructed of grey gneiss (quartz, feldspar and mica) stones, and its base was cut granite. The lantern was equipped with a fourth-order lens, showing a fixed red light. In 1874, its illuminant was a gas lamp.

At the base of the lighthouse was a crude inscription carved in the rock by John McCarthy; he was said to have been a patient at the nearby mental institution. It read, "This work was done by John McCarthy who built the light house from the bottom to the top. All ye who pass by may pray for his soul when he dies." Vandals later removed the inscribed stone.

The light continued to be maintained by New York City until the mid-1940's. In more recent years, the landmark has been illuminated at night by flood lights.

---

*Blackwell's Island Light can be seen from
the shore, off 1st Street in Astoria Queens.
A walkway on Roosevelt Island, leads directly
to the light.
NOAA Chart #12339*

6 *Gardiners Bay Lights*

GARDINERS ISLAND LIGHT

Appropriation: March 3, 1851 $6,000
Appropriation: August 31, 1852 $1,000
Established: 1854
First lighted: December, 1854
First keeper: Albert Edwards, appointed December 21, 1854
Illuminating apparatus: 1855, sixth-order Fresnel lens, fixed white light (FW)
Fog signal: none
Height of light above sea level: (1883) 33 feet
Discontinued: 1894

"I am happy to learn that you have obtained the site for 400 dollars, a much less sum than we expected to pay for it," wrote Fifth Auditor Stephen Pleasonton. The unstable sandy beach, purchased from the Gardiner in August of 1851, would prove, however, not to have been such a great deal.

Gardiners Island Lighthouse was established to guide vessels clear of the north end of the island. It stood on a beach, at the end of what is now a shoal. Rising just three feet above the high tide mark, the sandy beach extended three miles off the northeast end of the island. During storms or unusually high tides, parts of the beach were ordinarily awash.

Work on the light station began early in 1854 and was completed in December of the same year. The keeper's dwelling was twenty-eight square feet wide and stood one and a half-stories tall. The station's circular tower was attached at the rear of the residence; both structures were constructed of hard-burned bricks. The dwelling's roof was slate, and the tower's lantern was iron. Attached to the outside of the dwelling was a cistern, six feet in diameter and seven feet deep cistern, and a ten by twelve-foot washroom.

Access to the tower was from the outside; a wooden spiral stairway

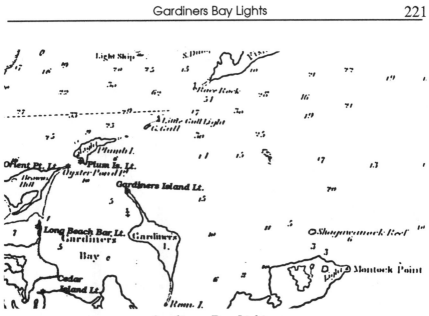

Gardiners Bay Lights

led to a platform just below the lantern, and a short ladder completed the way. Equipped with a sixth-order Fresnel lens, the lighthouse began showing its fixed white light in late December of 1854; although preparations were made to install a fog bell in 1870, the station was apparently never equipped with a signal.

Albert Edwards, appointed keeper on December 21, 1854, was the first of only four persons to serve in that capacity at Gardiners Island during the station's short history. Erosion of beach sands, brought about by the natural processes of wind and wave action, plagued the light station from the time of its establishment. In 1890, loss of beach accelerated to such a point that the high tide mark was approaching the lighthouse from the east at a rate of almost eleven feet per year! Proposals were made to move or rebuild the station, but, before a consensus could be formed, the forces of nature made the decision. With the sea lapping at its foundation, the station was abandoned on March 8, 1894. Two months later a gas-lighted buoy, moored in seventy-two feet of water, replaced the threatened beacon.

In response to the hostilities between the United States and Spain (the Spanish-American War), on April 5, 1898, the Secretary of the Treasury transferred the abandoned light to the War Department for the establishment of a gun battery.

Little remains of the Gardiner's Island Light; in 1987, its former site was marked as "ruins" on local nautical charts.

NOAA chart #13209

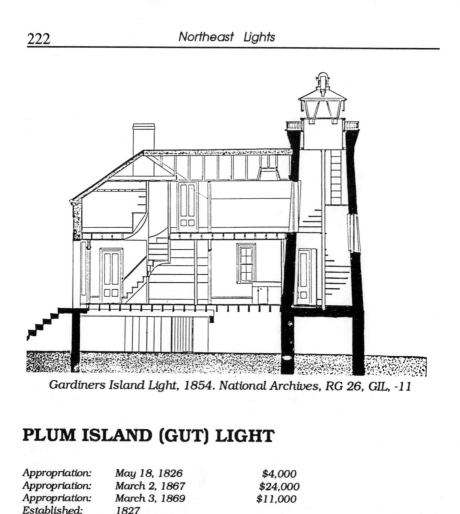

Gardiners Island Light, 1854. National Archives, RG 26, GIL, -11

PLUM ISLAND (GUT) LIGHT

Appropriation:	*May 18, 1826*	*$4,000*
Appropriation:	*March 2, 1867*	*$24,000*
Appropriation:	*March 3, 1869*	*$11,000*
Established:	*1827*	

Illuminating apparatus (IA): (1838) 10 lamps, 13" parabolic reflectors, revolving light (Rv)
IA: (1848) 10 lamps, 14" reflectors, Rv.
Refitted: 1856, fourth-order Fresnel lens, RV
Rebuilt: 1870
IA: 1870, fourth-order Fresnel, Rv every 30 seconds
IA: (1939) fourth-order Fresnel lens, flashing white 1 second, eclipse 6.5
*   seconds. Incandescent oil vapor, 24,000-candlepower (cp).*
Fog signal: 1871 fog bell, Steven's striking apparatus, sounded every 15 sec.
Height of tower: 1826, 30 feet
Height of light above sea level: (1873) 63 feet
Discontinued: 1978

William Chapell was an ordinary man who happened to enjoy the self-imposed isolation of a light station. He had served four years at Long Beach Bar before being transferred to Plum Island Light on July 15, 1913. Located at the west end of the island, the beacon marked the east side of Plum Gut, a narrow entrance to Long Island Sound known for its exceptionally strong tidal currents.

An earlier keeper at Plum Island, William Parks, did not have Chapell's dedication to duty. An inspection of the lighthouse in September of 1910 found the station in "scandalous condition." Four months later, an entry in the lighthouse log read, "Inspected the station and found that directions for its improvement which were written under date September 1, 1910, have been practically completely neglected or ignored." Keeper Parks was discharged shortly thereafter.

In January of 1876, the Third Light House District had received a petition for the removal of another keeper and his assistant, William Wetmore and his son, William Wetmore, Jr. An inspector was dispatched to the area where he interviewed all of those who had signed the petition. "Most of the signers of the petition could give no evidence of neglect or intemperance on the part of the Keepers," wrote the inspector. He concluded that "the petition was prepared and circulated for signatures by Benjamin H. Sisson, whose object it was to have the Keeper removed to obtain the place for himself." The senior Wetmore remained at Plum Island a total of thirty-four years. On September 23, 1903, he resigned his position, stating that he was ill with Bright's disease and could no longer carry on the lighthouse duties.

When William Chapell was first appointed keeper at Plum Island in 1913, he was able to purchase provisions from the commissary at Fort Terry, situated on the island just east of the light station. Three years later, however, he was informed that he could no longer obtain supplies from the military base. He was thus forced to travel two miles by small boat to Orient Point or, in some instances, all the way to New London, a distance of twelve miles across Long Island Sound. Similar rulings at other military bases prevented local keepers from obtaining supplies from commissaries. Intervention by the Lighthouse Service, which had to be done on a case-by-case basis, finally restored permission for most keepers.

During his term of duty at Plum Island, Keeper Chapell made many friends of sportsmen who fished the waters off the lighthouse. The keeper often housed and fed the fishermen when sudden storms forced them to seek refuge at the light, and, on several occasions, this "ordinary man" risked his own life rendering aid to sailors caught in Plum Gut's dangerous waters.

In 1930, the aging keeper casually complained to a visiting fisherman of an insufficient supply of coal to keep the lighthouse warm throughout the year. As a younger man, he had never minded the structure's damp and cold, but now they seemed to penetrate to his very bones. The sportsman, Franklin Overton of Peconic, NY, wrote United States Congressman Robert Bacon of the keeper's plight, and

Plum Island Lighthouse, 1988

the congressman, in turn, interceded on behalf of the keeper with the Light House Bureau.

Established, 1827

Plum Island Light was established in 1827. The original tower, built of rough stone, stood thirty-five feet high and was equipped with ten lamps with reflectors. Divided into two equal clusters that were arranged on two rotating copper tables, the mechanism for their rotation was identical to that of the lights at Point Judith and Watch Hill. The station's dwelling, which was separate from the tower, had eight rooms.

In 1867, the masonry of the dwelling and tower was found to be soft and crumbling, and both of the structures leaked badly. In March of 1869, funds were appropriated for a new lighthouse, and construction began almost immediately. With its completion in the following year, the station's sixth-order lens, which had been in use for fourteen years in the old tower, was transferred to the new facility.

Later changed to a fourth-order lens, the station operated until 1978, when the lighthouse was discontinued and replaced by a flashing white light, located on a brick shed. The station's lens, built in Paris by Barbier and Bernard, was removed and placed in storage.

The Army closed Fort Terry in 1956. The base was then turned over to the United States Department of Agriculture, which established the Plum Island Animal Disease Center.

Plum Island's flashing white light on a brick shed, together with the Orient Point Light, continues to direct mariners through the narrow, hazardous channel known as Plum Gut. In 1988 the lighthouse, which resembled the Norwalk Island Light, stood empty, decaying slowly as the result of neglect by its new owner, the United States Department of Agriculture.

> *The lighthouse on Plum Island can seen only from the water. The island itself is off limits to the public.*
> *NOAA chart #12354*

ORIENT POINT LIGHT
(Oyster Pond, Coffee Pot Light)

Appropriation:	*June 4, 1897 $30,000*
Appropriation:	*March 3, 1899 $3,000*
Established:	*1899*
First lighted:	*November 10, 1899*
First keeper:	*Ole N.A. Anderson, appointed October 20, 1899*
Illuminating apparatus (IA): 1899, fifth-order Fresnel lens	
Characteristic:	*November, 1899, fixed red (FR)*
Refitted:	*May 1, 1900, fourth-order Fresnel lens, (FR)*
IA:	*(1939) fourth-order Fresnel lens, FR, Incandescent oil vapor, 870 cp.*
IA:	*(1988) 190 mm lens, 2.03 amp lamp, flashing white light every 5 sec*
Fog signal:	*June 1, 1900, blower siren and trumpet*
Fog signal:	*February 4, 1905, second-class Daboll trumpet, blast 3 seconds, interval 17 seconds (Bl, I,).*
Fog signal:	*(1924) second-class reed horn, Bl 3 sec, I 17 sec*
Height of light above sea level: (1907) 64 feet	
Automated:	*1966*

Two hours after the tide begins to ebb at the Race, the waters of Long Island Sound rush through the deep and narrow gap between Orient Point and Plum Island. Developing currents that sometimes exceed five knots, known as Plum Gut, less than a mile wide, can present a formidable challenge to even a seasoned mariner.

The steamer *Halyoake* was sailing though Plum Gut in the early afternoon of August 30, 1912, when it suddenly lost steering. Swept by the Gut's strong currents, the vessel turned, and still under power, it headed straight for the Orient Point Light. Capt. Clarence Sherman gave the order to reverse the engines, and seconds became a lifetime as the steamer shuddered in a desperate effort to slow momentum. At the lighthouse, Keeper Charles Whitford, who had seen the crippled steamer turn, prepared himself for the inevitable

Orient Point Lighthouse under construction, June 6, 1899. First course erected. National Archives, 26-LG-13-37B

Orient Point Lighthouse, 1988

collision, but the captain's actions had come in time. Describing the incident Whitford wrote, "the bow ran up on the rocks surrounding the station, but the steamer backed off immediately, and no damage was done to either the steamer or the station."

Established, 1899

During the winter 1895-1896, ice floes, propelled by the currents, carried away the navigational beacon off Orient Point. The Light House Board proposed replacing the lost aid with a lighted beacon and fog signal, but, after considerable debate, it opted to erect a light-house. On June 4, 1897, Congress appropriated $30,000 for its establishment.

In October of 1898, forty-eight cast-iron plates were delivered at Orient Point for erecting the foundation's two lower courses. Assembly of the plates had proceeded smoothly, with the second course sunk in place, when a strong gale swept over the work site. Twenty of the iron plates were torn away and damaged beyond repair; nineteen others sustained considerable damage. Unable to proceed any further, construction was halted for the winter.

Work on the conical tower resumed in the following spring. Within two months, the foundation's new plates were bolted together, sunk, and filled with concrete. The project proceeded without interruption, and, by early autumn, the lighthouse was completed. Keeper Ole N. A. Anderson lit the station's fixed red, fifth-order light for the first time on November 10, 1899.

In its exposed position on the west side of Plum Gut, ice and storms were a continuous problem. During construction, 600 tons of riprap stone had been placed around the light to help shield it from the elements. From 1900 to 1903, an additional 10,047 tons of riprap were used at the base of the lighthouse and for building a protective breakwall.

Locally referred to as the Coffee Pot, the lighthouse was manned until the mid-1960s. Declaring that the station was a hazard to its keepers, the Coast Guard announced plans, in 1971, to demolish the landmark and replace it with a pipe tower, but citizens' protest saved the structure.

Still operational, the automated station displays a flashing white light; its fog horn sounds two blasts, every thirty seconds.

Orient Point Light can be approached on the water, being careful to avoid the shallow reefs that surrounds it. On land, it can be seen from a distance at Orient Point.
NOAA Chart #12358, 12354

LONG BEACH BAR LIGHT

Appropriation:	*July 15, 1870*	*$17,000*
Appropriation:	*June 10, 1872*	*$20,000*
Established:	*1871*	
First lighted:	*December 1, 1871*	
First keeper:	*William Thompson*	

Illuminating apparatus (IA): (1873) fifth-order Fresnel lens , fixed red light (FR).
IA: (1939) fourth-order Fresnel lens, FR, incandescent oil vapor. 870 cp.
Fog signal: 1871, cast-steel bell struck by machine every 15 seconds.
Height of light above sea level: (1883) 54 feet
Discontinued: 1948

L ong Beach Bar Lighthouse was established on December 1, 1871, to mark the entrance to Peconic Bay at the eastern end of Long Island. The first entry in the station's log read, "Only 70 gallons of oil on hand when I came." Apparently, Keeper William Thompson was not too happy with his assignment since ten days later, he wrote, "sent in my resignation as keeper."

The tower rose from the keeper's dwelling to a height of fifty-four feet above sea level and was equipped with a fifth-order, fixed red light; its fog signal consisted of a bell. The wooden dwelling had a kitchen, dining room, and sitting room on the first floor and three bedrooms and an oil room on the second floor. The cistern consisted of two tanks, with a capacity of 219 gallons each, which were located in the kitchen, and a 359-gallon tank, that took-up most of the first-floor hallway.

The station stood on a screw-pile foundation, which had been driven ten feet into the sandy bottom; it was at the mercy of wind, waves, and ice. In February of 1872, ice shook the entire structure and tore away the dock. A month later, the keeper and his assistant abandoned the lighthouse for two days, "on account of ice shaking it so bad."

Despite the construction of a protective breakwall, and placement of more than 3,000 tons of granite around the base of the structure, damage from the elements continued to be a problem. On February 20, 1881, George W. Fenton, who had been appointed keeper eight years earlier, described how the lighthouse was nearly destroyed in a storm: "Ice packed under the house from the east with flood tide, and broke three spikes [pilings], and nearly all of the braces. The ice was two feet thick. Had to steady the lamp lenses by hand to save them."

Long Beach Light,
to Greenport Harbor, L. I.

Long Beach Bar Lighthouse, undated. National Archives, 26-LG-12-63

Judging from the regular entries in the lighthouse log document-
ing the season's first catch of lobster and blackfish, Keeper Fenton's
favorite pastime seemed to have been those activities. Much to his
chagrin, however, storms often swept away his lobster pots.

Keepers were not always attentive to their assigned tasks. On
August 3, 1911, the steamer *Shinnecock* sailed from New York's East
River and proceeded up Long Island Sound toward Peconic Bay. As
it neared Cornfield Lightship, the vessel entered a fog bank. Capt.
George Rowland set a course for Plum Gut, and, having heard that
station's fog bell, he turned toward Long Beach Bar Light. The
steamer ran twenty-two minutes in the direction of the lighthouse
and then stopped to listen for its fog signal. Since the captain heard
nothing, the ship moved ahead slowly but ran aground within five
lengths of the light station. It was nearly a half hour after the
grounding before the fog bell was first sounded, and it then continued ringing long after the fog had lifted. The undamaged steamer, its
passengers unscathed, was later pulled off the sandbar; the keeper
was later severely reprimanded for not having sounded the fog bell.

In 1926, the keeper's dwelling was set on a concrete pier, and
refurbished extensively. By the following year, though, it had
become apparent that the sandbar had extended far beyond the
lighthouse, and the beacon could no longer be depended upon to

mark the channel's entrance. Despite its problems, the station continued to operate for another two decades; it was discontinued in 1948.

When the lighthouse was offered for sale in 1955, a group of citizens formed the Orient Point Marine Historical Association and purchased the property. About nine years later, during a Fourth of July celebration, the lighthouse mysteriously caught fire and was totally destroyed.

> *Only the foundation of the Long Beach Bar Light is left standing. Its remains are indicated on area navigational charts as "Lt Ho (ruins)."*
> *NOAA chart #12358*

CEDAR ISLAND LIGHT

Appropriation:	March 3, 1837	$1,000
Appropriation:	July 7, 1838	$2,500
Appropriation:	March 2, 1867	$25,000
Established:	1839	
First keeper:	Frederick King, appointed January, 1839	
Illuminating apparatus (IA):	(1842) 9 lamps, __ reflectors	
IA:	(1849) 9 lamps, 14" reflectors, fixed white light	
Refitted:	1855, sixth-order Fresnel lens, 270o, Argand lamp, fixed white light	
Rebuilt:	1869	
Fog signal:	1882, fog bell struck by machine every 20 seconds	
Height of light above sea level:	(1848) 32 feet. (1891) 45 feet	
Discontinued:	1934	

T he risks were great for the whalers who had begun to sail out of eastern Long Island around 1785, but for the shipowners, there was potential for immense wealth. Sailors approaching Gardiners Bay from the east, had no lighthouses to help them find their way; from the south and southwest, the nearest beacon stood at Sandy Hook, NJ. Thus, when Montauk Point Light was first lit on November 5, 1797, it must have been a welcome sight to those seafaring men. Ships travelling from Block Island to Montauk Point were warned of a dangerous shoal lying midway between the two, with only four and a half fathoms over its shallowest part. In storms, the waves usually broke over the rock reef. The area had many more hidden obstructions. A reef lay three miles within Montauk Point, and one and a half miles offshore, "there are 6 feet of water, which is very dangerous," wrote the Blunts in *American Coast Pilot*. On

Cedar Island Lighthouse, 1987

August 15, 1780, the English vessel *Bedford* was stranded on a shoal near Plum Island; the reef later became known as Bedford rock.

To aid vessels entering Sag Harbor, the area's developing whaling fleet began maintaining stake lights at Cedar Island around 1810; the keeper of these beacons was said to have been Capt. Joshua Penny. The harbor's maritime commerce continued to increase, and on August 20, 1838, the federal government purchased Cedar Island from the town of East Hampton for establishing a lighthouse. Estimates as to the size of the island vary, but it seems that it was, at the time, about two acres. Except for a small stand of cedar trees, the land was fairly barren. Ninety-eight years later, when the lighthouse reservation was put up for auction, erosion had reduced the island to less than an acre.

Samuel Eldridge was awarded the contract for the construction of the lighthouse, and it became operational in January of 1839. The tower rose from the keeper's dwelling to a height of thirty-four feet above sea level. Displaying a fixed white light, it served to mark the harbor's entrance. In 1848, the station was equipped with nine lamps and fourteen inch reflectors, and in 1855 it was refitted with a sixth-order lens.

On January 9, 1839, Fifth Auditor Steven Pleasonton sent a letter to the area's Collector of Customs, asking him to notify Frederick King that he had been appointed keeper of the Cedar Island Light. "You will inform him," he wrote, "that his salary is fixed at three hundred and fifty dollars per annum. You will also state to him the necessity of his residing and being himself steadily in the house provided for the Keeper."

In June of 1880, Keeper W. W. Seaman, who had been in charge of the station for eleven years, was removed from office. "When the station was last inspected," wrote Comdr. George Dewey, USN, "the house and tower were found dirty and neglected, and the lens was not properly cleaned. It appears from the report of inspection that the station has always shown signs of neglect by this Keeper, who is seldom found there." For the most part, however, the keepers of Cedar Island were dedicated to their charge. William F. Follett, a well-known figure in the local community, was credited with going to the aid of many area sailors. On July 13, 1919, he saved the lives of those aboard the yacht *Flyer*, after the boat exploded.

On March 2, 1867, Congress appropriated $25,000 for the construction of a new lighthouse at Cedar Island. Built of Vermont granite, the two-story, nine-room structure was completed in 1869. Like its predecessor, the tower was fitted with a sixth-order lens that continued showing a fixed white light. In 1882, the station was equipped with a machine-operated fog bell.

Erosion of the sandy island was a persistent problem, and over the years the small cedar grove was undermined and washed away. During the construction of the new lighthouse, several tons of riprap were set in place to protect both the structure and the property. From February of 1903 to September of 1906, an additional 6,600 tons of rock were delivered to the site, and by the early 1920's, further riprap had stabilized the sands. On September 21, 1938, the Great Hurricane reshaped the coastline, filling in the 200-yard gap between Cedar Island and the mainland; the newly created peninsula became known as Cedar Point.

The Cedar Island Light was discontinued in September of 1934, and its beacon was replaced by an automatic light atop a skeleton tower.

The Lighthouse Service offered to turn over the Cedar Island Light to the National Park Service in 1936, but it showed no interest. In the following year, the site was put up for auction, and a Manhattan lawyer, Phelan Beale, purchased it for $2,002. When questioned why he wanted the property, Beale, who had a lease on a nearby game preserve answered, "It would be a damn nuisance if strangers bought it" He was also quoted as saying that, "he wanted to preserve it as a monument to the past." In 1943, Beale sold the lighthouse to Isabelle Bradley, who had been renting it from him for about four years. It remained in her hands until 1967, when she sold it to Suffolk County.

On June 6, 1974, a fire set by vandals, swept through the 105-year-old structure, destroying its roof and its oak paneled walls, and cracking some of its stones. It was not the first blaze to beset the structure. In July of 1939, a fire started in the lighthouse's generator. Isabelle Bradley, who was living there at the time with her husband, set out by boat to Sag Harbor to get help; two passing fishermen and her husband remained to fight the blaze. Men from the East Hampton Fire Department were unable to reach the lighthouse; they were blocked by a locked gate leading to the property. By the time Isabelle had returned with help, the structure had been gutted.

Shortly after the 1939 fire, the lighthouse was refurbished, but after the 1974 fire, it was learned that Suffolk County had forgotten to insure the historic landmark. The roof was repaired, the windows were boarded up, and the doors were sealed. In the summer of 1988, the Sag Harbor Whaling Museum approached Suffolk County officials, requesting permission to restore the lighthouse. The museum received their blessing, and, within a short time, $100,000 had been raised toward the goal.

> Access to the Cedar Island Light is possible by four-wheel drive vehicle, or via shallow draught boat.
> NOAA chart #12358

Cedar Island Lighthouse, from its southwest side, 1987

7   *Long Island's Coastal Lights*

MONTAUK POINT LIGHT

Appropriation:	March 2, 1793	*$20,000*
Re-appropriated:	March 3, 1797	*$13,000*
Appropriation:	March 3, 1797	*$2,740.67*
Established:	1797	
First keeper:	Jacob Hand, appointed November 4, 1796	

Illuminating apparatus (IA): (1838), 18 lamps, 14.5" reflectors, fixed white light(FW).

IA:	(1842) 13 lamps, 18" reflectors, FW
IA:	(1850) 15 lamps, 21" reflectors, FW
Refitted:	1857, first-order Fresnel lens (1-order), fixed white light varied by flash (FW v Fl).
IA:	(1883) 1-order, FW v Fl; white flash every 2 min.
Refitted:	1904, (1907) three and a half-order bivalve lens, Fl W every 10 seconds, duration of flash 9/10 sec. Fixed red (FR sector) between SE 3/8 S and SSE 5/8 S, FR range lens.
IA:	(1939) 3.5-order bivalve lens, Fl W, flash .5 sec, eclipse 9.5 sec. Incandescent oil vapor lamp, 220,000 cp. FR sector, 4-order range lens, oil lamp, 3,500 cp.
Fog signal:	1792, steam fog signal.
Fog signal:	(1873) first-class Daboll trumpet operated by hot-air engine. Blasts 12 seconds, intervals 50 seconds.
Fog signal:	1898, first-class siren, Belt air compressor.
Fog signal:	(1939) air diaphragm horn, blast 2 seconds, silent 13 seconds.

Height of light above sea level: (1838) 160 feet. (1891) 169.5 feet

August 18, 1795: "The President has this day," wrote Commissioner of Revenue Finch Coxe, "approved the proposals for building a light House on Montauk Point, as made by you, on the 11th ultimo (July 11). You will therefore consider the same as mutually binding upon you and the United States." Four individuals had submitted bids ranging from $32,000 to $22,300; John McComb Jr.'s had been the lowest.

After having reviewed the plans for its construction, President Washington is often quoted as having predicted that the lighthouse

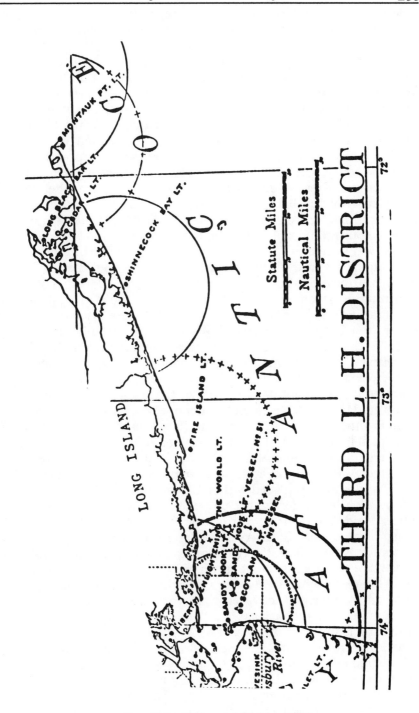

Long Island Coastal Lights, 1895

would stand for 200 years. The octagonal tower was built of Connecticut red sandstone, which was transported to the site by ship. The eighty-foot tall structure was seven feet thick at its base, and tapered to a width of three feet at the top. It was surmounted by an iron lantern, ten feet high and ten feet wide. A ball-like copper ventilator capped the lantern; it turned by means of a weather vane, allowing its built-in opening to point always to the leeward side.

The site for the Montauk Point Light, then known as Turtle Hill, was surveyed and chosen by Ezra L'Hommedieu. He warned that, though the land was good for a foundation, the bank would gradually erode from the action of the sea. The surveyor thus recommended that the lighthouse be "set a distance back for safety." Even before the completion of the lighthouse, John McComb was forced to take measures to slow erosion and since then, loss of the bluff sands has been a continual problem for the light station.

The tower's original lighting apparatus consisted of thirteen whale-oil lamps, arranged on two levels. In July of 1838, the tower was changed to eighteen lamps and parabolic reflectors, divided between two iron tables; ten were grouped on the upper table and eight on the lower table. In 1856, plans were made to refit the station with a first-order Fresnel lens. The apparatus was to have been lit on January 1, 1858, to coincide with the exhibition of Shinnecock's (Great West Bay) first-class light, but, to accommodate the new, twelve feet high by six feet in diameter lens, the lantern room had to be enlarged, and fourteen feet of height had to be added to the masonry tower. When completed in 1860, the station's immobile beacon was differentiated from Shinnecock's equally powerful fixed light by using a separate lens panel that rotated around the main lens. The mechanism produced a bright flash that interrupted the fixed light every two minutes. Along with other improvements to the tower, the wooden spiral stairs were replaced with a 137-step iron stairway.

Montauk's first-order light remained in operation until 1904, when it was decided to replace it with a more modern and powerful third-order bivalve lens. Similar to the lens installed at Highlands of Navesink, NJ, in 1898, the twin convex discs each had a bull's-eye lens, through which a single beam of light was focused. The apparatus flashed a white light every fifteen seconds. It continued to be revolved by a weight-activated clockwork mechanism until 1960, when an electric motor was installed.

Edmund Blunt, copublisher of *American Coast Pilot*, visited Montauk Point in 1837 with Colonel Livingston. The dwelling that was then being erected at the light station, was not to their liking. "The cellar walls are not laid in mortar, and improper sized stone filled in next the earth. The material generally, is bad for a work of that kind." In his letter to the Light House Establishment of November 30, 1837,

Montauk Point Lighthouse, 1987

Blunt went on, "The contractor differs in opinion from those who have seen the work, as to the measuring of the height of the brickwork from the floor." A new well had been dug by the contractor, but it was too shallow, yet he had filled in the old well over the objections of Keeper Patrick Gould. "Now, who is to blame? Certainly not the Collector of Sag Harbor; he resides many miles distant, and there is no provision for him to go there to attend to the details." In a thinly veiled reference to the administration of lighthouses by Superintendent of Lights Steven Pleasonton, Blunt finished that portion of his letter stating, "It is the system."

During Lt. Bache's inspection tour of Montauk in 1838, there were three dwellings at the site. The oldest, a wood-frame house, had only three rooms; it was said to be in poor condition. Another wooden dwelling had four rooms, and a new brick house had six rooms.

Jacob Hand, appointed on November 4, 1796, was Montauk's first keeper. Fifteen years later, Hand began thinking of stepping down, and his son, Jared, applied for the position. When the recommendation for Jared was made known to President Jefferson, the chief of state wrote: "I have constantly refused to give in to this method of making offices hereditary. Whenever this one becomes actually vacant, the claims of Jared Hand may be considered with those of other competitors." Apparently Jared was the best qualified applicant; he was appointed on January 28, 1812, but he served as head keeper for barely two years.

There were twelve more head keepers before James G. Scott was appointed on September 26, 1885. Scott, one of the station's best-known keepers, had held a position in the Light House Establishment before the Civil War. During the conflict, he served in the Army, and four years later he returned to his real love, keeping a light.

Scott kept diaries while at Montauk, in which he recorded birds sighted at the lighthouse. In one of his first entries concerning birds, he wrote, "Large number of winter gulls have lived on a shoal off the Point for two or three months past." The keeper watched for and made note of many species of birds, but his chief concern seemed to have been for the birds that ran into the light. Scott's daughter is said to have recalled that, in 1938, "thousands of birds would strike the Light. After one storm we counted 300 yellow warblers dead on the beach."

In his last few years at Montauk, friction developed between Keeper Scott and his first assistant, Evard Jansen. The first assistant considered the head keeper too old and claimed that he was not doing his share of the work. Some members of the Light House Board felt that the assistant might simply be vying for the sixty-nine-year-old man's position. Both men, however, had the reputation of being good keepers, but it was noted that Scott had become less efficient with his advancing age. In May of 1910, Keeper Scott was offered a transfer to the New Dorp Light, a station that would have required much less physical effort. The keeper declined and resigned on October 1, 1910; he had served twenty-five years in the Light House Service.

Until the late 1920s, the last few miles leading from Amagansett to Montauk Point consisted of a narrow, sandy road that could easily trap a vehicle. Only the more adventurous motorist made it out to the lighthouse. In its earlier history, getting supplies to the station meant a long trek by horse and wagon. There was an urgent appeal made to Congress in 1879 for funds to rebuilt the fallen-down barn, without which there was no place to shelter the horses. The appropriation was made that year.

The remoteness of Montauk Point Light did not help isolate its keepers, however, from the troubled times of the Prohibition years. "On February 10, 1925," wrote Assistant Superintendent Luther, "we proceeded to Montauk Point Light Station, to investigate the complaint of District Superintendent S. R. Sands, Coast Guard Service, regarding the lack of cooperation on the part of the Keepers at Montauk Point Light Station and the inference in his report that the two of said Keepers had violated the Prohibition Law."

In the early morning hours of January 20, 1925, the Ditch Plain

Coast Guard Station received a call from New York concerning two vessels, the *Linnie Bell* and the *Imperia.* They had gone aground on a nearby sandbar, and they were suspected of carrying cargoes of liquor. The guardsman on duty called Montauk Point, asking if the keepers had seen such a boat. Assistant Miller, the head keeper's son, responded that a passerby had reported a stranded vessel, that had, however, gotten itself off the beach. When the guardsman went to investigate the site, he found one totally wrecked boat, which was high and dry; around it lay empty liquor boxes. (Apparently, however, he did not see the second vessel, also wrecked on the beach.) A message was left to have Head Keeper John Miller return the guardsman's call, but, when he failed to do so, the Coast Guard's suspicion was aroused. (John E. Miller had been a New York City policeman for twenty-three years before being appointed to the Montauk Point Light. His father, Jonathan A. Miller, had also been the station's keeper from 1865 to 1869.)

Inspector Luther of the Third District made a thorough investigation. The two Millers' claim that they had not observed the grounded vessel(s) was found to be correct. During the entire day of the incident, there had been a heavy snowstorm; it was impossible to see within any distance from the station. Though it was concluded that Keeper Miller had not shown a "proper spirit of cooperation" by failing to return the Coast Guard's phone call, there was no evidence that implicated the keepers with the "illegal spirits." The matter was dropped.

Montauk was a natural observation post, a fact that did not escape the War Department in 1898, during its preparations for war with Spain. On April 30 of that year, the station's old fog signal house was converted to quarters for a contingent of Navy Signal Corps personnel. At the same time, a telephone was installed, and a telegraphic connection was made with the Western Union office. The telegraph was discontinued a few months later. Ezra L'Hommedieu in 1792 foresaw Montauk's erosion problem. At the time of construction, the tower was thought to have stood 297 feet from the bank's edge. By 1867, a survey of the property revealed that the distance had been reduced to a little over 200 feet. Though authorities had always recognized the problem, efforts to stem the progress of erosion were generally ineffective. Following a severe storm in 1944, during which a 12-foot section of sand cliff was lost, Army engineers constructed a 650-foot long sea wall at the foot of the sand bank; the measures taken could not stand up to heavy storms.

In 1965, the bank's edge had crept to only forty-five feet, nine inches from the tower. Landfill was dumped over the side, gaining about another twenty feet. The editor of a local newspaper predicted that the lighthouse would topple over the edge within five years, and he called for a "light-in" demonstration by concerned citizens; one thousand persons responded on that "foggy and rainy night." Some of the guardsmen did not share their fear of imminent disaster; "I wont hang by my thumbs waiting for the light to fall," one man stationed at Montauk was quoted as saying.

Help in controlling erosion came in the form of rock-filled wire baskets, "gambions," which were placed at the foot of the sand cliff. A gentle lady in her seventies, Gorgenia Reid, and other volunteers, supported by contributions and the Coast Guard's blessing, terraced some areas, using cedar planks staked into the sand bank. Behind each plank, a trench was dug, and sea grasses and shrubs were planted. The measures worked, but much more is needed to be done.

In February of 1987, Montauk's bivalve lens was removed from the tower and placed on display at the site's lighthouse museum; the 190-year-old sentinel was then automated.

The Montauk Point Lighthouse Museum is open to the public on a seasonal basis. Exhibits include the Fresnel bivalve lens, lighthouse photographs, and drawings. Visitors can also climb up the tower's spiral staircase to the watch deck, where the station's new lens can be seen.
NOAA chart #13209, 12300

GREAT WEST BAY - SHINNECOCK BAY LIGHT

Appropriation: *August 3, 1854*   *$35,000*
Appropriation: *August 18, 1856*   *$12,000*
Established: *1858*
First lighted: *January 1, 1858*
First keeper: *Charles A. Conly, appointed December 7, 1857*
Illuminating apparatus (IA):1858, first-class Fresnel lens (1-order), fixed white light.
Illuminant: *1907, changed from 5 wick oil lamp to incandescent oil vapor.*
        Power increase 12,188-candlepower (cp) to 45,690 cp
IA: *(1924) 1-order, group flash W 7.5 sec, 350,000 cp*
Fog signal: *none*
Height of light above sea level: (1891) 160 feet
Discontinued: *1931*

Duty at Shinnecock Bay Light was not for the very old or feeble; approximately one hundred seventy-eight steps and landings led to the base of the lantern. The red brick tower, built by Lt. J. C. Duane of the Corps of Engineers, rose 150 feet to the center of the lantern, and it was 160 feet above mean high water. It showed its fixed white light for the first time on January 1, 1858.

The station was located on Ponquogue Point, NY, approximately midway between the lights at Fire Island and Montauk Point. Shinnecock was part of an important system of improved coastal lights that included the installation of first-order lenses at all three of the stations.

The lighthouse was one of the tallest towers on the east coast, but standing on the beach about 200 feet from the water's edge, it rose only to about the height of a large vessel's mast. Seen from offshore, its fixed light could have easily been mistaken for a fishing vessel, or any other coastal craft —a situation that could have led to disaster.

In 1901, the Light House Establishment requested a change in the light's characteristic from fixed to flashing. At the time, incoming trans-atlantic steamers, approaching the coast at full speed, made for Shinnecock after sighting Nantucket Shoals. Ships generally did not steer for the Fire Island Light, located thirty-five miles to the west of Shinnecock. The beacon was considered too near the entrance to New York Harbor and the hazardous New Jersey coast.

The request for a change in the characteristic was repeated over a period of several years, but instead, in 1907, the intensity of the light was increased. By switching illuminants from oil to incandescent oil

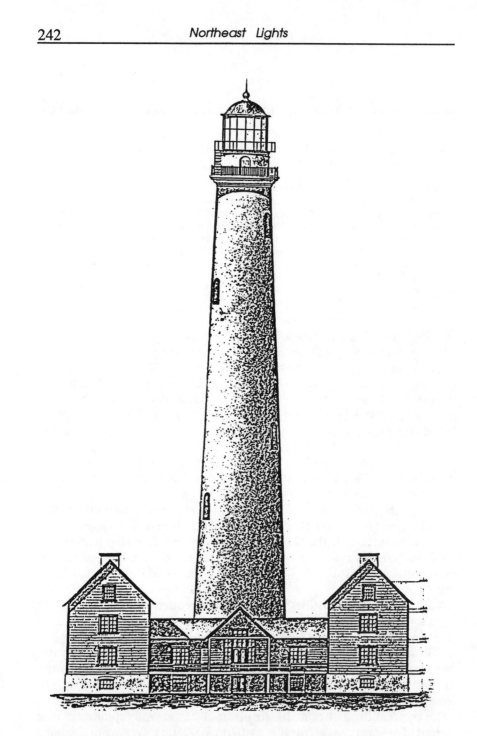

Great West (Shinnecock) Bay Lighthouse, 1857.
National Archives, RG 26, Great West Bay LH, NY. #2

vapor, the beacon's candlepower was raised from 12,188 to 45,690. The vapor illuminant also saved a great deal of oil; the old consumed 2,282 gallons per year, and the new used only 599 gallons per year.

The lighthouse reservation at Shinnecock consisted of about ten acres. Keeper John Raynor, who had been appointed to the post on October 14, 1893, used most of the land for grazing his five cows, and the outbuildings for housing his horse and eleven pigs. The first assistant keeper took over the unused oil house as his workshop, and with the second assistant, he shared two small, fenced-in parcels that they maintained as vegetable gardens.

When Maj. Charles Potter of the Third Light House District arrived to inspect the station in November of 1909, he was met by Keeper Raynor. As the two approached the old oil house, Maj. Potter asked what it was being used for. Before the keeper was able to answer, both were startled by a high-pitched female voice: "John uses that work shop and he's going to use it too as long as he's here." Trying to avoid further confrontation, Major Potter walked away and heard, "John you come here." He looked back and saw First Assistant John Potter leave what he was doing and go up to his quarters. The shrill-voiced woman fired off another salvo: "He's got every devilish thing at this station except that old oil house and now he's trying to get that. There ain't a devilish thing left for John. He's got everything filled with his hogs, his cows and his horse!"

Maj. Potter later recounted that as he walked away in disgust, "the voice followed me growing louder and louder as the distance increased but I purposely avoided hearing any more — I could not have felt more uncanny if I had been in an insane asylum."

Following the incident, Assistant Keeper Potter apologized for his wife's behavior. "I would not have had it if I could have helped it," he wrote, "but women get sore sometimes and talk a good deal more than they might."

Maj. Potter's first inclination had been to dismiss the assistant, a punishmant that may seem a bit drastic by modern standards, but not so at the time. After tempers cooled, he wrote, "I am rather loath to recommend drastic action in this case for such an old and faithful employee of the Board." In many ways, the problems of the keepers were no different from those of the rest of society.

Improvements in New York's main shipping channel made Shinnecock's beacon unnecessary, and in 1931 it was discontinued and replaced with a red skeleton tower. About five years later, the tower was turned over to the Bureau of Biological Survey of the Department of Agriculture, but it was later found unsafe and was ordered abandoned. Holes were drilled through the tower's walls, and a large section was removed from one side, near the base. Timbers, which had been put into place to shore up the missing section, were then thoroughly soaked with gasoline, and a fire was set. On December 23, 1948, the smoldering sentinel leaned over, hesitated, and then plunged to the ground.

NOAA chart #12353

FIRE ISLAND LIGHT

Appropriation:　　March 3, 1825　　　　　　$10,000
Appropriation:　　March 3, 1857　　　　　　$40,000
Established:　　1827
Illuminating apparatus (IA): circa 1827, 18 lamps, 15"　　reflectors, revolving (Rv)
Refitted:　　　　1842, 14 lamps, 21" reflectors, Rv 1.30 min.
IA:　　　　　　(1849) 14 lamps, 21" reflectors, Rv 1.30 min.
Rebuilt:　　　　1858
Refitted:　　　　1856, first-order Fresnel lens, Rv 1.00 min.
IA:　　　　　　(1873) first-order, flashing white (Fl W) 1 min.
IA:　　　　　　(1924) first -order, Fl W, incandescent oil vapor, 170,000 cp.
IA:　　　　　　(1939) first-order, Fl W 7.5 sec, electric, 280,000 cp
Fog signal:　　　none
Height of light above sea level: (1842) 89 feet. (1891) 168 feet

Prior to the creation of the Light House Board in 1852, there were few instructions available for new keepers. Correspondence notifying a keeper of an appointment stated the salary and emphasized the necessity of residing and being "steadily in the house provided for the keeper." The printed instructions covered when to light and extinguish the station's beacon and went into little else.

For a few individuals of that era, the responsibility of keeping the light was just an adjunct to their real occupation of farming, fishing, or a variety of other trades. Throgs Neck's first two keepers were known to have kept a bar for visiting sportsmen on lighthouse property, but they apparently were never caught or disciplined. Keeper Felix Dominy, however, lost his appointment after Superintendent Curtis discovered his activities at Fire Island Light.

"M. Dominy," wrote the superintendent in November of 1843, "entertains boarders and company at his dwelling on the Island and devotes so much of his time and care to that, and other business personal to himself, that the public charge committed to him, is not faithfully exercised; his Light House duties are made subordinate objects of attention." Superintendent Curtis further complained that through neglect, the keeper had damaged reflectors that had

Fire Island Lighthouse, old and new. National Archives 26-LG-11-62

Fire Island Lighthouse, 1987

recently been installed at the station. Lastly, he stated that Keeper Dominy provided spirits for his guests. The keeper was discharged, and on January 15, 1844, Eliphalet Smith was appointed in his place.

Established, 1827

Fire Island's first lighthouse was erected near the southwest end of the barrier beach, about 120 feet from the water. Constructed of Connecticut River bluestone between 1825 and 1826, the octagonal tower rose seventy-four feet from its base to the bottom of the lantern. It had six windows and a wood spiral stairway leading to the lantern. Originally equipped with eighteen lamps and reflectors, the tower was refitted in 1842, with fourteen lamps and twenty-one-inch reflectors; powered by a weight and clockwork, the light revolved every one and a half minutes.

The light marked the entrance to Fire Island Inlet and the eastern entrance to New York's lower bay; its maximum range was fourteen and a half miles in "ordinary weather." Because it was considered the most important beacon for vessels trading in New York, the recommendation was made to increase the height of the tower and equip it with the most powerful lens apparatus that could be procured.

Construction of the new lighthouse, under the direction of Lt. J. C. Duane, began in the summer of 1857 and continued until that December. In the spring, Lt. J. T. Morton took over the project and discovered that the foundation's concrete had many defects. Rather than start over, the officer doubled the number of reinforcing iron bands that were imbedded in the lower part of the tower. Using an estimated 800,000 bricks, the 168-foot tower was raised on a stone pier, 100 feet by 150 feet. The lighthouse's walls were made 11 feet thick at its base and 2 1/2 feet at the parapet; approximately 192 iron steps and nine landings led to the lantern room. A keeper's dwelling was built in front of and connecting to the tower; it had separate quarters for three keepers.

Fitted with a first-order Fresnel lens, its flashing white light was exhibited for the first time on November 1, 1858; it could be seen up to twenty-three miles. With the lighting of the new Fire Island tower, along with the towers at Montauk and Shinnecock, it was anticipated that the 120 miles of coastline to New York would be made "with ordinary care and precaution, entirely easy and safe." History proved those hopes to have been wrong.

In 1895, some of the Light House Board members became convinced that Fire Island had become the most important light for trans-atlantic steamers bound for New York. A bivalve lens built by Henry Lepaute of Paris, France, had been on display at the 1893 World's Columbian Exhibition in Chicago. Consisting of two, nine-feet-in-diameter range lenses, back to back, the makers claimed that, by using electricity, the apparatus would produce the most powerful flash along the entire coast. The board ordered preparations made to install the new lens at Fire Island.

Plans were made to show a fourth-order lens during the change. The boiler room and the engine room were built. Two boilers, one engine, and one dynamo were installed, and the ironwork necessary to adapt the lantern to the new apparatus was fitted. A narrow-guage railroad was laid from the beach to receive coal shipments, but then all work stopped. On December 21, 1896, the equipment was returned to the General Light-House Depot at Staten Island; it had been decided to install the bivalve lens at Highlands of Navesink instead. In December of 1907, the station's illuminant was changed from oil to incandescent oil vapor (see Great West Bay Light).

In April of 1912, the tower was inspected and found in poor condition. A large crack had developed in the upper part of the tower, 130 feet above the ground, and smaller ones were found farther down. Reinforcing bands were put into place around the tower and protective coating was applied. The tower was refaced in 1955, but, when the light was discontinued in January of 1974, the tower began to deteriorate rapidly. Under the leadership of Norma Murray Ervin, president of the Fire Island Preservation Society, restoration of the lighthouse was begun and on May 25, 1986, the tower again exhibited a light.

Fire Island Light is open to the public during the summer season, and by special arrangement. (516) 661-4876
NOAA chart #12300

FIRE ISLAND LIGHTSHIP

Established:	1896		
First lighted:	July 15, 1896		
Lightship LV 58:	1896-1897.	Built 1894, Toledo, Ohio.	$50,870
Lightship LV 68:	1897-1930.	Built 1897, Bath, ME.	$74,750
Lightship LV 114:	1930-1942.	Built 1930, Portland, OR	$223,121
Discontinued:	1942		

During the mid-1890's, transatlantic vessels bound for the Port of New York carried an estimated 450,000 passengers yearly, and 13 million dollars in cargo each week. Approaching the harbor in fog or heavy weather, it was difficult for navigators to determine their exact position. Sounding the bottom gave an indication of the proximity of land, but a miscalculation could mean grounding the vessel, or worse, on the shores of Long Island or New Jersey. A whistling buoy had been established six miles off Fire Island to aid mariners during reduced visibility, but the sailors complained that its signal was often barely audible. Thus in 1895, marine interests petitioned the Light House Board to replace the buoy with a lightship.

The 121-foot steam screw vessel, *LV 58*, took up its position at the newly established Fire Island lightship station, on July 15, 1896. It was equipped with a twelve-inch steam chime, and an emergency, hand-operated bell; from its two masts, it showed white lights. The ship remained posted at Fire Island for only fourteen months, and was replaced by *LV 68*. It was then reassigned to relief duty.

On December 5, 1905, *LV 58* was relieving the Nantucket Lightship, *LV 66*, when a strong northeaster swept over the region. In the midst of the relentless pounding, *LV 58* sprang several leaks in its fireroom compartment. The pumps were started, but they clogged so often that they were unable to keep up with the incoming water; within a short time, the ship's boilers had been extinguished. Capt. James Jorgensen sent out a call for help, and, for the next twenty-four hours, the crewmen bailed by hand. On the following morning, the tender *Azalea* took *LV 58* under tow, but in the mid-afternoon, some eighteen miles northwest of the station, the water-laden vessel succumbed to the sea.

The composite hull *LV 68* (steel ribs and wood bottom) was built in 1897 at the Bath Iron Works of Bath, ME. Capable of 8.5 knots under steam screw power, the vessel was also rigged for sail. Its two masts showed white lights, which were generated by electricity. In 1920, the electric lights were replaced with acetylene and later changed to 375-millimeter electric lens lanterns.

Most of *LV 68's* crewmen were still in their bunks on the morning of May 8, 1916, when the steamer *Philadelphian* crashed head-long into its side. The force of the collision had left a two-foot gash in the lightship, four feet below the waterline. The men reacted quickly. With the aid of the steamer's crew, tanks were emptied, coal was shifted, and lifeboats were swung out over the uninjured side and filled with water. Together, the measures made the vessel list sufficiently to raise most of the damaged side out of the water. With the pumps able to keep up with any further flooding, *LV 68* was taken under tow by the *Philadelphian* to a point just short of Ambrose Lightship. There, it was met by a lighthouse tender which took the damaged vessel to the lighthouse depot at Staten Island. That night, the light was shown from a tender, and, on the following day, a relief vessel took up the position off Fire Island. The vessel was repaired and returned to duty, but, eight years later, it was involved in yet another mishap.

A dense fog had settled over *LV 68* during the evening of March 29, 1923, and, by noon of the following day, it showed no sign of lifting. A radiobeacon, installed two years earlier, had been operating all night long as had the ship's submarine bell and fog whistle. "About 2:45 p.m.," the lightship's assistant engineer later reported, "I heard three ships, two off the port quarter and one off the stern. I went on deck looking for them and they continued blowing. I then heard a sudden rush of water coming straight toward us. I looked up and saw the steamer heading straight for us."

The assistant engineer barely had time to ring the alarm bell before the British steamer *Castillian* struck a glancing blow to the lightship's port quarter. A hole was left in its side, from the deck to the waterline. Recovering from the shock of the collision, the crew threw slings over the side of the lightship, and, using tarpaulins and planks, they were able to patch up the damage sufficiently, to allow the vessel to steam back to port.

A new lightship, *LV 109/WAL 530*, which was being prepared at Staten Island for the station at Five Fathom Bank, was repainted red overnight. On the following day, it took up the injured vessel's position and continued to be posted at that location, until the necessary repairs had been made. In 1930, *LV 68* was reassigned to relief duty, and, two years later, it was sold at public auction. Only four bids were received for the aging vessel. The lowest was for $22, and the winning bid was $825; it had been constructed at a cost of $74,750.

Fire Island's new lightship, *WAL 536*, was built at the Albina Marine Works, in Portland, OR. On July 15, 1930, Capt. J. Nielson took possession of the self-propelled lightship and began the long voyage to the lighthouse depot at Staten Island, NY.

The ship was first sailed to the lighthouse depot at Astoria, OR, were it was outfitted with a wireless and other navigational equipment. On the morning of August 5, 1930, *WAL 536* left the dock, bound for San Francisco. The 560 miles were uneventful, and Capt. Nielson noted in the lightship's log, an average speed of 9.3 knots. After remaining there for several days, the vessel proceeded for the Panama Canal, making one stop for oil and fuel in Los Angeles. By September 5, the lightship had cleared the canal, and, fifteen days later, it pulled in at Staten Island. Over the next three months, equipment was installed and tested. At 4:45 am, on Monday, December 1, 1930, *WAL 536* left the dock under the command of Capt. A. Bruggeman. Five hours later, it arrived on station, and it took over for Relief *LV 78*.

The 133-foot steel hull *WAL 536*, had a complement of five officers and ten crewmen. The captain's and radioman's quarters were located on the upper deck. The main deck provided spaces for the

Fire Island Lightship, LV 68, 1897-1930. National Archives, 26-LS-68-1

U. S. LIGHT-HOUSE TENDER "AZALIA."

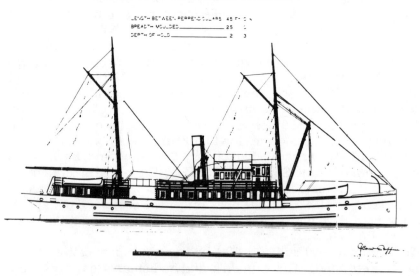

Tender Azalia. Light House Board, December, 1889

other personnel, officers' and crews' galleys, heads, windlass room and battery room. The engineer's workroom and storerooms were located below the main deck. The ship's freshwater tanks were capable of holding a three-month supply, and the oil tanks held enough to last one year. The vessel had two tubular lantern masts, equipped with 374-millimeter lens lanterns; they were each lit by 1000-watt incandescent lamps. The fog signal was a compressed-air diaphone.

Following the Japanese attack on Pearl Harbor, Fire Island Light-ship remained on station. On Christmas Day of 1941, the entries in the lightship's log reflected those of a nation at war.

> *7:30 am USCG plane UN 79 bound E.*
> *8:00 am carried out routine, holiday observed*
> *8:10 am USN Blimp K 4, bound E.*
> *8:12 am mast lights off 1 hour after sunrise.*
> *9:00 am anchored throughout watch.*
> *9:20 am motor boat from Fire Island Station close astern on search for reason for flares. Reported no flares seen by this station. Boats continued to search east.*
> *9:30 am USN Blimp TCM in vicinity.*
> *2:25 pm twin motor plane bound N.NW*
> *3:33 pm mast lights on 1 hour before sun set.*
> *4:00 pm anchored at station.*
> *10:10 pm US Bomber circled ship, departed west.*
> *11:35 pm red flares parachute type sighted by watch officer in charge, and radioman called 11:45 pm reporting same to Fire Island Station with information.*
> *Walter Fleck C.B.M.*

Throughout that night, the lookout reported more flares; Germany had declared war against the United States on December 11, 1941, and their U-boats had begun to prowl the waters just off Long Island. On January 11, 1942, *WAL 536* was taken off station and converted into an examination vessel. Armed with a single six-pounder, it was stationed at Bayshore, NY.

The lightship station at Fire Island remained discontinued at the end of the war. Its last vessel, *WAL 536*, was reassigned as a relief ship, and in 1958, it was posted at Pollock Rip, MA, remaining there for eleven years. It was then moved to Portland, ME, and was decommissioned in 1971. Four years later, the ship was transferred to the city of New Bedford, MA, where it was put on display under the pseudonym of "New Bedford."

WRECK OF THE OREGON LIGHTSHIP

Act of Congress: March 2, 1889,
Appropriation: never made
Established: 1886
First lighted: April 10, 1886
Lightship LV 20:   April 10, 1886 to November 1, 1886
Discontinued: November 1, 1886

Most of the 640 passengers were asleep aboard the luxury liner *Oregon* in the early morning hours of March 14, 1886. Built in 1883, the 502-foot, steel hull Cunard steamer was a record holder in its time; it had once made the Atlantic crossing in 6 days, 9 hours and 22 minutes.

As the *Oregon* approached the Long Island coastline, a heavily laden three-masted schooner suddenly emerged from the inky-black night. Steaming at full speed, the *Oregon's* lookout had no time to react before the schooner tore into its port side; within seconds, the unidentified vessel had slipped below the cold Atlantic waters with all hands still aboard. For the next eight hours, the crippled steamer drifted gradually away from shore. When it had become apparent that the *Oregon* was in mortal danger, the captain fired a series of distress rockets and ordered the ship abandoned. With all aboard safely away, the liner sank slowly, bow first, and settled to the sea floor with two of its mast still above water.

Though the masts were later cleared away, the sunken vessel still posed a hazard to navigation. To mark the obstruction, lightship *LV 20* was anchored 600 yards to the east of the *Oregon* on April 10, 1886. Seven months later, it was determined that there was sixty feet of water over the wreck, and it no longer presented a danger to shipping. The *LV 20* was thus withdrawn and returned to the Staten Island Depot, yet some in the Light House Establishment still felt that a lightship was needed in the vicinity of the wreck.

On March 2, 1889, an Act of Congress authorized establishment of a light vessel and steam fog signal for the wreck of the *Oregon*; it was never funded.

The *Oregon* lies in 130 feet of water, approximately 13 miles off Great South Beach, Long Island, NY. Much of the vessel has broken up and its bulkheads have collapsed to the sea floor, but some sections are still relatively intact. In the late 1980s, scuba divers were still finding a variety of artifacts from the once proud Cunard liner.

NOAA chart #12353. Loran C 26452.9 43676.6

8 Approach Lights — New York Harbor

HIGHLANDS OF NAVESINK -Twin Lights

Appropriation: May 18, 1826, $30,000
Appropriation: June 20, 1860 $72,941
Established: 1828
Purchased land from: Nimrod Woodward, $700.
Contractor: Charles H Smith, Stonington, CT
Contract for illuminating apparatus: David Melville
First keeper: Joseph Doty, appointed April, 1828
Rebuilt station: 1862

North tower:
Illuminating apparatus (IA): (circa 1828) 15 lamps, 14"reflectors, fixed white light (FW)
Refitted: March 1841, first-order Fresnel lens, FW.
IA: 1862, first-order Fresnel lens, FW.
Illuminant north tower: (1862) lard oil, 1883 kerosene.
North tower discontinued: 1898, held in reserve.

South tower:
IA: (circa 1828) 12 lamps, 14" reflectors, FW.
Refitted: March, 1841, second-order Fresnel lens, revolving.
IA: 1862, first-order, fixed lights.
Refitted: 1898, first-order bivalve lens, flashing white light.
Illuminant: (1862) lard oil. 1884, kerosene. 1898, electricity. 1917, changed to
                   incandescent oil vapor.
IA: (1939) second-order, Fl W, flash .3 sec,
                   eclipse 4.7 seconds, electric, 9,000,000 cp.
South tower discontinued: 1949
Fog signal: none
Height of towers, base to focal plane: 1826, 46 feet.
Height of towers, base to focal plane: 1862, 53 feet.

The first beacon(s) on the Highlands of Navesink was part of an "early warning system" erected in 1746 for the protection of Monmouth County and New York City. On seeing six or more vessels approaching the coast, the watchmen were instructed to ascertain their nationality. If they proved to be enemy ships, the beacon was lighted, and an observer in New York sounded the alarm. Shortly after its establishment, it was accidentally lit, but no one in

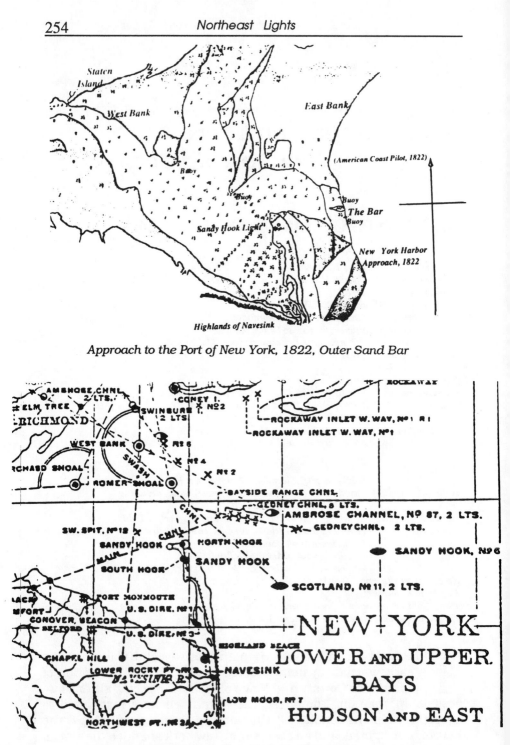

Approach to the Port of New York, 1822, Outer Sand Bar

Approaches to New York Harbor, 1895

New York took notice. Needless to say, steps were immediately taken to assure the vigilance of New York's watchmen.

Navesink's first lighthouse may have been predated by as many as sixty-six years by another lighthouse. Igniting the speculation was an early author's mention of the "erection of a commodious lighthouse" at Highlands of Neversink (in early documents, Navesink was spelled Neversink), the discovery on the site of a seventeenth-century cannon that may have served as a fog signal, and the occasional reference to the area as "Beacon Hill." In the absence of any real proof, however, the forty-six-foot-tall twin towers, which were erected between 1827 and 1828, are recognized as Navesink's first navigational lights.

The octagonal towers were built of blue split stone by Charles Smith of Stonington, CT. The keeper's dwelling, constructed of the same materials, was located about midway between the two and slightly to their rear.

The towers stood 320 feet apart. The north tower exhibited a fixed white light generated by fifteen lamps and fourteen-inch parabolic reflectors. The south tower's light, produced by twelve lamps with fourteen-inch parabolic reflectors, rotated every two and a half minutes; mariners, however, were warned that its rotation could vary from two to three and a half minutes.

Under the supervision of Commodore Perry, a first-order fixed catadioptric (using both refraction and reflection to bend the light rays in the desired direction) lens and a second-order revolving catadioptric lens were purchased for trial in Navesink's towers. When the lenses were installed in 1841, Navesink became the country's first light station to make use of the famous Fresnel lens. The cost of equipping the towers, which necessitated a French technician on site, was about $23,000, but the expense proved to have been worth it. The two lighthouses quickly gained recognition as the best lights along the entire United States coastline.

Care for the lighting systems was difficult. At each tower, a single lamp with three to four concentric wicks, supplied all of the illumination. William Lopez, an especially capable keeper, maintained, repaired, and made any necessary modifications to the apparatus and its clockwork, but his successor, James D. Hubbard, proved to be ill-prepared for the task. A report to the Light House Board in 1852 revealed that nearly all of the mirrors in the two towers were out of adjustment, resulting in a loss of candlepower. Keeper Hubbard had been appointed to the post without providing him with instructions; he had no idea how to maintain the equipment. The only printed manual given to him, translated from French, merely stated that the beacons were to be lit at sunset and extinguished at sunrise.

The station had only two extra lamps, but, rather than keeping

North tower, Highlands of Navesink, 1987

South tower, Highlands of Navesink, 1987

them filled and ready for use in the trimming room, the keeper kept them in a storage shed at a distance from the towers. Under those circumstances, if a light had gone out, it was estimated that it would have taken at least thirty minutes to replace the lamp.

Keeper Hubbard had four assistants to help with the lights. After having assigned the watches, he generally went to bed by 9:00 pm and expected to be awakened only in an emergency. In 1879, Keeper Grosham Van Allen also showed a preference for sleeping through the night, leaving the care of the lights solely in the hands of his three assistants. Though warned that head keepers were to participate in all lighthouse duties, Van Allen persisted in avoiding the watches. In July of that year, his penchant for retiring early, earned him an "early retirement" from the Light House Service.

The Light House Establishment was slow to adapt to new equipment, fuels, and techniques. As a result, its coastal beacons were decidedly inferior to those of France, Great Britain, and other European countries. Navesink's lights had been considered "state of the art" in 1841, but within a decade America's best light had become outdated in comparison to many of Europe's lights.

In 1852, there was a litany of shortcomings in the nation's lighthouse system. There were insufficient numbers of people with the specialized knowledge and skills required for the construction of light towers, leading all too often to badly built structures. The lighthouses frequently resembled each other, making it difficult for sailors to distinguish one from another. Lightships periodically broke away from their moorings, whereas the European vessels seldom lost anchorage. Buoys were insufficiently marked, and their positions were sometimes changed without notifying mariners. Fuel for lamps was at times poor, and there was no overall system for testing, purchasing, and distributing supplies. Despite the changes made over the next twenty years, Maj. George Elliot's inspection tour in 1873 of French and English lights indicated that the United States continued to lag far behind its overseas counterparts.

As a principal light for the port of New York, Highlands of Navesink was in the forefront of the nation's gradually improving lighthouse system. In 1861, the station's twin towers, which had deteriorated badly because of their poor construction, were replaced by new towers that rose fifty-three feet above the ground (248 feet above sea level). Their fixed white lights were first shown on May 1, 1862.

The eighteen-room keeper's dwelling, which was completed in the following year, connected directly with the two towers and allowed access to them without having to exit the buildings. Lacking only a moat and drawbridge, the ornate structures resembled a medieval castle whose occupants stood ready to defend the surrounding countryside against any seaborne invasion.

South tower's bivalve lens on exhibit at Highlands of Navesink

At the time of Maj. Elliot's inspection tour, the coastal lights of France and Great Britain had already converted from the less efficient vegetable and animal oils to mineral oil. In comparison to lard oil, mineral oil burned more cleanly, did not tend to thicken in the cold as did the latter, it did not require trimming during the night, and cost about one-third of the animal product. In the United States, however, it was not until 1883 that a first-order light, Navesink's north tower, made the conversion. The lamp's old illuminant, lard oil, developed 8,000-candlepower; the mineral oil (kerosene) produced 10,000-candlepower. The station's south tower was changed over to mineral oil on the following year.

In 1898, a bivalve lens was installed in the south tower in place of its first-order lens. Built in France, the rotating lens consisted of two convex discs joined at their edges by bands of thick brass; in the center of each disc was a bull's-eye lens. After having exhibited it at Chicago's World's Fair, Capt. Schley, chairman of the Light House Board, reportedly intended to place the massive lens at Fire Island. It was apparently transported there, but a decision was then made to use it at Navesink (see Fire Island Light).

An electric power plant was constructed behind the south tower, and, when completed on June 30, 1898, the bivalve lens was illuminated by an electric arc lamp. As the first coastal light in the

Spiral stairway leading up the north tower, 1987

country to be so lighted (see Sandy Hook East Beacon), it once again was America's most powerful beacon. Producing 25-million-candle-power, the revolving light was visible to the horizon, a distance of about tewnty-two miles. It was said that the reflection of its flashing light could occasionally be seen seventy-five miles out at sea. On September 15, 1898, the north tower was discontinued, but it was held in reserve as an emergency light.

As a cost-cutting measure, the electric arc lamp was replaced in 1917 by an incandescent oil vapor lamp. Ten years earlier, a large number of light stations in the Third District had converted from oil lamps to oil vapor, and the results had been spectacular. A first-order lamp, which produced 710-candlepower, showed a change to 10,879, and in most cases, operational costs were significantly decreased. At Navesink, the change to oil vapor proved disappointing; there was a decrease to 710,000-candlepower. The station continue to operate with the illuminant until 1931. It was then converted to electricity, and it was once more the nation's most powerful light.

The south tower continued to show a light until it was decommissioned in 1949. Three years later, the lens was acquired by the Boston Museum of Science, which placed it on exhibit. In 1979, the museum transferred it to Navesink, where it has been placed on permanent display in the small power plant building behind the south tower,

The twin-lights of Highlands of Navesink can be reached by taking the Garden State Parkway to exit 117 and following Route 36 to Highland. The museum is open from 9:00 am to

SANDY HOOK'S LIGHTS (NJ)
SANDY HOOK LIGHT (MAIN LIGHT), EAST HOOK BEACON (HOOK BEACON), WEST HOOK BEACON (SOUTH BEACON)

Sandy Hook Lighthouse (Main)
Ceded to United States: Act of August 7, 1789
Established: 1764
First lighted: July 11, 1764
Illuminating apparatus (IA): 1764, "48 oil blazes"
IA: (1827) 18 lamps, 18" reflectors
Refitted: 1842, 18 lamps, 21" reflectors, plate glass. Fixed white light (FW).
Refitted: 1857, third-order Fresnel lens (3-order), FW
Rebuilt keeper's dwelling, main light: 1883
Illuminant: 1907, change from 2-wick oil lamp to incandescent oil vapor. Power increase from 1,782-candlepower (cp) to 22,720 cp.
IA: (1939) 3-order, FW electric, 45,000 cp.
Height of tower (main) base to top: 1764, 103 feet.
Height of light above sea level: (1848) 90 feet, (1873) 90 feet.

West (South) Beacon, established: 1817
Refitted: 1842, 14 lamps, 14" reflectors, plate glass, FW.
Refitted: 1855, sixth-order Fresnel lens, FW
Rebuilt: 1867, new lantern with iron deck
IA: (1873) sixth-order, FW
IA: (1907) sixth-order lens, FW acetylene
Height of tower: (1848) 35 feet. (1873) 35 feet

East (Hook) (North Hook) Beacon, established: 1817
Refitted: 1842, 14 lamps, 14" reflectors, plate glass, FW.
IA: East and West Beacons: (1852), 7 lamps, 14" reflectors
Refitted: 1856, fifth-order Fresnel lens, FW
Rebuilt: 1867, burned, rebuilt
IA: (1873) fourth-order Fresnel lens, FW.
Rebuilt: 1880, iron tower
IA: (1883) fourth-order lens, FW
Illuminant: 1889, North Hook (East) electrified.
IA: (1907) 4-order, FW, with fixed red sector
Height of tower: (1848) 35 feet. (1873) 35 feet, (1883)
Height of light above sea level: (1883) 46 feet
Fog signal: (1863) fog bell.
Fog signal: 1868, steam-siren operated by 15-hp boiler.
Fog signal: 1871, first-class steam siren, blast 6 seconds, interval 40 seconds.
Fog signal: (1907) first-class automatic compressed-air siren, blast 3 seconds, silent 27 seconds.

Sandy Hook Fog Bell:
Established: 1892, wedge-shaped wooden skeleton tower built on NW point, bell struck by machine, triple blow every 10 seconds.

"On Monday Evening last [July 11, 1764] the NEW-YORK LIGHT-HOUSE, erected at Sandy-Hook, was lighted for the first Time." The article, which appeared in the June 18, 1764, issue of *New York Mercury*, described the tower as being octagonal in shape. Its base, which was thirty-nine feet in diameter, tapered to fifteen feet at the top. The structure's iron lantern was seven feet high, and it was lighted by "48 Oil Blazes."

Isaac Conro, a resident of New York City, was hired to build the lighthouse. He did his work well; Sandy Hook Light is the oldest original tower still in use in the United States.

In the late 1600s, the governor of New York, Edmund Andros, twice expressed to the governor of East Jersey, Philip Carteret, the need to establish "sea marks for shipping upon Sandy Hook." Other calls for a lighthouse were made, but they were not heeded until 1761, when a group of New York merchants banded together and petitioned Lt. Governor Caldweller Colden, president of His Majesty's Council of New York. The governor immediately recognized the need for a beacon, and representatives approached the owners of Sandy Hook to purchase a four-acre parcel. The asking price was described as "unreasonable," and nothing was done until the following year. On May 9, 1762, the New York Assembly authorized a lottery to provide the necessary funds, but the money raised was inadequate and a second lottery had to be held. After a lighthouse had been established, a tax of three pence per ton was levied on all vessels entering the Port of New York to help defray maintenance costs. Within forty-eight hours of arrival, ship masters had to report to Jonias Smith, the clerk of the Masters and Wardens for the harbor, who collected the fee.

During most of the Revolutionary War period, British troops occupied the lighthouse at Sandy Hook. In 1776, a band of local patriots, commanded by Maj. William Malcolm, managed to slip into the lighthouse and remove "eight copper lamps, two tactile falls, and blocks, and three casks and part of a cask of oil." The British immediately reequipped the beacon, and a small contingent of militia returned to destroy the lighthouse with cannon fire; the raid failed, and the tower survived the war.

In 1804, vessels approaching the port of New York were instructed to look for the promontory known as Highlands of Neversink (Navesink). They could then "run boldly in within 3 miles of the beach, and in steering along the northward, observe to keep in about 8 fathoms water, until you get the [Sandy Hook] light-house to bear W. by S. 1/2 S." Two buoys marked the area of greatest depth over the outer sandbar, and another was located at West Spit, where vessels would veer sharply toward the harbor. At least two other buoys directed mariners away from obstructions, and toward the Vandeventer Point (Verrazano Narrows).

Upon entering New York Harbor, mariners were bound by the port's "Orders and Regulations." All vessels tied up at wharves, and were directed "to lower their top-sail, have their fore and aft spars rigged

Sandy Hook Lighthouse, (main light), 1987

Sandy Hook East beacon, undated. National Archives, 26-LG-15-7

in, and their anchors taken up." There were a number of regulations governing vessels carrying combustible materials and the maintenance of fires aboard ship, while at dock side. Strict rules were in force concerning the discharge of ballast at any point between Sandy Hook and the harbor. Every ship captain was to "report in writing, and on oath, to the mayor of the city, names and occupations of every person who shall be brought into this port in his vessel." Fines for not complying were $50 for each person and $75 for each foreigner.

Each state had its own laws governing vessels entering its harbors. A Connecticut regulation stated that "any persons who shall bring into the state any poor and indigent persons, and leave him or her in any town within the same, of which town he or she is not an inhabitant... shall pay the sum of sixty-seven dollars for each person." Fines of $350 per person were imposed for bringing in anyone previously convicted of a crime.

In 1827, Sandy Hook Light was described in *American Coast Pilot* as being lighted with eighteen patent lamps, with eighteen-inch reflectors. "The strength of light in this lantern is greater than any other on the coast, and if properly attended, may be seen at a distance of 10 leagues." Sometime around 1817, two additional lighted beacons were erected at the site: The West Beacon ranged with a black buoy on the S.W. Spit, and the East Beacon, which ranged with a black buoy of the Middle: the buoy was located five miles from the beacon.

An inspection of the light station in July of 1838, found the keeper's dwelling "not worth repairing." Fifth Auditor Stephen Pleasonton directed New York's Collector of Customs to advertise for bids on a new residence, built of stone or brick, which, he hoped, would be finished by the middle of November of that year. In the same letter, he wrote, "If the Keeper cannot attend to the Beacons, and the principal Light in a proper manner, he must hire himself an assistant at his own expense, his salary having been increased to 600 dollars with that view. Any complaint against him for inattention will cause his removal, and you will inform him."

Only one keeper had been assigned to Sandy Hook. His responsibilities included the main light and two beacons. The East and West beacons, which were about a mile from each other, each had seven lamps and fourteen-inch reflectors; the main light had eighteen lamps and reflectors. "To perform the duty of lighting and extinguishing the 32 lamps at this station properly," it was reported to the Light House Board in 1852, "it would require the keeper to walk about three miles, morning and evening, to the entire neglect of the lamps first lighted; rendering it utterly impossible to attend properly upon them during the entire night." At that time, Highlands of Navesink, whose two towers stood a little more than 300 feet apart, had five keepers! Sandy Hook's keeper, David J. Patterson, had hired an assistant out of his own pocket, but the extra pay, which allowed him to do so, was insufficient. "the small amount allowed does not enable him to obtain the services of such a person as so responsible and important a trust demands." Uriah Smalley, appointed keeper on June 30, 1857, was assigned three assistants.

The East and West Beacons were wooden towers that stood on stone foundations. In 1855, the East Beacon was refitted with a fifth-order lens, and, in the following year, the West Beacon received a sixth-order lens. In 1857, the main light (Sandy Hook Light) was refitted with a third-order Fresnel lens.

A frame building, with the tower attached to the keeper's dwelling, replaced the East Beacon's wooden structure in 1867. First lit in April of that year, the structure was completely destroyed by a fire just two months later. The blaze had been set by an overheated smokestack in the fog signal's engine house. Within a short time, the entire structure was reconstructed, but a September 8, 1869, gale washed away a large portion of the beach in front of the beacon and water then threatened to topple it. It was moved 500 feet south on the following year, but erosion continued to plague the structure. In 1880, a new iron tower and keeper's dwelling were erected 400 feet back from the old site as the sea further encroached on the beacon. The old dwelling was then moved to the rear of the new structures, and it was occupied by one of the keepers. From that time on, the East Beacon was also referred to as Hook Beacon or North Hook Beacon.

The West Beacon also faced difficulties with erosion. In 1857, its foundation had been undermined by wave action and needed to be moved to a more secure site. Ten years later, jetties were constructed in an attempt to deal with the sea that was inching its way even closer toward the foundation. The beach then began to erode from the rear of the beacon, and the structure was set on oak piles, driven twenty-five to thirty feet into the sand. When the channel was dredged in 1889, the West Beacon was moved and made to range with Sandy Hook Light. Relocated 250 feet east, and 440 feet south of its old site, the West Beacon was then referred to as the South Beacon.

In 1888, the torturous and narrow Gedney Channel was one of only two waterways through which deep-draught, ocean-going vessels could enter New York Harbor; the other was by way of Long Island Sound, through Hell Gate. After dark, Gedney Channel, which was marked by unlit buoys, was nearly impossible to navigate on any but the clearest, moonlit nights. In 1884, Hell Gate had been illuminated with powerful electric lights from a 250-foot tower, but the experiment failed (see Hell Gate Light).

U.S. Life Saving Station, Sandy Hook, NJ.
Spermaceti Cove Visitor Center, Gateway National Recreational Area

During the summer of 1888, preparations were made to install six electrically lighted buoys in Gedney Channel. The dynamo was housed in a small brick building that was erected near the North Hook (East) Beacon. From there, an electrical line ran across the sea floor and was connected to each of the buoys. The lights, which were housed in brass lamps with thick, curved glass, alternated between red and white on each side of the channel. In January of 1889, the colors of the lamps were changed to all red lamps on the starboard side of the channel and white ones on the port side.

At first, the keepers of the electric buoys were quartered in a house belonging to U. S. Army Engineers. When asked to vacate the building, the three keepers and their families were forced to move in with North Hook's assistant keeper and his family. Some arrangements were made to relieve the intolerable crowding, and in 1891 an additional dwelling was constructed.

On April 16, 1889, North Hook Beacon was connected to the electric buoys' dynamo, and it became America's second lighthouse, after the Statue of Liberty, to use that source of power. Seven years later, electrical wires were extended to Sandy Hook Light (main light) and South Hook Beacon. At the main light, a 150-candlepower lamp was substituted for the tower's 77-candlepower oil lamp, and South Hook was equipped with a 100-candlepower lamp, replacing its former 50-candlepower oil lamp.

The electrically-lighted buoys were a success; during the first six months of operation, a total of 224 large vessels entered or exited the harbor after dark. The navigational aids were, however, difficult and costly to maintain. Storms, ice, and vessels running into the buoys often interrupted their operation. Thus, on March 15, 1903, they were replaced by gas buoys.

Throughout most of its history, Sandy Hook's strategic position near the Port of New York, made it the site of almost continual military presence. The armed forces' activities, however, were not always compatible with keeping the lights.

During the War of 1812, Sandy Hook's keeper complained of being put out of his home by Army personnel. Commissioner of Revenue Smith, wrote to the Secretary of War, asking him to "instruct General Porter to forbid the troops to occupy the dwelling house of the keeper of the light house, or to interfere with the light unless the enemy shall appear with intention of attacking the post."

In 1864, the East Beacon's lantern glass had been shattered so often by the firing of guns at the nearby fort that it was suggested that it would be best to move the tower. "Yesterday, the 9th inst.," wrote Keeper William Stanton in April of 1903, "notice was given me that firing would take place on that day, which enabled me to have all doors and windows open, and no damage." On the following day, however, the keeper received no notice; when the thirteen-inch guns were fired, they blew away the window sashes. The War Department paid for the damage, but there were many other similar instances.

In 1917, the North Hook Beacon found itself in direct firing line of Fort Hancock's new gun battery. The cast-iron conical tower was taken to a storage area and replaced by a thirty-five-foot skeleton tower. The old structure was later moved to Jeffrey's Hook, NY, where it became known to the nation's children as the Little Red Lighthouse.

Sandy Hook Light was extinguished for the duration of the Second World War. It was not the first time since the Revolutionary War that its beacon had gone unlighted. From April 28, 1898, to August 1 of that year, the War Department ordered all of Sandy Hook's lights extinguished; the nation was at war with Spain. The North Hook and South Hook beacons were last lit in 1923, but the sturdy old tower, automated in 1962, continues to serve mariners.

Gateway National Recreational Area is open to the public, year-round. Visitors are not permitted to enter Sandy Hook Light, but the site is a natural spot for swimming, fishing, picnics and just sight-seeing. NOAA chart #12326

SANDY HOOK LIGHTSHIP

Established:	*May, 1823. Discontinued: 1829*
Re-established:	*1838*
First keeper:	*Captain William Taylor*
Lightship LV "VV":	*1823-1829 Built 1822-1823, $17,702*
Lightship LV "WW":	*1838-1854 Built 1837, $15,900*
Lightship LV 16:	*1854-1891 Built 1854, $28,084*
Lightship LV 48:	*1891-1894 Built 1891, $57,280*
Lightship LV 51:	*1894-1908 Built 1892. $53,325*

Position moved to Ambrose: 1908

May 1, 1823: "The Floating Lights for Sandy Hook near New York being now ready for her Station," wrote Stephen Pleasonton of the Treasury Department, "I have the honor to enclose all the applications and recommendations received at this office for the office of Master or Keeper." Pleasonton recommended Capt. William Taylor for the post, and, two days later, President Thomas Jefferson appointed him to the post. The captain died in March of the following year, and he was replaced by Charles Barnard.

Sandy Hook's lightship was the nation's first to be stationed at a site which was exposed to the open sea. Built in New York at a cost of $17,702, the ninety-foot long, twenty-three-foot beam vessel had two masts, with lanterns on each. It was said to have been the nation's first lightship equipped with reflectors.

The vessel was moored in fourteen fathoms of water, about thirteen miles east, southeast of the lighthouse at Sandy Hook. Describing it in his publication, *American Coast Pilot,* Edmund Blunt remarked, "lights are placed in each lantern at sun-set, and kept burning until sun-rise. The vessel is provided with a large Bell and clock-work, which in stormy and foggy weather will be kept tolling at the rate of one stroke per minute." With the completion of the Highlands of Navesink's twin towers in 1829, the lightship was discontinued.

Pressure from maritime interests restored the lightship station at Sandy Hook in 1838. The new vessel, which was built in 1837, was ninety-eight feet, six-inches-long and had a beam of twenty-four feet, six-inches. The foremast light was thirty-seven feet above the deck, and the main mast rose forty feet. Each lantern was four-sided and used compass lamps that burned sperm oil. Henry B. Lunt, who took charge of Sandy Hook's light vessel in July of 1849, reported that it had parted its mooring and gone adrift eighteen times in a period of thirteen years. Following an 1852 inspection of the lightship, it was reported that it could be seen no "further than three to seven miles, and very dimly." The report went on: "The vessel from

Sandy Hook Lightship, LV 16, December 6, 1894-December 1, 1908.
National Archives, 26-LS-16-1

peculiarity of model, was represented to roll very heavily, and to be very uncomfortable in bad weather." Captain Lunt considered the vessel unsafe. Later designated lightship *LV WW*, the vessel remained posted at Sandy Hook until 1854.

For the next thirty-seven years, lightship *LV 16* was stationed at Sandy Hook. The 125-foot, 8-inch-long sail-schooner was the last United States lightship powered by sail only when it was finally retired from service in the early 1930s. Painted red, the vessel showed two lights; the foremast light was thirty feet above the deck, the aft light was at forty feet. The lanterns had eight oil lamps, each with reflectors, and the vessel's fog signal was a hand-operated fog bell.

On at least two separate occasions, the anchored *LV 16* was rammed and damaged sufficiently, to require immediate repairs. One accident occurred in 1874 and the other on May 2, 1888, when the outbound British bark, *Star of the East*, ran into it. For the most part however, life for the nine men aboard the lightship, as described by a *New York Times* reporter, was "exceedingly dull." Yet, when Keeper R. H. Pritchard, master of the Sandy Hook, was offered the position of keeper at the land-based Coney Island Light, he turned it down. "The lightship is good enough for me," he was quoted. The old mariner had, by then, spent twenty years aboard lightships.

The vessel's normal routine included hoisting the lights, sounding the fog signal, and maintaining the ship and its equipment. Once a month, the crew "sighted the bridles." The bridles were the vessel's two chains, forty-five fathoms in length, which were attached to 1000-pound mushroom anchors. Galvanic action, created by the action of salt water and the friction of metal link against metal link, tended to wear the chain. Their inspection was the most difficult and least popular task aboard the lightship, yet the ability of the vessel to stay on station depended entirely on their integrity.

The Sandy Hook lightship station, which was located off the entrance bar of New York Bay, was regarded as one of the most important light vessels on the Atlantic coast. Its role in guiding vessels into the New York Harbor prompted the proposal for a new vessel in 1887; it was to be equipped with the best light and fog signals of that era.

Lightship *LV 48* was one of three sister vessels built at about the same time by Harrison Loring Works, of South Boston, MA. It was placed on station on August 1, 1891. The old lightship, *LV 16*, was then relegated to relief duty for the rest of its operational life.

The steel and iron composite vessel was 120 feet, 10 inches long; it was sail-schooner rigged. Its foremast was fitted with an English revolving lens that produced a flashing red light; it was the first United States lightship to be so equipped. The main mast had a conventional lantern that showed a fixed red light. Its fog signal was a 12-inch steam whistle and a hand-operated 1000-pound fog bell.

Sandy Hooks last lightship, *LV 51*, was its most modern. The steel-hulled vessel had been stationed at Cornfield Point for two years before being transferred to Sandy Hook. On December 6, 1894, the self-propelled vessel took up its position at Sandy Hook; it was then the only lightship whose beacon was lighted by electricity. New York pilots reported that for the first time, as they approached New York from the east, they could see the lightship's beacon shortly after sighting Navesink's lights. The ease of spotting the vessel allowed a change in the Scotland Lightship's characteristic to a fixed light; it also helped to distinguish the two vessels.

The crew aboard the *LV 51* consisted of four officers, a captain, a mate, an assistant engineer, three firemen, four seamen, and a cook. Each member of the ship's company was allowed ten days ashore per month, weather permitting. For Seaman Thomas Lind, however, it was his first time ashore since joining the crew three months earlier.

Over the next twelve days, Seaman Lind visited his sister in New York City, spent time with friends, and made a few purchases to bring back with him to the ship. On October 2, 1904, he and Mate Eric Carlson started back for the lightship aboard a small sailboat. "When we got out a little ways the wind started to brace up, and Carlson said he was afraid to go out to the light-ship in such a strong wind, and we started to turn back again. I think part of the sheet got afoul of the rudder and lifted it out of place, and as the rudder came out the boat turned over."

For the next two hours, the pair clung to the overturned boat. Every time a swell washed over the boat, they were thrown off, and they had to struggle back. Seaman Lind managed to tie a handkerchief to the tiller and kept waving it, but no one saw it. As time went on, Mate Carlson began to tire. When the two were again swept off the boat, Lind helped him back up, but, in one large wave, the mate disappeared. A tug towing mud scows passed nearby, but Seaman Lind was unable to get their attention. Finally, after six hours in the water, the tug *Bee* with a barge in tow spotted the lone man waving his guernsey. He was picked up and returned ashore; the mate's body was never recovered.

Light vessel *LV 51* remained posted at Sandy Hook until the mooring site was moved in 1908. The station was then renamed Ambrose Lightship, and *LV 51* was relieved by *LV 87/WAL 512*. The former Sandy Hook Lightship, *LV 51*, was then assigned to relief duty until 1919, when the vessel itself met with tragedy (see Cornfield Lightship).

WRECK OF THE SCOTLAND LIGHTSHIP
SCOTLAND LIGHTSHIP

Established:	*1868*		
Lightship LV 20:	*1868-1870.*	*Built 1867,*	*$25,040*
Lightship LV 23:	*1874-1876.*	*Built 1857,*	*$7,500*
Lightship LV 20:	*1876-1881.*		
Lightship LV 7:	*1881-1902.*	*Built 1854,*	*$18,304*
Lightship LV 11:	*1902-1925.*	*Built 1853,*	*$13,462*
Lightship LV 69:	*1925-1936.*	*Built 1897,*	*$79,500*

In the early evening of December 1, 1866, the schooner *Kate Dyer*, carrying a cargo of guano, was bound for New York Harbor. The vessel was showing a light from its mast, and as the captain looked out over the water, he spotted the steamer *Scotland* approaching him off his starboard bow. At a point about ten miles southwest of Fire Island Light, the steamer suddenly turned toward the schooner — there was no time to react! The *Scotland's* bow dug deep into the vessel's starboard side, and within a few minutes, the schooner had gone to the bottom, taking thirteen crewmen. The steamer picked up sixteen survivors, but its bow had been badly damaged, and it began taking on water. Heading for Sandy Hook Bay, the captain was forced to run up on the Outer Middle (sandbar) when it became evident that his ship was also about to sink. A few days later, the steamer *Andrew Feltcher* reported that the *Scotland* was almost out of sight under water; much of its cargo of cheese had been found floating in the vicinity.

The wreck of the steamer *Scotland* lay about two and a half miles east-southeast of Sandy Hook Light and one half mile southwest by west of the southern black buoy of the Outer Bar. For the first two years, the navigational hazard was reportedly marked by a buoy, but, beginning in 1868, lightship *LV 20* was anchored nearby. The vessel, which had been built a year earlier, had two masts and lanterns and a hand-operated fog bell. During its first year, *LV 20* had operated as a relief vessel. It remained at the wreck of the *Scotland* until 1870, when the wreckage was removed to deeper water; *LV 20* then returned to relief duty.

Mariners had come to rely on the Wreck of the Scotland Lightship in making their approach to New York Harbor, and over the next few years, pressure mounted for its reestablishment. On June 23, 1874, Congress appropriated $40,000 for construction of a vessel to be stationed at the site, but the *LV 23*, which was immediately available, was assigned to the post instead. It began operating on the evening of September 10, 1874.

The ninety-four-foot *LV 23* had originally served as the brig *A. J. W. Applegate* during the Civil War. Following a raid by Confederate forces in which the Smiths Point Lightship (VA) was sunk, the brig was anchored at that station, and a light was shown from its mast. In its new role, it was said to have been manned by "a competent military guard." In 1862, the *A. J. W. Applegate* was officially converted into a lightship at a cost of $7,500, and it continued operating at Smiths Point for an additional six years. From 1868 to 1872, the vessel was posted at Willoughby Spit, VA, and, over the next two years, it served as the Wreck of the Scotland Lightship.

In 1876, *LV 23* was replaced by *LV 20*. Built in 1867, the newly assigned vessel was described as being "in good serviceable condition." In the following year, it was again said to have been in good condition, "and, escaping accident, [it] will not need repairs during the fiscal year." The lightship *LV 20* remained on station for over four years, and it was not involved in any serious collisions. The Light House Board, however, recognized their ships' vulnerability; many had been, and were later to be, heavily damaged or sunk in accidents while on station.

During the early part of 1880, *LV 7* had substituted for *LV 20* while it was in for repairs. Capt. Richard H. Pritchard, his mate and crew, expressed their greater liking for this vessel, and in the following year, it was permanently assigned to the station. In 1891, the

Wreck of the Scotland Lightship, LV 7, 1881-1902.
National Archives, 26-LS-7-1

station's position was moved one-half mile, and it was renamed Scotland Lightship.

While it operated as the Scotland Lightship, at least three vessels collided with *LV 7*. On December 29, 1892, it was run into by an Italian bark under tow. In 1900, the British schooner *Goldseeker* drifted into the anchored vessel, and, in April of 1902, a scow being towed by a tug rammed *LV 7*; in all three incidents however, damage was relatively minor.

Lightship *LV 11*, which succeeded *LV 7* in December of 1902, also showed a propensity for being the victim of collisions. The new vessel had been on station for only three months when a schooner ran into it, and, beginning with March of 1905, it was rammed three times within three months.

Fifty-two-year-old Ernest W. Borgstrom had served as Hog Island Shoal Light's first keeper, prior to being assigned to the Scotland Lightship. In his capacity as the master of *LV 11*, he had a record of good performance, but his thirteen-year career in the Light House Service was nearly ended over the requisitioning of a bottle of Duffy's malt whiskey.

In January of 1910, the *Scotland's* cook ordered the whiskey, along with a number of other food items; he planned to use the alcoholic beverage for preparing desserts. As for all items purchased for the lightship, the requisition was signed by the vessel's master. When the Light House Inspector, Capt. Thomas, accidentally discovered the order, he promptly recommended Keeper Borgstrom's dismissal, but cooler heads prevailed. Borgstrom was reminded that all malt, vinous, or spirituous liquors, except those for the treatment of actual illness, were expressly forbidden aboard light vessels. Taking into account his years of faithful service, the keeper received only a reprimand, but he was warned that any further offense of an equally serious nature would result in his immediate dismissal. Keeper Borgstrom remained in command of *LV 11*, until October of 1925, when the lightship was replaced by *LV 69*. Two years later, *LV 11*, the oldest lightship then in service, was decommissioned and sold. Scotland's *LV 69* was built in 1897 at the Bath Iron Works, Bath, ME. The steam screw, composite hull vessel, had two masts and a stack at midships. At the time of construction, the 122-foot, 10-inch-long vessel, was also rigged for sail. During the Spanish-American War, the Navy took over the tender Maple, and for four months, *LV 69* was used as a lighthouse tender. In its temporary role, it steamed 3,400 miles.

The hurricane that swept over the Atlantic coast in August of 1899, nearly destroyed lightship *LV 69*. Stationed at the time at Diamond Shoal, NC, the vessel began to drag its moorings. The captain ordered *LV 69's* engines ahead at full speed, but despite all efforts, wind and waves slowly pushed the vessel toward the coast. On August 18, the lightship was driven ashore near Creeds Hill Lifesaving Station, NC. Following the storm, the vessel was refloated and repaired in Baltimore, MD.

_LV 69_ served as the Scotland Lightship until 1936, and it was sold in the following year for the sum of $3,030. Its replacement was _LV 87/WAL 512._

The new lightship had begun its career at Ambrose Channel in 1908. It remained there until 1932 and spent the next four years as a relief vessel. Built in 1907 at Camden, NJ, _WAL 512_ had a wood pilothouse and deckhouse, a steel hull, and two masts. Its illuminating apparatus was initially a cluster of three oil lens lanterns hoisted to each masthead, and its fog signal consisted of a twelve-inch chime whistle. In 1921, the lightship was equipped with a radiobeacon, and in 1945 it was fitted with radar.

On January 10, 1942, the Coast Guard announced that the Fire Island and Scotland lightships were to be taken off station as a war measure, and replaced by lighted bell buoys. During most of the Second World War, Scotland's _WAL 512_ was stationed at Fort Hancock, where, armed with a single one-pounder, it served as an examination vessel. In 1944, the lightship was reassigned to Vineyard Sound to take the place of _LV 73_ which had been lost to the September hurricane (see Evolution of the Nation's Lighthouse System).

Scotland Lightship Station was reactivated in January of 1946 with the transfer of _WAL 512_ to the site, but, three years later, a public hearing was held to discuss its proposed discontinuance. The Coast Guard felt that its elimination would save $80,000 per year, while towing companies, barge lines, and other coastal maritime interests argued that shipping safety would be greatly impaired by its elimination. The mariners won the day and the vessel continued operating another seventeen years.

In 1966, the vessel was replaced by a 140-ton buoy, whose tower rose to a height of 38 feet. The unmanned navigational aid was equipped with a 7,500-candlepower light, a fog signal, and a radiobeacon. Powered by a continuously operating diesel generator that used propane gas, it had to be refueled only once a year. The "super-buoy" was built by General Dynamics Corporation at a cost of about $250,000; a modern lightship would have cost approximately $3 million, and would have required fifteen to nineteen men, as well a support personnel ashore.

Lightship _WAL 512_ was decommissioned on March 4, 1966, and three years later, it was donated for use as a floating exhibit to the South Street Seaport in New York City.

AMBROSE LIGHTSHIP

Appropriation: *Act of June 20, 1906,*   *$115,000*
Established: *1908*
First keeper: *Captain Gustave Lange*
Lightship LV 87/WAL 512:   *1908-1932.*   *Built 1907, $79,000*
Lightship LV 111/WAL 533:   *1932-1952.*   *Built 1926, $219,883*
Lightship WLV 613:   *1952-1967.*   *Built 1952, $500,000*
Amborse lightship discontinued: August 23, 1967
Ambrose tower automated: *1988*

D ense fog, haze, and intermittent heavy rains had plagued the New York City area on the evening of June 30, 1960, causing long delays at the city's major airports. At 10:45 pm, Central Gulf Steamship Corporation's freighter, *Green Bay*, weighed anchor from Port Newark, bound for the Red Sea. Loaded with a general cargo, the ship began to make its way slowly toward Ambrose Channel.

Sometime earlier, Ambrose Lightship *WLV 613* had been withdrawn from the station for its annual maintenance, and Relief *WAL 505*, one of two relief vessels in the Coast Guard's Third District, had taken its place eight miles southeast of Rockaway Point. Built in 1904 by the New York Shipbuilding Company, *WAL 505* was identified by the word RELIEF, painted on both of its sides. Except for the duration of the Second World War, when it was used as an unarmed examination vessel, the 129-foot steel hull ship had always been used for relief duty.

On that summer night in 1960, Capt. Thomas Mazzella, master of the *Green Bay*, heard the lightship's fog signal and picked it up on his radar, but somehow he had miscalculated its position.

Boatswain's Mate Bobby Pierce was on duty in *WAL 505's* pilothouse at 4:00 am, when he saw the *Green Bay* emerge from the fog less than 100 feet away! He barely had time to sound the general alarm before the 10,270-deadweight-ton freighter had smashed into the anchored vessel. The *Green Bay* struck the lightship's starboard side, just behind the midsection, leaving a twelve-foot gash in its side. A deluge of seawater quickly followed the excruciating sound of metal being torn away from the bulkheads, and within a short time, the engine room and adjoining compressor room were flooded. The nine crewmen had time neither to get fully dressed nor to collect personal items. Scrambling for an emergency inflatable raft, they shoved off, and, using their hands, they paddled furiously to escape

Ambrose Lightship LV87/WAL 512, 1908-1932.
National Archives, 26-G-21043

the grip of the whirlpool that would soon surround the sinking ship. Ten minutes after the collision, "she sank stern first, kicked up her nose and went straight down." All hands had made it to safety.

Relief *WAL 505*, landed upright in about 100 feet of water. In the late 1980's, the vessel was still relatively intact (Loran C 43695.7-8, 26903.4-6). Scuba divers regularly dive the wreck, but poor visibility and silt have made it dangerous for anyone but the most experienced and well-prepared divers to penetrate its rusting hull.

Established, 1908

The 2,000-foot wide and 45-foot-deep Ambrose Channel was dredged under an 1899 appropriation of $4 million. In 1908, the Sandy Hook lightship station was moved to eight miles east of Rockaway Point and renamed Ambrose. Its former light vessel, *LV 51*, was reassigned to Cornfield Point, and *LV 87/WAL 512* was anchored at the newly designated site.

The 135-foot, 5-inch-long steel hulled lightship, *WAL 512*, was built in 1907 at a cost of $99,000. It was originally equipped with three oil lens lanterns shown from each masthead, but in 1908 they were replaced with electric lights. Its fog signals consisted of a twelve-inch steam whistle chime and a hand-operated fog bell, and it was later equipped with a submarine bell, a two-way radio (1918), and a radiobeacon (1921). In October of 1932, *WAL 512* was taken out of service for an extensive overhaul; at that time, its original main engine was replaced by a Winton diesel.

Gustav A. Lange, a resident of Staten Island, was Ambrose Lightship's master from about 1910 to 1932. While the captain was ashore on September 14, 1914, a tug pulled alongside *WAL 512* and left a package of newspapers and a letter for the British warship *Essex*. A short time later, a boat from the *Essex* arrived and picked up the materials. When Capt. Lange reported the incident to his superiors, he was informed that such an action might be viewed as a breach of the nation's neutrality. In the future, he was instructed, the lightship should neither receive nor deliver mail, or any other materials for British or other foreign war vessels. The United States entered the war three years later.

The usual entries in the lightship's log were wind direction and strength, barometric pressure, weather, and temperature. On February 20, 1927, Capt. Lange recorded a severe storm.

"Snowy NE gales with hail and snow," began the entry. The winds picked up to force 9, and the lightship pitched wildly at its mooring. "At 10:30 am, seas broke over mid-ship," and much of the equipment on deck was lost overboard. As the ship heaved to the stern with its bow clearly out of the water, it broke away from its mooring and drifted off station. The captain radioed his situation and headed in for the Lighthouse Depot at Staten Island. Seven days later, the vessel resumed its post.

While on station, lightships were always at risk of being rammed, but it seems that *WAL 512* was not necessarily safe even while tied up at a dock. In the spring of 1924, the light vessel had made its way to Staten Island for maintenance. While there, a steam lighter parted its stern line, and, carried by the current, it swung around and struck the lightship. Though *WAL 512's* plates and railings were severely damaged, no one was hurt.

In 1932, *WAL 512* was reassigned as a relief vessel, and it was replaced by *LV 111/WAL 533*. The former Ambrose lightship spent the next four years in its new role and was then reassigned as the Scotland Lightship (see Scotland Lightship).

The new lightship had previously served at Northeast End, NJ, from 1927 until August 31, 1932, when that station was discontinued. Built in 1926, the 132-foot, 4-inch-long vessel was powered by a diesel engine, whose maximum speed was 9 knots. The lightship had a complement of five officers and ten crewmen.

Ambrose Lightship must have been the last place anyone would ever have wanted to be as one of the century's worst hurricanes headed for the Atlantic coast. At 8:00 am on September 21, 1938, a north-northwest wind was blowing at force 3, and the barometer recorded 29.76; the barometric pressure began to drop rapidly.

force	miles per hour	sea description
0	0-3 mph*	calm, like glass
1	3-8 mph	light air, ripples
2	8-13 mph	light breeze, 0-1 ft waves
3	13-18 mph	gentle breeze, 1-2 ft waves
4	18-23 mph	moderate breeze, 2-4 ft waves
5	23-28 mph	fresh breeze, 4-8 ft waves
6	28-34 mph	strong breeze, 8-13 ft waves
7	34-40 mph	moderate gale, white foam from breaking waves.
8	40-48 mph	fresh gale, very rough 13-20 ft waves
9	48-56 mph	strong gale, 20 ft+ waves
10	56-65 mph	whole gale, 20-30 ft waves
11	65-75 mph	storm, 35-45 ft waves
12	75 mph +	hurricane, 45 ft + waves

Table 1: Wind scale and sea contitions. * Often given in knots rather than miles per hour. Source: Lightship log, *LV 111/WAL 533*

Seemingly ignoring the approaching storm, the tender *Spruce* arrived at 10:00 am to deliver the mail and provisions; the winds were then at force 5, and the barometer registered 29.58. Immediately after the tender's departure, Capt. Kalb Skari ordered all equipment, ports, boats, and gear secured; the crew then went below and prepared themselves to ride out the storm. By 2:00 pm, the winds had picked up to force 9, and the barometer read 28.66. Over the next two hours the winds reached a maximum of force 11. "Full storm forces with heavy rains," wrote the captain in the log. "Vessel riding storm very easily." The winds gradually subsided, and *WAL 533* emerged from the Great Hurricane, relatively unscathed.

During the Second World War, the unarmed Ambrose Lightship remained on station for the duration. U-boats did not bother the lightship, since it probably aided them as much as it helped the nation's shipping. On January 3, 1944, however, the destroyer *USS Turner*, which was anchored about midway between lightship *WAL 533* and Rockaway Point, took two enemy torpedoes. The initial blast killed all of the ship's officers, and, fed by the warship's magazines, a second explosion sent the warship to the bottom in sixty feet of water.

In August of 1952, *WAL 533*, which had served twenty years at Ambrose, was withdrawn and replaced by a relief vessel. Its permanent replacement, *WLV 613*, arrived in October of that year; it was the last lightship posted at Ambrose. The old vessel, which had survived the 1938 hurricane, a war, and ramming three times in a period of just ten months, was refurbished and reassigned to

Portland, ME; it remained there until 1969.

The new lightship, *WLV 613*, built at the Coast Guard Curtis Bay Station, was launched on August 4, 1952. The diesel-powered 126-foot vessel was capable of 10.5 knots. It had a duplex 375 mm electric lens lantern mounted above the gallery on the foremast, and its fog signal consisted of twin diaphones mounted aft of the pilothouse.

The vessel remained stationed at Ambrose until August 23, 1967, when a $2.5 million tower took its place. Built by Tidewater, Raymond, and Kiewit, the structure was supported by four legs, driven 190 feet into the sea bottom. Standing some 90 feet above the water's surface, the tower reportedly was made to withstand winds in excess of 125 knots and waves of 65 feet in height. In 1986, its flashing white light, shown from a point 136 feet above sea level, could be seen at a maximum of 24 miles. The tower was manned by a crew of six Coast Guardsmen, with four men always "on board." It was automated in 1988.

9   *New York Lower Bay Range Lights*

M ountain peaks, trees, or any other prominent points on a shoreline formed natural ranges that were in use long before the introduction of beacons for marine navigation. By constructing two beacon towers, the back one higher than the front, a mariner could then line himself up on the two and be assured that the waterway was safe for navigation. Still in use, range lights or leading lights showed distinctively colored lights that could be seen only within a narrow area from one side to the other. If a mariner went too far to the right, the rear light appeared to drift to the right of the front range; if he went to the left, the rear drifted left. As a sailor made his way up a channel, he changed at a specific point from one set of ranges to another.

The British were probably the first, in the early 1800s, to make extensive use of range lights. In the United States, one of the earliest was established in 1820 at Wolf Island, GA. The range lights constructed at Morris Island, SC, in 1837, were made "portable" to accommodate the shifting channel.

Congress in 1852 authorized the establishment of six light-houses for New York Bay, four of which were located on the New Jersey shores and the others on Staten Island, NY. Erected by Richard Calrow, Jr., the lighthouses, in pairs, formed Gedney's Channel Range (Point Comfort/Waackaack), Main Channel Range (Conover-/Chapel Hill), and Swash Channel Range (Elm Tree/New Dorp). They became operational in November of 1856. With the dredging of the seven and one-half-mile-long Ambrose Channel, Congress appropriated funds in 1906, for the Ambrose Channel Range (Staten Island/West Bank).

The wide sandbar, reaching from Sandy Hook to Coney Island, lay dangerously close to the water's surface along most of its length. Even after construction of the Lower Bay Ranges, larger vessels navigating the channels across the New York Bar, usually required

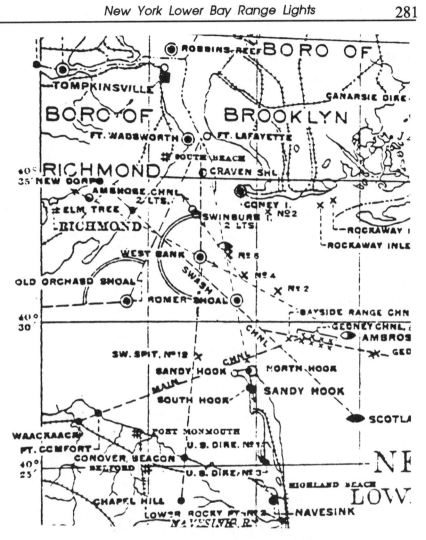

New York Lower Bay Ranges, 1895

the guidance of a harbor pilot. Twenty-one years earlier, Lt. R. T. Gedney had surveyed the sand bar and discovered an alternate route, with twenty-three feet of water at low tide. Bearing his name, Gedney's Channel was the best route into New York Harbor until the dredging of Ambrose Channel.

Ships traveling Gedney's Channel lined themselves up on Point Comfort/Waackaack Lights until, (as one of a number of alternatives) they picked up the Conover/Chapel Hill Lights. The Elm Tree/New Dorp Lights directed sailors through Swash Channel, and vessels navigating the Main Ship Channel from the SW Spit to the Narrows, lined up on the Conover/Chapel Hill Lights (see chart).

POINT COMFORT/
WAACKAACK RANGE LIGHTS

Act of Congress (both): August 31, 1852 $30,000
Established (both):   1856
Contractor (both):   Richard Calrow, Jr.

Point Comfort Beacon:
Purchased land from: Lydia and Catherine Tilton
First keeper: James Seeley, appointed October 15, 1855
Illuminating apparatus (IA): 1856, third-order lens, fixed white.
IA: (1891) range lens, fixed white (FW).
Illuminant: 1907, changed from oil to incandescent oil vapor.
                            Power increase from 3,636-candlepower (cp) to 27,272 cp.
IA: (1924) range lens, FW, 55,000 cp.
Height of light above sea level: (1891) 45 feet

Waackaack Beacon:
Purchased land from: Andrew Wilson, July 30, 1853, and Ezekiel and
                            Ann Thompson, September 2, 1853
First keeper: Andrew Wilson, appointed October 15, 1855
IA: 1856, second-order lens, FW.
IA: (1891) range lens, FW.
Illuminant: 1907, same as Point Comfort.
IA: (1939) 2 range lenses, FW.
                            102 feet 60,000 cp, 96 feet 14,000 cp.
Height of light above sea level: (1891) 76 feet. (1939) 102 feet and 96 feet.

L ocated near the beach at Point Comfort in Keansburg, NJ, the
    Point Comfort Light functioned as the front range; its beacon
    was shown from forty-five feet above sea level. The lighthouse
was a duplicate of the Chapel Hill and New Dorp stations. Its tower
rose from the middle of the frame dwelling and was accessible via a
wooden ladder. The dwelling had four rooms and a built-on kitchen.
  Charles Redfern was posted at Point Comfort in June of 1911. The
keeper became well known for several daring rescues on the water,
and for his involvement in the community as the local fire chief. His
status with the community, however, did not insulate him from
being suspected of violating the prohibition laws. A letter from a
Keansburg woman in 1924 charged that the keeper was selling
alcohol to young men and boys, including her own son. An under-
cover investigator was dispatched, but, when he found that the
accusation had been made under an assumed name and that there
appeared to be no substance to the allegations, the matter was
dropped. Suspicion of rum-running in the case of Keeper William
Baker of Orient Point Light, however, may have been closer to the
truth. An inspector found some irregularities in the station's log that

Point Comfort Range Light, undated. National Archives, 26-LG-14-14

Conover Range Light, undated National Archives, 26-LG-11-33

the keeper could not explain, but before the investigation proceeded any further, Baker submitted his resignation.

Waackaack's hexagonal tower was similar that of the Conover and Elm Tree beacons. Constructed of wood, the towers were separate from the keeper's dwellings. Waackaack's beacon, situated on Creek Road in Keansburg, NJ, stood three-quarters of a mile to the rear of Point Comfort and rose to seventy-six feet above sea level. Both of the stations showed fixed white lights.

Except for the lack of a tower rising from the middle of their roofs, the two-story keeper's residences at Waackaack, Conover, and Elm Tree resembled those at Point Comfort, Chapel Hill, and New Dorp. A little over two years after Waackaack's first keeper, Andrew Wilson, occupied the dwelling, it was consumed by fire; the structure was rebuilt in that same year.

In 1894, as part of a project that called for forming a range with the Old Orchard Shoal Light, Waackaack's wood tower was moved forward a short distance and kept in range with Point Comfort Light. The new iron skeleton tower, constructed on the site of the old structure, was equipped with two fixed white lights, one at 105 feet and the other at 95 feet above sea level. The original tower was then torn down and used as firewood by the keeper.

Elm Tree Light, undated. National Archives, 26-LG-11-50

CONOVER/CHAPEL HILL RANGE LIGHTS

Act of Congress (both):   August 31, 1852 $30,000
Established (both): 1856
Contractor (both):   Richard Calrow, Jr.

<u>Conover Beacon:</u>
First keeper: Marsh L. Mount, appointed October 8, 1855
IA: 1856, third-order lens, fixed white and red.
IA: (1891) range lens, fixed white.
Illuminant: 1907, change from oil to incandescent oil vapor.
                   Power increase from 3,636 cp to 27,272 cp.
IA: (1939) 375 mm range lens, FW, electric, 130,000 cp.
Height of light above sea level: (1891) 60 feet

<u>Chapel Hill Beacon:</u>
First keeper: John Morris, appointed October 8, 1855
Illuminating apparatus (IA): 1856, second-order lens, fixed white (FW).
IA: (1891) range lens, FW.
Illuminant: 1907, same as Conover
IA: (1939) 4-order range lens, FW, electric, 1,000,000 cp
Height of light above sea level: (1891) 224 feet

The Chapel Hill Range was built on three acres of land purchased in 1853 from Timothy Mount. The station was located off Hosford Avenue, next to the cemetery in Leonardo, NJ. Standing 1.4 miles to the rear of Conover Range, its fixed white light was shown from 221 feet above sea level. Conover's hexagonal tower, also located in Leonardo, stood near the beach on Roop Avenue. It also showed a fixed white light.

Over the years, ships' captains entering New York Lower Bay had frequently complained that the range lights were difficult to see on a clear day and useless in haze or stormy weather. In July of 1923, all of the ranges serving Lower Bay were discontinued, and the channels were marked by gas-lighted buoys.

It was not the first time that the ranges had been extinguished. For a three-month period during the Spanish-American War (1898), the beacons ceased operating by order of the War Department. In 1923, less than four months after their discontinuance, tugboat captains towing barges clamored that "the ranges were absolutely necessary to counteract the side drift of the current through the channels." The Chapel Hill/Conover, Point Comfort/Waackaack, and Elm Tree/ New Dorp ranges were reestablished in December of that same year, but Staten Island Light, which ranged with West Bank, awaited electrification before it exhibited a light once more.

The Conover Range was converted to electricity in 1924. With the change, the position of keeper was abolished, and Keeper Peter M. Peterson was placed in charge of both stations. Shortly thereafter, the property at Conover was sold at auction.

Waackaack and Point Comfort were also electrified in 1924, but it was five years before Chapel Hill followed suit. The four lights, all within four miles of each other, were then placed under the care of one keeper. A portion of Waackaack's property had been sold in 1925. When the remaining parcel, which included the two-story keeper's dwelling, was put up for auction, it was purchased by former keeper, Charles Redfern; he was able to retire to surroundings that had been so familiar to him.

ELM TREE/NEW DORP RANGE LIGHTS

Act of Congress (both):	*August 31, 1852 $30,000*
Established (both):	*1856*
Contractor (both):	*Richard Calrow, Jr.*

Elm Tree Beacon:

Purchased land from:	*Harriet Lord*
First keeper:	*William Hooper, appointed October 17, 1855*
Illuminating apparatus (IA):	*1856, third-order lens, fixed white light (FW).*
IA:	*(1891) range lens, FW.*
Illuminant:	*1907, changed from oil to incandescent oil vapor. Power increase from 3,636 cp to 27,272 cp.*
Rebuilt:	*1937*
IA:	*(1939) sixth-order range lens, FW, electric 80,000 cp*
Height of light above sea level: (1891) 62 feet	

New Dorp Beacon:

Purchased land from:	*William Ebbitt, George Ebbitt, and David Ebbitt.*
First keeper:	*John B. Fountain, appointed October 17, 1855*
IA:	*1856, second-order, fixed red (FR).*
IA:	*(1891) range lens, FW.*
Illuminant:	*1907, same as Elm Tree.*
IA:	*(1939) sixth-order range lens, FW, electric, 80,000 cp.*
Height of light above sea level: (1891) 192 feet	

T he New Dorp Light, with its tower rising from the center of the dwelling, stood on the crest of a hill on Staten Island. Bounded by the Moravian Cemetery on its east side, it was otherwise surrounded by a tree-lined, rugged terrain. The government's right-of-way leading through the cemetery, from the public road to the property, was barely a path; it was impassable by horse and wagon. In the past, the keepers had been allowed to use the winding cemetery road from the lighthouse to Richmond Road, but in 1878 the cemetery's trustees rescinded their permission. They wanted to expand and improve the burial grounds, but negotiations with the government over the tract of land covered by the right-of-way had become deadlocked. For nearly eleven years, Keeper John Langston was forced to carry most of the supplies to the station in his arms or on horseback. The government, which had been unwilling to appropriate the necessary funds to build a road to the station, finally agreed to give up its right-of-way to the trustees, in exchange for use of the cemetery road.

New Dorp Light was located to the rear of the Elm Tree Light. Together, they formed a range for Swash Channel, beginning from the outside of the sandbar to the Main Channel. Sailing through the Swash Channel, mariners were instructed to bring the range lights "in one" and steer for them until the Conover and Chapel Hill Beacons came into range. They were then to haul-up and steer on that range to clear West Bank.

New Dorp remained operational until 1964, when it was boarded up and abandoned to vandals. Ten years later, the Government put the property up for auction, and it was purchased by a young Staten Island engineer, John Vokral, for $32,000. The new owner found that the structure had been thoroughly "raped" by intruders, and he had to virtually rebuild it. He "sanded and painted every square inch of the clapboard himself, and hammered every peg into the old floors upstairs — all 1,286 of them."

Designated a city landmark, the New Dorp Light can be seen at the top of Altamont Street, off Richmond Avenue, on Staten Island. It is maintained as a private home, and its exterior has been kept exactly as it was during its 108 years as a range light.

J acob Swain(m) had been keeper of the Elm Tree Range Light for nearly fourteen years when, in his late sixties, he married Sarah, a widow with two children. During the next few years, the couple had two more children, and Sarah, in addition to her homemaking chores, assisted Jacob in keeping the light. On February 14, 1906, the keeper died, leaving behind his wife and four children; the oldest was fourteen and the youngest was only three.

Left penniless, Sarah applied for the position of keeper. It was the general custom to allow the widow to assume the post, but Swain's application was turned down in favor of Edward B. Burge. He had been keeper of the isolated West Bank Light for about six years.

Jacob Swain had made many friends while at Elm Tree, and, when George Cromwell, president of the Borough of Richmond, Staten Island, learned of the widows plight, he enlisted others to join him in a petition to have the Light House Service reconsider the appointment.

In defending his decision, Capt. R. Mackenzie, the area's Light-

New Dorp Light, Staten Island, NY.
A private residence, 1987.

house Service Inspector, wrote that though hard-hearted, "as a business proposition the Light House Establishment must pay more attention to living keepers than to the relatives of dead ones." The captain went on to point out that the widow "married Mr. Swain some seven or eight years ago when he was about seventy years old and cannot herself be said to have any great claim on the Light House Establishment." He continued by relating that the widow of another keeper, Mary Elizabeth Clark, was applying for keepership at Black Rock (Fairweather Light). "I think her case is more deserving than Mrs. Swain's because Mrs. Clark has lived so much longer at Black Rock than Mrs. Swain at Elm Tree" Edward Burge became keeper of Elm Tree on April 14, 1906.

Elm Tree Light was located near the water on the south side of Staten Island. During the 1920s, the tower stood within the perimeter of Miller Field (airfield), and the dwelling was located opposite it across a public road. When first established in 1856, the dwelling and tower were within a short distance of one another, but a shift in the course of the Swash Channel made it necessary to move the tower in 1899. In 1939, the wooden tower was torn down, and the beacon was moved to a sixty-five foot concrete tower, which also functioned as an "aviation tower." Maintained by New York City, it showed alternating white and green lights for the benefit of aircraft; the ships' light was visible on range only — the range was discontinued in 1964.

OLD ORCHARD SHOAL/
WAACKAACK RANGE LIGHTS

Appropriation: March 3, 1891 $60,000
Established: 1893
First lighted: April 25, 1893
First keeper: Alfred L. Carlow, appointed April 23, 1893
Illuminating apparatus (IA): (1907) fourth-order Fresnel lens,
  fixed white light with eclipse.
IA: (1939) 4-order, occulting white (W) 11 sec,
  eclipse 4 sec. W 2,900 cp, R 870 cp.
Fog signal: 1896, (1907) compressed-air siren.
Fog signal: (1939) electric diaphragm horn, blast 3 seconds, silent 7 seconds.
Height of light above sea level: (1907) 50.5 feet

Construction of a railroad bridge across Staten Island Sound in the late 1800s, brought with it a large increase in shipping traffic through Prince's Bay. In the winter, when the sound was closed off by ice, an estimated 15,000 tons of shipping traveled the narrow channel per day. Because of the narrow waterway, tugs towing barges in the direction of West Bank were forced to hug the Staten Island shoreline. In doing so, however, they came dangerously close to the Old Orchard Shoal. Though the shallows had for some time been marked by a lighted buoy and a bell buoy, the aids were widely regarded as inadequate. The Light House Board thus went to Congress in 1891, asking for funds to establish a lighthouse at Old Orchard Shoal. At the same time, the board requested money for erecting a new tower at Waackaack that would be made to range with the new lighthouse; Congress appropriated $60,000 on March 3, 1891.

Construction of the conical lighthouse was completed in the opening months of 1893; it was equipped with a fourth-order lens and later fitted with a fog signal. The station became operational on April 25 of that same year. In 1907, Old Orchard Shoal was listed as showing a fixed white light for twelve seconds with eclipse for three seconds to the southeastward (S 30 57'W and S 84 42' E) and a fixed red for twelve seconds with eclipse for three seconds in the remaining sector; its fog signal was an air siren.

Alfred L. Carlow, the station's first keeper, had previously been assistant keeper aboard the Sandy Hook Lightship and had served for about a year in the same capacity on the Scotland Lightship; he had performed well at both of those posts. The confinement of the cast-iron structure, however, became too much for the man to bear; on September 1, 1902, Keeper Carlow was hospitalized at the United States Marine Hospital in New York, for "nervous exhaustion." He was relieved by Adolph Norostrom and never returned to active duty in the Light House Service.

The Old Orchard Light stood about three miles off Staten Island. The station's keepers often went to the assistance of ill-equipped sport fishermen in small boats, who were caught in the Lower Bay's sudden squalls. Keeper Andrew Zuius had made many rescues from the lighthouse when, on June 26, 1927, he set out in a fierce storm to save the lives of four men. Their motorboat had sprung a leak, and, by the time the keeper had reached them, it had sunk to its gunnels. Typical of so many other keepers, Zuius provided food and overnight shelter for his unexpected guests.

Though Old Orchard Shoal no longer forms a range with the Waackaack Beacon, its flashing white light with a red sector, continues to warn mariners of the area's dangerous shoals; the station no longer has a fog signal.

Old Orchard Shoal Light, off Great Kills Harbor, Staten Island, can be approached only by boat. NOAA chart #12327

Old Orchard Shoal Lighthouse, undated. National Archives, 26-LG-13-35

WEST BANK/STATEN ISLAND
(Ambrose Channel) RANGE LIGHTS

Appropriation: June 4, 1897 $50,000
Established: 1901
First lighted: January 1, 1901
First keeper: Edward B. Burge, appointed December 6, 1900
Illuminating apparatus (IA): 1901, fourth-order Fresnel lens (4-order),
                     fixed white with red sector.
Rebuilt: 1908
IA: (1939) 4-order, occulting white (W), 5 sec, with red (R) sector.
                     Incandescent oil vapor, W 2,900 cp, R 870 cp.
Fog signal: June 1, 1901, compressed-air siren
Fog signal: (1939) electric diaphragm horn, 2 blasts every 15 seconds.
Height of light above sea level: (1907) 59.5 feet

T he weather was clear on the evening of December 28, 1904, as Assistant Keeper Frederick Nielson went about the station's chores. He no doubt had heard the tug *America's* engines as it passed the iron tower, but he probably had not become conscious of the vessel's presence until he felt the blow. There were the sounds of glass crashing to the deck and the screech of metal against metal as the tower's railings were torn away. Keeper Nielson sprinted for the balcony and arrived just in time to see the bark *Carrie Winslow*, under tow, as it was moving away from the lighthouse.

Subsequent investigation revealed damage to the lighthouse in excess of $1,200, and there was a large gash in the bark's bow; the tug's owners were made responsible for all of the damages. Eleven years later, another tug's tow collided with the lighthouse, tearing away a section of cast iron from the tower's base.

The lighthouse at West Bank was established as part of a series of New York Harbor improvements. Construction of the conical tower began in August of 1900, with the first four sections of cylindrical foundation plates sunk into position. The sections were then filled with concrete, and workmen began assembling the remaining five sections. Following their completion, the tower's 135,000-pound iron superstructure was lifted into place. The station began to display its fixed white, fourth-order light on January 1, 1901, and, in June of the same year, it was fitted with a fog siren.

Five years after the lighthouse became operational, Congress appropriated funds for lighting the nearly completed Ambrose Channel. The Act of June 20, 1906, called for establishing the Ambrose Lightship and a tank light-vessel, moving the North Hook Beacon, and raising the height of the West Bank Light to bring it into range

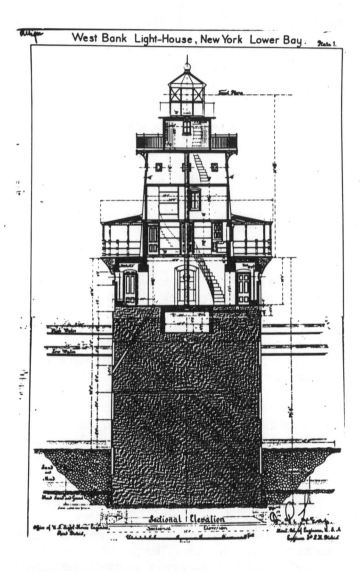

West Bank Light-House, New York Lower Bay.

Sectional Elevation

West Bank Lighthouse. Light House Board, 1889

with the proposed Staten Island Light. The appropriation also included funds for a stone beacon at Craven Shoal and thirteen gas beacons for the Ambrose Channel.

The height of West Bank's tower was increased during the latter part of 1907 by adding two stories between the watchroom and the deck below. While work was being done at the lighthouse, a temporary beacon was erected.

West Bank's last civilian keeper, Otto Banks, was stationed there with Coast Guard personnel until his retirement in 1956. The lighthouse continued to be manned into the early 1980s, when it was automated. At that time, it was the last of six manned stations in the Third Coast Guard District.

> *West Bank Light stands near the junction of Ambrose Channel and Chapel Hill North Channel. It can be approached only by boat.*
> *NOAA chart #12327*

West Bank Lighthouse, 1987

Second-order range lens, Staten Island Lighthouse, 1915.
National Archives, 26-LG-16-52

Staten Island Range Light
(West Bank/Staten Island)

Appropriation: *June 30, 1906*
Established: *1912*
Purchased land from: Julia Chaffanjon, April 3, 1908, $5,000
First lighted: *April 15, 1912*
Illuminating apparatus (IA): (1915) second-order range lens with prism reflectors.
           Maker, Chance Brothers & Co., identified by USLHE, #206.
IA: *(1939) second-order range lens, FW, electric 350,000 cp.*
IA: *(1986) range light, FW, visible on range only*
Fog signal: *none*
Height of light above sea level: 1912, 231 feet

S taten Island Light was built on Richmond Hill, a little more than five miles to the rear of West Bank Light. From its vantage point 141 feet above sea level, the octagonal tower rose an additional 90 feet. When first lit on April 15, 1912, the new lighthouse was hailed by the *New York Times* as "destined to take its place among famous beacons of the world, such as Eddystone Lighthouse, on the Eddystone Rocks, about fourteen miles from Plymouth, England."

Second-order range lens, Staten Island Lighthouse, 1915.
National Archives, 26-LG-16-55

Staten Island Lighthouse, 1987

The lighthouse was equipped with a kerosene vapor lamp that produced a light of only 1,500-candlepower, but its intensity was multiplied 200 times by means of a large reflector of glass prisms, that completely surrounded a central bull's-eye lens. The rays were concentrated and projected in a narrow beam of white light that was visible "on range" only for a distance of about twenty-one miles.

The octagonal tower was built of light-colored vitrified bricks, with grey limestone base and trim. The keeper's dwelling, situated 150 feet east of the lighthouse, was constructed of the same materials. It had a kitchen, pantry, living room, parlor, three bedrooms, and a large attic. An electric call bell ran from the tower's watchroom to the dwelling.

It was often said when first constructed, that the stately lighthouse would have been more at home on a rugged coastline than inland, high on a hill. As Staten Island's population grew, only the top of the tower remained visible over the surrounding homes, making it seem more out-of-place than it had once been considered. Though the Staten Island Light never attained the fame hoped for by the *New York Times*, it was designated a New York City Historical Landmark in 1968.

The automatic beacon is expected to continue to be an important aid to ships entering New York Harbor for the foreseeable future.

The lighthouse stands in Richmondtown, Staten Island, between Edinboro Road and Manor Court. A short cobblestone access road leads to the tower from the foot of Manor Court. The beacon is not open to the public. The keeper's dwelling, a private home, stands behind the tower and faces Edinboro Road.   *NOAA chart #12327*

10 NEW YORK LOWER BAY NEW YORK HARBOR LIGHTS

CONEY ISLAND (Nortons Point) LIGHT

Appropriation: *March 2, 1889* $25,000
Established: *1890*
First lighted: *August 1, 1890*
First keeper: *Thomas Higgenbotham, appointed June 30, 1890*
Illuminating apparatus (IA): 1890, fourth-order Fresnel lens,
               flashing red light (Fl R) every 10 seconds.
IA: *(1924) 4-order, FL R, 5 seconds, 54,000-candlepower (cp).*
IA: *(1986) Fl R, 5 seconds, electric.*
Fog signal: *(1891) fog bell struck by machine every 15 sec.*
Height of light above sea level: 1890, 76.5 feet

F rank Schubert was the Coast Guard's last civilian keeper. He began his lighthouse career in 1938 aboard the buoy tender *Tulip.* When the Coast Guard took over the Light House Service in 1939, Schubert was transferred to the Old Orchard Light, joining two other civilians at the station. During his three and a half years there, the crewmen rotated twenty-six days at the light, followed by six days ashore.

With the outbreak of the Second World War, Schubert was assigned to the Army Transportation Service; he was given the billet after proclaiming that he'd "had enough of boats for a while." He served in the Pacific and returned to keep the lights at Governors Island. While there, civilian Keeper Schubert and two enlisted men maintained the station's three lights and two fog signals.

Frank and Marie Schubert and their three children moved into their new quarters at Coney Island in July of 1960. The seven-room dwelling was a palace in comparison to the four-room apartment which they had occupied while Frank served at Governors Island.

"We've gone from one extreme to the other," said Marie Schubert to a *New York Times* reporter. "We never used to see Frank. Now he

New York Lower Bay - New York Harbor Lights

never leaves home." The Schuberts seldom left Coney Island after they moved there, and, when they did, the light was always attended by another family member or a Coast Guardsman. "We haven't been to the movies since 1946," recounted Keeper Schubert in 1986, "and we haven't taken a vacation in 20 years." "Twenty-five," proclaimed Marie Schubert emphatically. A short time later, Marie passed away.

Until approximately 1976, Coney Island Light had a radiobeacon that permitted ships to calibrate their directional finders. There were five transmitters at the station for which Keeper Schubert was responsible. The lighthouse was also equipped with a 1000-pound fog bell, and in an emergency it could be sounded, as the keeper explained, "with a sledge hammer." It was later discontinued.

Keeper Schubert liked to compare the light's rotating mechanism to a grandfather clock. "The weight comes down through the center of the tower and turns the clockwork. Now it has an electric motor, but it has pinion gears in case the power goes out." Under those circumstances, the weights could still rotate the lens.

The light itself was generated by shore power, but kerosene lamps were on hand in case of a power outage. "It takes about fifteen minutes to change from one to the other," explained Schubert. In

Coney Island (Nortons Point) Lighthouse, 1987

1987, a quarts iodide, 1000-watt lamp was the source of the beacon's light. "When it burns out, the bulb makes a great TV antenna," he exclaimed.

Established, 1890

The lighthouse at Coney Island was established as a rear range light in 1890. Its purpose was to guide steamers to the island's piers and to direct sanitation scows to their dumping grounds.

When representatives of the Light House Board approached the landowners to purchase the sites of the proposed beacons, the asking prices were twice their estimated values; the properties were thus condemned and obtained for $3,500.

The rear beacon, a square skeleton tower, was erected between what are now B47 and B48 streets at Sea Gate. The front range was at an undetermined distance away; it was discontinued in 1896.

On August 1, 1890, the rear range, equipped with a fourth-order Fresnel lens, began to exhibit its flashing red light. Standing seventy-one and a half feet above sea level, it could be seen at a maximum distance of a little over fourteen miles.

Following dredging of the Ambrose Channel, currents were diverted, and erosion began to take away materials from the front of the station's property. In 1915, a 600-foot stone wall was erected for protection, but six months later a northeast storm undermined most of the structure. It was backfilled, yet erosion continued. On April 11, 1918, Superintendent Yates received an urgent call from Coney Island's keeper; the fog bell building that stood near the water's edge was about to topple over. The superintendent arrived just in time to see it go over the bank and fall into the water. The bell was retrieved, but it was replaced a year later with a pyramidal skeleton tower that was equipped with a 1,200-pound bell. The site was then protected by several tons of riprap.

At the time the station was built, there were no other buildings or roads in the vicinity. By 1921, however, there had been so much construction that there no longer was any means of getting in and out of the station except by water. The Light House Service was thus forced to purchase a right-of-way at a cost of $5,000.

The Coast Guard announced in 1988 that it intended to fully automate Coney Island Light by 1989; the "young" seventy-two-year-old keeper, Frank Schubert, hoped that he would be allowed stay on at the lighthouse to guard against vandalism.

> *Coney Island Light is located at Sea Gate, on Coney Island. It is directly off Surf Avenue between B47 and B48 Streets. NOAA chart #12327*

ROMER SHOALS LIGHT

Appropriation:	March 3, 1837	$15,000
Appropriation:	July 7, 1838	$10,000
Appropriation:	March 3, 1849	$10,000
Appropriation:	September 28, 1850	$30,000
Appropriation:	August 3, 1854	$25,000
Appropriation:	March 3, 1867	$45,000
Established:	1838. (daymark)	
Established:	1886, lighted beacon	
First lighted:	July 15, 1886, compressed gas, unmanned	
Illuminating apparatus (IA):	(1891) fifth-order lens, fixed red	
Rebuilt:	1898	
First keeper:	Albert H. Porter, appointed September 26, 1898.	
IA:	1898, fourth-order Fresnel lens, flashing white light (Fl W).	
IA:	(1907) fourth-order (4-order), Fl W, oil lamp.	
IA:	(1924) 4-order, group Fl W, 18 sec, 15,000 cp	
IA:	(1939) 4-order, Grp Fl W, 18 sec, incandescent oil vapor, 37,000 cp.	
Fog signal:	February 20, 1899, 1,300-pound bell	
Fog signal:	(1939) air-diaphone, blast 2 sec, silent 13 sec	
Height of light above sea level:	(1886) 41 feet. (1898) 54 feet	
Automated:	1966	

It could not have been more unwelcomed news; the message received from Capt. Gedney indicated that the twenty-five-foot granite tower that was nearly completed "was put in the wrong place." His assessment was confirmed by Captains Kearney and

Perry, and a war of words broke out between the Navy and the Light House Establishment. The two naval officers had previously examined the proposed site but had not commented on it, leaving the Light House Establishment to believe that their surveyor, Winslow Lewis, had made the right choice. As the argument heated up, Congress stepped in and allowed the beacon's completion. It was later determined, however, that the 1838 Romer Shoals day-beacon, intended to mark the Swash Channel, was in fact about a mile from its correct position. Mariners bound for New York were thus instructed during the mid-1850s not to "run for the beacon, or they would infallibly get on shore."

Despite its being at the wrong end of the shoal, the beacon became an important navigational aid as mariners became accustomed to its position. In 1877, the structure was found to have settled considerably to one side, and, though temporary steps were taken to shore it up, a replacement had to be erected. Built on the opposite side of the channel, the new beacon had a thirty-foot- diameter iron pier on top of which was a twenty-five-foot-high skeleton tower. First lit on July 15, 1886, the light had a ninety-day supply of compressed gas and required no keeper. With time, however, the cost-saving light station broke down more and more frequently, prompting the decision to erect a lighthouse in its place.

Construction of the new structure began in May of 1898. In less than six months, the fifty-four-foot-high lighthouse was completed, and it was equipped with a fog bell and fourth-order flashing white light. Built of cast iron, the conical tower had accommodations for three keepers.

During the First World War, the *USS Amphitrite* patrolled the entrance to New York Harbor near what is now Ambrose Tower. From its position, it kept track of all incoming and outgoing vessels. At the end of the war, the Navy decided to discontinue the guard ship and requested permission to assign from five to six signal quartermasters at Romer Shoals Light. From the lighthouse, the men were to report on ship traffic by telephone to the Daily Shipping Bulletin Office.

In May of 1919, six enlisted men moved in with the three keepers at the light station; the sailors were quartered in a single room that was only seventeen feet in diameter. Fortunately, the men remained there for just a little over a month before being withdrawn because of shortage of Navy personnel. About a year later, the Navy took over the entire light station, assigning three quartermasters to both make ship observations and to keep the light. The Navy men had hardly any time to settle in, however, before tragedy struck.

It was noon on Saturday, November 13, 1920, as the U.S. Submarine *Chaser #137* approached Romer Shoals to deliver provisions.

Romer Shoals Lighthouse, 1987

The wind was brisk, and the seas were choppy, preventing the vessel from tying up at the lighthouse. Quartermaster William Walker set out for the sub-chaser and was alongside when a wave surge pushed both of the vessels toward the nearby rocks. Reacting quickly, the commanding officer of *#137* ordered the engines reversed, but in doing so the vessel's prop wash swamped the small boat, and sucked the quartermaster below the surface. The unfortunate sailor was lost. Following the accident, the Navy continued to maintain the light until October 16, 1921, when its care was returned to the Light House Service.

In September of 1938, the Great Northeast Hurricane developed off Puerto Rico and moved up the Atlantic coast. Winds that began that Wednesday morning as "moderate, to west, to strong northerly," soon developed into gale-force winds, and Keeper Herman Westgate noted in the margin of the lighthouse log that the barometer had fallen to 28.72. "The water was black due to this gale. I have never witnessed such a storm in my ten years in the lighthouse. I was expecting any minute to see the new platform and the 20-foot motor boat to take a ride over the rip-rap." Though Romer Shoals sustained damaged in the hurricane, in comparison to that of other light-houses farther up the coast, it escaped relatively unscathed.

The Coast Guard took over the light station in 1939, assigning four men to keep the light; three stayed at the light while one remained on shore for a week's leave. The routine varied little from day to day with the usual lighthouse chores consisting of maintaining equipment, painting, washing down the decks, and making once-a-week trips to shore for supplies, mail, and rotation of personnel. When questioned by a reporter concerning duty at the lighthouse, one of the guardsmen replied, "About the only excitement we have is running the launch out in heavy seas, or going out to help a boat with a broken-down engine. That doesn't happen very often. But it's not so bad here. And how many people get a week's vacation every month?"

Romer Shoals Light was automated in 1966.

Romer Shoals Light can only be seen close up only by small boat. A favorite site for fishermen and scuba divers, it can be safely approached, being sure to avoid a shallow rocky area to its northeast.   *NOAA chart #12327*

PRINCE'S (Princess) BAY LIGHT

Appropriation:	*May 18, 1826*	*$30,000*
Appropriation:	*March 2, 1867*	*$24,200*
Established:	*1828*	

Illuminating apparatus (IA): (1842) 12 lamps, 14" reflectors, fixed white light (FW).
Refitted: 1857, three and a half-order Fresnel lens, fixed varied by flash.
Rebuilt: 1864
Characteristic change: July 18, 1883, to fixed white light varied by white flash at intervals of 45 seconds.
Refitted: 1890, fourth-order Fresnel lens, flashing white every 5 seconds.
Fog signal: none
Height of light above sea level: (1891) 106 feet
Discontinued: August 31, 1922

From about the late 1700s to the early 1900s, oystering played an important part in the history of Prince's Bay. It supplied local citizens with an income and food, and crushed oyster shells supplied lime, which was used in the construction of Staten Island homes. Overfishing, human waste, agricultural runoff, and pollution from industrialization, however, decreased the yield and eventually destroyed the commercial fishery.

With an increasing amount of shipping entering the port of New York, Prince's Bay was chosen in 1828 as one of three sites for the establishment of a lighthouse. The other two were at Highlands of Navesink and Fort Tompkins.

Prince's Bay Lighthouse, undated. National Archives, 26-LG-14-24

Prince's Bay Lighthouse, 1987

The lighthouse at Prince's Bay was erected on that shoreline's highest point. Built of rubble stone, it rose to 106 feet above sea level and showed a fixed white light. In 1837, a Navy commission, consisting of Captains Kearney, Perry, and Sloat, surveyed the station and observed that, since it was visible only from a north-northeast to south-southwest direction, it could serve only vessels bound to and from New York. They suggested that, by placing additional reflectors facing westward, the light would also direct mariners traveling in the upper part of Prince's and Raritan bays. Furthermore, they noted, Prince's Bay Light was of great use in the winter, for, when the Arthur Kill was frozen over, steamers and coasters bound from ports in New Jersey to New York had to pass on the south side of Staten Island. Their recommendations were carried out a short time later.

During their inspection of the light station itself, the Navy commissioners had found it well maintained by Keeper Rawson, but a successor Silas Bidell, appointed on July 18, 1849, was ill prepared for the assignment. Bidell had been previously employed as a stagecoach driver, and, when he arrived at the lighthouse, he received no instruction on its care. The keeper was in the habit of leaving his daughter in charge of the light while he pursued another trade. It was thus not surprising that, during an 1851 inspection of the station, the buildings were said to have been dirty and the lanterns were said to be in poor condition. The keeper was described as "ignorant of his duties, and evidently not aware of the importance of keeping a good light." In the following year, another inspector was even less complimentary. "Keeper nothing extra," was his comment. Bidell did, however, manage to remain one more year at Prince's Bay, and then he was relieved by Homer Phelps.

In 1863, the tower was found to be in such poor condition that it had to be rebuilt. Work began almost immediately, and, during construction, a temporary light was shown from a wood-frame tower. From nearly the beginning, the station's illuminating apparatus had consisted of ten to twelve lamps with reflectors; in 1857, it was refitted with a 3.5-order lens that flashed every two seconds. With completion of the new brown-stone tower in 1864, the Fresnel lens was transferred to the structure. Some twenty years later, the station was reequipped with a fourth-order Fresnel lens.

In 1868, a brownstone dwelling was built and attached to the tower, and the former keeper's dwelling was torn down. The first floor of the new dwelling, consisted of a kitchen, pantry, dining room, and sitting room. The second floor had four rooms, and the attic was divided into two rooms.

A cast-iron staircase, which wound around a central pillar, led to the lantern. The lens rotated by means of a weight-activated clockwork, whose ropes ran through the center of the deck, across to one side of the tower, and down a narrow groove cut into the brick lining; it had to be rewound every four hours.

Following the establishment of acetylene lights in Raritan Bay in 1922, Prince's Bay Light was deemed unnecessary, and it was discontinued on August 31 of that year. The eight-acre lighthouse reservation bordered an often used beach, and, to guard from vandalism, the keeper remained there until November of 1922, when was he was transferred to Watch Hill, RI.

The other sides of the lighthouse property were surrounded by the Mission of the Immaculate Virgin, a residence and school for seventeen hundred orphans. Its director, Rev. Mallick Fitzpatrick, feared that the reservation might be made into a "bungalow village" or turned into a public park. This development, he felt, would interfere with the care of the children, and he thus pleaded to have the property sold directly to the mission. Rev. Fitzpatrick was informed, however, that the property could be sold only by sealed bids or at public auction. After at least three postponements and a great deal of lobbying by various interest groups, the government held a public auction in April of 1926. The highest bid received was that of the mission.

In 1953, a rear range light was erected on the mission property, southeast of the lighthouse. As rental for the small parcel occupied by the navigational aid, the government pays the mission $32 per annum.

Partially hidden by trees, the Prince's Bay Light is located at Mount Loretto, Hylan Boulevard, Staten Island, NY. The lantern, which was removed at the time that the station was discontinued, was replaced by a statue of the Virgin Mary. NOAA chart #12327

GREAT BEDS LIGHT (NY)

Appropriation: *June 20, 1878*   *$34,000*
Established: *1880*
Cession of jurisdiction: March 20, 1880
First lighted: *November 15, 1880*
First keeper: *David C. Johnson, appointed November 3, 1880*
Illuminating apparatus (IA): (1883) fourth-order Fresnel lens (4-order), fixed red light (FR).
IA: *(1924) 4-order, FR, 150 cp.*
Fog signal: *June 20, 1898, 1,227-pound fog bell, struck by machine.*
Fog signal: *(1924) fog bell, 1 stroke every 15 seconds.*
Height of light above sea level: (1883) 57 feet

L ocal mariners petitioned the Light House Establishment in 1868 to mark the shoal off Ward's Point in Raritan Bay. The request was viewed as reasonable, but a decade passed before Congress acted upon it. After a careful survey of the area, the site selected was located at the extreme end of the shoal known as Great Beds; it lay about three-quarters of a mile southeast of Staten Island.

In 1879, an iron tower and 1,000 barrels of cement were assembled at a local dock, but construction was delayed by confusion as to which state, New Jersey or New York, actually had jurisdiction over the underwater property. On April 8, 1880, the state of New York ceded the site to the United States, and, before the year was out, the lighthouse became operational. Equipped with a fourth-order Fresnel lens, the tower showed a fixed red light. In 1898, a 1,227-pound fog bell was added to the station.

David J. Johnson, a native of Philadelphia, was appointed keeper of Great Beds Light on December 17, 1894; he was replacing Mortimer Wood, who had been removed from office for an undisclosed reason.

When Civil War broke out in April of 1861, Keeper Johnson, then a young man of twenty-one years, joined the Pennsylvania cavalry, and during most of his four years in the conflict, he served as scout and wagon master. In 1891, he entered the Light House Service and was employed as assistant keeper at Shinnecock, and later at Montauk Point; at both stations, the keeper had performed well.

On April 8, 1898, Keeper Johnson and his assistant John Anderson, received word that they were being relieved of their post. "Sir," wrote Keeper Johnson to the Secretary of Treasury, "On the 8th inst., I was relieved of my position as Keeper of the Great Beds Light House, without notice and not letting me know the cause."

In the investigation that followed, Keeper Johnson accused his

Great Beds Lighthouse, undated. National Archives, 26-LG-12-8

assistant of being drunk and using indecent language in the presence of his family. The assistant charged the keeper with misappropriation of government property.

Keeper Johnson defended himself saying that he had given half of his alloted rations to his family "and replaced them with other things from the grocery store for a change." After having completed his investigation, Lt. J. M. Roper, assistant to the inspector, concluded that, in the case of the assistant, "while the charge of drunkenness was not proved, that of using indecent language in the presence of the Keeper's family was." Referring to the head keeper, he wrote, "There was found an inexcusable looseness in the care of public property." Neither man was reinstated.

In the early morning of January 25, 1906, Keeper John Osterdahl was on watch when he was jolted from his chair. Going out on the tower's main deck, he saw a large group of barges moving eastward away from the lighthouse; they were being towed by a Pennsylvania Railroad tug. It was not the first time since he had taken over the light from David Johnson that a vessel had collided with the lighthouse. In July of 1901, the schooner *Paul* had run itself up on the station's riprap, and, over the next nine years, collisions averaged about one per year.

Damage to the lighthouse was usually confined to the station's boat or to the ladder leading up from the pier; if anything, the collisions probably broke up an otherwise very dull routine. In the tradition of any governmental matters, however, the investigation and the paperwork that followed an accident were anything but routine.

Subsequent to the January 25 incident, statements were taken from the keeper, his assistant, William Aichele, and a variety of crewmen aboard the Pennsylvania tug. The tender *Nettle* made its way out to the lighthouse to inspect the damage, and a small mountain of paperwork later, the investigation was concluded. The towing company was assessed $20 for the damage done to the station's landing ladder.

In 1988, Great Beds Light continued to exhibit its flashing red light, every four seconds.

> *Great Beds Light stands just off Staten Island's Wards Point. It can be approached safely by small boat.*
> *NOAA chart 12332*

Fort Thompkins Lighthouse, circa 1880. National Archives 26-LG-11-69

FORT TOMPKINS and
FORT WADSWORTH LIGHTS

<u>Fort Tompkins (FT) and Fort Wadsworth (FW)</u>
Appropriation (FT):   May 18, 1826 $30,000
Appropriation (FT):   June 10, 1872 $13,400
Appropriation (FW):   June 11, 1896 $1,500
Appropriation (FW):   March 3, 1901 $12,900

<u>Fort Tompkins Light</u>
Established: 1828
Illuminating apparatus (IA): (1842) 12 lamps, 14" reflectors, fixed white light (FW).
Refitted: 1849, 9 lamps, 21" reflectors.
Refitted: 1855, fourth-order Fresnel lens, (4-order) FW.
IA: 1890, 4-order, flashing alternately white and red (Fl alt R W).
Rebuilt: 1873. Became operational, December 20, 1873.

<u>Fort Wadsworth Light and Fog Signal</u>
Fog signal: May 16, 1898 1,200-pound fog bell
Keeper of fog signal: William Boyle, appointed June 11, 1898
Established (light): May 11, 1903
IA: 1903, 4-order, Fl alt W R).
IA: (1924) 4-order, Fl alt W R, 10 seconds.
        W 24,000-candlepower (cp), R 7,200 cp.
IA: (1939) 4-order, Alt W and green sector (G) 10 sec. Incandescent oil
        vapor, W 24,000 cp, G 7,200 cp.
Height of light above sea level (FT): (1863) 89 feet. 1873, 90 feet.
Height of light above sea level (FW): (1907) 75 feet

J ohn Jennings was described as already being an "old man"
when he took charge of Fort Tompkins Light on July 11, 1849;
he had spent most of his adult life as a boatman and seaman.
His predecessor, Jacob B. Earle, had spent eight years at the station,
and he was in a hurry to leave –he stayed on only one more night to
instruct Jennings on how to light and maintain the lamps.

Lighting of the beacon at Fort Tompkins had been awaited with
great expectation by mariners entering New York Harbor. After
bringing the soon-to-be-completed twin lights of Highlands of
Navesink into range, navigators received the following instructions:
"You will be up with the Can Buoy of the S.W. Spit, and may then
alter your course to N. by E. 1/4 E. for the bluff of Staten Island,
where a light-house is to be built by December, 1827, showing a
fixed light."

Fort Tompkins Light was equipped with twelve lamps and reflectors. In 1843, they were described by New York Superintendent of
Lights, E. Curtis, as "much worn, and new ones are wanted. The light
is not a good one; I have had an opportunity to observe it for nearly

two months this summer." Going on, he stated, "the glass in the lantern is of the poorest quality, and would impair and destroy the most brilliant light." Later that year, the lantern was refitted, and in 1849 it received nine brass lamps equipped with twenty-one-inch parabolic reflectors. The station's illuminating apparatus was updated in 1855 to a fourth-order Fresnel lens.

The station's original tower rose forty feet from its base to the bottom of the lantern. The dwelling and tower stood so closely to the fort that, in 1863, artillery practice seriously damaged the lantern glass. Construction at the fort during the 1860s forced a change of site for the lighthouse, and on December 20, 1873, the handsome, new gingerbread dwelling and light tower, became operational. The old structures were then torn down, and their sites were returned to the jurisdiction of the fort.

The new lighthouse had been operating for only nineteen years when it was determined that the light was too far back from the point to be effective. It was thus proposed to move it to an angle off Fort Wadsworth and also to erect a fog signal there. A fog bell, which had been established at Fort Lafayette in 1873, served vessels bound to and from Coney Island, but it was too far away for those traveling through the Verrazano Narrows.

Nothing was done for the next three years, but construction of a gun battery directly to the rear of the lighthouse made the move all the more expedient. An appropriation was made for the removal of the light in 1896, yet further delays and war with Spain postponed the project. On April 28, 1898, the light was extinguished for four months as a war measure.

Construction of the new tower on the northeast salient of Fort Wadsworth began in October of 1902. The structure consisted of a seventy-five-foot-tall semi-cylindrical brick tower with a black lantern, and a square brick building to its rear. Equipped with a fourth-order lens, its flashing red and white light could be seen fourteen miles in clear weather. The station became operational on March 1, 1903, and, a short time later, the keeper's dwelling was moved to a new location.

The light and fog signal continued to operate at Fort Wadsworth until the mid-1960s; construction of the Verrazano Narrows Bridge had made the station obsolete.

NOAA chart #12327

ROBBINS REEF LIGHT

Established:	*1839*
Contractor:	*D. Haselton Co.*
First keeper:	*Issac Johnson, appointed October 25, 1839*
Illuminating apparatus (IA): (1842) 9 lamps, 14" reflectors	
IA:	*(1849) 15 lamps, 16" reflectors, fixed white light*
Refitted:	*1855, fourth-order Fresnel lens, 360o, with valve and moderator lamps.*
	Fixed white light (FW).
IA:	*1883, fourth-order Fresnel lens (4-order), flashing white (Fl W) every 6 sec.*
Rebuilt:	*1883. Became operational, July 10, 1883*
IA:	*(1939) 4-order, Fl W, flash 0.8 sec, eclipse 5.2 sec.*
	Incandescent oil vapor, 24,000 -candlepower.
Fog signal:	*(1863) fog bell*
Fog signal:	*1883, bell struck by machine every 15 seconds.*
Fog signal:	*(1907) compressed-air siren, blast 3 seconds, silent 3 seconds.*
Fog signal:	*(1939) diaphragm horn, electric. Blast 3 seconds, silent 7 second.*
	Emergency bell rung by hand.
Height of light above sea level: (1863) 66 feet. 1883, 58 feet.	

J acob Walker was assistant keeper at Sandy Hook when he met a young German immigrant, Katherine (Katie) Gortler. The slender woman of no more than one hundred pounds could speak very little English, yet the two fell in love and were married. The couple settled down at Sandy Hook, and Katie gave birth to Jacob, the first of their two children. About two years later, on December 30, 1885, Walker was transferred to Robbins Reef Light and was named keeper.

It took a long time for Katie to get accustomed to their new home. At Sandy Hook, she'd had a garden and a few chickens, but there was no possibility for such amenities at the isolated Robbins Reef station.

In the early winter of 1890, Jacob Walker caught a cold that quickly progressed to pneumonia. With his condition steadily deteriorating, he was taken to the Smith Infirmary on Staten Island. Though Katie was torn by concern for her ailing husband, she also realized that someone had to tend to the light. Suppressing her feelings, she remained at the station. On a cold evening in February of 1890, the middle-aged woman saw a small boat making its way toward the lighthouse. She knew instinctively that it was bad news; Jacob had succumbed to his illness.

The Light House Board offered the keeper's position to David Decker and Christian Hansen, but they both declined. Katie, who had remained at the station as acting keeper, was finally appointed keeper a short time later.

Robbins Reef Lighthouse, 1987

During her long residence at Robbins Reef, Katie Walker raised her two children, tended the light, and may have saved as many as fifty lives. One of those rescues, however, stood out in her mind above all of the others. During a gale, a three-masted schooner struck the reef and rolled over on its side. The keeper set out in her small boat and took aboard the vessel's crew of five. As the fifth man climbed into the boat, he asked "Where's Scotty?" The question was answered with a quiet whimper, and Katie reached over the side to pick up a small dog. "I'll never forget the look of his big brown eyes as he raised them to mine," she recounted years later to a reporter. At the lighthouse, she wrapped the animal in her shawl and force-fed him some warm coffee. The grateful animal again gazed directly into her eyes as if he was thanking her. When the storm had subsided, the crew made its way back to land, and the captain returned for Katie's new-found friend three days later. Though the animal was with her for only a short time, the two had formed a strong bond. As the captain carried Scotty down the lighthouse ladder, the dog looked back at the keeper and whined. "Then I learned that dogs really weep. There were tears in Scotty's eyes." Katie was keeper at the light for thirty years. She died in 1930, at the age of eighty-four.

Established, 1839

Built in 1839 by D. Haselton, Robbins Reef's original lighthouse was an octagonal white stone tower that rose to sixty-six feet above sea level. It had accommodations for one keeper and his family. In 1842, the station's illuminating apparatus consisted of nine lamps and reflectors; it was refitted with a fourth-order Fresnel lens in 1855.

The old structure was torn down in 1883 and replaced with a cylindrical iron tower. During construction, relief lightship *LV 25*, which had seen duty at Choptank River, MD, was anchored nearby to mark the reef and to house the construction crew. Two years after serving at Robbins Reef, the aging lightship was declared too small for service, and it was sold at public auction.

The new lighthouse exhibited a light for the first time on July 10, 1883. Standing on a stone pier, the tower was equipped with a clockwork operated fog bell and a fourth-order Fresnel lens that produced a flashing white light. The structure's first four decks were connected by spiral stairs, and a ladder led to the last deck, the tower's lantern. The cellar, built within the pier, had a storeroom and cistern. The first deck consisted of a kitchen and sitting room, and the next two decks served as sleeping quarters; the fourth deck housed the fog signal's machinery.

When the Coast Guard took over the Lighthouse Service in 1939, four men were assigned to the station. Three men remained at Robbins Reef, while the fourth rotated ashore for five days of leave. The three on duty stood daily watches of eight hours, with sixteen hours off. In the mid-1960s the station's personnel were removed, and the lighthouse was then run remotely via a cable from the Coast Guard Station at St. George, Staten Island.

Robbins Reef can be seen from the Statue of Liberty, standing about two miles to its southwest. It can also be approached by small boat.   **NOAA Chart #12327**

STATUE OF LIBERTY
(Liberty Enlightening the World)

Established: *1886*
Illuminant: *electricity*
Height of light above sea level: (1891) 305 feet
Discontinued: *March 1, 1902*

I n the strict sense of the word, she was anything but a lighthouse, but on November 16, 1886, President Grover Cleveland directed the Secretary of Treasury to place the Statue of Liberty under the care of the Light House Board, "henceforth maintained, lighted and tended in accordance with such rules and regulations as now exist applicable." The twelve-acre Bedloe Island, upon which the Statue of Liberty had been erected, was divided into three

Statue of Liberty, 1988

separate jurisdictions. With the exception of a section enclosed by the walls of an old star fort, the War Department controlled the east end of the island; it also held police powers at the statue. The Light House Board occupied some three acres at the northwestern end of the island and exercised an undefined control over the statue as a light station. The American Statue Committee looked after the outside of the statue and its grounds and provided a ferry service for visitors.

The statue became operational as an aid to navigation on November 22, 1886, and for a short time, an engineer of the American Electric Manufacturing Company maintained the light. Two days after Christmas, that same year, Albert E. Littlefield was named as the station's head keeper. Because of his specialized knowledge of electricity, his salary was set at $1000 per annum, $200 to $300 per year more than that of keepers posted at the most remote lighthouses of the time. The station's head keeper, and its two to three assistant keepers and their families, were housed in the three-story brick post hospital; it stood at the northwest end of the island.

The statue's dynamo, designed and built by James Wood of American Electric Manufacturing Company, generated the electricity for the nine arc lamps shown from the torch. Standing 305 feet above sea level, Lady Liberty's light could be seen from about twenty-four miles out at sea.

Members of the Light House Board were not entirely pleased with their assigned task. The Statue of Liberty was never regarded as an important aid to navigation, and in 1889 it was not even listed as one of New York Harbor's lights. The cost of its maintenance as a lighted beacon was about $10,000 per year, and, despite repeated requests for funds to finish the statue's pedestal and to make other needed improvements, Congress was not forthcoming.

By 1901, the American Statue Committee had been reduced in number to only two members: Richard Butler, an aging invalid, and Cornelius Bliss, who was forced to shoulder all of the "committee's" responsibilities. The probability of the Statue Committee being able to raise funds for improvements from private sources, was thus considered remote.

Visitor approaches to the statue were incomplete, even though fifteen years had passed since the statue had opened to the public. Of four entrances, three were boarded up with rough planks; the fourth and only access was an unpainted wood stairway. The steps leading to the crown were dimly illuminated by kerosene lanterns. Lamenting the condition of the statue and its surroundings, Post Commander A. C. Taylor wrote a letter to his superiors: "When it is remembered that hundreds of visitors, climb these dark narrow stairs daily and breathe the suffocating, nauseating air, it is remarkable that so few casualties occur –it is strange that so many people risk their lives by climbing to its head." Outside the statue, the grounds were composed mostly of cinders with occasional patches of wild grass. At one site, a cistern had caved in, presenting visitors with an additional hazard. The only toilet facility provided for visitors was a single, unisex, ten-foot by ten-foot shed that overhung the seawall!

When the War Department asked the Light House Board to relinquish its jurisdiction over the statue in November of 1901, there was no argument; it was by then regarded as being of little use to mariners. On March 1, 1902, the Statue of Liberty was discontinued as an aid to navigation.

> *Going from Battery Park in Manhattan by*
> *excursion boat, one can visit the Statue of Liberty*
> *year-round, except on Christmas day.*
> *NOAA chart #12327*

BERGEN POINT LIGHT (NY)

Appropriation: March 3, 1849 $5,000
Appropriation: August 18, 1856 $20,000
Established: 1849
First keeper: Joseph Lopez, appointed August 29, 1849
Illuminating apparatus (IA): (1850) 7 lamps, 15" reflectors, fixed white light (FW).
Refitted: 1855, sixth-order Fresnel lens, 300o, and Argand lamp. FW.
Refitted: December 14, 1904, fourth-order Fresnel lens (4-order). FW
                   with eclipse.
IA: (1907) 4-order, FW 5 sec, eclipse 5 sec.
IA: (1939) 4-order, occulting white, 10 sec.
                   Incandescent oil vapor, 2,900-candlepower.
Fog signal: (1863) hand-struck fog bell. 1873, machine struck bell.
Height of light above sea level: (1863) 53 feet. (1907 45.5 feet.
Discontinued: 1948

Major Delanfield of the Corps of Engineers had been directed in 1853 to survey the lighthouse at Bergen Point; what he found was discouraging. The two-story frame dwelling with its tower rising from its center, was only four years old, yet it was already in great need of repairs. The quadrangular wharf of crib-work on which it stood had been only partially filled with stone. It was described as being "in a very precarious condition, being constructed of very light stuff, and negligently framed." In that short time, ship worms had laced the wharf's pilings with their destructive tunnels, leaving the dwelling and wharf sagging toward the center. The ceilings in both the hall and upstairs rooms were cracked, and large sections of plaster had fallen to the floors. "The dwelling house is sufficiently commodious," asserted Major Fraser, who confirmed the other officer's findings, "but its condition, as well as that of the wharf, is too bad for me in asking anything for their repairs." Estimating the cost of complete restoration at $20,000, he recommended rebuilding.

Two years later, the station was reexamined and found by then to be in such poor condition that it was expected that an ice floe could sweep it away at any time. Work on a new lighthouse, however, began only in 1857; it was completed two years later. Standing on a stone pier, the structure consisted of a forty-one-foot-tall stone tower, with an attached two-story dwelling.

The Bergen Point Light had been established to mark the entrance to Newark Bay through the Kill Van Kill (Kuhl). The original lighthouse was equipped with seven lamps and fifteen-inch reflectors; it was refitted in 1855 with a sixth-order Fresnel lens, exhibiting a

Bergen Point Lighthouse, undated. National Archives, 26-LG-11-19

fixed white light. In the early 1900s, the station's illuminating apparatus was upgraded to a fourth-order lens, showing a flashing white light.

John Carlson (Carlsson) was twenty-eight years old when he joined the Light House Establishment. His career began aboard the Sandy Hook Lightship, *LV 51*, where he remained for six years. He was then transferred to the tender *Larkspur*, a twin-screw steamer that was used as a buoy tender and that resupplied and inspected light stations in the Third District. His stay aboard the tender was brief, and he moved on to a three-year tour of duty at Latimer Reef Light, off Stonington, CT. On March 10, 1906, Carlson was named keeper of the Bergen Point Light.

The Carlson family was elated; though the lighthouse was surrounded by water, it was the first family quarters to which John had ever been assigned. The dwelling had a kitchen, a dining room, and sitting room on the first floor and three bedrooms on the second floor. To get to school, the couple's daughter, Annie, rowed her small boat back and forth to the mainland.

Keeper Carlson's responsibilities at the lighthouse included the care and operation of the station's fourth-order Fresnel lens and the machine-operated fog bell. He also maintained the lighthouse and made any small repairs. Like most other keepers, Carlson never hesitated to go to the aid of mariners in distress. In 1913, he spotted two boys whose skiff had capsized in the Kill Van Kill. Reaching the site in the station's boat, he managed to pull one of the boys from the water, but the other had already slipped below the surface.

In 1948, Army engineers began to widen the Kill Van Kill, and dredge it to a depth of thirty-five feet. During the operation, the point on which the lighthouse stood was to be cut off. The lighthouse was thus automated, and, as the channel improvements neared completion, the station was demolished and replaced by a skeleton tower.

NOAA chart #12327

PASSAIC LIGHT (NJ)

Appropriation:	March 3, 1849	$5,000
Appropriation:	August 18, 1856	$20,000
Established:	1849	
First keeper:	Michael P. Nerney, appointed September 3, 1849	
Illuminating apparatus (IA): (1850) 5 lamps, 15" reflectors.		
Refitted:	1853, sixth-order lens, fixed white light (FW)	
Rebuilt:	1859	
IA:	(1873) sixth-order, FW	
Refitted:	1894, fifth-order Fresnel lens	
IA:	(1907) fourth-order, flashing white light every 5 seconds.	
Fog signal:	(1863) fog bell struck by hand	
Fog signal:	(1873) fog bell struck by hand	
Fog signal:	(1891) fog bell struck by machine every 20 sec	
Height of light above sea level: (1863) 51 feet		
Discontinued:	April 4, 1914	

During the mid-1850s, Passaic Light was one of four light stations that served mariners plying the waters of Newark Bay. The first one encountered, Bergen Point Light, stood on a rock reef at the entrance of the bay. A stake light, known as Corner Stake, marked the port side of the channel; it was situated on the edge of a mud flat, opposite Elizabeth, NJ. Farther up the bay, Passaic Light, the near-twin of Bergen Point's lighthouse, stood at the mouth of the Passaic River; it marked the mud flats on the west side of the channel. The last station, a stake light named Elbow Beacon, was located on a shoal near the Passaic and Hackensack rivers.

Like Bergen Point, Passaic Light was erected in 1849. It consisted of a two-story frame building with a wooden tower rising from its center. The entire structure rested on a wharf that stood some six feet above high water.

Both light stations were poorly built, and, within less than a decade, they were about to topple over. In 1859, Bergen Point and

Passaic Lighthouse, 1885. National Archives, 26-LG-13-39

Passaic light stations were rebuilt; as with the original stations, the new structures were near replicas of each other.

Passaic was originally equipped with five lamps and fifteen-inch reflectors, but in 1853 it was refitted with a sixth-order Fresnel lens. In 1894, the illuminating apparatus was upgraded to a fifth-order lens. The station's fog signal consisted of a hand-operated fog bell, which was later mechanized.

Women played an important role in "keeping the light" at Passaic. When William Bonnell was appointed keeper on June 8, 1870, his wife, Anna, was named assistant keeper; over the next eleven years, four more wives of other keepers served in that same capacity. During the entire history of the Lighthouse Service, women were seldom appointed head or sole keeper of a lighthouse without first becoming the widow of a keeper. It was thus surprising that New London Superintendent of Lights, Charles F. Lester, made note of the value of their labors in 1843. Submitting his report in July of that year, he wrote, "Three of the five light-houses in this district are kept by women, the widows of the former keepers; and I have to add, that, in point of efficiency, they are fully equal, and, indeed, superior to the men."

Eliza MacCashin was appointed assistant keeper at Passaic, eight months after her husband, Dennis, had taken over the station. For the next twenty-two years, Eliza was a mother, a homemaker, and an assistant keeper. When Dennis passed away in 1903, she assumed his post and stayed on as custodian after the lighthouse was abandoned on April 4, 1914.

Over the years, the river shifted its course, and vessels no longer passed near the light. In 1905, the Light House Board proposed the construction of a new lighthouse and fog signal at the edge of the channel, near the Lehigh Valley Railroad Bridge. In erecting the new station, workers were to drive pilings fifty feet into the river bed and then imbed them in a concrete pier. The lighthouse was to consist of a brick dwelling, similar to the structure erected at Stepping Stones in Long Island Sound. When test borings were made of the site, it was determined that it would require a much deeper foundation than had been planned and the anticipated additional cost was more than had been appropriated for the entire project. Faced with long delays in obtaining supplementary funding and persuaded by local mariners, who felt that post lamps would better serve the area, the Light House Board reversed itself. Four small flashing acetylene post lights and a fog signal were erected, and, following their establishment, Passaic Light was discontinued.

Eliza MacCashin died in September of 1914, and position of custodian was assumed by her son Hugh; he remained there until June of 1933. In the following year, an attempt was made to sell the property at auction, but the light could only be reached at high tide, and thus no one showed any interest in the decaying structure. It was left unattended, and eventually it was demolished.

NOAA chart # 12327

11 Husdon River Lights

JEFFREY'S HOOK LIGHT
(Little Red Lighhouse)

Appropriation: *(Hudson River Lights)   July 1, 1916*
Established: *1889*
Illuminating apparatus (IA): two tubular lanterns, 10 feet apart vertically
                     (30 and 20 feet high). Fixed red
Rebuilt: *1921. Became operational October 10, 1921*
IA: *1921, fifth-order red acetylene light, flashing.*
Fog signal: *1921, 1,000-pound fog bell*
Height of light above sea level: 1921, 61 feet
Discontinued: *1947*

N ew York City's best known lighthouse was its smallest. Made famous in a children's book, the Little Red Lighthouse at Jeffreys Hook portrayed the conflict between a David which seemed insignificant, in the shadow of a Goliath, the Great Gray, George Washington Bridge.

Vessels traveling the Hudson River usually followed the shoreline on the east side of the waterway, but, in doing so, they often passed dangerously close to the rock reef that lay just below the surface at Fort Washington Point. To mark the hazard, a stake light was established in 1889; it consisted of a black iron post with two lanterns, showing fixed red lights. They were hung one above the other, some ten feet apart. A small storage shed was erected to the rear of the post, but no provision was made for keeper's quarters. Nearby housing was probably not difficult to find, however, since the light station stood at the edge of New York City.

Within a short time after establishment of the stake light, it became apparent that the beacon was inadequate; a stronger light and a fog signal were needed. A recommendation for a change was first made

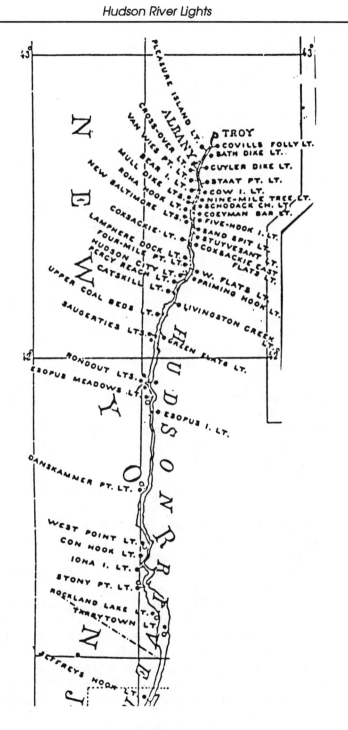

Hudson River Lights, 1895

in 1895 and repeated yearly for over two decades, but Congress was not moved. In 1909, it was suggested that a lighthouse be erected, similar to another farther up the Hudson River. "This will not be an ideal station but it will give good lights, a fog signal and a room where a keeper can sleep. He can probably obtain meals at a short distance away. The station at Danskammer (Point) is attended by a keeper with the same accommodations and no place where he can get meals." Despite a petition from the American Association of Masters, Mates and Pilots and the support of the Light House Board, the proposal was turned down.

The Act of July 1, 1916, appropriating $100,000 for the improvement in aids to navigation on the Hudson River, finally brought action to Jeffrey's Hook. In 1918, the Department of Commerce applied to New York City's Department of Parks for a permit to erect a small lighthouse and fog signal. Permission was granted with the stipulation that, should the lighthouse at any time outlive its usefulness, or should it be removed, or the permit revoked, the federal government would agree to remove the tower and return the property back to its original condition. In 1921, a cast-iron cylindrical tower, which had served as the North Hook Beacon, was moved to the site. Standing on a concrete base, the forty-foot red tower became operational on October 10, 1921. From a height of sixty-one feet above sea level, the station's fifth-order red acetylene light flashed for one second, with a three-second eclipse; its 1,000-pound bell was struck by machinery, one blow every fifteen seconds.

Little is known about the keepers of Jeffrey's Hook. In 1912, Lamplighter H. J. Whitley maintained the stake light at an annual salary of $240. The new station, erected in 1921, required a great deal more time for care and maintenance; thus the position was changed at that time to Lamp Attendant, with a base pay of $540 per year.

The Little Red Lighthouse had looked out over Fort Washington Point for less than six years when it was announced that one of the piers of a new Hudson River bridge was to occupy the site on which it stood. Arrangements were made to have the tower moved during construction and to relocate it on a special foundation when the bridge was completed. On September 21, 1927, loudspeakers were installed around the tower's deck for the bridge's ground-breaking ceremony. When it was completed in 1931, George Washington Bridge rose 600 feet above the Hudson River; the small lighthouse had truly become insignificant next to the towering giant. Though dwarfed by the Great Gray Bridge, Little Red continued to direct mariners up and down the Hudson for another sixteen years. It was discontinued in 1947.

On July 10, 1951, the Coast Guard announced its intention to sell

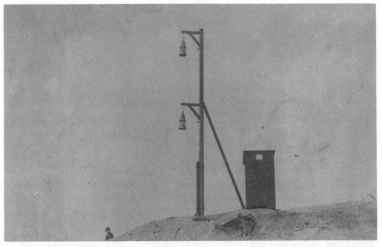

Jeffrey's Hook Light, circa 1900. National Archives, 26-LG-12-40

the Little Red Lighthouse to the highest bidder; it was not prepared for the chorus of protest that arose from the nation's youngest citizens. Made famous by Hildegarde Swift and Lynd Ward's picture book (*The Little Red Lighthouse and the Great Gay Bridge*), the story told children that even the smallest of things could feel "useful and important." The Coast Guard was flooded with letters from the youngsters saying that they were sad that the lighthouse was soon to be taken away. A child psychiatrist joined the protest, claiming that the structure had "become a symbol of security for many of the city's children." With an increasing public awareness of the lighthouse's importance, New York City Park Commissioner Robert Moses, requested its transfer to the city. His action came none too soon; it was to have been put up for auction on the following day.

After the Coast Guard turned over Jeffrey's Hook Light to the city, its door was welded shut, and it became the victim of benign neglect. Vandals had always been a problem. In 1934, while the station was still operational, someone had peppered the lantern's windows with rifle fire; with the tower unattended, it became a convenient billboard for graffiti.

In August of 1982, the city announced that the lighthouse was to be repainted and the park grounds were to be improved. Though it was to be three more years before that was accomplished, the Little Red Lighthouse was finally able to say that "it was VERY VERY PROUD."

> *The Little Red Lighthouse stands beneath the George Washington Bridge, at Fort Washington Park, New York City. NOAA chart #12343*

Jeffrey's Hook Lighthouse, 1989

TARRYTOWN LIGHT

Appropriation:	March 3, 1847	$4,000
Appropriation:	August 18, 1856	$7,000
Established:	1883	
First lighted:	October 1, 1883	
First keeper:	Jacob Ackerman, appointed October 4, 1883	

Illuminating apparatus (IA): 1883, fourth-order Fresnel lens (4-order), fixed white light (FW).

Refitted:	May 1, 1902 clockwork mechanism, flashing red light (Fl R).
IA:	(1907) 4-order, Fl R every 5 seconds.
IA:	(1924) 4-order, Fl R, 2 seconds, 800-candlepower (cp).
IA:	(1939) 4-order, Fl R, flash 0.9 seconds, eclipse 1.1 sec.
	Incandescent oil vapor, 3,200 cp
Fog signal:	(1891) fog bell struck by machine every 20 sec.
Fog signal:	(1907) fog bell struck by machine every 30 sec.

Height of light above sea level: 1883, 56 feet
Discontinued: 1961

On March 3, 1847, $4,000 was appropriated for establishing a lighthouse at Tellers Point, near Sing Sing. In the following year, however, officials of the Light House Establishment changed their minds and transferred the funds to Tarrytown; its lighthouse was to be a boiler-plate iron structure, on iron piles. The decision was not final. "On consulting the Pilots and Captains of steam Boats," wrote Fifth Auditor Stephen Pleasonton, "the Collector [of New York] learnt that it was the general opinion of those persons, that the Light instead of being put upon Tarrytown Point, should instead be placed upon Beekmans Point." After the land-owner of the alternate site declared that he wanted the princely sum of $3,000 for his two-acre parcel, the project was abandoned.

A lighthouse was again proposed for Tarrytown in 1855, but it was 1883 before one was finally erected. When the site's cast-iron tower became operational on October 1, 1883, Jacob Ackerman was appointed its keeper. Prior to assuming the· post, he had been captain of at least three different vessels, had held a variety of positions in the local government, and had worked at a Tarrytown feed store.

The tower's first deck (floor) was eighteen feet in diameter; it was divided into a kitchen, dining room, and living room. A spiral stairway led to the next two decks; they served as sleeping quarters. On the fourth deck, there were an additional bedroom and a work-shop/oil room. The fifth deck housed the fog bell's machinery and opened to an outside walkway; above it was the lantern. When first lit, the forty-four-foot tower displayed a fixed white, fourth-order light that could be seen at a distance of thirteen miles; its fog bell was sounded by machine every twenty seconds. On May 1, 1902, the tower's Fresnel lens was equipped with a clockwork mechanism, changing the station's characteristic to a flashing red light.

Life at the lighthouse was usually quite routine, with little to occupy the keepers other than the station's duties. Visitors often made their way out to Tarrytown Light during the summer, but in the winter the beacon's isolation was most apparent.

Keeper Ackerman sometimes dramatized important events at the lighthouse by giving them a title in the station's log. "The Tremen-dous North East Storm April 20th, 1893," he wrote of that spring day. In the page's margin, he added another title, "Lost Row Boat in the Gale and Storm." The keeper then began his entry: "The Storm of this day, and more particularly the wind from the East North East was the Heaviest Gale ever known at this Place. The Storm commenced at 4 am moderate and then continuously increasing in rain and wind until about 3 pm when the Gale was fearful strong." Keeper Ackerman went on to describe how the station's rowboat broke away from its davits and went adrift. "The highest tide for many years and with a Violent Gale. The cellar of the station overflowed, and for two hours we kept carrying out water before we gained much on it."

The April 26, 1893, entry was entitled, "4 Men Saved from Drown-ing." The keeper recounted how fishermen, while tending their nets, had capsized their boat. Recording the incident as if he was speaking of someone else, he wrote: "All of a sudden, the keeper heard a terrible outcry for help. All the men were clinging to the boat, but

Tarrytown Lighthouse, 1986

much frightened, and in danger of their lives. The keeper of the light station immediately lowered his skiff, the only boat he had. After lowering the station's boat in the least time, he went to their rescue and saved them all. He took them to shore and also their boat, with many thanks for the keeper's timely assistance in the rescue." In August of 1904, Ackerman submitted his resignation, effective October 1 of that year; he had spent twenty-one years at Tarrytown Light. Following his retirement, the former keeper built himself a home on North Washington Street, Tarrytown, where he remained until his death in 1915.

With completion of the Tappan Zee Bridge in 1955, the light's importance as an aid was greatly reduced. When the beacon was automated in 1959, the intensity of its flashing red light was reduced from 7,000 to 1,500-candlepower, and its fog signal was silenced. A foghorn and navigation lights were then installed on the center span of the bridge.

Tarrytown Light was discontinued in 1961, and a few years later, it was declared surplus property and transferred to the state of New York. On September 18, 1974, Westchester County purchased the light from the state for the sum of $1.

When first constructed, Tarrytown Light had stood a quarter mile offshore, but railroad construction projects and the building of the

General Motors plant eventually extended the shoreline to within fifty feet of the tower. During the late 1970s, the tower was connected to the shore via a small footbridge.

> *The Tarrytown Lighthouse is maintained by Tarrytown's Parks Department. It is open to the general public on a scheduled basis and to groups by special arrangement.*
> *NOAA chart #12343*

ROCKLAND LAKE LIGHT

Appropriation: *March 3, 1893*   *$35,000*
Established: *1894*
First lighted: *October 1, 1894*
First keeper: *Jonathan A Miller, appointed September 1, 1894*
Illuminating apparatus (IA): 1894, fourth-order Fresnel lens, 300o.
                      Occulting light, fixed white 5 seconds, eclipse 5 seconds.
Fog signal: *1896, fog-bell operated by machine*
Height of light above sea level: (1907) 50 feet
Discontinued: *1923, replaced by red skeleton tower on white tank house.*
IA (skeleton tower): (1939) 375 mm lens, occulting 10 sec. Acetylene, 390-candlepower.
Fog signal (skeleton tower): 1,000-pound bell, 1 stroke every 15 seconds

T he shallows off Rockland Lake Landing known as Oyster Bed had not been a problem for the shallow-draught, side-wheel steamers, but, as mariners changed to deep-draught, steam-screw vessels, the shoal became a threat. In 1888, Hudson River pilots and other maritime interest groups petitioned the Light House Board to have a lighthouse erected at the eastern end of the shoal. With a light and a fog signal at the site, it was argued, a steamer leaving Stony Point could lay a course close to Rockland Lake Landing and aim directly for the light. When Kingsland Point Light came into view, the vessel would then make its turn down the river. The cost of erecting the new station was estimated to be $35,000.

Over the next few years, a proposal for its establishment was repeatedly placed before Congress, and, on March 3, 1893, the necessary funds were appropriated.

Soundings of the site were made in July of 1893 by Third District Engineer, William Ludlow. "I tested the foundation" he wrote, "by using a 1 3/4" iron pipe 50 feet below the bottom; had the pipe been longer I would have driven it further." The riverbed consisted of a

Rockland Lake Lighthouse, circa 1897. National Archives, 26-LG-14-34

crust of oyster shells, whose thickness varied from eight to twelve feet; it overlay a deep stratum of mud that was practically solidified. The bottom's instability, and the river's currents and ice fields would later haunt the structure.

Construction of the conical, cast-iron lighthouse began by driving sixty-six piles, in concentric rows, into the river's bottom. An outside circle of piles, twenty-five feet in diameter, supported the iron caisson, and the tops of the inner circle of posts were imbedded in the concrete that filled the foundation cylinder. The lower part of the tower was completed on June 30, 1894, and, by mid-September, the superstructure was in place. Fitted with a fourth-order Fresnel lens, the station began showing its occulting white light on the first of the following month. Two years later, the lighthouse was equipped with a machine-operated fog bell.

During construction of the foundation, 200 tons of riprap were placed around the structure to help protect it from erosion. In November and December of 1894, 1,236 tons of stones were deposited on the tower's northeast side to act as an "icebreaker." At about the same time, inspectors noted that the tower was leaning in a northeasterly direction, "about 9 inches in 30 feet," and, over the next two years, the tower leaned farther, to a point that one side was 9 3/16 inches lower than the other. Engineers speculated that the heavy riprap had settled into the bottom, and had caused the tower to lean in that direction. Measurements continued to be made, and by 1897 the "leaning tower" of Rockland Lake had finally become stable.

Ice and currents persisted in playing havoc with the exposed lighthouse, and in 1906, another 3000 tons of rock were deposited around the structure. Despite its problems, however, Rockland Lake Light continued to operate until 1923, when it was demolished and replaced by a skeleton tower.

STONY POINT LIGHT

Appropriation:	*May 26, 1824* $4,500
Established:	*1826*
First keeper:	*Cornelius W. Lansing, appointed October 26, 1826*
Illuminating apparatus (IA): 1826, 8 patent lamps, 12" reflectors.	
IA:	*(1838) 7 lamps, 14" reflectors, fixed light.*
Refitted:	*1855, fifth-order Fresnel lens (5-order), fixed white light (FW).*
IA:	*(1891) 5-order, FW*
Refitted:	*November 1, 1902. Fourth-order Fresnel lens 270°, manufactured by Barbier and Feinstre (1891), identified by L.H.B./ B.F. No. 95. FW.*
Fog signal:	*1855, fog bell.*
Fog signal:	*1876, fog bell suspended from bracket on tower.*
Fog signal:	*1890, tower and fog bell. Struck by machine every 15 seconds.*
Height of tower, base to focal plane: (1863) 22 feet	
Discontinued:	*1925*

Stony Point lower light established: November 29, 1902, fixed red lens lantern light.
IA (skeleton tower): 300 mm lens, fixed green, electric 750 cp.

"I Capt. Frank Guyette of the Stony Point lighthouse, have a new housekeeper, and it seems to worry the people of Stony Point who she is. If you will please be so kind as to be in the park at 3 o'clock Thursday, the 30th, my housekeeper and myself will take a walk through the park and you will see who she is."

The crusty, seventy-one-year-old Vermonter had served at Juniper Light on Lake Champlain before being assigned to Stony Point on December 1, 1905. Everyone in Haverstraw knew that the keeper's robust, bespectacled, and not all that attractive forty-three-year-old wife had run off a few months earlier with a Haverstraw policeman; it was the talk of the town. When the local citizens learned that

Keeper Guyette had hired a housekeeper, every busybody in the county just had to know who she was! "They peeked in at the windows and hid in the woods in efforts to find out who I had engaged. Neither Henry [his nineteen-year-old son] or I could stir out of the house without falling over some of them."

Nettie Bulson, a widow from Stony Point, had answered the keeper's ad. After inspecting his home, she agreed to begin work on that Thursday. The keeper's invitation to come out to see the "mystery lady" was published in a Haverstraw paper; it brought out a huge crowd. They came by carriage, automobile, by boat and on foot. More people made their way to the state park, "than had been seen there in many a moon."

The widow had been expected at 3:00 pm, but by 6:00 pm, she had not turned up; apparently, she had spotted the throng. "I reckon she's got cold feet," commented the keeper, but he was undaunted. "If she doesn't show up tomorrow I'll hire some one else and parade her." Newspaper accounts did not reveal the outcome, but Frank Guyette probably did get his way.

The station's first keeper, Cornelius W. Lansing, had been selected from a group of eight candidates. Appointed on October 26, 1826, he arrived to find that the station had not yet been completed. Three months earlier, a contract had been signed with Thomas Phillips for the construction of the lighthouse; the builder was to finish the work by December of that year. The plan specified that the octagonal tower was to be built of "blue splitstone, and the best quality quicklime and sand mortar." The structure had three floors; the first floor was made of flat stones, and the next two were built of white pine. Wooden stairs led to just below the lantern, and a ladder was used to reach the lamps. The keeper's dwelling, built of the same material as the tower, was a one-story structure, "thirty-eight feet wide and twenty-two feet deep." Though Keeper Lansing probably maintained a temporary beacon until the tower was completed, he did not sign for materials to equip the tower until March 14, 1827. The list included eight patent lamps, eight twelve-inch reflectors, one iron stand fitted to hold the lamps and reflectors, and a host of other supplies.

Stony Point Light had been erected on the west side of the Hudson River, below West Point. From its position on a promontory, the light exhibited from the twenty-four-foot structure could be seen from an approach from the north "at the turn of the Dunderberg" (Jones Point —a distance of about three miles), and, from the south, it was visible to a maximum distance of nearly twenty-two miles. The light was especially important to vessels approaching from the south. From that direction, it served to point out a narrows on the waterway that otherwise was difficult to discern against the uniform topography of that side of the river.

Stony Point Lighthouse, 1838. National Archives, 26-LG-17-3

Stony Point Lighthouse, 1989

In 1838, the station's lighting apparatus was listed as having seven lamps with spherical reflectors, arranged on two horizontal tables. The apparatus was updated in 1855 to a fifth-order Fresnel lens, and, on November 29, 1902, a more powerful fourth-order lens was installed; it had previously been used at Tarrytown. At that same time, a second light was established at the end of the point; it consisted of a lens lantern showing a fixed red light, and it was erected on the roof of the fog bell tower.

The station's first fog signal, a machine-operated fog bell, had been established in 1855. Twenty years later, the signal tower was in such poor condition that the fog bell was suspended from a bracket on the light tower; a new signal tower was built in 1890.

During his 1838 inspection tour of the station, Lt. George W. Bache described the stone tower as being "at present in a very bad condition, the mortar used in its construction was not hardened; the masonry over the cellar window is cracked; the stone lintel over the door is broken and timbers over the door frame, and the beams and rafters on the floors, are very much decayed." The keeper's dwelling was in better condition, but it needed some repairs.

The tower was refurbished, and in 1879 a new keeper's dwelling was constructed of brick. With the quarters completed, the old stone building was torn down, and most of its materials were used in filling in its former cellar.

Keeper Cornelius Lansing apparently never developed the type of relationship with his neighbors that was later attained by the Rose family. In April of 1829, Fifth Auditor Stephen Pleasonton received a petition from citizens of Haverstraw, requesting Keeper Lansing's removal from office. In their letter, they complained of his "conduct." Though the nature of the misdeed(s) was not disclosed, following an investigation, Pleasonton dismissed him and appointed a new person, Robert Parkinson.

Alexander Rose was appointed keeper of Stony Point Light on April 22, 1853, and, when he died four years later, his widow, Nancy, was appointed to the post. Their daughter Melinda was only two years old at the time of her father's death, and, as she grew into her teens, the young lady began to assist in keeping the light. Never married, Melinda remained on at Stony Point and eventually assumed all of the station's duties from her aging mother. On May 17, 1904, her mother passed away, and Melinda took over as temporary keeper, pending the appointment of a permanent keeper. When she applied for that position, she was informed that, at age fifty-three, she was too old to apply.

Melinda and her parents were well known and liked in the surrounding community. When her plight came to the attention of United States Congressman Thomas W. Bradley, he wrote a letter to the Light House Board in her behalf. Third District Inspector, Captain Mackenzie, also supported her. "Melinda Rose has been practically keeper of the light, and it has been kept well," wrote Capt. Mackenzie. "I respectfully submit my opinion that this is a case justifying a request for the suspension of Civil Service Rules." The age limit was waived, and Melinda stayed on at Stony Point for another eighteen months; her successor was Frank Guyette.

The old stone light tower was discontinued in 1925, after a new steel skeleton tower had been erected at the water's edge. The station continued to be manned until 1973. John J. Kerr, who served at Stony Point from 1959 to 1968, was the station's last civilian keeper; he was succeeded by Coast Guard personnel.

In 1895, there were forty-eight light stations on the Hudson River, from Jeffrey's Hook to Troy, NY. Of those, twelve were lighthouses (eventually thirteen); the remainder were post lamps, towers, or dolphins. At one time or another, all of them were serviced by keepers, though a number of them were maintained by the same person(s). When the Stony Point light station was automated in 1973, Terry Dixon, a twenty-two-year-old Coast Guardsman, was the station's and the Hudson River's last keeper.

The Stony Point Battlefield State Historic Site is open to the public in season. It is located off Route 9W in Stony Point, NY. NOAA chart #12343

WEST POINT LIGHT

Appropriation:	August 14, 1848	$150
Appropriation:	March 3, 1871	$1,500
Established:	1853	
First keeper:	John A. Ellis, appointed December 8, 1853	
Illuminating apparatus (IA):	(1863) stake light, sixth-order lens, fixed white (FW).	
Rebuilt:	1872. Became operational September, 1872	
Refitted:	1872, sixth-order Fresnel lens, 270o. FW.	
IA:	(1939) sixth-order, FW, oil lamp, 65-candlepower.	
Fog signal:	1888, fog bell struck by machine every 20 seconds.	
Height of light above sea level:	(1863) 38 feet. 1872, 40 feet	
Discontinued:	1946	

West Point Light was erected under an appropriation which provided for the establishment of two other lights on the Hudson River: one was erected at Pryme's Hook, two miles north of Hudson, NY, and the other was at a bend of the river, two

West Point Light, circa 1880. National Archives, 26-LG-17-46

miles north of Catskill Landing.

The original light at West Point Light, built in 1853, was a thirty-two-foot-high iron beacon post that was equipped with a sixth-order lens; it showed a fixed white light. The structure was erected at Gees Point, on the/west side of the river. From the shoreline, the waterway dropped to a depth of fifty to eighty feet, allowing ships to cut in close to the point.

In 1872, a wooden hexagonal tower was erected in place of the stake light. Rising to only twenty feet from its base, the structure was also equipped with a sixth-order lens that showed a fixed white light. Sixteen years later, a machine-operated fog bell was added to the station.

The fog signal house stood near the water's edge, so close, in fact, that, in July of 1921, the schooner *Philip Mehrhof* smashed into the building, causing some structural damage. The vessel had grounded itself south of the station, and, when it was able to get off, the tide swept it up on Gees Point.

Certain officials of the Light House Board were, at times, capricious and petty in dealings with their subordinates.

Keeper A. P. Andersen had been forewarned in August of 1918 of the Secretary of Commerce's impending sail-by aboard the steamer *Kilkenny.* Despite the lack of quarters at the lighthouse, the keeper had remained on site from August 10 to 15, yet there was no sign of the secretary. On the morning of August 16, Andersen left the station on an errand, aboard the U.S. Military Academy's motor boat. About one-half-mile south of the lighthouse, he spotted the *Kilkenny* making its way up the Hudson. He asked to have the motorboat pull up alongside the steamer, and there was an exchange of greetings, but the motorboat was slow, and it was unable to get back to the station before the Secretary of Commerce had sailed past. Two days later, as the steamer approached West Point on its return trip, Keeper Andersen gave the proper salute, and he was answered by the ship's whistle. The Secretary of Commerce, who was standing on deck, saluted by dipping his hat, and the keeper responded in kind. Despite his efforts, Keeper Andersen was later "called to task" for not having saluted the vessel as it was making its trip up river. Third District Superintendent of Lighthouses, J. Yates, came to the keeper's defense. "The keeper has no quarters at the station," was his response to the Secretary of Commerce's letter, "and consequently cannot be at the station at all times."

In 1922, Keeper Andersen was commended for having saved the lives of two boys, who were drifting down the river with their small boat partially filled with water. Later that same summer, he pulled a man from the river whose canoe had capsized near the station. The keeper's predecessor, Louis A. Peterson, and his successor, Stephen J. Nolan, were also involved in a number of rescues.

West Point Light was discontinued in 1946. It was replaced by a black skeleton tower with a white central column and white tank house.

NOAA chart #12343

DANSKAMMER POINT LIGHT

Appropriation:	*August 7, 1882*	*$5,000*
Established:	*1885*	
First lighted:	*June 1, 1885*	
First keeper:	*James C. Tole (actg) June, 1885*	
First keeper:	*John Cox, appointed September 15, 1885*	
Illuminating apparatus (IA): 1885, tubular lantern, fixed white light (FW).		
IA:	*(1907) post lantern, FW*	
IA:	*(1924) post lantern, FW, 40-candlepower.*	
Fog signal:	*1885, bell struck by machine.*	
Fog signal:	*(1907) bell struck by machine every 15 sec.*	
Height of light above sea level: (1891) 44 feet		
Discontinued:	*1925*	

On the evening of July 11, 1914, Keeper James H. Wiest was sitting at his desk watching a heavy downpour when suddenly the wooden tower was enveloped in a deafening roar and a blinding flash! Lightning had hit the structure's skeleton top, and, running down one of the posts, it shattered the strut about two-thirds of the way down. Roof shingles scattered, and the bolt entered through the south window, striking the keeper. Wiest was thrown from his chair, and, for a short time after, he was left paralyzed on his right side. "I summoned help," the keeper later recalled, "and was able to stay at my post until daybreak." He then crawled to his house and called for a doctor. Upon examination, he was found with a broad streak reaching from under his right arm, down his right side and leg, and to his ankle. The bolt had passed through him and through the floor.

Following repairs to the tower, a lightning rod was installed, but, a year later, another bolt hit the structure. "I found on reaching the L.H. that it had been struck in 4 places," wrote Wiest in a letter to the Light House Inspector. "The west end of the cap on the tower slightly shattered, the bottom strip of siding on north side of weight box slightly shattered." The keeper was no doubt happy that he had been away from the tower during that storm.

Established, 1885

An appropriation for the light and fog signal at Danskammer Point had been made in August of 1882, and two years later the land was purchased. The plot was a circle, merely fifty feet in diameter, with a right-of-way access to the nearest highway. Erected on the west side of the river, at Danskammer Point, the lighthouse stood about sixty feet inland from the high tide mark. The structure stood on a brick foundation laid on rocks; it was thirty feet square on the bottom and rose to forty-four feet above sea level. Its illuminating apparatus consisted of a tubular lantern suspended from the front of the tower; its machine-operated fog signal was located on a platform that was attached to the structure.

When the light station became operational on June 1, 1885, James C. Tole was appointed acting keeper, but, apparently after seeing the tower's one-room quarters, he chose not to stay; his replacement, John Cox, took over on September 15, 1885. The new keeper remained for less than a year and was succeeded by James Wiest; he chose to live with his family in a nearby private dwelling. In November of 1919, Keeper Wiest submitted his resignation, and his successor, Harry Lewis, was appointed as laborer in charge.

Danskammer Point Light was discontinued in 1925. It was replaced with a pyramidal skeleton tower that was erected about fifteen feet to its east. Rising to fifty-three feet above high water, the new structure was equipped with a flashing acetylene light and a more powerful fog bell.

ESOPUS MEADOWS LIGHT
ESOPUS ISLAND LIGHT

Appropriation:	*March 3, 1837*	*$3,000*
Appropriation:	*July 7, 1839*	*$3,000*
Appropriation:	*July 15, 1870*	*$25,000*
Established:	*1839*	

Illuminating apparatus (IA): (1842) 5 lamps, 14" reflectors, fixed white light (FW)
Refitted: *1854, sixth-order steamer lens, 225o, and Argand lamp, FW.*
Rebuilt: *1872. Became operational August, 1872.*
Refitted: *1872, fifth-order Fresnel lens (5-order), 270o. FW.*
IA: *(1924) 5-order, FW, oil lamp, 350 cp.*
IA: *(1939) 5-order, FW, dark sector. Oil lamp, 350 cp*
Fog signal: *(1907) bell struck by machine every 10 seconds.*
Height of light above sea level: (1863) 38 feet. 1872, 58 feet.
Discontinued: *1974*

Esopus Meadows Light stood on a pier, nine feet above the mud bottom, on the western side of the river. An appropriation of $3,000 had been made for its construction on March 3, 1837, but the amount proved insufficient, and in the following year, an additional $3,000 was made available. The lighthouse, with its tower rising four feet above its roof, was essentially a duplicate of the Rondout Creek Light. Equipped with four lamps and reflectors, the station showed a light for the first time in 1839.

In 1855, there were five Hudson River lighthouses located above Poughkeepsie (Esopus Meadows, Rondout, Saugerties, Coxsackie, and Stuyversant), that stood on wooden crib piers. The lighthouses were located on marshes, on an island or on a shoal. In the winter, ice floes played havoc with their piers, and, in the spring of that year, George Dutton of the Corps of Engineers found all of them in poor condition. He estimated the cost of their repair in excess of $5,000.

The pier at Esopus Meadows was forty-one by fifty feet. It had been protected on its north end by a triangular, "icebreaking," fifty-foot extension, but its south end was unshielded. With a southeast wind and a flood tide, ice tended to pile up at that end of the pier. To protect it better, an extension was created, using additional piles driven into the riverbed. Timbers and ties were set on top of the piles, and the sides were faced with three-inch chestnut planks; the corners were covered by stout iron bands and sheet iron. The space between the piles was then filled with stone quarried at New Baltimore, NY.

Over the next decade, the pier was battered by the elements, and in 1867 the site was described as being "in ruinous condition." Nothing was done and two years later the pier was said to have been

Esopus Meadows Lighthouse, undated. National Archives, 26-LG-11-52

in such a state that "it is feared the whole will be taken away by the ice and freshets [flooding] during the coming winter. The keeper's house," the report went on, "is unfit for occupancy in the winter, even if the foundation pier were safe enough to justify its occupancy." Funds for a new lighthouse were made available in July of 1870, but Keeper Charles M. Yates, who had been posted there from 1866, apparently had had enough; he was relieved by Jonathan Cole a month before the appropriation was approved by Congress. Delays postponed the start of construction until the following year; it was completed in August of 1872.

The new structure stood on a pier of rock-faced granite. The keeper's dwelling, a wood-frame building with a mansard roof, had a kitchen, dining room, and sitting room on the first floor and bedrooms on the second floor. The sixth-order lamp that had been in use in the old tower from 1855 was removed to storage, and the new tower received a fifth-order Fresnel lens. In the following year, the original lighthouse was torn down.

In 1892, a beacon post was established at Esopus Island, about three miles downriver from Esopus Meadows. Two lanterns, one above the other and fifteen feet apart, were hung from the structure. A small house, eight by ten feet, was erected nearby to store oil and to serve as a refuge for the keeper in stormy weather.

On October 1, 1901, Robert A. Snyder, president of the Saugerties and New York Steamboat Company, wrote to the Third District complaining that the post lights were often extinguished. Two days later, when Lt. Spencer Wood went out to inspect the station aboard the tender *Gardinia*, he found the lights burning brightly. The keeper lived about two and a half miles from the beacon post, and it was impossible for her to see the lights from there. "No entry had been made of the lights having gone out," wrote the lieutenant in his report, "although the Keeper admitted that they had been found out once or twice lately. She supposed that the wind had blown them out." In inspecting the oil house, the naval officer found it dirty and the stores in bad order; he reminded her that she already had been warned of its bad condition on a recent site visit.

Lt. Wood interviewed other rivermen concerning the post lights; some said that they had never seen them out, while others said the opposite. "There seems to be a disinclination to remember which almost indicates a desire to shield another from trouble." He dismissed the keeper and recommended John Waldron of Hyde Park in her place.

In 1909, an experiment was conducted at the beacon post with a pressed glass Fresnel lens, produced by the Corning Glass Works. Compared to the plain globe then used at post lanterns, the new device gave an fivefold increase in intensity with a white light and a threefold increase with a red light. The post lamp continued to operate until 1919, when it was replaced by a skeleton tower.

"Last night about 10:30 P.M.," wrote Esopus Meadow's keeper on December 23, 1929, "a large field of ice drifting down on the ebb tide, struck the pier about under the Northeast corner of the dwelling, shaking the station considerable." The pipe to the kitchen stove had been knocked out of the wall, and dishes and canned food had fallen from their shelves. Large fields of ice, two inches thick, often drifted up against the station's stone pier, and in one area it had piled up to a height of five to six feet. "I have not been able to leave the station long enough to go to Kingston for food since December 6th," continued Keeper Andrew McLintock. "I have a good supply of ordinary food, but it is impossible to keep such perishable necessities as yeast, meat and butter on the station. And I cannot get ashore unless a west or northwest gale blows the tide down two feet or more below normal low tide mark. Then I have to walk through the mud as I did on the 19th of December." In its answer to the keeper, the Third District office stated that the conditions were nothing new for the station. "This station together with many others in this District which are similarly effected by the ice, etc. are in need of rip rap protection." On the following year, the station received several tons of riprap, at a cost of $6,850.

On August 14, 1965, the Coast Guard announced the automation of Esopus Meadows Light, and in 1974 it was replaced by a twenty-six-foot steel pipe tower.

NOAA chart #12347

RONDOUT (Creek) LIGHT

Appropriation:	*March 3, 1837*	*$5,000*
Appropriation:	*July 28, 1866*	*$22,000*
Appropriation:	*July 17, 1910*	*$40,000*
Established:	*1838*	
Illuminating apparatus (IA): 1838, 7 lamps, parabolic reflectors.		
IA:	*(1842) 5 lamps, 14" parabolic reflectors.*	
IA:	*(1850) 4 lamps, 16" reflectors.*	
Refitted:	*1854, sixth-order lens, 300o, and Argand lamp.*	
	Fixed white light (FW).	
Rebuilt:	*1867*	
IA:	*(1873) sixth-order lens, FW*	
Rebuilt:	*1915*	
IA:	*1915, fourth-order Fresnel lens (4-order), fixed red light (FR)*	
IA:	*(1924) 4-order, FR, oil lamp, 150-candlepower (cp)*	
IA:	*(1939) 4-order, FR, incandescent oil vapor, 870 cp*	
Fog signal:	*1915, 1,000-pound fog bell, operated by clockwork.*	
Fog signal:	*(1924) bell, 1 stroke every 20 seconds.*	
Height of light above sea level: (1863) 38 feet. (1891) 42 feet. 1915, 42 feet.		
Automated:	*1954*	

Rondout Light was erected on a mud flat, some three and a half miles upriver from the Esopus Meadows Light. Situated on the south side of the north entrance to Rondout Creek, it marked the entrance to the Delaware and Hudson Canal.

The idea for the canal had emerged from the efforts of William and Maurice Wurts, who wanted to find a route to transport their Pennsylvania coal to market in New York City. The brothers ultimately concluded that the only practical way was to dig a canal from the Delaware to the Hudson River.

Work on the canal began in July of 1825, and, in October of 1828, the first boat made the 106-mile journey to Rondout, carrying 10 tons of coal. Before the close of that season, 7,000 tons of coal had been shipped on the new waterway. At first, the canal was only twenty-eight feet wide and four feet deep; it could accommodate vessels carrying no more than twenty-five to thirty tons. As demand grew however, the canal was enlarged to allow barges handling as many as 140 tons. By the 1860s, the docks at Rondout held

Rondout Lighthouse, undated. National Archives, 26-LG-14-42

enormous piles of coal unloaded from canal boats. The fossil fuel was then carried to market aboard schooners and barges.

It was during that same time that Rondout Creek became home port to one of the Hudson's best known and fastest steamers, the *Mary Powell*. Leaving Kingston in the early morning, the vessel arrived in New York Harbor by noon. Its return trip generally began at 3:00 pm, and it was welcomed by the Rondout Light sometime after dark.

Funds were appropriated for a lighthouse at Rondout nine years after the opening of the Delaware and Hudson Canal; the beacon became operational in 1838. The station's first structure consisted of a keeper's frame dwelling with the tower rising from it; it stood on rectangular pier, forty-two by fifty feet (see Esopus Meadows Light). The lantern was at first equipped with seven lamps and reflectors, but the number of lamps was later reduced to four and then changed to five. In 1854, the tower was refitted with a sixth-order lens and Argand lamp.

Winter ice floes and natural deterioration forced the Light House Establishment to make major repairs to the pier in 1855. Ten years later, however, the entire station was found to be in such a poor state that the decision was made to rebuild. Congress, in July of 1866, appropriated $22,000 for its reconstruction, and work on a stone pier began a short time after.

Erected next to the original lighthouse, the new structure was a two-story stone dwelling, with its tower attached. From its lantern thirty-eight feet above sea level, the station's sixth-order light could be seen for eleven miles.

In the early 1870s, Army engineers built two dikes at the entrance of Rondout Creek. During construction, the engineers had marked the north dike with a light, and, with its completion in 1875, it was obvious that a beacon would continue to be necessary to help vessels avoid colliding with the structures. In 1880, three stake lights were established to mark the dikes; two were located on the north dike and one on the south dike.

Vessels traveling in either direction on the Hudson had traditionally run for Rondout Light. Changes in the river's flow, however, gradually left the lighthouse nearly high and dry at low tide. With construction of the dikes, the station found itself 1,070 feet inside the north dike and 660 feet inside the south dike; the lighthouse thus became of marginal importance as an aid to navigation. It was thus proposed to erect a new light and fog signal at the end of the north dike. From there, it was reasoned, the lighthouse could serve river traffic and the ferry that between Rhinebeck and Rondout Creek.

The new structure was located inside the point of the north dike. Its foundation consisted of a reinforced concrete pier within a sheet-steel cofferdam; in its center, forty-foot-long wooden piles were driven into the riverbed to help prevent any chance of undermining. The pier, which rose six feet above high tide, had an open area in its center to accommodate a cistern and storage room. The dwelling's first floor had a sitting room, dining room, kitchen, and a large pantry; the second floor had three bedrooms and a bathroom. The third floor served as an attic. The station was equipped with a fourth-order Fresnel lens showing a fixed red light, and a fog signal consisting of a 1,000-pound bell operated by clockwork. It became operational on August 25, 1915.

Rondout's old lighthouse had barely been discontinued when various parties began to vie for the purchase or lease of the handsome structure. Franklin D. Roosevelt, then Assistant Secretary of the Navy, wrote to the Lighthouse Bureau on behalf of friends from Kingston. They were eager to obtain the property for use as a yacht club. Another man wanted to lease the lighthouse to erect an advertising signboard. Though the government was inclined to dispose of the property, all interested parties were informed that, with its sale, the "land" on which it stood automatically reverted to the state of New York. Anyone purchasing the lighthouse would thus have to either remove the structure or obtain a grant for the site from the state. In 1917, the old structure, with its lantern removed, was put up for auction; there were no bids received. On February 14, 1935, the unused building was again put up for sale, and again no bids were received. Without maintenance, the structure deteriorated rapidly, and, after the roof collapsed during the 1950s, the Coast Guard had it torn down.

Rondout Light was automated in 1954. It was taken over and maintained as a museum by the Maritime Center at Kingston in 1984; it continues to function as a local aid to navigation.

> *Rondout Light may be visited during the summer months by contacting the Maritime Center, Kingston, NY.*
> *NOAA chart #12347*

SAUGERTIES LIGHT

Appropriation:	June 30, 1834	$5,000
Appropriation:	March 2, 1867	$25,000
Established:	1836	
Contractor:	Charles Hooster	
Illuminating apparatus (IA):	(1838) 5 lamps, 14" parabolic reflectors, fixed white light (FW).	
IA:	(circa 1850) 4 lamps, 15" parabolic reflectors.	
Refitted:	1854, sixth-order steamer lens (6-order), 225o, and Argand lamp, FW.	
Rebuilt:	1869	
IA:	(1873) 6-order, FW	
IA:	(1939) 6-order, FW, oil lamp, 240-candlepower.	
Fog signal:	(1924) fog bell, 1 stroke every 5 seconds.	
Height of light above sea level:	(1863) 42 feet. (1873) 42 feet.	
Discontinued:	1954	

"During the Summer of 1837," wrote Fifth Auditor and Superintendent of Lights Stephen Pleasonton, "I was informed that the Keeper of the Saugerties Lighthouse (Esopus Creek) Mr. Abraham Persons had for some time past hired out the Lighthouse, and lived some miles distant from it himself." Pleasonton directed the local superintendent to investigate the allegation and report back to him. "He replied that the fact was admitted by the Keeper, but that he had promised for the future to reside in the house provided for the Keeper, and perform the duty himself." In keeping with a strict policy that obligated a keeper to reside at his assigned post and attend to it himself, Persons was dismissed from office, and George Keys was appointed in his place. Congress appropriated funds for the establishment of a lighthouse at Saugerties in June of 1834, and, several months later, as Stephen Pleasonton was about to award the contract for its construction to the lowest bidder, he received a letter from that person stating that he had made an error in his proposal; it should have read, the builder pleaded, $3,700 instead of $2,700. The fifth auditor then signed a contract with the next lowest bidder, Charles Hooster of Saugerties; his bid was $2,988.

Construction began in 1835, and, as the stone dwelling neared completion, an agreement was signed with Charles Morgan to supply the station with oil and other necessary materials. Morgan was informed that Saugerties Light was to be equipped with five lamps and reflectors. In 1854, the station's lighting apparatus was upgraded to a sixth-order steamer lens and an Argand lamp.

The original structure stood at the edge of a mud flat, on a forty by fifty-foot pier. Like other Hudson River lighthouses, it had an "ice-breaker" extension at one end. In 1855, extensive work was done to the ice-damaged pier.

Congress appropriated $25,000 for rebuilding Saugerties Light in 1867. The stone pier and the outside of the dwelling were completed by the end of the following year, and the new lighthouse became operational in 1869. The two-story dwelling had a kitchen, dining room, and sitting room on the first floor and three bedrooms on the second floor; access to the tower was via wooden stairs from the second floor hallway. In 1871-1872, the old structure was town down, and the pier was then used as a public wharf.

In the spring of 1909, the American Association of Masters, Mates, and Pilots petitioned the Third District to have a fog bell established at Saugerties. As vessels passed the lighthouse, the association members argued, they ordinarily made a change-of-course correction of two points on the compass. In foggy weather, ships usually did not risk going any farther and had to lie at anchor, "but if there was a bell at this point," it was contended, vessels could still safely proceed. Later that year, a 10,000-blow fog bell was installed.

There were two women that kept the light at Saugerties: Mrs. Shoonmaker, who apparently took over the station after her husband's death in 1846 (1846-1849), and Katie A. Crowley (1873-1885). Ed Pastorini was the station's last keeper. Reportedly, there were tears in his eyes when he and his family moved out of the lighthouse in 1954. The station was then replaced by a "drab square tower on the southeast corner of the dwelling." In 1972, that structure was succeeded by a single pipe structure showing a flashing white light.

> *Saugerties Light is maintained by the Saugerties Lighthouse Conservancy.*   *NOAA chart #12347*

HUDSON CITY LIGHT

Appropriation:	June 10, 1872	$35,000
Established:	1874	
First lighted:	November 1, 1874	
First keeper:	Henry D. Best, appointed September 19, 1874	
Illuminating apparatus (IA):	1874, sixth-order lens, 360o. Fixed white.	
IA:	(1924) sixth-order, FW oil lamp, 110-candlepower (cp).	
Refitted:	1926, fifth-order Fresnel lens (5-order). Identification, USLHS #512. Revolving light.	
Illuminant:	1926, kerosene	
IA:	(1939) 5-order, flashing white, flash 0.3 sec, eclipse 1.7 seconds, om, 2,100 cp.	
Fog signal:	(1907) bell struck by machine every 15 seconds.	
Height of light above sea level:	1874, 54 feet	
Automated:	November 10, 1949	

I t was an unlikely place for a whaling town, yet in 1784 an adventurous band of New Englanders founded the city of Hudson, some 100 miles north of New York City. From Claverack Landing, whalers sailed in quest of the beautiful levia-thans; kindled by the products of their hunts, the city grew, prospered, and became an important river port.

The nearly two mile-long Middle Ground Flats, which lay just off Hudson City, had long been recognized as a hazard to navigation, but it was not until 1872 that Congress appropriated funds for a lighthouse to mark the site. Before the year's end, a preliminary survey was made of the southeast end of the flats, and, on May 11, 1874, the state of New York ceded jurisdiction of a parcel, 100 feet in diameter, for construction of the lighthouse.

Work began by driving pilings into the riverbed and surrounding them with a protective granite pier; within the pier, a 6,500-gallon brick and cement cistern stored rainwater collected from the roof. The keeper's dwelling, of red brick and stone, had a kitchen, pantry, dining room, and sitting room on the first floor and three bedrooms on the second; the dwelling's outhouse was at pier level, at the back of the building. In 1938, the station was finally equipped with an indoor bathroom and a central heating system.

The structure's tower, which rose from the front of the dwelling, reached a height of forty-six feet above sea level. Its lantern was initially equipped with a sixth-order lens showing a fixed white light, and in 1926 it was refitted with a fifth-order Fresnel lens, showing a flashing white light. The station's fog signal consisted of a

Hudson City Lighthouse, undated. National Archives, 26-LG-12-31

clockwork-operated fog bell.

The station's first keeper, Henry D. Best, was appointed to the post in September of 1874, two months before the station became operational. He kept the light until his death in January of 1893 and was succeeded by his son, Frank.

Frank Best was credited for several rescues during his time at the light. On Saturday, July 8, 1905, the keeper noted in the station's log that he had gone to the aid of a young lad, who apparently showed no gratitude for being plucked from the river: "Saved boy from drowning 10:00 am. Sherman Rockefeller. No thanks." In 1912, the keeper removed eleven women to safety from the steamer *Isabella;* it had collided with a tug near the lighthouse. Frank died on August 10, 1918, and his widow, Nellie, took over the station for about two months. During that short time, the Best family was involved in yet one more rescue from the lighthouse. Frank and Nellie's daughter, Mrs. Harvey D. Munn, saved the lives of a man and his son, whose boat had swamped a short distance from the lighthouse. Nellie turned over the station to William J. Murray, on October 5, 1912.

Coast Guardsman, G. E. Speaks, EM3, was Hudson City Light's last keeper (Emil Brunner was the last civilian keeper); the station was automated on November 10, 1949. Except for its navigational equipment, the structure stood empty until 1984, when the Hudson-Athens Lighthouse Preservation Committee took over the maintenance of the structure. The nonprofit organization raised funds and made considerable repairs to the old structure; it hoped to open it to the public by the late 1980s.

> *Hudson/Athens Lighthouse Preservation Committee*
> *725 Warren Street, Hudson, NY 12534*
> *NOAA chart #12347*

FOUR MILE POINT LIGHT

Appropriation:	March 2, 1829	$4,000
Established:	1831	
Contractor:	Ruel Clapp	
Illuminating apparatus (IA): (1838) 7 lamps, reflectors. IA:		
	(1842) 6 lamps, 9" reflectors.	
IA:	*(1863) sixth-order lens, fixed white light (FW).*	
Rebuilt:	1880	
IA:	*(1883) sixth-order Fresnel lens, FW.*	
IA:	*(1907) sixth-order, FW.*	
Fog signal:	none	
Height of light above sea level: (1873) 35 feet. (1883) 93 feet.		

Vessels approaching Four Mile Point on the Hudson River, had to run close to shore to avoid a shallow mud flat that extended out from the opposite side. Responding to the concerns of river captains and pilots, Congress in 1829 appropriated funds to establish a lighthouse to mark the site. In the following year, New York's collector of customs was directed by Fifth Auditor Stephen Pleasonton to select sites for proposed lighthouses at North Brothers Island (East River) and Four Mile Point. In both cases, the collector had less difficulty in selecting the appropriate sites than in purchasing the needed property. The owner of North Brothers Island simply did not want to sell (see North Brothers Island). Four Mile Point's owner wanted to sell just enough land for construction of a tower and he suggested that he should then be appointed keeper; since he lived nearby, he reasoned that there was no need for a keeper's dwelling.

Stephen Pleasonton was not impressed. "Should the proprietor (of Four Mile Point) object to sell the quantity of land we want at a fair price, without the privilege of Keeping the Lighthouse, you will apply to the Legislature [of New York] without delay, for an act to condemn." Addressing an alternative suggestion that the keeper could rent quarters from the landowner, the fifth auditor wrote, "We must have a dwelling house for a keeper erected, as we could not render ourselves dependent upon him or any other individual for the accommodation of a Keeper."

The landowner finally relented and sold the property on the government's terms. In April of 1831, a contract was signed with Ruel Clapp for construction of a stone tower and dwelling, and separate agreement was made with Cornell and Althouse for fitting the lantern with patent lamps and reflectors. The lighthouse became operational later that year.

In 1838, the station's illuminating apparatus consisted of seven lamps and parabolic reflectors arranged on two horizontal tables; the light was visible from both directions along the river and across the channel. In 1854, the tower was refitted with a sixth-order lens.

Following an inspection of the station in which the stone tower was described as "dilapidated and unsightly," funds were made available for its reconstruction. The new structure, erected in 1880, was a twenty-five-foot iron tower. An acetylene light was installed in the tower around 1918. It then continued to operate until about 1928, when it was discontinued and replaced by a steel tower that was erected at the water's edge. The property was sold at auction in 1932 to Donald Greene for $1,100. Nothing of either tower remains, but the keeper's dwelling is still standing and continues to be occupied by a member of the Greene family. The stone end of the stone and frame structure was probably part of the original kitchen; it now serves as a dining room.

NOAA chart #12348

COXSACKIE LIGHT

Appropriation:	*May 23, 1828*	*$8,000*
Appropriation:	*July 28, 1866*	*$22,000*
Established:	*1830*	
Illuminating apparatus (IA): (1838) 7 lamps, 14" reflectors, fixed white light (FW).		
IA:	*(1842) 5 lamps, 14" reflectors, FW*	
Refitted:	*1854, sixth-order steamer lens, 225o, and Argand lamp, FW.*	
Rebuilt:	*1868*	
IA:	*(1924) sixth-order lens, FW, 270-candlepower (cp).*	
IA:	*(1939) sixth order lens, FW, oil lamp, 270 cp.*	
Fog signal:	*none*	
Height of light above sea level: (1863) 38 feet. (1873) 38 feet		
Discontinued:	*1939*	

A cold winter wind stung Keeper Jerome McDougall's weathered face as he set out for the dolphin at Coxsackie East Flats. Carried by the current, he found it easy to row the half-mile downriver from the lighthouse. A post light had been erected at East Flats in July of 1890, but, during the winter following its establishment, a heavy ice floe destroyed it, and a dolphin was put up in its place. Two decades later, it too was carried away as an ice jam broke up; the second dolphin light became operational on April 8, 1903. Over the next twenty years, the structure was gradually weakened by intermittent onslaughts of winter ice and spring floods.

On that day in 1923, Keeper McDougall tied up his skiff to one of the dolphin's pilings and began to climb it to change the lantern's reservoirs. As he was reaching the top, the structure suddenly gave way under his weight and hurled him head first into the near-freezing waters. The keeper first attempted to swim to shore, but, slowed by his water-soaked winter clothing and the river's current, he opted to return to his skiff. Too exhausted by then to lift himself out of the water, he clung to the small boat's bow, uncertain if he would ever see his loved ones again.

The captain of the Standard Oil tug had seen the keeper struggling in the river and ordered his vessel brought up alongside the skiff. A line was thrown out to McDougall, but his hands were frozen stiff, and he couldn't grasp it. Somehow thought, he managed to wind it a half-turn around his arm, and, taking hold of the line with his teeth, he was pulled from the frigid Hudson!

Established, 1829

The lighthouse at Coxsackie was established in 1829. Located at the northeastern end of Rattlesnake Island, two miles above Coxsackie Landing, it served to guide vessels through the narrow channel between the island and a mud flat that extended from the eastern bank of the river. In 1838, the light exhibited from the keeper's dwelling consisted of seven lamps and reflectors, which were arranged around two horizontal tables. The beacon was visible along the river from both directions. In 1854, the station was refitted with a sixth-order steamer lens and an Argand lamp.

The banks surrounding the lighthouse gradually eroded, and, though protective riprap was placed along the shoreline, the decision was made in 1866 to rebuild the thirty-seven-year-old lighthouse. Completed two years later, the new structure was erected on a pile foundation, surrounded by a protective stone pier. Rising thirty-two feet from its base to the center of the lantern, the tower was located on the northeast corner of the two-story dwelling. Its lantern was equipped with a sixth-order lens showing a fixed white light.

During the winter of 1901-1902, an ice gorge formed on the Hudson River between the Coxsackie and Stuyversant light stations; the resulting "lake" soon flooded Stuyversant's dwelling. When the ice jam broke up on March 2, 1902, the cascading torrent of jagged

Coxsackie Lighthouse, undated. National Archives, 26-LG-11-35

Stuyversant Lighthouse, undated. National Archives, 26-LG-17-19

blocks of ice and water rushed towards Coxsackie Lighthouse. The north wall of the dwelling "dissolved" in the onslaught, "making a clear hole nearly the entire width of the building." As ice rushed in through the opening, it filled the first floor and caused the west wall to budge and crack. Heavy foundation stones were displaced, and some were pushed out into the river. One of the station's outhouses went for a ride down the river, while the other was crushed where it stood. The tower, however, emerged intact, and, though some of its lamps were damaged, its light continued to burn. By the end of June, all of the repairs had been completed; the tower's color was changed from red to white, and a new set of lamps was delivered.

Coxsackie Light was discontinued in 1940 and replaced by a black skeleton tower and a white tank house. The old structure was then torn down.
NOAA chart #12348

STUYVERSANT LIGHT

Appropriation:	*May 23, 1828*	*$8,000*
Appropriation:	*March 2, 1867*	*$20,000*
Established:	*1829*	
Rebuilt:	*1837*	
Illuminating apparatus (IA): (1838) 5 lamps, 13 3/4" reflectors		
IA:	*(1842) 5 lamps, 14" reflectors, fixed white (FW)*	
IA:	*(1850) 5 lamps, 16" reflectors, FW.*	
Refitted:	*1854, sixth-order Fresnel lens (6-order), FW.*	
Rebuilt:	*1868*	
IA:	*(1873) 6-order, FW*	
IA:	*(1907) 6-order, fixed red light (FR).*	
IA:	*(1924) 6-order, FR, oil lamp, 50 cp.*	
Fog signal:	*none*	
Height of light above sea level: (1863) 38 feet.		
Discontinued:	*1933*	

S tanding as it did on the edge of a marsh that extended out from the east side of the Hudson River, the lighthouse at Stuyversant was at the mercy of winter ice floes and spring floods. The station had been established in 1829 to mark the nearby narrow channel, but tragedy struck in March of 1832. An ice jam, which had formed up river, broke up releasing a "tidal wave" that carried away everything in its path. There was no warning for Stuyversant's keeper, and, in the ensuing deluge, the lighthouse and four members of the keeper's family were swept downstream.

A new four-room stone structure was built in 1835-1836; it showed its light from the keeper's dwelling. In 1838, the lantern was equipped with five lamps and reflectors arranged on two horizontal tables. Like many of the other Hudson River lighthouses, Stuyversant was refitted with a sixth-order lens in 1854.

Stuyversant's lighthouse was rebuilt for a third time in 1868. Set upon pilings and a granite pier, the station's square red tower rose from the southwest angle of the two-story dwelling. After its completion, the old dwelling was used as a shed; during the winter, it housed portable beacons that had been taken off station while the river was closed to navigation.

In the early part of 1902, an ice jam developed on the river between Coxsackie and Stuyversant. As water backed up from the ice dam, Stuyversant's first floor flooded; ice that formed in the temporarily abandoned building grew to a thickness of three and a half feet! When the ice jam broke on March 2, 1902, the old dwelling was swept into the river along with a small bridge that connected the property to the mainland. The lighthouse's west wall was pushed in, and the opposite wall bulged out, but there was only minor damage to the tower. Later that month, repairs were begun, and, by the end of June, the station was again fully operational.

Keeper Edwin M. McAllister was luckier than his predecessor seventy years earlier; he and his family were safely away from the lighthouse when the ice gave way. He did, however, lose all of his furniture on the first floor, including the family's prized possession and source of diversion, a Bordman and Gray piano. Writing to Capt. William Folger, inspector for the Third District, the keeper asked if he could be reimbursed for his losses. "My loss in personal property," he pleaded, "amounting to between six and seven hundred dollars is a most severe one for a poor man." There was precedent for such reimbursement, and Keeper McAllister was repaid.

Stuyversant Light was discontinued in 1933 and replaced with a skeleton tower. The lighthouse was torn down shortly thereafter, and some of its foundation stones were used for the base of the porch of the Stuyversant Falls Post Office.

NOAA chart #12348

12 *New Jersey 's Coastal Lights*

SEA GIRT LIGHT

Appropriation:	*March 2, 1888*	*$20,000*
Established:	*1896*	
First lighted:	*December 10, 1896*	
First keeper:	*Abram S. Yates, appointed December 2, 1896*	

Illuminating apparatus (IA): (1907) fourth-order Fresnel lens (4-order).
Identification number, HL #305, clock made in shop
of General Depot, 1896. Flashing red every six seconds.

Illuminant:	*June 24, 1912, changed from oil to incandescent oil vapor.*
Radiobeacon:	*1921-1927 3 dashes.*
IA:	*(1924) 4-order, flashing white (Fl W) .3 sec, eclipse .7 sec. 11,000 cp.*
IA:	*(1939) 4-order, Fl W, 1 seconds Electric, 100,000 cp.*
Fog signal:	*none*

Height of light above sea level: (1907) 52 feet
Discontinued: 1945

The lighthouses at Barnegat and Highlands of Navesink stood some thirty-eight miles apart, but their beacons were visible simultaneously only when a vessel ventured close to shore and only under the best weather conditions. If a lighthouse was established in the vicinity of Squam Inlet, it was argued, it would light up the "dark spot" that existed between the two others, thereby facilitating navigation along that part of the coast. Furthermore, mariners could obtain a fix on their positions by obtaining a cross-bearing on the lights. The estimated cost of erecting a light in that area was set at $20,000.

Congress authorized the establishment of a lighthouse at Squam Inlet on October 19, 1888, but, after the proposed location was examined, it was found unsuitable. Difficulties in finding another site and obtaining the title delayed the project further, and it was not until the spring of 1896 that work began.

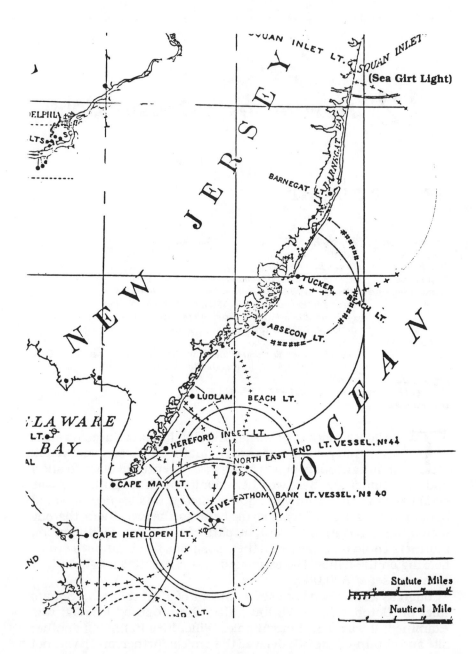

New Jersey Coastal Lights, 1895

The lighthouse was erected on Sea Girt's beach at the intersections of Ocean and Bellevue (Ocean and Beacon) avenues. When inspected in 1907, the location was termed convenient; the railway station was a little over a mile away, and a streetcar line passed only four blocks from the light station.

Sea Girt became operational on December 10, 1896. Constructed of red brick, the lighthouse consisted of a six-room, two-story dwelling with a square tower rising from the front. The station's fourth-order Fresnel lens, identified in 1907 by the inscription "HL 305," showed a flashing red light every six seconds.

The station's logs suggested that life at Sea Girt was quiet. Very few entries were made other than the usual weather observations and details on equipment and station maintenance. On May 29, 1910, Harriet Yates noted in the station's log that her husband, Abram, had passed away. She took over the keeper's duties and remained there until relieved by John L. Hawkey on July 24, 1910. The widow was the only woman to keep the light at Sea Girt.

On May 21, 1921, the Lighthouse Service installed three radio-fog signal stations at the approaches to New York Harbor. Transmitters were placed aboard Fire Island and Ambrose lightships and at Sea Girt Light. It was the first practical use of radiobeacons by the Lighthouse Service.

The French had initiated their first radiobeacons in 1912, and, in that same year, the Lighthouse Service had also begun exploring their use. In 1917, an experimental transmitter was installed at Highlands of Navesink, and another receiver was placed on board the tender *Tulip*. The results were promising, but the First World War interrupted any further work on the system by the Lighthouse Service.

As part of the radiobeacon installation at Sea Girt in 1921, two large antennas were erected on each side of the lighthouse, and the keeper was placed in charge of the transmitter. The signals were operated primarily in thick or foggy weather, but they were also transmitted on clear days, (a half-hour in the morning and a half-hour in the afternoon) to allow ships to try out their equipment under good conditions. The stations were identified by the characteristic of their signals. Ambrose sent one dash, Fire Island had a group of two, and Sea Girt's signal was three dashes. Sea Girt maintained a radiobeacon until the late 1920s, when a transmitter was installed aboard the Barnegat Lightship.

At 4:30 am on September 8, 1934, an S. O. S. was received by the steamer *Monarch*; the liner *Morro Castle* was ablaze just northeast of Sea Girt! Nearly every ship in the area responded to the call for help. When the *Monarch* arrived on the scene, several vessels were already picking up survivors. Some of the *Morro Castle's* passengers

Sea Girt Lighthouse, 1989.   *Photo by Herb Segars*

and crew were able to board the liner's few lifeboats that were
launched, but many more had to jump into the water to escape the
inferno. Of the 562 persons aboard, 134 perished; some of the
survivors were sheltered at the Sea Girt Lighthouse.

During the Second World War, Sea Girt Light was occupied by the
Coast Guard. The station served as an observation post to guard
against Nazi agents and saboteurs who came in by submarine. The
lighthouse was decommissioned in 1945, and, in August of 1956,
the station was sold to the borough of Sea Girt.

In 1981, the Sea Girt Lighthouse Committee obtained a twenty-
five-year lease from the borough; it has refurbished and maintained
the historic landmark since then.

---

*Sea Girt Lighthouse is used for local club meetings, and the Sea Girt
Lighthouse Committee plans to open the building to the public
sometime in the future.*
` NOAA chart #12300, 12323, 12324`

BARNEGAT LIGHT

Appropriation:	June 30, 1834	$6,000
Appropriation:	August 18, 1856	$45,000
Established:	1835	

Purchased land from: Bornt Slaught, October 25, 1834, $300
Superintendent of construction: Nathan S. Crane
First keeper: Henry V. Low, appointed August 3, 1835
Illuminating apparatus: (1842) 11 lamps, 14" reflectors.
IA: (1850) 11 lamps, 15" reflectors.
Refitted: 1854, fourth-order Fresnel lens, 360o.
Rebuilt: 1858. Became operational January 1, 1859
Contractor: Engineer W.F. Reynolds
Refitted: 1858, first-order Fresnel lens (1-order), revolving light, 0.10 minutes.
IA: (1891) 1-order, flashing white light (Fl W), every 10 seconds.
IA: (1924) Fl W 10 seconds; flash 2.5 seconds, eclipse 7.5 seconds, 80,000-candlepower (cp).
IA: (1939) three and a half-order, Fl W 10 sec. Electric, 11,000 cp.
Height of tower, from base to lantern: (1842) 40 feet
Height of light above sea level: (1863) 165 feet
Discontinued: January 1, 1944

From almost the time of its establishment, there had been a long list of complaints voiced by ships' captains concerning Barnegat Light. When they were asked in 1852 what they thought of it and other United States lights, Fifth Auditor and Superintendent of Lights, Stephen Pleasonton, could not have been pleased with their answers; most were negative.

Vessels bound to and from New York along the New Jersey coastline, depended on Barnegat Light to avoid a shoal that extended out from shore. Its beacon was so dim, however, that it was frequently mistaken for a vessel's light. "After leaving the Hook or Highlands lights (the latter I believe to be the best on our coast)," wrote Capt. William Berry of the *Vicksburg*, "I generally steer for Barnegat, frequently passing without seeing it, owing no doubt to the low position (inferiority) of the light." Capt. E. R. Smith, master of the *Tropic*, lamented that, when the weather was the least bit hazy, there was nothing to distinguish the Barnegat Light from the Egg Harbor Light (Tucker Beach). "I came very near losing my ship in consequence. It is reported red, but it is not so, and may lead to some fatal mistake." (At that time, Tucker Beach exhibited a fixed red light, and Barnegat had a fixed white light —the two lights stood eighteen miles apart.)

Barnegat Lighthouse, undated. National Archives, 26-LG-10-52

In June of 1834, Congress had appropriated $6,000 for establishing a lighthouse on or near the shoals of Barnegat, and in the following month, Pleasonton directed George Tucker to select and purchase the necessary site. The forty-foot-tall lighthouse was erected on a low beach, a little over 100 yards from the water's edge. Equipped with eleven lamps and reflectors, it became operational on July 20, 1835.

The tower had been built on the south side of Barnegat Inlet, near the entrance. The channel shifted position so often, however, that the lighthouse was of no practical use for marking the waterway, and it thus functioned mainly as a seacoast light. Attesting to the importance of the coastal beacon, Keeper James Fuller reported 3,000 large sailing ships and steamers passing the station during a nine-month period in 1855. The total did not take into account an even greater number of coastal vessels.

The old light tower was poorly constructed, and gradually its walls began to bulge; mortar was lost, and bricks fell out. To help appease the demand for a brighter beacon, a fourth-order Fresnel lens had been installed in 1854, and the structure was sufficiently patched up to last until a new tower could be erected.

Congress appropriated funds for the station's second lighthouse on August 18, 1856. Erected under the direction of W. F. Reynolds, an engineer, the focal plane of the masonry tower was 165 feet above sea level; its lantern was equipped with a powerful first-order Fresnel lens. During construction, the beach in front of the old tower had eroded to such an extent that the tower had to be abandoned, and a temporary wood frame beacon was erected. About one year after the second tower became operational, the original structure toppled over and was destroyed in the pounding surf.

The new tower exhibited its light for the first time on January 1, 1859. It had been constructed about 900 feet from shore, but, just seven years later, erosion had reduced that distance to about 450 feet. Brushwood jetties were built to protect the site, but storms tore them away almost as fast as they could be erected. By 1869, nine jetties had been built, yet loss of beach continued to be a problem. Semi-monthly measurements made of the high tide mark, and they showed that the jetties had checked the erosion directly in front of the lighthouse, but, to the south, loss of sand was becoming serious. In less than a decade, the shoreline had receded on that side approximately 50 to 100 feet. Additional measures were taken, but in 1880 it was predicted that "Unless this abrasion can be entirely checked, the ultimate destruction of the lighthouse buildings is inevitable."

In 1888, a new jetty was constructed at the southeast corner of the property; it was three hundred forty-eight feet long, and twenty to thirty feet wide, and averaged four feet in height. For a time, the beach sands were stabilized.

During an unusually high tide in April of 1919, the channel diverted itself and cut through the beach between the jetty and lighthouse. Just four days earlier, the water had been 140 feet from the raised ground that surrounded the lighthouse reservation; with the storm waves, water reached to just 50 feet of the raised base. "Isn't it time something was done?" questioned the editor of the *New Jersey Courier*. "This light will not stand the summer out, without some protection," he wrote Bureau of Light Houses Commissioner, G. R. Putnam. "The mariners on the coast are looking to you for action."

A recommendation was made to abandon the threatened station and establish a lightship in its place, but popular sentiment was with the lighthouse. Temporary measures were taken to hold back the sea while the government considered still another option, the construction of a 100-foot steel beacon tower.

Frustrated local residents took matters in their own hands. They raised over $2,000 to construct a small jetty, which proved to be successful for at least a short time. The battle of the encroaching sea may finally have been won in the mid-1930s, however, when the federal government and the state of New Jersey joined forces to build a bulkhead and dredge the channel inlet.

The Barnegat Light property was transferred to the state of New Jersey in 1926, and, in the following year, the beacon was made automatic. The lighthouse continued to exhibit a light, though of a lower intensity, until January 1, 1944.

As part of Ocean County's 100th anniversary, the sentinel was re-lit on February 15, 1950. Masked from the open sea so as not to confuse mariners, the light was shown landward for the rest of the year. The famous lighthouse was commemorated that same year with the issuance of a postage stamp.

> *Part of Barnegat Lighthouse State Park, the tower, and its museum are open to the public from May to October. The site can be reached from exit 62 on the Garden State Parkway, via Route 72 and the Long Beach Island Boulevard. NOAA chart #12323*

BARNEGAT LIGHTSHIP

Established: *1927*
First lighted: *August 15, 1927*
Lightship LV 79/WAL 506:   *1927-1942.*   *Built 1904 $89,030*
Lightship LV 79/WAL 506:   *1945-1967*
Discontinued: *1967*

On a clear night, Barnegat Light was visible to a maximum distance of nineteen miles, yet, because of frequent haze and fog along the New Jersey coastline, it often could be seen only seven to ten miles away. A light vessel posted seven miles, 93° true of Barnegat Lighthouse, argued Acting Secretary of the Navy, Franklin D. Roosevelt, in 1918, "would enable coastwise traffic to proceed from Northeast End light vessel, off the Delaware Capes, to Ambrose light vessel, off New York Harbor entrance, ...clear of all dangers."

The site off Barnegat Light was widely regarded as one of the most important change-of-course points for coastal vessels. It was estimated at that time that over seventy million tons of shipping passed there annually, and, over a twenty-year period, there had been at least fifty strandings on the area's shoals. Barnegat's lighthouse had no fog signal, but, even if it had been so equipped, vessels could not risk approaching that close to shore to pick up its sound. By equipping the vessel with a fog signal, a submarine bell, lights and (as later suggested) a radiobeacon, the lightship station, it was reasoned, would become the most important aid to navigation established on the Atlantic coast in many years. At about the same time, it had become apparent that beach erosion might soon topple Barnegat Lighthouse. Establishment of a light vessel was thus an attractive option to rebuilding or further protecting the lighthouse.

The Department of Commerce, then in charge of the Lighthouse Service, was in favor of establishing the lightship station, but many of the existing vessels were old and needed replacing. Though six were being constructed, none was available for a new station.

Lightship *LV 79/WAL 506* had served twenty years at Five Fathom Bank before being assigned to relief duty. In June of 1927, its hull was painted black, with the name Barnegat inscribed in white letters on each side. It took up its new station on August 15, 1927.

Built in 1904 at Camden, NJ, at a cost of $89,030, the 129-foot steam-propelled vessel had a compliment of five officers and eight crewmen. The original oil lanterns atop its two masts were replaced with acetylene lens lanterns in 1921, and converted to electric beacons seven years later. At Barnegat, *LV 79* was equipped with a steam chime whistle that gave a single blast for two seconds, every twenty seconds. It also had a submarine bell and a radiobeacon.

During the Second World War, the lightship was taken off station and was posted at Edgemoor, DE, where it served as an examination vessel. It returned to Barnegat in 1945 and remained there until 1967, when the station was discontinued. The vessel was decommissioned and later that year, donated to the Chesapeake Maritime Museum, Saint Michaels, MD. The museum held *LV 79* for about three years, but because of the expense of maintaining it, the vessel was sold to the Philadelphia Ship Preservation Guild (Heritage Ship Guild), Penns Landing, Philadelphia, PA.

> *In 1988, LV 79 was still in possession of the Ship Preservation Guild at Philadelphia. It was in great need of restoration and was not yet open to the public.*

TUCKER BEACH LIGHT
(Little Egg Harbor Light)

Appropriation:	March 3, 1847	$6,000
Appropriation:	July 28, 1866	$5,000
Established:	1848	
First keeper:	John Hall, appointed October 18, 1848	

Illuminating apparatus (IA): 1848, 15 lamps, 15" reflectors, fixed white light (FW).

Refitted:	July 1, 1854, fourth-order lens, 350o (4-order), varied by alternate red and white flashes.
Discontinued:	1859
Reestablished:	June 20, 1867
IA:	(1883) 4-order, fixed white (FW) 1 min., varied by six consecutive red flashes (Grp Fl R) at intervals of 10 seconds.
IA:	(1907) fourth-order Fresnel lens with inscription, Henry Le Paute, Paris, 1872. Lens actuated by clockwork on ball bearings.
IA:	(1924) 4-order, FW Grp Fl R. W 2,900 cp R 3,200 cp
Fog signal:	none

Height of tower from base to lantern: 1848, 40 feet
Height of light above sea level: (1883) 46 feet

Discontinued:	September 30, 1927

Established in 1848, Tucker Beach Light stood near the water's edge, about eighteen miles south of Barnegat Light, and ten miles northeast of Absecon Light. The station's fixed light, generated by fifteen lamps and reflectors, was so dim that it was often difficult to distinguish it from small coastal vessels. Capt. H. K. Davenport, USN, of the U.S. mail steamer *Cherokee,* echoed the feelings of other ships' captains. "As for Egg Harbor Light [Tucker Beach]," he wrote in 1852, "that had better be put out than kept as it is now, a decoy to draw vessels into difficulty looking for it. It is not as bright as the light I carry at my masthead."

Tucker Beach was refitted in 1854 with a fourth-order Fresnel lens, whose light was varied by alternating red and white flashes. Following the lighting of the first-class light at Absecon, however, the station became obsolete; it was discontinued in 1859.

In the summer of 1866, Congress appropriated $5,000 for the repair and relighting of the Tucker Beach Light. Work began in the spring of the following year with the construction of a new cistern and the laying of new floors in the keepers dwelling. A fourth-order lens was reinstalled, and, on June 20, 1867, the station became operational once more.

Eben Rider was appointed to Tucker Beach on May 29, 1867. He

Tucker Beach Lighthouse, 1891. National Archives, 26-LG-17-33

and his family and one assistant were cramped into a one-story house (thirty by twenty feet) that had but two rooms, a small detached kitchen and an attic. Despite repeated appeals by the Light House Board for larger or additional quarters, Congress was slow to respond. Finally in 1879, the keeper's residence was expanded, and a new tower was built that rose from the dwelling's roof. The old tower, which had been taken down, was then converted into an oil storage shed.

Over the next quarter century, the keeper's dwelling was expanded to eleven rooms. The station was located at one end of Sea Haven, a community consisting of little more than a schoolhouse and a few dwellings.

On March 22, 1906, Keeper Arthur H. T. Rider, who had taken over the station from his father, received word that the position of assistant keeper was being abolished. Keeper Rider protested. The nearest grocery store, post office, and railroad station were six miles away at Beach Haven; obtaining other household necessities meant a nine mile boat trip to Tuckerton. "All errands from this station must be done by boat," wrote the keeper to the Light House inspector at Philadelphia, "there are no men near the Station except those employed in the Life Saving Service, therefore they cannot be called on to take my place in case of my disability." Besides his son Joseph, who was the assistant keeper, Keeper Rider's father and mother were residing with him at the lighthouse. Both parents were elderly and too ill to assist with the light. The keeper went on, stating "a trip to Tuckerton and return by Sunset is a very uncertain undertaking – it often happens that we are delayed by calms, fogs, headwinds and tides, as well as heavy winds that make it unsafe to return." The Light House inspector was unmoved; though he admitted that the station

Tucker Beach Lighthouse, 1927. National Archives, 26-LG-17-34A

was isolated, he felt that it was no worse than some of the other stations in the district. Assistant Keeper Joseph Rider was transferred to Barnegat Light.

On February 20, 1927, Tucker Beach was struck by a fierce winter storm. "Nearly all of the foundation was washed from the front of the porch," wrote Keeper Arthur Rider. He pointed out that unless the lighthouse was moved immediately, it would be lost. "I might add," he continued, "that the old hotel that stood about 200 feet away and another house about 500 feet away, was washed down and totally destroyed." He then suggested that someone from the Light House Service make an inspection of the site.

An inspection was made, but not before another storm struck on August 26 of that same year. "The front porch is resting on only one broken pier action and is pulled away from the posts, leaving the roof and posts hanging in air 7 feet above ground." The storm continued to rage, and, on the next day, fearing that the building could collapse at any time, Keeper Rider asked for permission to vacate the lighthouse. On August 28, the keeper wrote, "Front porch of this station was washed down and carried away by the sea yesterday afternoon."

By that time, the service had decided to discontinue Tucker Beach and install a steel tower at Little Egg Inlet. Keeper Rider, however, was instructed to keep the light in operation until the new beacon was completed. On September 30, 1927, Tucker Beach was discontinued, and the keeper retired.

On at least three more occasions, Arthur Rider wrote letters to the Third District office concerning his old charge.

October 10, 1927: "Tucker Beach Lighthouse is so much undermined that it has started to sag and lean toward the ocean."

October 13, 1927: "Tower and dwelling except dining room and kitchen upset in the surf yesterday and was broken up and washed away by the sea."

October 14, 1927: "The dining room and kitchen of the Tucker Beach Lighthouse, which was badly wrecked when the main part of the building pulled from it and upset in the surf, was completely destroyed by fire yesterday afternoon." Apparently a passerby had ignited the old structure.

NOAA chart #12318, 12316

ABSECON (Absecum) LIGHT

Appropriation:	August 3, 1854	$35,000
Appropriation:	August 18, 1856	$17,436.62
Established:	1857	
First lighted:	January 15, 1857	
First keeper:	Daniel Scull, appointed November 25, 1856	
Illuminating apparatus (IA):	1857, first-order Fresnel lens (1-order), fixed white light (FW).	
Illuminant:	1910, oil to incandescent oil vapor (iov).	
IA:	(1924) 1-order, FW, iov, 13,000-candlepower (cp)	
Illuminant:	1925, electric, 70,000 cp.	
Fog signal:	none	
Height of light above sea level:	(1891) 167 feet	
Discontinued:	July 11, 1933	

A first-class light was needed, Congress was informed, "in the vicinity of Absecum Inlet, to guide navigators clear of Absecum and Brigantine shoals." Legislators responded by appropriating $35,000 on August 2, 1854, and an additional $17,436.32 two years later.

Construction of the lighthouse began in June 1855, with the excavation of an eight-foot-deep foundation. As workers neared half that depth, water from an adjoining salt marsh began to seep in, and eventually flooded the hole. At first, the work crew tried using buckets and a hand pump, but they could not keep up with the incoming water. A steam-driven centrifugal pump capable of removing 12,000 gallons an hour was brought in, and, working it around the clock, the contractor finally managed to pour the concrete foundation.

When completed, 400,000 bricks and 800 barrels of cement had been used to erect the 167-foot tower; 225 cast-iron steps led to its summit. Equipped with a first-order Fresnel lens, the station began operating on January 15, 1857, under the care of Keeper Daniel Scull.

In June of 1910, the lantern's light source was changed from a wick lamp to incandescent oil vapor; an electric light was installed in 1925, increasing the candlepower from 13,000 to 70,000.

The lighthouse had been built 1,300 feet from the water's edge, but a report in 1864 revealed that the beach in the vicinity of the lighthouse was eroding rapidly. Bimonthly measurements of the beachfront were initiated, and over the next four years, erosion became somewhat stabilized, but, in September of 1868, a storm washed away a large portion of the beach.

By 1876, the high tide line had crept up to only seventy-five feet from the lighthouse. "One ambitious contractor," it was said, "made a bid of ten thousand dollars to move the light one mile and keep it burning." Fourth District Engineer A. A. Schenck felt, however, that the fastest and the cheapest way to stabilize the problem was to use brush weighted down with stone. Trainloads of brush were brought in from the mainland and cellar stone from New York City was transported to the site by schooners.

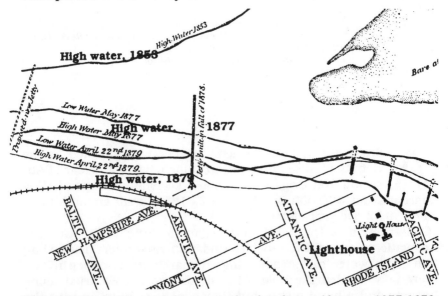

Construction of jetties and changes in the shoreline at Absecon, 1877-1879

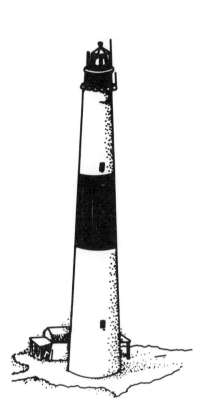

Absecon Lighthouse
by Linda Vallerie

At about the same time, seven jetties, 150 feet apart, were erected in the vicinity of the lighthouse. Though regarded as experimental, they probably did forestall the possible loss of the lighthouse. The structures, however, had not been extended below the low tide line, and they proved ineffective against winter storms. In 1877, $25,000 was requested to build a more effective, deep water jetty.

The Light House Board did not get the amount they had wanted, but measures taken did slow beach loss below the lighthouse reservation, but not above. "If it is not checked," warned the board, "it will eventually work around the site and destroy the light-house, as well as much valuable property in Atlantic City." Some voiced the opinion that it might be cheaper to rebuild on a new site; the estimated cost was $100,000.

In November of 1878, a long jetty was built north of the light station. The results, as far as the lighthouse was concerned, were "eminently successful," and, by mid-1880, the low water line had returned to its 1854 level.

The lighthouse reservation at Absecon had nearly two acres, and in 1906 most of it was used "simply for ornamental purpose." The light station, at that time, was staffed by two keepers (usually three) and a hired laborer whose sole function was care of the grounds. There were two keeper's dwellings on the property and a greenhouse, ten feet by thirty feet, which was located on the north side of the reservation. The greenhouse was used for growing flowers that were planted around the site.

Absecon had become a major tourist attraction, and, from July to September of 1912, 10,339 persons registered at the station. Averaging about that same number each year, it was the most often visited lighthouse in the service. The station's popularity with tourists continued until the early 1950s.

As Atlantic City grew and matured, the sentinel that once stood among sand dunes, surrounded by only a few fishing shacks, found itself on Pacific Avenue between Vermont and Rhode Island Avenues. In 1932, lights from neighboring tall buildings blended in with those of the lighthouse, making it of little use to sailors. In that year, the decision was made to discontinue Abescon Light.

The station ceased operating on July 11, 1933, and the lighthouse was eventually turned over to the state of New Jersey. The tower was relit briefly in 1954, when Atlantic City celebrated its centennial, but, having become surrounded by a less desirable neighborhood, Absecon Light no longer attracted hordes of tourists.

Absecon Light is open to the public during the summer season.
NOAA chart #12318, 12316

LUDLAM BEACH LIGHT

Appropriation:	July 7, 1884	$5,000
Established:	1885	
First lighted:	November 3, 1885	
First keeper:	J. H. Reeves, appointed October 20, 1885	

Illuminating apparatus (IA): (1891) fourth-order Fresnel lens (4-order), flashing white (Fl W) every 15 seconds.

IA: (1924) 4-order, Fl W, flash 2 sec., eclipse 3 sec, red sector (R). W 24,000-candlepower (cp), R 7,200 cp.

Fog signal: none
Height of light above sea level: (1891) 40 feet
Discontinued: 1924

A large crowd of onlookers had gathered along Atlantic City's shoreline to watch the unusually strong surf. Around 4:00 pm, on September 8, 1889, the water momentarily receded below the low tide line, leaving some fish "high and dry." Without further warning, an immense wave hurled itself toward the beach and broke seventy feet beyond any previous high water! In that instant, the festive atmosphere was replaced with the frightened screams of men, women, and children, who had become trapped in the wake of water rushing seaward. Miraculously, there were no lives lost, but, at Sea Isle City, a young Philadelphia man was trapped by the same wave and lost his life. The "tidal wave," as it was later referred to in many newspapers, was just a prelude to what was to come.

The tropical disturbance, which had begun a few days before the tidal wave, grew to a hurricane as it moved up the coast. The storm's center remained stalled off the Virginia coast for several days, and its wind, rain, and waves battered the shoreline as far north as Maine. Sea Isle City was completely submerged, forcing residents to evacuate to a hotel that was farther back from the sea. As the storm grew in intensity, Ludlam Beach Lighthouse was undermined and nearly lifted from its foundation. Its bulkhead was destroyed, and water covered the ground floor. Fearing that the lighthouse was about to be destroyed, Keeper J. H. Reeves removed the illuminating apparatus and abandoned the structure.

From the time it was first lit on November 3, 1885, the lighthouse at Ludlam Beach had always been at the mercy of storms. The station was located on a barrier beach, some fifteen feet from the water's edge. To protect it from onshore waves, a timber bulkhead that was back-filled with sand and gravel surrounded it. Though the lighthouse survived the hurricane of 1889, it suffered storm-related damage on a number of other occasions during the years that it operated.

Ludlam Beach was purchased from the Ludlam family in 1880, by Charles K. Landis. Largely through his efforts, the borough of Sea Isle City was created. As the community grew, the once isolated light station found itself at the intersection of Atlantic Street (Ninety-first Street) and Marine Place. A lifesaving station stood some 340 feet southwest of the lighthouse.

The keeper's dwelling was a seven-room structure, with an oil shed and privy at its rear. Had it not been for the light tower that rose from the front of its roof, the white frame building, with its lead- colored trim and green shutters, could have been easily mistaken for any seaside home.

The tower's lantern was equipped with a fourth-order Fresnel lens, showing a flashing white light every fifteen seconds. It rotated by means of a weight-actuated clock, which had to be rewound every five hours. The station, however, was never outfitted with a fog signal.

Ludlam Beach Light was situated eleven miles north of Hereford Inlet and seventeen miles south of Absecon Light. Coastal vessels were instructed to keep the light in sight to clear a shoal off Townsend Inlet. When Ludlam's light was no longer visible or bore north, navigators were to steer south until Hereford Inlet came into view; at that point, they were clear of the shoal.

Following a 1914 storm that caused some damage to the protective bulkhead, the Lighthouse Service was reluctant to make repairs. "This station is not a very important station," wrote Superintendent J. T. Yates, "and it is not considered that a great deal should be expended in protecting same, until more urgent cases have been cared for elsewhere." A 1923 fire sealed the lighthouse's fate. On the evening of November 21, the keeper went to bed, leaving an unattended lighted kerosene lamp on the kitchen table. At midnight, he arose to check the tower's beacon; as he opened his bedroom door, he was greeted by thick, acrid smoke. Closing the door, he slipped

Ludlam Beach Lighthouse, 1921. National Archives, 26-LG-12-66B

out the bedroom window and went to the kitchen; once there, he found it engulfed in flames. The keeper first tried using an extinguisher, and then a garden hose, but he could make no headway against the spreading inferno. He made his way to the Coast Guard station (the former lifesaving station), and, with the help of its personnel and that of local fire fighters, the blaze was finally extinguished.

An investigation later revealed that the fire had been set by the kerosene lamp; apparently the keeper's cat or dog, which had been locked in the room, had knocked it over. About one-third of the dwelling's roof was lost, and the kitchen was gutted. The lens and lantern were slightly damaged, but the station was able to continue to show its light. Repairs were made, but a March 11, 1924, storm tore away the temporarily repaired roof, making further occupancy of the station impossible. Shortly thereafter, the light was discontinued and replaced by a forty-foot steel tower, displaying a flashing acetylene light. The old dwelling was sold and moved to the corner of Thirty-first Street and the beach. Sometime around the 1940s, it was moved to its present location.

The former keeper's dwelling stands at 3414 Landis Avenue, Sea Isle City, NJ. It is a private home. NOAA chart #12300

HEREFORD INLET LIGHTHOUSE

Appropriation: *June 10, 1872 $25,000*
Established: *1874*
First lighted: *May 11, 1874*
First keeper: *John Marche, appointed April 25, 1874*
Illuminating apparatus (IA): 1874, fourth-order Fresnel lens (4-order),
                  fixed white light (FW).
IA: *(1907) fourth-order Fresnel lens. Maker: Le Sautter Lemunonier,*
                  Paris. Identification, USLH Depot, 3 Dist. Lamp Shop,
                  Staten Island, NY.
IA: *(1924) 4-order, group flash white (Grp Fl W) 15 seconds,*
                  red sector (R) flashes west of 226o. W 47,000 cp, R 320,000 cp.
IA: *(1939) 4-order, Grp Fl W, R. Electric, W 1,100,000 cp, R 320,000 cp*
Fog signal: *none*
Height of light above sea level: (1924) 53 feet
Discontinued: *1964*

T he risks of traveling back and forth by small boat to an offshore light station were all too often evident. John Marche who had taken charge of Hereford Inlet Light four days before it became operational, was caught in a squall while returning from the mainland; the keeper's craft capsized, and he drowned. Earlier that year, four other men from the Five Fathom Bank Lightship had similarly lost their lives. Throughout the history of the Light House Service, many more were to perish.

Hereford Inlet Light was established to mark the harbor's sheltered anchorage used by small coastal vessels and also to serve steamers navigating the Delaware Bay and river. The keeper's dwelling stood on the south side of the inlet, with its tower rising to fifty-seven feet above sea level. On May 11, 1874, the station's fixed white, fourth-order light was shown for the first time.

Following the keeper's accident, John Nickerson, the station's custodian during its construction, returned to Hereford and kept the light for about a month. Freeling H. Hewitt was then appointed to the post.

As a young man, the new keeper seemed not to always show the dedication to his charge that was expected of all keepers. On September 16, 1878, Hewitt received a letter from the Lighthouse inspector concerning his absence from the station on ten separate occasions. Two years later, he was again cited for the same infraction. Commenting on the incident, Inspector G. W. White wrote: "Neither keeper, nor substitute was at the station. Previous to this, the keeper had been warned about having this station without a person in charge." Apparently, Keeper Hewitt had a satisfactory

Hereford Inlet Lighthouse, undated. National Archives,26-LG-12-26

explanation for his absence, since he remained at Hereford Inlet for an additional thirty-nine years.

At times, nature seemed to conspire against the lighthouse. In October of 1878, Keeper Hewitt and the station's personnel were forced to abandon the lighthouse as hurricane-driven waves washed it off its block foundation. In an 1889 storm, though completely surrounded by water, eighteen neighbors took refuge at the light station after their own homes were either severely damaged or destroyed. Twenty-four years later, a gale damaged the structure's foundation to such an extent that the lighthouse had to be moved 150 feet westward.

As Hewitt advanced in age, entries in the lighthouse log became progressively more difficult to read. He began his last entry on March 31, 1919, as he always had begun them during his long years at the light station: "This day came in" The penmanship that had flowed so artistically in the hands of a young man was now labored and barely legible.

For just two months in 1926, Hereford Inlet Light was kept by a woman, Laura Hedges, who took over the station following the death of her husband. Her replacement, Ferdinand Heinzman, had previously served at Peck Ledge, CT, and Great Captain Island, CT.

Fire twice nearly destroyed the seven-room frame lighthouse. In

1902, flames were discovered in the roof over the kitchen. Fortunately, Keeper Hewitt and his assistant were able to extinguish the blaze before it engulfed the entire structure. During Keeper Heinzman's next-to-last year at Hereford Inlet, fire again threatened the station.

Coast Guard personnel near the lighthouse were first to spot thick smoke coming from an upstairs bedroom. Keeper Heinzman was outside painting; his wife and daughter, Anna, were in the kitchen. A guardsman alerted the lighthouse and notified the local fire department. The keeper, hearing Anna call, "fire," picked up an extinguisher and made his way to the bedroom, but heat and smoke drove him back. Grabbing a hose, he climbed a ladder and managed to douse the flames through an open window. Investigation later determined that the fire, which had started in Anna's bedroom closet, was due to spontaneous combustion.

The lighthouse was discontinued in 1964 and replaced by a white skeleton tower; the grounds and buildings were transferred to the state of New Jersey. Though part of the complex was occupied by the marine police, the lighthouse itself was boarded up and neglected. Largely through the efforts of Mayor Anthony Catanoso and concerned citizens, care for the attractive Victorian structure was turned over to the city in 1982. Using city funds and private donations, restoration was begun almost immediately. In the spring of 1986, the Coast Guard dismantled the skeleton tower and reactivated the beacon, which is now shown from the old lighthouse tower.

> *Hereford Inlet Lighthouse is located in the community of North Wildwood, NJ, at First and Central avenues. The structure serves as North Wildwood Tourist Center and lighthouse museum. NOAA Chart #12318*

NORTHEAST END LIGHTSHIP
(Northeast end of Five Fathom Bank)

Established: 1882
First lighted: June 1, 1882
Keeper (1884): Joshah L Falkenburg, appointed January 7, 1884
Lightship LV 44:   1882-1926 Built 1882, $49,999.58
Lightship LV 111/WAL 533: 1927-1932 Built 1926, $219,833.00
Lightship station discontinued: August 31, 1932

The coastwise steamer *Roanoke*, of the Old Dominion Line, was bound from Norfolk, VA, to New York on September 10, 1889, when, eighteen miles north of Cape Charles, it sailed into the fringes of the hurricane. The winds were blowing from out of the north-northwest, and steep waves began to batter the vessel broad-

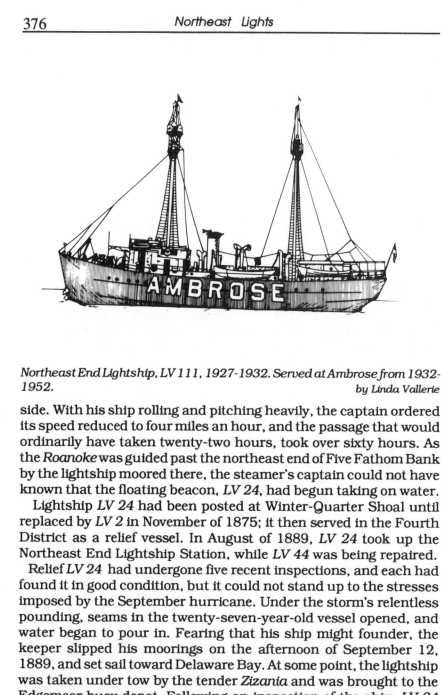

Northeast End Lightship, LV 111, 1927-1932. Served at Ambrose from 1932-1952.
                                                          by Linda Vallerie

side. With his ship rolling and pitching heavily, the captain ordered its speed reduced to four miles an hour, and the passage that would ordinarily have taken twenty-two hours, took over sixty hours. As the *Roanoke* was guided past the northeast end of Five Fathom Bank by the lightship moored there, the steamer's captain could not have known that the floating beacon, *LV 24*, had begun taking on water.

Lightship *LV 24* had been posted at Winter-Quarter Shoal until replaced by *LV 2* in November of 1875; it then served in the Fourth District as a relief vessel. In August of 1889, *LV 24* took up the Northeast End Lightship Station, while *LV 44* was being repaired.

Relief *LV 24* had undergone five recent inspections, and each had found it in good condition, but it could not stand up to the stresses imposed by the September hurricane. Under the storm's relentless pounding, seams in the twenty-seven-year-old vessel opened, and water began to pour in. Fearing that his ship might founder, the keeper slipped his moorings on the afternoon of September 12, 1889, and set sail toward Delaware Bay. At some point, the lightship was taken under tow by the tender *Zizania* and was brought to the Edgemoor buoy depot. Following an inspection of the ship, *LV 24* was deemed unworthy of repair, and she was ordered condemned. The Fourth District, which extended from Squam Inlet, NJ, to Metomkin Inlet, VA, had three lightship stations in the open ocean;

it had been left without a relief vessel.

Established, 1882

On June 1, 1882, *LV 44* was towed out to the newly created lightship station at Five Fathom Bank's northeast end. Built by Pusey and Jones Company, Wilmington, DE, the sail-schooner-rigged, iron-hulled vessel, had two masts. The foremast exhibited a fixed red light, and the main mast showed a fixed white light; both had a hoop-iron day mark, surmounted by a black ball. The words NORTHEAST END were painted on the starboard and port sides of the ship, and the number forty-four appeared at its stern. The lightship's fog signal consisted of a twelve-inch steam whistle and an emergency hand-operated bell.

Lightship *LV 44* was the first iron vessel in the service and, after only two years, its rivets were showing a great deal of corrosion. "It is evident," it was reported to the Light House Board, "that it will be necessary to bring her in every year to clean and paint her bottom. The rapid deterioration of the iron raises a question as to the wisdom of building more iron light-ships without sheathing." The ship was apparently brought in for repainting every year until 1890, and it was then done at two-year intervals.

In late December of 1926, Capt. Theodore P. Maffia and his crew were transferred from *LV 44* to *LV 111/WAL 533*, and on January 5, 1927, the new lightship arrived at its station. The old vessel, *LV 44*, was then reassigned to Cornfield Point, Long Island Sound.

As payment for a lightship sunk by one of its barges (see Cornfield Lightship, *LV 51*), the Standard Oil Company paid for construction of *LV 111's* hull. After it was built at Bath Iron Works, Bath, ME, the steel hull was towed to the General Depot at Staten Island for completion.

The 132-foot, 4-inch long vessel had a steel house constructed around its foremast, consisting of a raised pilothouse and captain's quarters. Another house, built around the mainmast aft, served as the radio room and for battery storage. The main deck included quarters for the officers (aft) and crew (forward), and the galley and mess. The lower deck housed storerooms, provision lockers, and machinery storerooms.

The lightship was powered by an eight-cylinder diesel engine that developed 450-horsepower; it was the first in the Lighthouse Service to be equipped with a diesel engine. Its illuminating apparatus consisted of 375-mm lens lanterns and 150-watt lamps, located on both mastheads. Its fog signals were a six-inch air siren operated by compressed air, a submarine bell also operated by compressed air, and an emergency 1,000-pound fog bell mounted on the forward deck.

On August 31, 1932, the last entry was made in *LV 111's* log as the Northeast End Lightship: "8:30 am received orders from the tender *Spruce* to leave station. Pulled up anchor at 8:45 am." The lightship station at Five Fathom Bank's northeast end had been discontinued. On September 22, 1932, the ship was turned over to the crew of *LV 87*, and *LV 111* was posted at Ambrose Channel. It remained there for twenty years and spent the next seven years at Portland, ME. In 1970, the lightship was sold to Uruguay, and it was renamed *Banco Ingles*. The vessel is believed to have been retired two or three years later.

FIVE FATHOM BANK LIGHTSHIP

Established: 1839
Lightship LV 18:   1839-1869.   *Built at Stonington, CT.* $14,584
Lightship LV 37:   1869-1876.   *Built 1869,* $100,000 (?)
Lightship LV 39:   1876-1877.   *Built 1875,* $42,200
Lightship LV 40:   1877-1904.   *Built 1875,* $39,200
Lightship LV 108/WAL 530: 1924-1942. Built 1923, $200,000
                      1947-1970
Lightship WLV 189: 1971-1972.
Discontinued: 1972

One can only imagine the difficulties experienced in 1839 by the crewmen of lightship *LV 18*; the ninety-foot vessel, which marked Five Fathom Bank, was constantly exposed to the full force of the sea. Constructed at Stonington, CT, the two-masted sail-schooner was not suited for open water, and, as a result, it was often driven off station. Writing of his experience with the errant lightship, Capt. Robert Bosworth of Bath, ME, reported that he had seen *LV 18* off Cape May, while bound for St. Johns, VI, and Europe in May of 1851, but, on his return trip, the lightship was nowhere to be found. Approaching Five Fathom Bank at night, the captain thought he saw the lightship's two lights, one above the other, but, when he ordered one of the crewmen to sound the bottom, the depth did not agree with what it should have been. The captain tacked his ship and stood off until daylight. "To our amazement, the lightship was not there, and it was Cape Henlopen light we saw, and but not for lead[1] we should have gone ashore with three hundred and sixty souls and a valuable cargo on board." A few months earlier, another vessel had mistaken Cape Henlopen Light for the absent lightship; it was wrecked on shore. "A relief ship should always be in readiness

---

1. Capt. Bosworth was referring to the lead line used in determining depth.

in case of removal by accident or for repairs—such is always the case in England." Captain Bosworth's remarks were true for most of the nation's lightships of that time, and his complaints were echoed by many other captains.

Lightship *LV 18* remained on duty at Five Fathom Bank until 1869, and, over the next six years, it served as relief vessel. It was decommissioned in 1875 and was then turned over to the Navy for use in target practice.

The ninety-eight-foot *LV 37* was the next light vessel to be stationed at Five Fathom Bank. On January 16, 1874, a strong winter storm swept over coastal New Jersey. Laboring heavily at its mooring, *LV 37* suddenly parted its cables and began drifting in a southeasterly direction. It was later located and brought in for repairs. On March 2, it was returned to its station and, just six weeks later, tragedy struck the lightship's crew.

On the morning of April 23, 1874, Keeper John Reeves and three of his crewmen left the lightship aboard the station's sailboat; they were headed for shore. As they were crossing Cold Spring Bar, a strong gust caught the sail of the small vessel and capsized it; the four were thrown into the cold water, and only Keeper Reeves survived. The incident was, however, but a prelude to what was to come aboard *LV 37*, nineteen years later.

The 119-foot *LV 39*, which had previously been stationed at Vineyard Sound, took up the post at Five Fathom Bank on June 24, 1876. A year later, it was replaced by *LV 40*. During the mid-summer of 1893, *LV 40* was taken off station for repairs, and *LV 37* returned as relief vessel.

Left in charge of Relief *LV 37*, the inexperienced assistant keeper was not prepared for the August hurricane of 1893; he had neither battened down the hatches nor had he ordered the vessel's cables let out to full scope.

The seas had begun increasing in height overnight and, on the morning of August 23, waves were breaking on Five Fathom Bank. At 10:00 pm that evening, the seas had begun washing over the ship's deck, and the winds had picked up to near hurricane strength. "Every time a sea boarded the ship it was noticed, after she had freed herself, that she had a list to port. As soon as she would free herself from one sea, another would board her." Around midnight, two of *LV 37's* boats were swept overboard, and the third was lost at about 1:00 am. Hatches were torn off, and the ship took on water. At 1:45 am, there seemed to be a momentary lull in the storm, and the ship turned broadside just in time to catch an immense wave. She rolled over to port, and water gushed in through the open hatches; moments later, *LV 37* went to the bottom.

Trapped aboard the sinking ship, the assistant engineer somehow

Five Fathom Bank Lightship LV 37, 1869-1876. Served at Fenwick Island Shoal from 1888-1892. Sank at its mooring on August 23, 1893. National Archives, 26-LS-1-37-1

Five Fathom Bank Lightship, LV 108/WAL 530, undated. National Archives, 26-G-126-21133

managed to break away from death's grip, and, once at the surface, he crawled onto the main hatch cover, which was floating nearby. One of the crewmen, who had been thrown into the water as the ship rolled over to its side, swam to another floating hatch cover, but it was already occupied by three crewmen. He then tried floating on several different pieces of wood, but each one proved to be too small to hold him. Nearing exhaustion, he spotted part of the lamp house and then clung to it for some sixteen hours; he and the assistant engineer were finally picked up by a pilot boat. The other three men and the assistant keeper had perished.

LV 37, was the first United States lightship to have foundered at its mooring. On August 27 of that same year, the Rattlesnake Shoal Lightship had broken away from its mooring and was driven up on a beach. The vessel's hatches had been so securely battened down that it was later found with only a few inches of water in its bilge. "If the hatches of Five Fathom Bank light-ship had been battened down as thoroughly, and her chain had been veered to the bitter end as that of the Rattlesnake Shoal light-ship, it is believed," concluded the Light House Board, "that she would have ridden out the storm." On October 16, 1893, the USS *Vesuvius* dynamited the submerged wreck.

Lightship *LV 40* remained at Five Fathom Bank until 1904, when it was permanently relieved by *LV 79/WAL 506*. The new lightship, built in Camden, NJ, was a 129-foot steel-hulled vessel. Powered by steam screw, it was also initially rigged for sail. It remained at Five Fathom Bank until 1924, and it was then designated relief vessel. In August of 1927, it was assigned to the newly created lightship station off Barnegat, NJ.

The Bath Iron Works of Bath, ME, constructed the station's next vessel, *LV 108/WAL 530.* The 133-foot steel-hulled vessel, propelled by steam screw, was capable of nine knots. When built, it was equipped with a radio and radiobeacon. Its lighting apparatus consisted of special 150-watt incandescent lamps within 375-mm lenses, located on each mast. The ship's storerooms, provision lockers, and machinery stores were located on the lower deck; the upper deck housed the galley, messroom, heads, and officers' and crews' quarters. The lightship was manned by six officers and ten crewmen.

Lightship *LV 108* remained at Five Fathom Bank until April 16, 1942, when it was transferred to the Coast Guard Station at Curtis Bay, MD. Once there, it served in training personnel for engineering and deck ratings.

---

2. *Lightship LV 108/WAL 530's* designation was changed to *WLV 530* in January 1945.

On February 1, 1947, *LV 108* resumed its post at Five Fathom Bank, and it remained at that station until it was decommissioned on August 31, 1970.[3] Five years later, it was scrapped at Norfolk, VA.

Five Fathom Bank's last lightship, *WLV 189*, had previously served at Diamond Shoal, VA, and New Orleans, LA. The diesel-powered, 128-foot-long steel-hulled vessel, spent only one year at the "Bank" before the lightship station was discontinued. It was then assigned to Boston, MA, where it remained until decommissioned three years later.

Five Fathom Bank's fifth lightship, LV 79, is located at Penns Landing, Philadelphia, PA. In 1988, it was still in great need of restoration.   NOAA chart #12214

CAPE MAY LIGHT

Appropriation:	March 7, 1822	$5,000
Appropriation:	March 3, 1823	$5,750
Appropriation:	March 3, 1857	$40,000
Established:	1823	
Illuminating apparatus (IA):	(1832) 15 lamps, reflectors, revolving light (Rv) every 3 min.	
IA:	(1842) 15 lamps, 16" reflectors, Rv.	
Refitted:	1853, first-order Fresnel lens (1-order), Rv .30 min.	
Rebuilt:	1859. Became operational October 31, 1859	
IA:	(1907) first-order Fresnel lens. Identification; Henry Le Paute, Paris. Flashing white every 30 seconds.	
IA:	(1891) 1-order, flashing white light (Fl W) every 30 seconds.	
IA:	(1924) 1-order, Fl W 30 sec., 130,000 cp.	
IA:	(1939) 1-order, Fl W flash 4 sec, eclipse 26 sec. Electric, 250,000 cp.	
IA:	(1989) "reflector lens," 1000 watt lamp	
Fog signal:	none	
Height of light above sea level: (1842) 80 feet. (1891) 167 feet		

From the late 1700s, a windmill located near the tip of Cape May helped direct mariners into Delaware Bay. "You may run for Cape May till within three-quarters of a mile of the windmill," wrote the publishers of *American Coast Pilot* in 1800. There were several homes in the same vicinity, most of which were occupied by pilots. "As soon as you sight the Cape, and are in want of a pilot, you had better hoist some signal, as those who do not are considered not in want of one."

There is some evidence that a beacon may have existed at Cape May around 1785. Papers recorded in September of that year read,

---

3. Other USCG records indicate that *LV 108* was not decommissioned until November 1, 1971

"Thomas Hand, 2nd gentleman, conveys to the Board of Port Wardens, City of Philadelphia, for a certain consideration, a tract of land for the purpose of erecting thereon a beacon for the benefit of navigation." It is widely accepted, however, that the tower erected in 1823, at the extreme southwest point of Cape May, was the site's first lighthouse.

In 1832, the beacon at Cape May was described as a revolving light of fifteen lamps, which made a revolution every three minutes. Shown from eighty feet above sea level, it was claimed by Fifth Auditor and Superintendent of Lights, Stephen Pleasonton, that its light was visible to a maximum distance of twenty-seven miles. Impossible, retorted Edmund and George Blunt, publishers of *American Coast Pilot!*

In a feud that came to a boil in 1837, the Blunt brothers (as well as many sea captains), and Pleasonton were at odds over the efficiency of American lights, versus most of those in Britain and France (see Evolution of the Lighthouse System). The superintendent relied almost exclusively on information relayed to him by Winslow Lewis, "a gentleman who for many years has had the furnishing of patent lenses, patent lamps, patent parabolic reflectors, and erecting light-houses."

To prove that the nation's lights were better than those of the French, Stephen Pleasonton gave the distances that the French lights were visible and compared them "with the estimate Mr. Lewis states American lights can be seen."

Winslow Lewis, who had a vested interest in not introducing European improvements in the United States lighthouse system, "forgot" to include the curvature of the earth in calculating the maximum distance at which an American light could be seen. If a shipboard observer was standing fifteen feet above sea level, then the light at Cape May, eighty feet above sea level, should have been visible to a maximum distance of only 14.70 miles, twelve miles less than Lewis' calculations! (See Table 2.) The contractor also stated that Cape Henlopen Light, which rose to 180 feet above sea level, could be seen to maximum distance of 30 miles. Commenting on his figure, the Blunts wrote, "Mr. Lewis must himself have been elevated in the air no less than 160 feet." Despite the controversies, however, the lighthouse system grew tremendously during Stephen Pleasonton's thirty-two years as its head.

Cape May, as were most of New Jersey's coastal lighthouses, was susceptible to the erosive action of the sea. In 1847, the loss of beach had advanced to the point that high tide was but a short distance from the base of the tower. It thus had to be removed and rebuilt some 400 yards northeast of the original site. Standing on a six-foot base, the tower rose to eighty-eight feet above sea level.

Cape May Lighthouse, 1988.   *Photo by Herb Segars*

Height of light above sea level, in feet.	maximum distance seen in nautical miles.
10	8.06
20	9.57
30	10.72
40	11.69
50	12.55
60	13.32
70	14.03
80	14.70
90	15.32
100	15.91
120	17.00
140	18.01
150	18.46
200	20.66

Table 2: Maximum visible range. Distance (range) at which a light is visible, as calculated from a deck height of 15 feet.
(After *Modern Lighthouse Practice*)

Downes E. Foster's story as keeper was a familiar one for its time. Prior to his appointment in February of 1850, he had worked as a carpenter, and, when he took over the post at Cape May, he had received neither training nor any printed instructions. It was therefore not surprising that the station's general maintenance and record keeping were not to the liking of Lighthouse Inspector, Captain Howland, during his site visit in June of 1851.

The problems of the site's second lighthouse, however, reflected much more than just the keeper's inexperience. Built by Samuel and Nathan Middleton, the wood inside the tower was described as "rough beyond anything seen before; supports to stairway not planed; everything rough and unfinished; the tower damp from base to lantern." The keeper's dwelling, which was built at the same time, also showed poor workmanship. "Leaks through walls in a stream" was among the inspector's comments.

When the new tower had been completed in 1847, it was equipped with the same apparatus that had existed in the original structure. The light, mariners complained in 1852, was inferior to the third-order light at Brandywine Shoal. Under most atmospheric conditions, Cape May's beacon could be seen for only seven to eight miles. "Make Cape May and Henlopen lights first order lights, with proper elevations, and navigators will be able to place vessels in position for receiving pilots without the risk of shipwreck on the dangerous Five-fathom bank" was the general consensus of area navigators. In 1853, the station was refitted with a first-order Fresnel lens, and, just four years later, Congress appropriated funds to build a taller tower for Cape May.

The new structure, constructed of brick, was 158 feet, six inches, from the ground to the top of the lantern. Equipped with a first-order Fresnel lens, manufactured by Henry Le Paute of Paris, France, the tower exhibited its light for the first time on October 31, 1859. The entire lens, which revolved by means of a weight-actuated clock, flashed a white light every thirty seconds. The old tower was left standing, but it was feared that it might be misleading to mariners, it was dismantled in 1862.

In January of 1876, Downes Foster, who by then had been keeper for twenty-six years, was reprimanded for having given away "refuse oil and certain small quantities of alcohol." Keepers were kept strictly accountable for their station's supplies, and Foster was notified that he had been saved from dismissal only because of his many years of faithful and honest service. A year later, his actions came under close scrutiny once again.

A site visit, made by Commander Brigman in July of 1877, found conditions at the station not to his liking. The inspector concluded that the seventy-year-old keeper was "too old and feeble to do the work which seems to have been left almost entirely to the two Assistants, neither of whom is very competent." Foster, the inspector felt, had become indifferent; he was replaced in September of the same year by Samuel Stilwell.

In June of 1933, the Lighthouse Service made the decision to automate Cape May Light. Keeper Harry H. Palmer, who had spent about forty of his years at the station as assistant keeper and another five as head keeper, was allowed to retire with a pension. His assistant, Floyd Schmierer, was then transferred to the tender Iris and later to the tender Lilac, where he served as quartermaster. Keeper Palmer, his wife, and two grown daughters remained at the station, and his wife was named custodian.

A 1907 survey of the lighthouse reservation indicated that there were three keepers' dwellings on the property, listed as dwellings number 1, number 2, and number 3. Number one stood almost thirty-five feet from the tower; it had seven rooms and an enclosed porch. Number 2 was thirty-six feet to the other side of the tower, and it also had seven rooms and an enclosed porch. Number three had eight rooms and a bath. A year after the tower's automation, the Coast Guard moved and reconditioned the main keeper's dwelling.

Cape May Light was extinguished during the Second World War, and the military occupied the lighthouse reservation; it was used as a coastal observation and defense post. The station's first-order lens was removed from the tower sometime around the mid-1940s, and it was turned over to the Cape May County Historical Museum were it is kept on exhibit. During the mid-1980s, the Mid-Atlantic Center of the Arts took over maintenance of the light tower, and, though it is still operational, visitors can climb its 199 spiral steps for a spectacular view of the Atlantic coast.

> *Cape May's first-order Fresnel lens is on exhibit in season or by special arrangement at the Cape May County Historical Museum. Cape May Lighthouse is open to the public, in season. NOAA chart #12200, 12214*

BIBLIOGRAPHY

Absecon Light (NJ)
Correspondence of the Light-House Board. RG 26, 48, file 1139, 2046E. DC:NA
Correspondence of the Bureau of Lighthouses. RG 26, 50, file 2046A, 2046E. DC:NA
Light List. 1863, 1891, 1933.
Lighthouse Service Bulletin. October 1912.
Lighthouse Site Files. RG 26, 66 Absecon light station, NJ. DC:NA
New York Times. December 1, 1936
New York Times. October 28, 1979
New York Times. June 24, 1973
Report of the Light-House Board. Sketch of Absecon Light Station: Changes in Shoreline. 1879.

Ambrose Lightship (NY)
Bachand, Robert G. *Scuba Northeast, Vol 2.* Norwalk, CT: Sea Sports Publications. 1986
Correspondence of the Bureau of Lighthouses. RG 26, 50, file 2626. DC:NA
Light List. 1910, 1956, 1986
Lighthouse Service Bulletin. September 1, 1927. 3:205-209
Lighthouse Service Bulletin. December 2, 1929.   3:315
Logs of lighthouse vessels. RG 26, 79, LV 87/WAL 512, LV 111/533. DC:NA
New York Times. October 6, 1952
New York Times. June 25, 1960
New York Times. August 6, 1964
New York Times. March 8, 1964
New York Times. February 22, 1972

Avery Point Light (CT)
Light List. 1946, 1953, 1966, 1967.
United States Coast Guard Training Center. Reporting aboard booklet, April, 1965.

Barnegat Light (NJ)

American Coast Pilot. New York: Blunt. 1847
American Coast Pilot. New York: Blunt. 1850
Barnegat Lighthouse State Park. New Jersey Department of Environmental Protection. 1982
Correspondence of the Bureau of Lighthouses. RG26, 50, file 1246E.DC:NA
Letters from the Secretary of Treasury, 1844-1852. Doc. #114. Washington, DC: Government Printing Office.
Letters Regarding Light House Service. RG 26, 18, Vol 10. DC:NA
Light List. 1842, 1863, 1944, 1945.
Lighthouse Service Bulletin. May 1, 1933. 4:151
Lighthouse site file, RG 26, 66, Barnegat light station, NJ. DC:NA
New Jersey Courier (Toms River). May 23, 1919
New York Times. October 27, 1931
New York Times. September 27, 1936
New York Times. July 17, 1938
New York Times. January 19, 1950
New York Times. October 28, 1956
New York Times. July 12, 1957
New York Times. April 7, 1960
New York Times. August 31, 1975
Philadelphia Record. May 17, 1919
Providence Bulletin. (RI) May 17, 1919

Barnegat Lightship LV 79 (NJ)

Correspondence of the Bureau of Lighthouses. RG 26, 50, file 374. DC:NA
Flint, Willard. Lightship Data. Held by the U.S. Coast Guard Academy Library.
Light List. 1928, 1944, 1967.
Lighthouse Service Bulletin. July 1, 1927. 3:197
Lighthouse Service Bulletin. May 1, 1933. 4:151
Report to the Secretary of Commerce. 1927-1928, 1930-1935
Staff, Philadelphia Ship Preservation Guild. Personal communications, 1988.

Bartlett Reef Lightship (CT)

Correspondence of the Light-House Board. RG 26, 48, file 1099, 2464. DC:NA
Johnson, Arnold Burgess. *Modern Lighthouse Service.* U.S. Government Printing Office. 1889
Letters Regarding Light House Service. RG 26, 18, Vol 11, Vol 16. DC: NA
Lighthouse Service Bulletin. February, 1918.
Logs of lighthouse vessels. RG 26, 79, LV 13, LV 23
Notice to Mariners. No. 77 of 1903
New York Times. January 13, 1890
Report to the Light House Board. 1872-1906

Beavertail Light (RI)
Compilation of Public Documents and Extracts from Reports and Papers Relating to Lighthouses, Light-vessels, et al. 1789-1871. Washington, DC: Government Printing Office. 1871.
Correspondence of the Light-House Board. RG 26, 48, file 7729. DC:NA
Correspondence of the Bureau of Lighthouses. RG 26, 50, file 394E. DC:NA
Coughtry, Jay. *The Notorious Triangle.* Philadelphia: Temple University Press. 1981
Evening Bulletin. (Providence, RI) December 10, 1931
Kelley, Robert, EP2. U.S. Coast Guard, Aids to Navigation Team, Bristol, RI. Personal communications, 1988.
Lighthouse Service Bulletin. April, 1939. 5:169-172
Lighthouse Site Files. RG 26, 66, Beavertail light station, RI. DC:NA
Newport Daily News. (RI) March 28, 1972
Providence Journal Bulletin. (RI) May 29, 1985

Bergen Point Light (NY)
Light List. 1863, 1907, 1950
Lighthouse Site Files. RG 26, 66, Bergen Point light station, NY. DC:NA
New York Times. June 24, 1934
New York Times. March 2, 1948
Report of the Commissioner of Lighthouses. 1913

Black Rock Light (see Fairweather Island Light) (CT)

Blackwell's Island Light (NY)
Duffy, Francis J., Miller, William H. *The New York Harbor Book.* Falmouth, ME: TWB Books, 1986.
Light List. 1873, 1874, 1939.
New York Municipal Gazette. January 18, 1849

Block Island North Light (Sandy Point Light) (RI)
American Coast Pilot. New York: Blunt. 1833
American Coast Pilot. New York: Blunt. 1850
American Coast Pilot. New York: Blunt. 1863
Compilation of Public Documents and Extracts from Reports and Papers Relating to Lighthouses, Light-vessels, et al. 1789-1871. Washington, DC. Government Printing Office. 1871.
Correspondence of the Light-House Board. RG 26, 48, file 1102. DC:NA
Correspondence of the Bureau of Lighthouses. RG 26,50, file 1104E.DC:NA
Letters Regarding Light House Service. RG 26, 18, Vol 11. DC: NA
Light List. 1848, 1863, 1870, 1980
Lighthouse Site Files. RG 26, 66 Block Island, (north end) RI. DC:NA
New York Times. November 25, 1984

Block Island Southeast Light (RI)
Bachand, Robert G. *Scuba Northeast, Vol 2.* Norwalk, CT: Sea Sports

Publications. 1986
Block Island Times. (RI) July 31, 1987
Correspondence of the Bureau of Lighthouses.RG 26, 50, file 1104E.DC:NA
Lighthouse Site Files. RG 26, 66, Block Island, (southeast) RI. DC:NA
Lighthouse Station Logs. RG 26, 80, Block Island South East Light Station.
1938-1944 DC:NA
Philadelphia Inquirer. February 13, 1939
Providence Journal. (RI) June 2, 1946

Brenton Reef Lightship (RI)
Champlin, Richard L. "Brenton Reef Lightship." *Bulletin Newport Historical
Society.* Spring, 1971, 44:42-50
Clipping Files. Brenton Reef Lightship. Providence Public Library, RI.
Correspondence of the Light-House Board. RG 26, 48, file 2143. DC:NA
Flint, Willard. Lightship Data. Held by the U.S. Coast Guard Academy
Library.
Kelley, Robert, EP2, U.S. Coast Guard, Aids to Navigation Team, Bristol, RI.
Personal communications, 1988.
New York Times. December 4, 1873
Report to the Light House Board. 1872-1902

Bridgeport Breakwater Light (Bug Light, Tongue Point Light) (CT)
Bridgeport Standard. (CT) January 16, 1891
Clipping Files, lighthouses. Bridgeport Public Library, CT
Correspondence of the Light-House Board. RG 26, 48, file 1134. DC:NA
Lighthouse Site Files. RG 26, 66, Bridgeport Breakwater light station, CT.
DC:NA

Bridgeport Harbor Light (CT)
Bridgeport Post. (CT) December 15, 1920
Bridgeport Post. (CT) May 14, 1922
Bridgeport Post. (CT) November 26, 1922
Bridgeport Post. (CT) September 4, 1927
Bridgeport Post. (CT) July 31, 1935
Bridgeport Post. (CT) May 30, 1937
Bridgeport Post. (CT) December 20, 1953
Correspondence of the Light-House Board. RG 26, 48, file 2479. DC:NA
Lighthouse Site Files. RG 26, 66,Bridgeport Harbor light station, CT. DC:NA
Lighthouse Station Logs. RG 26, 80, Bridgeport Harbor. 1898. DC:NA
McNeil, John.*Bridgeport Harbor 1846-1900.* Bridgeport Harbor,circa 1900.
New York Times. August 25, 1953
New York Times. August 27, 1953
New York Times. September 16, 1953
New York Times. November 10, 1953
New York Times. December 21, 1953
Norwalk Hour. (CT) December 15, 1920

Bristol Ferry Light (RI)
Correspondence of the Light-House Board. RG 26, 48, file 4259. DC:NA

Correspondence of the Bureau of Lighthouses. RG 26, <u>50</u>, file 2857A, 2857E. DC:NA
Lighthouse Service Bulletin. February 1918.
Lighthouse Site Files. RG 26, <u>66,</u> Bristol Ferry, RI. DC:NA
Lighthouse Station Logs. RG 26, <u>80,</u> Bristol Ferry. 1917-1925 DC:NA
Notice to Mariners. No. 98 of 1902

Bullock Point Light (RI)
Correspondence of the Light-House Board. RG 26, <u>48</u>, file 2206. DC:NA
Lighthouse Service Bulletin. October, 1938. 5:135
Lighthouse Site Files. RG 26, <u>66,</u> Bullock Point light station, RI. DC:NA

Cape May Light (NJ)
American Coast Pilot. Newburyport, MA: Blunt. 1800
American Coast Pilot. New York: Blunt. 1833
Clipping Files, Cape May Lighthouse. Cape May County Public Library.
Correspondence of the Bureau of Lighthouses.RG 26, <u>50,</u> file 2122E.DC:NA
Delinquencies of Keepers. RG 26, <u>84</u>, 1876, 1877.
Descriptions of Lighthouses. RG 26, <u>71</u>, 1907. DC:NA
Letters from the Secretary of the Treasury, 1844-1852. Reprint Documents
Light-House Establishment, March 3, 1838. Washington, DC. Government Printing Office.
Lighthouse Papers. U.S. Government Printing Office. 1852
Lighthouse Site Files. RG 26, <u>66</u>, Cape May light station, NJ. DC:NA
List of Lighthouse Keepers, 1845-1912. RG 26, Micro Copy #1373, Rolls 1 & 2. DC:NA
Johnson, Arnold Burgess. *Modern Lighthouse Service.* Washington, DC: U. S. Government Printing Office, 1889.
New York Times. May 18, 1984
The Press. (NJ) May 25, 1976
Winterick, Douglas. Personal communications. 1989

Castle Hill Light (RI)
Eldridge, F.R. History of Castle Hill Light Station. USCG Hist. Soc. 1950 (Held by National Archives -DC:NA)
Lighthouse Site Files. RG 26, <u>66</u>, Castle Hill light-station, RI. DC:NA

Chapel Hill Light (rear range) (NJ)
American Coast Pilot. New York. Blunt. 1864
Correspondence of the Bureau of Lighthouses. RG 26, <u>50</u>, file 766E, 767A, 2241. DC:NA
Descriptions of Lighthouses. RG 26, <u>71</u>, 1907. DC:NA
Ellis, Franklin. *History of Monmouth County, New Jersey.* Philadelphia: R.T. Peck & Co. 1885
Jelliffe, Thelma. *Achter Call to Zoning: Historical Notes on Middletown, NJ:* Middletown Academy Press, 1982
Leonard, Thomas H. "From Indian Trail to Electric Rail." *Atlantic Highlands Journal,* 1923.
Lighthouse Site Files. RG 26, <u>66</u>, Chapel Hill Beacon, NJ. DC:NA

New York Times. November 15, 1959
Red Bank Register. (NJ) June 1, 1914

Cedar Island Light (NY)

American Coast Pilot. Newburyport, MA: Blunt. 1800
American Coast Pilot. New York: Blunt. 1857
Correspondence of the Bureau of Lighthouses. RG 26,<u>50</u>, file 1265A.DC:NA
Delinquencies of Keepers. RG 26, <u>84</u>, 1880.
Letters Regarding Light House Service. RG 26, <u>18</u>, Vol 13, Vol 14. DC: NA
Light List. 1848, 1870, 1939.
Lighthouse Site Files. RG 26, <u>66</u>, Cedar Island light station, NY. DC:NA

Conanicut Light (RI)

Champlin, Richard L. "Conanicut Light." *Bulletin Newport Historical Society* Spring 1971, 44:55-57.
Correspondence of the Bureau of Lighthouses. RG 26, <u>50</u>, file2798E.DC:NA
Lighthouse Site Files. RG 26, <u>66</u>, Conanicut Island Light, RI. DC:NA

Coney Island Light (Nortons Point Light) (NY)

Correspondence of the Light-House Board. RG 26, <u>48</u>, file 8712. DC:NA
Correspondence of the Bureau of Lighthouses. RG 26, <u>50</u>, file 321E. DC:NA
Fasulo, John. "Last Civilian Keeper." In Notice to Mariners. *The Keeper's Log.* 4:30 Winter, 1988
Light List. 1891, 1932.
Lighthouse Service Bulletin. May 1, 1918. 2:21
Lighthouse Site Files. RG 26, <u>66</u>, Coney Island light station, NY. DC:NA
New York Times. December 18, 1961
New York Times. February 16, 1986
Schubert, Frank. Personal communications. 1987

Conimicut Light (see Nayatt Point Light) (RI)

Conover Light (front range) (NJ)

American Coast Pilot. New York: Blunt. 1864
Correspondence of the Bureau of Lighthouses. RG 26, <u>50</u>, file 766E, 767A, 1104E, 2241. DC:NA
Lighthouse Service Bulletin. March 1 1933. 4:147
Lighthouse Site Files. RG 26, <u>66</u>, Conover Beacon (front), NJ. DC:NA
New York Journal of Commerce. November 5, 1928
New York Times. September 7, 1941

Cornfield Point Lightship (CT)

Correspondence of the Light-House Board. RG 26, <u>48</u>, file 2112, 7742. DC:NA
Light List. 1863, 1891, 1939
Lighthouse Service Bulletin. May 1, 1919. 2:73
Lighthouse Service Bulletin. June 1938. 5:118
Lighthouse Service Bulletin. May 1939. 5:180-181
Logs of lighthouse vessels. RG 26, <u>79</u>, LV 44, LV 48. DC:NA

New York Times. April 25, 1919
New York Times. July 15, 1956

Coxsackie Light (NY)
Correspondence of the Light-House Board. RG 26, 48, file 1969, 4169.
DC:NA
Glunt, Ruth Reynolds. *Old Lighthouses of the Hudson River.* Moran, 1969.
Light List. 1848, 1873, 1891, 1939, 1940.
Lighthouse Service Bulletin. January, 1923. 2:264
Lighthouse Site Files. RG 26, 66, Coxsackie light station, NY. DC:NA

Danskammer Point Light (NY)
Correspondence of the Light-House Board. RG 26, 48, file 2030, 6869.
DC:NA
Correspondence of the Bureau of Lighthouses. RG 26, 50, file2606E.DC:NA
Descriptive List of Lighthouse Stations. RG 26, 63, 1887. DC:NA
Light List. 1891, 1907, 1939.
Lighthouse Service Bulletin. 1914.   :134
Lighthouse Site Files. RG 26, 66, Danskammer Point light station, NY.
DC:NA

Dutch Island Light (RI)
Correspondence of the Light-House Board. RG 26, 48, file 2721. DC:NA
Correspondence of the Bureau of Lighthouses.RG26, 50, file 2007D.DC:NA
Light House Letters Series P RG 26, 35, May 5, 1843. DC:NA
Light List. 1979, 1980.
Lighthouse Site Files. RG 26, 66, Dutch Island light station, RI. DC:NA
New York Times. October 30, 1977
Newport Daily News. (RI) March 15, 1972

Eatons Neck Light (NY)
American Coast Pilot. Newburyport, MA: Blunt. 1800
American Coast Pilot. New York: Blunt. 1857
*Compilation of Public Documents and Extracts from Reports and Papers
Relating to Lighthouses, Light-vessels,* et al. 1789-1871. Washington, DC:
Government Printing Office. 1871.
Correspondence of the Light-House Board. RG 26, 48, file 1106. DC:NA
Correspondence of the Bureau of Lighthouses. RG 26 50, file 2594E.DC:NA
Descriptive List of Lighthouse Stations. RG 26, 63, 1880. DC:NA
Knowles, Howard N. *A Lighthouse of Stone.* Northport, NY: Northport
Historical Society. 1978.
Letters Regarding Light House Service. RG 26, 18, Vol 2, Vol 17. DC:NA
Lighthouse Site Files. RG 26, 66, Eatons Neck light station, NY. DC:NA
New York Times. November 29, 1965
New York Times. May 6, 1973
New York Times. September 24, 1972

Eel Grass Lightship (see Latimer Reef Light) (NY)

Elm Tree Light (front range) (NY)

Correspondence of the Light-House Board. RG 26, 48, file 1186. DC:NA
Correspondence of the Bureau of Lighthouses. RG 26, 50, file 771E. DC:NA
Light List. 1863, 1961, 1964.
Lighthouse Site Files. RG 26, 66, Elm Tree (front range) light station, NY. DC:NA

Esopus Meadows Light - Esopus Island Light (NY)

Correspondence of the Light-House Board. RG 26, 48, file 2113, 6968. DC:NA
Correspondence of the Bureau of Lighthouses. RG 26, 50, file 603. DC:NA
Letters Regarding Light House Service. RG 26, 18, Vol 13, Vol 25. DC: NA
Light List. 1974
Lighthouse Site Files. RG 26, 66, Esopus Meadows light station, NY. DC:NA
Lighthouse Station Logs. RG 26, 80, Esopus Meadows 1911-1919. DC:NA
New York Times. August 15, 1967

Execution Rocks Light (NY)

Compilation of Public Documents and Extracts from Reports and Papers Relating to Lighthouses, Light-vessels, et al. 1789-1871. Washington, DC: Government Printing Office. 1871.
Correspondence of the Light-House Board. RG 26, 48, file 4163, 1951. DC:NA
Correspondence of the Bureau of Lighthouses.
RG 26, 50, file 1274E. DC:NA
Klar, Flavia. "Sentinel in the Sound." Sea Frontiers. November 1977, 361-364.
Letters Regarding Light House Service. RG 26, 18, Vol 12, Vol 17, Vol 24, Vol 25, Vol 26, Vol 30, Vol 31. DC: NA
Light House Letters Series P. RG 26, 35, 1848, 1849. DC:NA
Lighthouse Site Files. RG 26, 66 Execution Rocks light station, NY. DC:NA
Lighthouse Station Logs. RG 26, 80, Execution Rocks 1919-1923. DC:NA
New York Herald. December 9, 1918
New York Times. December 9, 1918

Fairweather (Fayerweather) Island Light (CT)

American Coast Pilot. New York: Blunt. 1828
Bridgeport Telegram (CT) April 12, 1933
Bridgeport Post (CT). July 18, 1934
Correspondence of the Bureau of Lighthouses. RG 26, 50, file 2881. DC:NA
Justinius, Ivan. History of Black Rock 1644-1955. Black Rock Civic and Business Mens Club Inc. 1955.
Letters Regarding Light House Service RG 26, 18, Vol 3, Vol 6, Vol 10, Vol 11. DC:NA
Light List. 1863, 1907, 1931
Lighthouse Site Files. RG 26, 66 Black Rock light station, CT DC:NA

Falkner (Faulkner) Island Light (CT)

Correspondence of the Light-House Board. RG 26, 48, file 11150. DC:NA
Correspondence of the Bureau of Lighthouses. RG 26, 50, file 1989E. DC:NA
Letters Regarding Light House Service. RG 26, 18, Vol 2, Vol 15. DC:NA
Light List. 1848, 1863, 1874, 1891, 1988
Lighthouse Site Files. RG 26, 66, Falkner Island light station, CT. DC:NA
New York Times. March 16, 1976

Fire Island Light (NY)

Bang, Henry R. *Fire Island Light.* March 1981
Correspondence of the Bureau of Lighthouses. RG 26, 50, file 1264E. DC:NA
Light House Letters Series P RG 26, 35, November 7, 1843. DC:NA
Lighthouse Site Files. RG 26, 66, Fire Island light station, NY. DC:NA
New York Times. June 26, 1955
New York Times. April 24, 1974

Fire Island Lightship (NY)

Correspondence of the Bureau of Lighthouses. RG 26, 48, file 4241. DC:NA
Flint, Willard. Lightship Data. Held by the U.S. Coast Guard Academy
Library.
Light List. 1891, 1941.
Lighthouse Service Bulletin.. June 1916, :217.
Lighthouse Service Bulletin.. April 1923.
Logs of lighthouse vessels. RG 26, 79, Fire Island LV 1930-1941.
DC:NA
New York Times. December 30, 1932
New York Times. May 9, 1916
Report of the Light House Board. (LV 68) 1895-1897, 1899-1907

Five Fathom Bank Lightship (NJ)

Flint, Willard. Lightship Data. Held by the U.S. Coast Guard Academy
Library.
History Sheet. USCG WLV-530. Public Affairs Division, United States Coast
Guard.
Letters from the Secretary of the Treasury, 1844-1852. Doc. #114. Washing-
ton, DC: Government Printing Office.
Light List. 1842, 1863, 1891, 1907, 1939, 1972.
List of Lighthouse Keepers, 1845-1912. RG 26, Micro Copy #1373, Rolls 1
& 2. DC:NA
Report of the Light-House Board. 1872, 1874-1878, 1880-1891, 1893-
1902, 1905-1906.

Five Mile Point (CT) (see New Haven Harbor Light)

Fort Tompkins/Fort Wadsworth Lights (NY)

American Coast Pilot. New York: Blunt. 1827.
Correspondence of the Light-House Board. RG 26 48, file 2001. DC:NA
Correspondence of the Bureau of Lighthouses. RG26, 50, file 3080E. DC:NA
Letters from the Secretary of the Treasury, 1844-1852. Doc. #38. Washing-

ton, DC: Government Printing Office.
Light List. 1842, 1849, 1863, 1891, 1894, 1964, 1968.
Lighthouse Site Files. RG 26, 66, Fort Thompkins light station, NY. DC:NA
Lighthouse Site Files. RG 26, 66, Fort Wadsworth light station, NY. DC:NA
Notice to Mariners. No. 62, of 1873.
Yancy, Thomas R. "Fort Wadsworth." *Staten Island Historian.* July-September 1967.

Fort Wadsworth Light (see Fort Tompkins Light)

Four Mile Point (NY)
Greene, Tom. Personal communications, 1988.
Letters Regarding Light House Service. RG 26, 18, Vol 8, Vol 13. DC:NA
Light List. 1848, 1863, 1873, 1907, 1919, 1920, 1923.
Lighthouse Site Files. RG 26, 66, Four Mile Point light station, NY. DC:NA

Fuller Rock/Sassafras Point Lights (RI)
Descriptive List of Lighthouse Stations. RG 26, 63, 1873. DC:NA
Lighthouse Site Files. RG 26, 66, Fuller Rock light station, RI. DC:NA
Lighthouse Site Files. RG 26, 66, Sassafras Point light station, RI. DC:NA
Providence Journal.(RI) August 8, 1911
Providence Journal.(RI) February 6, 1923
Providence Journal.(RI) June 22, 1924
Providence Journal.(RI) August 2, 1936

Gardiners Island Light (NY)
Letters Regarding Light House Service. RG 26, 18, Vol 30, Vol 31. DC:NA
Light List. 1863, 1873, 1891.
Lighthouse Site Files. RG 26, 66, Gardiners Island light station, NY. DC:NA

Gould Island Light (RI)
Compilation of Public Documents and Extracts from Reports and Papers Relating to Lighthouses, Light-vessels, et al. 1789-1871. Washington, DC: Government Printing Office. 1871.
Correspondence of the Light-House Board. RG 26, 48, file 3395. DC:NA
Correspondence of the Bureau of Lighthouses. RG 26, 50, file 2582. DC:NA
Kelley, Robert, EP2, U.S. Coast Guard, Aids to Navigation Team, Bristol, RI. Personal communications, 1988.
Light List. 1891, 1907, 1939, 1959, 1986.
Lighthouse Site Files. RG 26, 66, Gould Island light station, RI. DC:NA
Lighthouse Station Logs. RG 26, 80, Gould Island 1889-1944. DC:NA
Stebbins Illustrated Coast Pilot: Atlantic and Gulf Coast. Boston, MA: N.L. Stebbins, 1896

Great Captain Island Light (CT)
Clipping files, lighthouses. Greenwich Public Library. CT
Correspondence of the Light-House Board. RG 26, 48, file 323A, 1100. DC:NA
Correspondence of the Bureau of Lighthouses. RG 26, 50, file 323E. DC:NA

Descriptive List of Lighthouse Stations. RG 26, <u>63</u>, 1880. DC:NA
Greenwich Times. (CT) October 4, 1966
Greenwich Times. (CT) October 31, 1968
Greenwich Times. (CT) January 29, 1970
Letters Regarding Light House Service. RG 26, <u>18</u>, Vol 8, Vol 13. DC;NA
Light List. 1848, 1871, 1907, 1986.
Lighthouse Site Files. RG 26, <u>66</u>, Great Captain Island light station, CT. DC:NA
New York Herald. June 19, 1905

Great Beds Light (NY)
Correspondence of the Light-House Board. RG 26, <u>48</u>, file 3239, 8376. DC:NA
Correspondence of the Bureau of Lighthouses. RG 26, <u>50</u>, file 1786E. DC:NA
Light List. 1891, 1988.
Lighthouse Site Files. RG 26, <u>66</u>, Great Beds light station, NY. DC:NA
Lighthouse Station Logs. RG 26, <u>80</u>, Great Beds Light 1897-1935 DC:NA

Great West Bay Light (see Shinnecock Bay Light) (NY)

Greens Ledge Light (CT)
Correspondence of the Light-House Board. RG 26, <u>48</u>, file 8937. DC:NA
Correspondence of the Bureau of Lighthouses. RG 26, <u>50</u>, file 2788. DC:NA
Light List. 1907.
Lighthouse Site Files. RG 26, <u>66</u>, Greens Ledge light station, CT. DC:NA
Norwalk Hour. (CT) January 20, 1902

Gull Rocks Light (RI)
Correspondence of the Bureau of Lighthouses. RG 26, <u>50</u>, file 2081. DC:NA
Light List. 1891, 1907
Lighthouse Site Files. RG 26, <u>66</u>, Gull Rocks light station, RI. DC:NA
Lighthouse Station Logs. RG 26, <u>80</u>, Gull Island Light 1887-1938 DC:NA
New York Times. January 9, 1970

Hell Gate Light (NY)
Journal of Commerce. (NY) September 11, 1851
Journal of Commerce. (NY) November 8, 1851
Light List. 1874, 1884, 1891.
Lighthouse Site Files. RG 26, <u>66</u>, Hell Gate light station, NY. DC:NA
New York Municipal Gazette. January 18, 1849
New York Municipal Gazette. March 1850
New York Times. July 11, 1867
New York Times. June 12, 1875
New York Times. August 25, 1874
New York Times. June 12, 1875

Hereford Inlet Light (NJ)

Correspondence of the Bureau of Lighthouses. RG 26, 50, file 1456C, 1456E. DC:NA

Descriptions of Lighthouses. RG 26, 71, 1907. DC:NA

Light List. 1874, 1891, 1939

Lighthouse Site Files. RG 26, 66, Hereford Inlet light station, NY. DC:NA

Lighthouse Station Logs. RG 26, 80, Hereford Inlet. May 6, 1874-1939. DC:NA

MacDonald, Stephen. Hereford Inlet Lighthouse. (Pamphlet) City of North Wildwood, NJ. (undated)

New York Times. February 16, 1986

Hog Island Shoal Light and Lightship (RI)

Correspondence of the Light-House Board. RG 26,48, file 744, 2477, 3080A. DC:NA

Instructions to Lighthouse Keepers. Washington, DC: Government Printing Office.July, 1881

Light List. 1891.

Lighthouse Site Files. RG 26, 66, Hog Island Shoal light station, RI. DC:NA

Report of the Light House Board. 1902, 1903

Horton Point Light (NY)

Correspondence of the Light-House Board. RG 26, 48, file 2580. DC:NA

Correspondence of the Bureau of Lighthouses. RG 26, 50, file 2046D, 1255E. DC:NA

Light List. 1863, 1891, 1939.

Lighthouse Site Files. RG 26, 66, Horton Point light station, NY. DC:NA

Long Island Traveller. April 21, 1977

New York Times. May 29, 1933

Hudson City Light (NY)

Bacon, Edgar Mayhew. *The Hudson River.* New York: G.P. Putnam, 1907.

Correspondence of the Bureau of Lighthouses. RG 26, 50, file 1981A, 1981C. 1981E. DC:NA

Descriptions of Lighthouses. RG 26, 71, 1930. DC:NA

Light List. 1874, 1930, 1986.

Lighthouse Site Files. RG 26, 66, Hudson City light station, NY. DC:NA

Lighthouse Station Logs. RG 26, 80, Hudson City. 1900 November 10, 1949. DC:NA

New York Times. March 4, 1984.

New York Times. November 24, 1986.

Notice to Mariners. No. 43, of 1874.

Report of the Commissioner of Lighthouses. 1919.

Jeffrey's Hook Light - Little Red Lighthouse (NY)

Correspondence of the Light-House Board. RG 26, 48, file 6968, 8597. DC:NA

Correspondence of the Bureau of Lighthouses. RG 26, 50, file 603. DC:NA

Light List. 1907, 1939, 1947.

Lighthouse Service Bulletin. 1927 :212
Lighthouse Site Files. RG 26, 66, Jeffrey's Hook light station, NY. DC:NA
Lighthouse Station Logs. RG 26, 80, Jeffrey's Hook. 1932-1947. DC:NA
Mooney, Michael. "Li'l Red." *Sea Frontiers.* July, 1985. 236-240
New York Times. July 11, 1951
New York Times. July 12, 1951
New York Times. July 14, 1951
New York Times. July 19, 1951
New York Times. August 27, 1982
Swift, Hildegarde H. and Ward, Lynd. *The Little Red Lighthouse and the Great Gray Bridge.* New York: Harcourt Brace Janovich. 1942.
Report of the Commissioner of Lighthouses. 1920

Latimer Reef Light - Eel Grass Lightship (NY)
Correspondence of the Bureau of Lighthouses. RG 26, 50, file 2423. DC:NA
Lighthouse Service Bulletin. September 1, 1927. 3:205-209
Lighthouse Site Files. RG 26, 66, Latimer Reef light-station, NY. DC:NA
Light List. 1863.
Report of the Light House Board. LV #25. 1872, 1882, 1885.
U.S. Coast Survey. Fishers Island, 1838

Liberty Enlightening the World (see Statue of Liberty)

Lime Rock Light - Ida Lewis Rock Light (RI)
Correspondence of the Bureau of Lighthouses. RG 26, 50, file 1752E, 3070. DC:NA
Harrington, Frances. "The Heroine of Lime Rock." *Oceans,* 1985. 6:24-27
Lighthouse Site Files. RG 26, 66, Lime Rock Light Station. DC:NA
New York Times. October 22, 1911
New York Times. December 18, 1911
Snow, Edward Rowe. *Lighthouses of New England.* 2nd ed. New York: Dodd, Mead, 1973

Little Gull Island (NY)
Correspondence of the Light-House Board. RG 26, 48, file 1105, 8288. DC:NA
Correspondence of the Bureau of Lighthouses. RG 26, 50, file 1109E. DC:NA
Letters Regarding Light House Service. RG 26, 18, Vol 3, Vol 4. DC:NA
Lighthouse Site Files. RG 26, 66, Little Gull light station, NY. DC:NA
New York Herald Tribune. June 19, 1920
New York Herald Tribune. June 2, 1926
New York Times. June 8, 1977

Lloyd Harbor Light (NY)
Correspondence of the Light-House Board. RG 26, 48, file 2570, 6968. DC:NA
Descriptions of Lighthouses. RG 26, 71, 1912. DC:NA
Descriptive List of Lighthouse Stations. RG 26, 63, 1880. DC:NA
Lighthouse Site Files. RG 26, 66, Lloyd's Harbor light station, NY. DC:NA

New York Times. December 26, 1934
New York Times. February 16, 1986

Long Beach Bar Light (NY)
Correspondence of the Bureau of Lighthouses. RG 26, <u>50</u>, file 1523E, 2858. DC:NA
Descriptive List of Lighthouse Stations. RG 26, <u>63</u>, 1873. DC:NA
Griffing, Eugene. "Passing of a Lighthouse." *Long Island Forum.* April 1956.
Lighthouse Site Files. RG 26, <u>66</u>, Long Beach Bar light station, NY. DC:NA
Lighthouse Station Logs. RG 26, <u>80</u>, Long Beach Bar. December 2, 1871-1889. DC:NA
New York Herald Tribune. December 22, 1944
New York Times. November 27, 1955

Ludlam Beach Light (NJ)
Bailey, Harriett Reardon. Personal communications, 1987.
Correspondence of the Bureau of Lighthouses. RG 26, <u>50</u>, file 2019A, 2019E. DC:NA
Descriptive List of Lighthouse Stations. RG 26, <u>63</u>, 1907. DC:NA
Light List. 1891, 1939.
Lighthouse Site Files. RG 26, <u>66</u>, Ludlam Beach light station, NJ. DC:NA
New York Times. September 9, 1889.
New York Times. September 11, 1889.
New York Times. September 13, 1889.

Montauk Point Light (NY)
Barrick, Thomas V. "Letters from Montauk." *Long Island Forum.* May 1987.
Compilation of Public Documents and Extracts from Reports and Papers Relating to Lighthouses, Light-vessels, et al. 1789-1871. Washington, DC: Government Printing Office. 1871.
Correspondence of the Light-House Board. RG 26, <u>48</u>, file 2028, 2572. DC:NA
Correspondence of the Bureau of Lighthouses. RG 26,<u>50</u>, file1546E. DC:NA
Harper's New Monthly Magazine. "Montauk Point." September 1871. 479-493
Hefner, Bob. "History of the Lighthouse." *The Beacon.* Montauk Historical Society. 1987
Letters Regarding Light House Service. RG 26, <u>18</u>, Vol 1. DC: NA
Light List. 1863, 1907, 1988.
Lighthouse Site Files. RG 26, <u>66</u>, Montauk Point light station, NY. DC:NA
New York Herald. August 31, 1932
New York Times. January 24, 1958
New York Times. September 24, 1967
New York Times. July 12, 1979
New York Times. May 17, 1981
New York Times. June 21, 1981
New York Times. September 22, 1985

Morgan Point Light (CT
Black, Ken . Shore Village Museum. Personal communications, 1988.
Correspondence of the Bureau of Lighthouses. RG 26, 50, 1916. DC:NA
Descriptive List of Lighthouse Stations. RG 26, 63, 1880. DC:NA
Letters Regarding Light House Service. RG 26, 18, Vol 10, Vol 19. DC: NA
Lighthouse Site Files. RG 26, 66, Morgan Point light station, CT. DC:NA
Morgan's Point Lighthouse. *Noank Historical Society Bulletin.* June 1968,
2:3-4

Musselbed Shoals Light (RI)
Correspondence of the Bureau of Lighthouses. RG 26, 50, file 3044E DC:NA
Light List. 1873.
Lighthouse Site Files. RG 26, 66, Mussel Bed Shoals. DC:NA
Notice to Mariners. No. 33, of 1873

Nayatt Point Light - Conimicut Light (RI)
Correspondence of the Bureau of Lighthouses. RG 26, 50, file 2798E.
(Conimicut) DC:NA
Descriptive List of Lighthouse Stations. RG 26, 63, 1873, 1887. DC:NA
Letters Regarding Light House Service. RG 26, 18, Vol 7. DC:NA
Lighthouse Site Files. RG 26, 66, Nayat Point Light and Conimicut Light.
DC:NA

New Dorp Light (rear range) (NY)
Correspondence of the Bureau of Lighthouses. RG 26, 50, file 3086. DC:NA
Lighthouse Site Files. RG 26, 66, New Dorp, rear range, NY. DC:NA
Lighthouse Station Logs. RG 26, 80, New Dorp Light. 1874-1877. DC:NA
New York Times. April 9, 1975
New York Times. April 2, 1978

New Haven Light (Five Mile Point Light) (CT)
Correspondence of the Bureau of Lighthouses. RG 26, 50, file 1963. DC:NA
Letters Regarding Light House Service. RG 26, 18, Vol 21. DC:NA
Light List. 1848, 1863, 1871.
Lighthouse Site Files. RG 26, 66, New Haven light station, CT. DC:NA

New Haven Long Wharf (CT)
Correspondence of the Light-House Board. RG 26, 48, file 862, 863. DC:NA
Correspondence of the Bureau of Lighthouses. RG 26,50,file 1849A. DC:NA
Light List. 1863, 1891, 1907, 1980.
Lighthouse Site Files. RG 26, 66, New Haven Long Wharf light station, CT.
DC:NA

**New Haven Outer Breakwater Light (New Haven Light, Sperry Light)
(CT)**
Correspondence of the Light-House Board. RG 26, 48, file 511, 729E, 3340.
DC:NA
Correspondence of the Bureau of Lighthouses. RG 26, 50, file 1696. DC:NA

Lighthouse Site Files. RG 26, <u>66</u>, New Haven Breakwater light station, CT. DC:NA
New Haven Register. (CT) November 2, 1913

New London Harbor Light (CT)
Correspondence of the Light-House Board. RG 26, <u>48</u>,file 2013. DC:NA
Correspondence of the Bureau of Lighthouses. RG 26, <u>50</u>, file 1209. DC:NA
Letters Regarding Light House Service. RG 26, <u>18</u>, Vol 10. DC:NA
Lighthouse Site Files. RG 26, <u>66</u>, New London light station, CT. DC:NA
Lighthouse Service Bulletin. May 1939 5:178-180
Petition by Gurdon Saltonstall. October 1760. CT State Library.

New London Ledge Light (CT)
Correspondence of the Bureau of Lighthouses. RG 26, <u>50</u>, file 857A. DC:NA
Lighthouse Site Files. RG 26, <u>66</u>, Black Ledge, New London Harbor, CT. DC:NA
Lighthouse Station Logs. RG 26, <u>80</u>, New London Ledge 1909-1938 DC:NA
New York Times. June 7, 1964
New York Times. August 9, 1981

Newport Harbor Light (Goat Island Light) (RI)
Champlin, Richard L. "Some Guardians of the East Bay." *Bulletin Newport Historical Society.* Spring 1971, 44:29-32
Correspondence of the Light-House Board. RG 26, <u>48</u>, file 8982. DC:NA
Letters Regarding Light House Service. RG 26, <u>18</u>, Vol 14. DC:NA
Light List. 1848, 1863, 1873, 1907, 1923
Lighthouse Site Files. RG 26, <u>66</u>, Newport Harbor light station, RI. DC:NA

North Brother Island (NY)
Correspondence of the Light-House Board. RG 26, <u>48</u>, file 2562, 7078. DC:NA
Correspondence of the Bureau of Lighthouses. RG 26, <u>50</u>, file 1041E, 2595E. DC:NA
Letters Regarding Light House Service. RG 26, <u>18</u>, Vol 8, Vol 9, Vol 10, Vol 26. DC:NA
Lighthouse Site Files. RG 26, <u>66</u>, North Brother Island light station, NY. DC:NA
New York Times. June 16, 1904
New York Times. June 18, 1904
New York Times. June 22, 1904
New York Times. June 24, 1904
New York Times. June 17, 1905
New York Times. November 17, 1938
Rosenkratz, Barbara ed. *The Carrier State.* New York: Arno Press. 1977

North Dumpling Light (NY)
Correspondence of the Bureau of Lighthouses. RG26, <u>50</u>, file 1104E.DC:NA
Letters Regarding Light House Service. RG 26, <u>18</u>, Vol 21, 26, 28. DC:NA
Light House Letters Series P RG 26, <u>35</u>, November 11, 1848. DC:NA

Light List. 1849, 1863, 1891, 1959, 1960.
Lighthouse Site Files. RG 26, 66, North Dumpling light station, NY. DC:NA

Nortons Point Light (see Coney Island Light) (NY)

Norwalk Islands Light (Sheffield Island Light) (CT)
Correspondence of the Light-House Board. RG 26, 48, file 2573. DC:NA
Letters of Keeper Norris Wilcox. September 10, 1845, October 6, 1845. Held
by Connecticut State Library Archives.
Letters Regarding Light House Service. RG 26, 18, Vol 7. DC:NA
Lighthouse Site Files. RG 26, 66, Norwalk Islands light station, CT. DC:NA
New York Times. January 10, 1954
Norwalk Gazette. (CT) August 15, 1826
Title Papers, State of Connecticut. Patrick Reef File #26. Held by National
Archives. DC:NA

Northeast End Lightship (Northeast end of Five Fathom Bank, NJ)
Light List. 1883, 1926, 1927, 1932.
Logs of lighthouse vessels. RG 26, 79, LV 44, LV 111/533. DC:NA
New York Times. September 13, 1889.
Report of the Light-House Board. 1876, 1882-1884, 1886-1891, 1893-
1902.
Report to the Secretary of Commerce. 1926-1928, 1930, 1932.

Old Field Point Light (NY)
American Coast Pilot. New York: Blunt. 1833
Correspondence Concerning Delinquencies of Board Employees. RG 26,
84, 1886. DC:NA
Correspondence of the Bureau of Lighthouses. RG 26, 50, 1510 DC:NA
Cummings, Robert E. Personal communications. 1987
Letters Regarding Light House Service. RG 26, 18, Vol 6, Vol 10. DC: NA
Lighthouse Site Files. RG 26, 66, Old Field Point light station, NY. DC:NA

Old Orchard Shoal (NY)
Correspondence of the Light-House Board. RG 26, 48, file 5273, 8202.
DC:NA
Light List. 1891, 1988.
Lighthouse Site Files. RG 26,66, Old Orchard Shoal light station, NY. DC:NA

Orient Point Light (NY)
Correspondence of the Light-House Board. RG 26, 48, file 1063. DC:NA
Correspondence of the Bureau of Lighthouses. RG 26,50, file 1822E.DC:NA
Lighthouse Site Files. RG 26, 66, Orient Point light station, NY. DC:NA

Passaic Light (NJ)
Correspondence of the Bureau of Lighthouses. RG 26, 50, file 1732. DC:NA
Letters from the Secretary of Treasury, 1844-1852. Doc. #14, Doc. #38.
Washington, DC. Government Printing Office.
Light List. 1850, 1863, 1907, 1915.

Lighthouse Site Files. RG 26, <u>66</u>, Passaic light station, NJ. DC:NA

Peck Ledge Light (CT)
Correspondence of the Light-House Board. RG 26, <u>48</u>, file 2403. DC:NA
Correspondence of the Bureau of Lighthouses. RG 26,<u>50</u>, file 1722E. DC:NA
Notice to Mariners. July 10, 1906
The Norwalk Hour. (CT) May 26, 1905
The Norwalk Hour. (CT) July 11, 1906
The Norwalk Hour. (CT) December 7, 1921
Report to the Light House Board. 1896, 1901, 1902, 1903, 1906.

Penfield Reef Light (CT)
Bridgeport Post. March 16, 1972
Bridgeport Post. March 17, 1972
Bridgeport Telegram. July 4, 1970
Clipping Files -Penfield Reef Lighthouse. Fairfield Historical Society, CT
Correspondence of the Bureau of Lighthouses. RG 26,<u>50</u>, file 1312A.DC:NA
Descriptive List of Lighthouse Stations. RG 26, <u>63</u>, 1880. DC:NA
Lighthouse Site Files. RG 26, <u>66</u>, Penfield Reef light station, CT. DC:NA
Lighthouse Station Logs. RG 26, <u>80</u>, 1915-1920. DC:NA
Norwalk Hour. (CT) October 20, 1930
New York Times.   November 7, 1969
Notice to Mariners.   No. 2 of 1874

Plum Beach Light (RI)
Correspondence of the Light-House Board. RG 26, <u>48</u>, file 1112. DC:NA
Correspondence of the Bureau of Lighthouses. RG 26,<u>50</u>, file 1341E.DC:NA
Lighthouse Site Files. RG 26, <u>66</u>, Plum Beach light station, RI. DC:NA
Newport Daily News. (RI) September 23, 1970

Plum Island Light (NY)
Correspondence of the Light-House Board. RG 26, <u>48</u>, file 1129, 1063.
DC:NA
Correspondence of the Bureau of Lighthouses. RG 26,<u>50</u>, file 1106D.DC:NA
Delinquencies of Keepers. RG 26, <u>84</u>, 1876
Lighthouse Site Files. RG 26, <u>66</u>, Plum Island light station, NY. DC:NA
Lighthouse Station Logs. RG 26, <u>80</u>, September 1, 1910, January 18, 1911,
March 20, 1911. DC:NA
New York Times. December 4, 1977

Point Comfort Light (front range) (NJ)
Albion, Robert G. *The Rise of the Port of New York.* New York: Schribner.
1967.
Correspondence of the Bureau of Lighthouses. RG 26, <u>50</u>, file 778E, 768E.
DC:NA
Light List. 1863, 1883, 1891, 1902, 1903.
Lighthouse Site Files. RG 26, <u>66</u>, Point Comfort light station, NJ. DC:NA

Point Judith Light (RI)

American Coast Pilot. Newburyport, MA: Blunt. 1812
Champlin, Richard L. "Point Judith - The Early Years." *Bulletin Newport Historical Society.* #148, 1972
Correspondence of the Light-House Board. RG 26, 48, file 5849. DC:NA
Ellery, William: Letter Book #3. September 29, 1815. Held by Newport Historical Society.
Evening Bulletin (Providence, RI) October 24, 1939
Lighthouse Site Files. RG 26, 66, Point Judith light station, RI DC:NA

Poplar Point Light (see Wickford Harbor Light) (RI)

Pomham (Pumham) Rocks Light (RI)

Correspondence of the Light-House Board. RG26,48, file 700, 1173. DC:NA
Descriptive List of Lighthouse Stations. RG 26, 63, 1873. DC:NA
Evening Bulletin. Providence, RI. April 4, 1934
Evening Bulletin. Providence, RI. August 2, 1946
Lighthouse Site Files. RG 26, 66, Pumham Rock light station, RI DC:NA

Prince's (Princess) Bay Light (NY)

Correspondence of the Bureau of Lighthouse RG 26, 50, file 769E. DC:NA
Descriptive List of Lighthouse Stations. RG 26, 63, 1887. DC:NA
Kollmer, Burton. "The Yesterday of the Oysterman." *Staten Island Historian.* July, 1940. 3:17
Letters from the Secretary of Treasury, 1844-1852. Doc. #14. Washington, DC: Government Printing Office.
Lighthouse Site Files. RG 26, 66, Prince's Bay light station, NY DC:NA
Notice to Mariners. No. 22, of 1883.

Prudence Island Light (RI)

Correspondence of the Light-House Board. RG 26, 48, file 3228, 1954. DC:NA
Correspondence of the Bureau of Lighthouses. RG26,50, file 2774E. DC:NA
Evening Bulletin (Providence, RI) Sept. 24, 1938
Lighthouse Site Files. RG 26, 66, Prudence Island Light. DC:NA

Race Rock Light (NY)

Correspondence of the Light-House Board. RG 26, 48, file 1104, 4547. DC:NA
Correspondence of the Bureau of Lighthouses.RG 26,50, file 1960E. DC:NA
Descriptive List of Lighthouse Stations. RG 26, 63, 1880. DC:NA
Letters Regarding Light House Service. RG 26, 18, Vol 1, Vol 14 DC: NA
Lighthouse Site Files. RG 26, 66, Race Rock light station, NY. DC:NA
Lighthouse Station Logs. RG 26, 80, Race Rock, April 26, 1931. DC:NA
Washington Star, April 5, 1936

Ram Island Lightship (CT)
Light List. 1891, 1907
Lighthouse Service Bulletin. September 1, 1927. 3:205-209
Logs of lighthouse vessels. RG 26, 79, Ram Island LV 1922-1924.
DC:NA
Report of the Light House Board. 1887, 1892, 1895.

Robbins Reef Light (NY)
Correspondence of the Bureau of Lighthouses. RG 26, 50, file 452E. DC:NA
Gallant, Cliff. "Mind the Light, Katie." *The Keeper's Log.* Summer 1987. 16-18.
Letters Regarding Light House Service. RG 26, 18, Vol 12, Vol 15. DC:NA
Light List. 1842, 1883, 1891, 1964.
Lighthouse Site Files. RG 26, 66, Robbins Reef light station, NY. DC:NA
Literary Digest. "At Seventy She Keeps the Light of New York's Inner Harbor." July 13, 1918
List of Lighthouse Keepers, 1845-1912. RG 26, Micro Copy #1373, Rolls 1 & 2. DC:NA
New York Times. November 2, 1964
New York Times. March 6, 1965

Rockland Lake Light (NY)
Correspondence of the Light-House Board. RG 26, 48, file 3221. DC:NA
Lighthouse Site Files. RG 26, 66, Rockland Lake light station, NY. DC:NA

Romer Shoal Light (NY)
Correspondence of the Bureau of Lighthouses. RG 26, 50, file 285A, 2595E. DC:NA
Letters Regarding Light House Service. RG 26, 18, Vol 13, Vol 15. DC:NA
Lighthouse Service Bulletin. January 3, 1921. 2:161-162
Lighthouse Site Files. RG 26, 66, Romer Shoal light station, NY. DC:NA
Lighthouse Station . RG 26, 80, Romer Shoal Light Station. 1938. DC:NA
New York Times. September 15, 1949

Rondout (Creek) Light (NY)
Barry, Elise, Wheeler, Wayne. "Hudson River Lighthouses Get a New Lease on Life," Part lll. In Notice to Keepers. *The Keeper's Log.* Summer, 1987
Carmer, Carl. *The Hudson.* New York: Farrar and Rinehart, 1893.
Correspondence of the Light-House Board. RG 26, 48, file 2609, 5694, 6968. DC:NA
Correspondence of the Bureau of Lighthouses. RG 26, 50, file 561, 616. DC:NA
Harlow, Alvin F. *Old Towpaths.* New York, D. Appleton, 1926.
Letters Regarding Light House Service. RG 26, 18, Vol 13. DC:NA
Light List. 1848, 1873, 1914, 1916.
Lighthouse Site Files. RG 26, 66, Rondout Creek light station, NY. DC:NA
Maritime Center at Kingston, staff. Personal communications, 1988.
New York Times. September 9, 1984

Rose Island Light (RI)
Champlin, Richard L. "Rose Island Centennial." *Bulletin Newport Historical Society.* Summer, 1970, 65-70
Correspondence of the Light-House Board. RG 26, 48, file 5859. DC:NA
Correspondence of the Bureau of Lighthouses. RG 26, 50, file 879E. DC:NA
Johnson, Charlotte. Rose Island Lighthouse Foundation. Personal communications, 1988.
Lighthouse Site Files. RG 26, 66, Rose Island light station, RI. DC:NA
Lighthouse Station . RG 26, 80, Rose Island, RI. 1876. DC:NA

Sabin's (Sabine) Point Light (RI)
Evening Bulletin. Providence, RI. August 28, 1924
Lighthouse Site Files. RG 26, 66, Sabines Point light station, RI. DC:NA
Lighthouse Station Logs. RG 26, 80, Sabines Point, 1874-1938. DC:NA
New York Times. July 5, 1968
Providence Journal. (RI) November 28, 1943

Sakonnet Point Light (RI)
Correspondence of the Light-House Board. RG 26, 48, file 211. DC: NA
Correspondence of the Bureau of Lighthouses. RG 26, 50, file 885A. DC:NA
Herald News,(Fall River, MA) July 11, 1956
Lighthouse Site Files. RG 26, 66, Sakonnet Point light station. DC:NA
"Sakonnet Lighthouse." In Notice to Mariners. *The Keeper's Log.* Fall, 1985

Sands Point Light (NY)
American Coast Pilot. New York: Blunt. 1827
Correspondence of the Light-House Board. RG 26, 48,file 4249, 4547. DC: NA
Delinquencies of Keepers. RG 26, 84, 1881
Light List. 1848, 1863, 1891, 1907
Lighthouse Service Bulletin. April 1, 1924. 3:17
Lighthouse Site Files. RG 26, 66, Sands Point light station, NY. DC:NA
New York Times. February 1, 1924

Sandy Hook Light (NJ) (Main Beacon, East Beacon and West Beacon)
American Coast Pilot. Newburyport, MA: Blunt. 1800
American Coast Pilot. Newburyport, MA: Blunt. 1806
American Coast Pilot. New York: Blunt. 1827
Compilation of Public Documents and Extracts from Reports and Papers Relating to Lighthouses, Light-vessels, et al. 1789-1871. Washington, DC. Government Printing Office. 1871.
Correspondence of the Light-House Board. RG 26, 48, file 1968. DC: NA
Correspondence of the Bureau of Lighthouses. RG 26, 50, file 10263, 770E, 2241. DC:NA
Houghton, George. *Sandy Hook in 1879.* Golden Co. Outbooks. 1981.
Letters Regarding Light House Service. RG 26, 18, Vol 4, Vol 13. DC:NA
Lighthouse Site Files. RG 26, 66, Gedney's Channel, NY Harbor.

DC:NA
Lighthouse Site Files. RG 26, 66, Sandy Hook light station, NJ.
DC:NA
Lopez, John. "Sandy Hook Lighthouse."*The Keeper's Log* .2:2-7 Winter,1986.
Mills, Robert. *American Pharos.* 1832
New York Mercury. June 18, 1764
New York Times. July 31, 1942

Sandy Hook Lightship (NJ)
American Coast Pilot. New York: Blunt. 1827
American Coast Pilot. New York: Blunt. 1857
Correspondence of the Light-House Board. RG 26, 48, file 1849. DC:NA
Flint, Willard. Lightship Data. Held by the U.S. Coast Guard Academy Library.
Harpers Weekly. May 11, 1895
Letters Regarding Light House Service. RG 26, 18, Vol 6. DC:NA
Lighthouse Service Bulletin. September 1, 1927. 3:205-209
New York Times. November 11, 1890
Report of the Light House Board. 1872, 1874-1878, 1880, 1881, 1883-1892, 1896, 1897, 1898, 1902, 1903, 1907.

Sassafras Point Light (see Fuller Rock Light) (RI)

Saugerties Light (NY)
Correspondence of the Light-House Board. RG 26, 48, file 2606. DC:NA
Correspondence of the Bureau of Lighthouses. RG 26, 50, file 603. DC:NA
Glunt, Ruth Reynolds. *Old Lighthouses of the Hudson River.* Moran Printing, 1969.
Letters Regarding Light House Service. RG 26, 18, Vol 10, Vol 13. DC:NA
Lighthouse Site Files. RG 26, 66, Saugerties light station, NY. DC:NA
Steen, Cliff. Personal communications, 1988.

Saybrook Breakwater Light (CT)
Correspondence of the Light-House Board. RG 26, 48, file 1130. DC:NA
Correspondence of the Bureau of Lighthouses. RG 26, 50, file 1687, 2595E DC:NA
Lighthouse Service Bulletin.. December 1938. 5:145-146
Lighthouse Site Files. RG 26, 66, Saybrook Breakwater light station, CT. DC:NA
Lighthouse Station. RG 26, 80, Saybrook Breakwater Light Station. 1904-1940. DC:NA

Scotland Lightship (see Wreck of the Scotland)

Sea Girt Light (NJ)
Descriptions of Lighthouses. RG 26, 71, 1907. DC:NA
Franklin, Samuel E. Personal communications. 1989

Light List. 1900, 1922, 1939.
Lighthouse Site Files. RG 26, 66, Sea Girt light station, NJ. DC:NA
Lighthouse Station Logs. RG 26, 80, Sea Girt Light. 1906-1925.
DC:NA
New York Times. September 9, 1939
New York Times. February 27, 1955
Report of the Commissioner of Lighthouses. 1921

Shinnecock Bay Light (NY)
Correspondence of the Light-House Board. RG 26, 48, file 1289. DC:NA
Light List. 1863, 1907, 1988
Lighthouse Site Files. RG 26, 66, Great West or Shinnecock Bay light station
DC:NA
New York Times. December 23, 1948

Southwest Ledge Light (CT)
Clipping Files -lighthouses. New Haven Historical Society, CT.
Correspondence of the Bureau of Lighthouses. RG26,50, file 1080A. DC:NA
Johnson, Arnold Burgess. *Modern Lighthouse Service.* Washington, DC:
U.S. Government Printing Office. 1889
Letters Regarding Light House Service. RG 26, 18, Vol 26. DC:NA
Light List. 1883, 1891
Lighthouse Site Files. RG 26, 66, Southwest Ledge light station. DC:NA
New Haven Register. January 22, 1908
New Haven Register. July 16, 1933

Stamford Harbor Light (CT)
Clipping Files -Stamford Harbor Light. Ferguson Public Library, Stamford,
CT
Hartford Currant. February 18, 1984
Lighthouse Site Files. RG 26, 66, Stamford Harbor light station, CT. DC:NA
Lighthouse Station Logs. RG 26, 80, Stamford Harbor Light. 1882-1940.
DC:NA
New York Times. June 16, 1949
New York Times. June 16, 1953
New York Times. January 26, 1955
Stamford Advocate. (CT) August 16, 1931
Stamford Advocate. (CT) August 18, 1931
Stamford Advocate. (CT) April 11, 1955
Stamford Mail. (CT) July 31, 1986

Staten Island Light (NY)
Correspondence of the Light-House Board. RG 26, 48, file 10272. DC:NA
Correspondence of the Bureau of Lighthouses. RG 26, 50, file 315E. DC:NA
Dayton, Thaddeus S. "An Inland Lighthouse."*HarpersWeekly*, July 13,
1912
Descriptions of Lighthouses. RG 26, 71, 1915. DC:NA
Lighthouse Service Bulletin. April 1938. 5:109

Lighthouse Site Files. RG 26, <u>66</u>, Staten Island light station, NY. DC:NA
New York Times. April 15, 1912
New York Times. May 17, 1968

Statue of Liberty (NY)
Correspondence of the Light-House Board. RG 26, <u>48</u>, file 1857, 1864.
DC:NA
List of Lighthouse Keepers, 1845-1912. RG 26, Micro Copy #1373, Rolls 1
& 2. DC:NA
Light List. 1891.
New York Times. March 27, 1956
Perrault, Carole. "Liberty Enlightening the World." *The Keeper's Log.* Spring
1986, 2:2-15, Summer 1986, 2: 6-18.
Report of the Light House Board. 1887-1893, 1903.

Stepping Stones Light (NY)
Correspondence of the Light-House Board. RG 26, <u>48</u>, file 3233. DC:NA
Daily Advocate (Stamford, CT). January 2, through March 2, 1934.
Lighthouse Site Files. RG 26, <u>66</u>, Stepping Stones light station, NY. DC:NA
New York Times. March 2, 1934.
Report of the Light House Board. (Hart Island) 1872, 1883, 1896-1901.

Stonington Harbor Light - Stonington Breakwater Light (CT)
American Coast Pilot. New York: Blunt. 1833
Correspondence of the Bureau of Lighthouses. RG 26, <u>50</u>, file 906E. DC:NA
Letters Regarding Light House Service. RG 26, <u>18</u>, Vol 26. DC:NA
Lighthouse Site Files. RG 26, <u>66</u>, Stonington Harbor light station, CT -
Stonington Breakwater Light, CT. DC:NA

Stony Point Light (NY)
Bedell, Cornelia F. *Now and Then and Long Ago.* Historical Society of
Rockland County, 1941.
Bergen Record. (NJ) August 31, 1973
Clipping Files, Hudson River Lighthouses. New City Public Library, NY
Clipping Files/Historical Files, Stony Point Light. Stony Point Battlefield,
State Historic Site (Museum), Stony Point, NY
Correspondence of the Bureau of Lighthouses. RG 26, <u>50</u>, file 702, 1097.
DC:NA
Dubitsky, Doina. Personal communications, 1989.
Letters Regarding Light House Service. RG 26, <u>18</u>, Vol 7, Vol 8, Vol 13.
DC:NA
Light List. 1848, 1863, 1883, 1891, 1926.
Lighthouse Site Files. RG 26, <u>66</u>, Stony Point light station, NY. DC:NA
Report of the Light House Board. 1895
Rockland County Journal News (NY). September 24, 1962.

Stratford Point Light (CT)
Bridgeport Sunday Post (CT). March 13, 1938

Connecticut Courier. June 20, 1821
Correspondence of the Light-House Board. RG 26, 48, file 1131. DC: NA
Lighthouse Site Files. RG 26, 66, Stratford Point light station. DC:NA

Stratford Shoal (Middle Ground) Lightship (NY)
Stratford Shoal (Middle Ground) Light
Compilation of Public Documents and Extracts from Reports and Papers Relating to Lighthouses, Light-vessels, et al. 1789-1871. Washington, DC: Government Printing Office. 1871.
Correspondence of the Light-House Board. RG 26, 48, file 349, 7841 DC:NA
Letters Regarding Light House Service. RG 26, 18, Vol 8, Vol 12. DC:NA
Lighthouse Service Bulletin. March, 1933. 4:146
Lighthouse Site Files. RG 26, 66, Stratford Shoal (Middle Ground) light station, NY
Norwalk Hour. (CT) February 10, 1933
Norwalk Hour. (CT) February 11, 1933
Report of the Light House Board. (LV 15) 1867, 1872, 1874-1877.

Stuyvesant Light (NY)
Correspondence of the Light-House Board. RG 26, 48, file 1969, 5648. DC:NA
Correspondence of the Bureau of Lighthouses. RG 26, 50, file 603. DC:NA
Glunt, Ruth Reynolds. *The Old Lighthouses of the Hudson River.* Moran Printing, 1969.
Letters Regarding Light House Service. RG 26, 18, Vol 10. DC:NA
Light List. 1848, 1873, 1907, 1933.
Lighthouse Site Files. RG 26, 66, Stuyversant light station, NY. DC:NA

Tarrytown Light (NY)
Correspondence of the Light-House Board. RG 26, 48, file 617. DC:NA
Letters Regarding Light House Service. RG 26, 18, Vol 25, Vol 26. DC:NA
Light List. 1891, 1907, 1958, 1963, 1964.
Lighthouse Site Files. RG 26, 66, Tarrytown light station, NY. DC:NA
Lighthouse Station Logs. RG 26, 80, Tarrytown Light Station. October 1, 1883-1893. DC:NA
New York Times. January 29, 1959
New York Times. October 6, 1967
New York Times. October 3, 1982
New York Times. May 15, 1983
Notice to Mariners. September 5, 1883
Notice to Mariners. April 11, 1902
Roe, Charles Henry. "The Tarrytown Lighthouse." *The Westchester Historian.* 1968. 44:73-78

Throgs Neck Light (NY)
Correspondence of the Light-House Board. RG 26, 48, file 1936. DC:NA
Letters Regarding Light House Service. RG 26, 18, Vol 7, Vol 10. DC:NA
Light List. 1848, 1863, 1891, 1907, 1936

Lighthouse Site Files. RG 26, 66, Throgs Neck light station, NY. DC:NA

Tongue Point Light (see Bridgeport Breakwater Light) (CT)

Tucker Beach Light (NJ)
Correspondence of the Light-House Board. RG 26, 48, file 1275. DC:NA
Correspondence of the Bureau of Lighthouses. RG 26, 50, file 2021E.
DC:NA
Descriptive List of Lighthouse Stations. RG 26, 63, 1907. DC:NA
Light List. 1849, 1873, 1930.
Lighthouse Site Files. RG 26, 66, Tucker Beach light station, NJ. DC:NA

Waackaack Light (rear range) (NJ)
Albion, Robert G.*The Rise of the Port of New York*. New York: Schribner.
1967.
Correspondence of the Light-House Board. RG 26, 48, file 1007. DC:NA
Correspondence of the Bureau of Lighthouses. RG 26, 50, file 768E, 778E.
DC:NA
Light List. 1863, 1883, 1891, 1902, 1903.
Lighthouse Site Files. RG 26, 66, Waackaack light station, NJ. DC:NA

Warwick (Neck) Light (RI)
Correspondence of the Light-House Board. RG 26, 48, file 1548. DC:NA
Evening Bulletin. (Providence, RI) August 6, 1932.
Gleason, Sarah. "Warwick Neck Lighthouse." *The Keeper's Log.* 2:29-30.
Spring, 1986.
Letters Regarding Light House Service. RG 26, 18, Vol 7, Vol 9. DC:NA
Lighthouse Site Files. RG 26, 66, Warwick (Neck) light station, RI DC:NA

Watch Hill Light (RI)
Inventory of Federal Archives, Series 10, #38, Rhode Island. Held by
Providence Public Library, Providence, RI.
Letters Regarding Light House Service. RG 26, 18, Vol 1, Vol 3. DC:NA
Lighthouse Site Files. RG 26, 66, Watch Hill light station, RI DC:NA

West Bank Light (NY)
Correspondence of the Light-House Board. RG 26, 48, file 324. DC:NA
Lighthouse Service Bulletin.. September 1, 1931. 4:83
Lighthouse Site Files. RG 26, 66, West Bank light station, NY DC:NA
New York Herald. January 1, 1917
New York Times. January 12, 1910
New York Times. October 10, 1982
New York Times. June 22, 1975

West Point Light (NY)
Correspondence of the Bureau of Lighthouses. RG 26, 50, file 1828. DC:NA
Light List. 1863, 1873, 1891, 1939,

Lighthouse Service Bulletin. July 1, 1935. 4:211
Lighthouse Site Files. RG 26, <u>66</u>, West Point light station, NY. DC:NA
Report of Commissioner of Lighthouses. 1922

Whale Rock Light (RI)
Clipping files. Lighthouses. Providence Public Library, Providence, RI
Correspondence of the Light-House Board. RG 26, <u>48,</u> file 207 DC:NA
Descriptive List of Lighthouse Stations. RG 26, <u>63,</u> 1887. DC:NA
Lighthouse Service Bulletin. December 1938. 5:146-147
Lighthouse Site Files. RG 26, <u>66</u>, Whale Rock light station, RI DC:NA

Wickford Harbor Light - Poplar Point Light (RI)
Correspondence of the Light-House Board. RG 26, <u>48,</u> (Wickford) file 8941.
DC:NA
Descriptive List of Lighthouse Stations. RG 26, <u>63,</u> 1887. DC:NA
Letters Regarding Light House Service. RG 26, <u>18</u>, Vol 8. DC:NA
Lighthouse Site Files. RG 26, <u>66,</u> Poplar Point light station, RI. DC:NA
Lighthouse Site Files. RG 26, <u>66,</u> Wickford Harbor light station, RI. DC:NA
Providence Journal. October 9, 1932
Providence Journal. June 21, 1940

Wreck of the Oregon Lightship (NY)
Bachand, Robert G. *Scuba Northeast, Vol 2.* Norwalk, CT: Sea Sports
Publications. 1986
New York Times. March 15, 1886
Report of the Light House Board. 1886, 1887, 1889.

Wreck of the Scotland Lightship - Scotland Lightship
Correspondence of the Bureau of Lighthouses. RG 26, <u>50</u>, file 480, 52820.
DC:NA
Evening Post. (NY) December 6, 1866
Evening Post. (NY) December 14, 1866
Lighthouse Service Bulletin. September 1, 1927. 3:205-209
Logs of lighthouse vessels. RG 26, <u>79</u>, Scotland LV 1923-1937.
DC:NA
New York Times. December 3, 1866
New York Times. September 6, 1866
Notice to Mariners. No. 31 of 1874.
Report of the Light House Board. 1874, 1876, 1878-1882, 1886, 1891-
1903, 1906, 1907.
Report of the Secretary of Commerce. 1932, 1938
World. (NY) December 3, 1866

Lighthouse Agencies, Museums, Societies and Publications

A partial listing.

Barnegat Lighthouse State Park
P.O. Box 167
Barnegat, NJ 08006

Battery Point Lighthouse
Box 1149
Crescent City, CA 95531

Block Island Lighthouses
Block Island Historical Society
P.O. 79
Block Island, RI 02807

Bluff Point Lighthouse
Clinton County Historical Assn.
Box 332
Platsburg, NY 12901

Cape May County Historical
Museum
Route 9
Cape May Courthouse
Cape May, NJ 08210

Cape May Lighthouse
Mid-Atlantic Center for the Arts
P.O. Box 340
1048 Washington Street
Cape May, NJ 08204

Columbia River Maritime Museum
1792 Marine Drive
Astoria, OR 97103

Concord Point Lighthouse
Friends of the Lighthouse
P. O. Box 212
Havre de Grace, MD 21078

Department of Transportation
United States Coast Guard
G-TPA Historian
Washington, DC 20590

East Point Lighthouse
Maurice River, NJ

Fairport Marine Museum
129 Second Street
Fairport Harbor, OH 44077

Friends of Fenwick Island Lighthouse
142nd Street
Ocean City, MD 21842

Fire Island Preservation Society
99 Maple Street
Bayshore, NY 11706

Hereford Inlet Lighthouse
North Wildwood, NJ 08260

Highlands of Navesink
Twin Lights Historic Site
Highlands, NJ 07732

Horton Point Lighthouse
P.O. Box 1
Southhold, NY 11971

Hudson/Athens Lighthouse
Preservation Committee
725 Warren Street
Hudson, NY 12534

LLoyd Harbor Lighthouse
Save Huntington Lighthouse
P.O. Box 2454
Huntington, NY 11743

Montauk Point Lighthouse
Montauk Historical Society
PO Box 386
Montauk, NY 11954

Newport Historical Society
(Ida Lewis memorabilia)
82 Tours St.
Newport, RI 02840

Old Lighthouse and Museum
5295 Lake Road
Presque Isle, Mich. 49777

Old Mackinac Point Lighthouse
Fort Michilimacknac Complex
Mackinaw City, Michigan 49701

Point Iroquois Lightstation
Bay Mills-Brimley, Michigan

Point Montara Lighthouse
American Youth Hostels
16th Street Cabrillo Hwy
Montara, CA 94037

Ponce de Leon Inlet Lighthouse
4931 South Peninsula Drive
Ponce Inlet, FL 32019

Rhode Island Department of
Environmental Management
9 Hayes Street
Providence, RI 02908

Rhode Island Parks Association
P.O. Box 6606
Providence, RI 02940

Rondout Lighthouse
Maritime Center
One Rondout Landing
Kingston, NY 12401

Rose Island Lighthouse Foundation
P.O. Box 1419
Newport, RI 02840

Sandy Hook Lighthouse
Gateway National Recreation Area
Sandy Hook Unit
P.O. Box 437
Highlands, NJ 07732

Saugerties Lighthouse Conservancy
P.O. Box 654
Saugerties, NY 12477

Sea Girt Lighthouse Citizens
Committee
P.O. Box 83
Ocean Avenue
Sea Girt, NJ 08750

Sheffield Island Lighthouse
Norwalk Seaport Association
92 Washington Street
Norwalk, CT 06854

Shore Village Museum
104 Limemark Street
Rockland, ME 04841
Publication:
Shore Village Museum Newsletter
Curator: Ken Black

South Street Seaport Museum
207 Front Street
New York, NY 11038

Split Rock Lighthouse
East Star Route
Two Harbors, MN 55616

St. Simons Lighthouse
Museum of Coastal History
Box 1136
St. Simons Island, GA 31522

Stonington Lighthouse Museum
7 Water Street
Stonington, CT 06355

Stony Point Lighthouse
Stony Point Battlefield
State Historic Site
PO Box 182
Stony Point, NY 10980

U.S. Lighthouse Society
244 Kearny Street
San Francisco, CA 94108
Publication: The Keeper's Log
Editor: Wayne Wheeler

Wind Point Lighthouse
Lighthouse Drive
Racine, Wis

Allied Publications, Agencies, and Associations

Maritime Center at Norwalk
10 North Water Street
South Norwalk, CT 06854

Mystic Seaport Museum
Greenmanville Avenue
Mystic, CT 06355

National Maritime Historical Soc.
132 Maple Street
Croton-on-Hudson, NY 10520

Oceans Magazine
2001 W. Main Street
Stamford, CT 06902

Sea Frontiers
International Oceanographic
Foundation
3979 Rickenbacker Causeway
Miami, Fla. 33149

Index